YVES CONGAR
THEOLOGIAN OF THE CHURCH

Louvain Theological and Pastoral Monographs is a publishing venture whose purpose is to provide those involved in pastoral ministry throughout the world with studies inspired by Louvain's long tradition of theological excellence within the Roman Catholic tradition. The volumes selected for publication in the series are expected to express some of today's finest reflection on current theology and pastoral practice.

Members of the Editorial Board

The Executive Committee:

International Advisory Board:

LOUVAIN THEOLOGICAL & PASTORAL MONOGRAPHS
——————————— 32 ———————————

YVES CONGAR
THEOLOGIAN OF THE CHURCH

edited by

Gabriel Flynn

PEETERS PRESS
LOUVAIN – PARIS – DUDLEY, MA

W.B. EERDMANS

2005

Library of Congress Cataloging-in-Publication Data

Yves Congar: theologian of the Church / edited by Gabriel Flynn.
    p. cm. -- (Louvain theological & pastoral monographs)
Includes bibliographical references and index.
ISBN 90-429-1668-0 (alk. paper)
    1. Congar, Yves, 1904- I. Flynn, Gabriel, 1960- II. Series.

BX4705.C76Y85 2005
230'2'092--dc22   2005052003

© 2005, Peeters, Bondgenotenlaan 153, 3000 Leuven, Belgium

ISBN 90-429-1668-0 (Peeters Leuven)
D. 2005/0602/103

ACKNOWLEDGEMENTS

My thanks are due first of all to the contributors to this volume, for their graciousness in accepting this extra duty amidst their myriad responsibilities, and above all for the quality of their contributions. Thanks are also due to Frère Éric de Clermont-Tonnerre, OP, Director of Les Éditions du Cerf, Paris; and Professor Terrence Merrigan, editor of the "Louvain Theological and Pastoral Monographs Series," at Peeters Publishers, Louvain. I wish to thank Mr. Paul Peeters, Director of Peeters Publishers, for his support for the project. I express my gratitude to the translators, without whom this volume could not have been brought to completion. I wish to thank my friends Owen Brennan and Alice Stanton, Beauparc, Co Meath, Ireland, for their generous support of this project. I also acknowledge my gratitude to the members of the Staff Research Fund Committee of the Milltown Institute of Theology and Philosophy, Dublin who also provided sponsorship. I thank my Mother and family, my colleagues and students for their encouragement. Lastly, I wish to acknowledge the kind support of Dr Michael Smith, Bishop of Meath.

"Freedom is a system based on courage."   *Charles Péguy*

"Whatever you can do or dream, you can do, begin it. Boldness has genius, power and magic in it. Begin it now."   *Goethe*

"Caught by the rain outside, sheltering under a tree waiting for a clearing, I started weeping bitterly. Shall I be forever a poor, lonely fellow, dragging my bags hither and thither, having no friend, despoiled of everything, an orphan? 'Dominus autem assumpsit me': these tears: will God notice them? Will he show himself as a Father?"   *Yves Congar*

"As for me, in my justice I shall see your face
and be filled, when I awake, with the sight of your glory."   *Ps 17:15*

"Only the eternal is always appropriate and always present, is always true."
                    Søren Kierkegaard

"The Second Vatican Council was a providential event, whereby the Church began the more immediate preparation for the Jubilee of the Second Millennium... No Council had ever spoken so clearly about Christian unity, about dialogue with non-Christian religions, about the specific meaning of the Old Covenant with Israel, about the dignity of each person's conscience... The best preparation for the new millennium, therefore, can only be expressed in a renewed commitment to apply, as faithfully as possible, the teachings of Vatican II to the life of every individual and of the whole Church."
Pope John Paul II, Tertio Milllennio Adveniente, 10 November 1994

"With the Great Jubilee the Church was introduced into the new millennium carrying in her hands the Gospel, applied to the world through the authoritative re-reading of Vatican Council II. Pope John Paul II justly indicated the Council as a 'compass' with which to orient ourselves in the vast ocean of the third millennium. I too, as I start in the service that is proper to the Successor of Peter, wish to affirm with force my decided will to pursue the commitment to enact Vatican Council II... Precisely this year is the 40th anniversary of the conclusion of this conciliar assembly (8 December 1965). With the passing of time, the conciliar documents have not lost their timeliness; their teachings have shown themselves to be especially pertinent to the new exigencies of the Church and the present globalized society."
Pope Benedict XVI, First Message in the Sistine Chapel, Rome, 20 April 2005

TABLE OF CONTENTS

NOTES ON CONTRIBUTORS

Contributors of Prefaces

Avery Cardinal Dulles, SJ is the Laurence J. McGinley Professor of Religion and Society at Fordham University, New York. An internationally acclaimed author and lecturer, he has served as President of the Catholic Theological Society of America and the American Theological Society. He has been a member of the International Theological Commission and the United States Lutheran/Roman Catholic Coordinating Committee. In 2001, he was created a cardinal by Pope John Paul II. His recent publications include *The Splendor of Faith: The Theological Vision of Pope John Paul II* (New York: Herder and Herder, 1999; new ed. 2003); *The New World of Faith* (Huntington, IN: Our Sunday Visitor, 2000); and *Newman* (New York: Continuum, 2002). Address: Faber Hall, Fordham University, Bronx, New York 10458, USA.

Marc Lienhard is the Honorary Dean of the Protestant Faculty of Theology of Strasbourg and formerly President of the Directoire of the Church of the Confession of Augsburg of Alsace and Lorraine. He has participated in numerous ecumenical conferences, notably, in the elaboration of the Concord of Leuenberg (1973), a statement of concord between the Lutheran and Reformed Churches of Eastern and Western Europe. His publications include *Martin Luther: La passion de Dieu* (Paris: Bayard, 1999); and, in collaboration with Mathieu Arnold, *Luther: Œuvres*, de la Pléiade (Paris: Gallimard, 1999). Address: 17 rue de Verdun, F-67000 Strasbourg, France.

Kenneth Stevenson is the Anglican Bishop of Portsmouth and Chairman of the Church of England Board of Education, and Vice Chair of the Churches Porvoo Panel, dealing with Anglican-Lutheran relations. A specialist in liturgy and historical theology, his recent publications include *The Lord's Prayer: A Text in Tradition* (London/Minneapolis, MN: SCM Press/Fortress Press, 2004); and *Love's Redeeming Work:*

The Anglican Quest for Holiness (Oxford: Oxford University Press, 2001; 2nd ed. 2004), a work he compiled in collaboration with Geoffrey Rowell and Rowan Williams. Address: Cathedral House, St Thomas's Street, Portsmouth, Hampshire PO1 2HA, UK.

Kallistos Ware is Bishop of Diokleia (Ecumenical Patriarchate of Constantinople) and a Fellow of Pembroke College, University of Oxford, where he taught Orthodox theology from 1966-2001. A convert to Orthodoxy, he is a committed ecumenist and a prolific author. His publications include *The Orthodox Church* (Harmondsworth: Penguin Books, 1963; new ed. 1993); and *The Orthodox Way* (Crestwood, NY: St Vladimir's Seminary Press, 1979). Address: 19b Northmoor Road, Oxford OX2 6UW, UK.

Contributors of Articles

Bruno Bürki, a Reformed Pastor, is former Professor of Theology at the University of Fribourg in Switzerland. He is a specialist in liturgy and ecumenism. Among his recent publications, in collaboration with the Catholic scholar Martin Klöckener, are *Liturgie in Bewegung/Liturgie en movement* (Geneva/Fribourg Labor et Fides/University of Fribourg Press, 2000); and *Tagzeitenliturgie/Liturgie des heures: Ökumenische Erfahrungen und Perspektiven /Expériences et perspectives oecuméniques* (Fribourg Academic Press Fribourg, 2004). Between 1991 and 1998, he was Vice-President of the Council of the Swiss Federation of Protestant Churches. Address: Faculté de théologie, Institut de sciences liturgiques, Université Miséricorde, Avenue de l'Europe 20, CH-1700 Fribourg, Switzerland.

Georges Cardinal Cottier, OP is Theologian of the Pontifical Household. He was a *peritus* at Vatican II and a consultor to the then Council for Dialogue with Non-Believers. He is currently director of the journal *Nova et Vetera* (Geneva), founded by Cardinal Charles Journet. He was formerly Visiting Professor at the University of Montreal and at the University of the Catholic Institute in Paris. In 1986, he was appointed to the International Theological Commission and became its secretary in 1989. In 2003, he was created a cardinal by Pope John Paul II. Address: Palazzo Apostolico, V-00120 Città del Vaticano.

Stephen Fields, SJ, is Associate Professor of Theology at Georgetown University, Washington, DC. He is the author of *Being as Symbol: On the Origins and Development of Karl Rahner's Metaphysics* (Washington, DC: Georgetown University Press, 2000). His areas of specialization include philosophical and historical theology, mysticism, Newman, and Balthasar. He has published scholarly articles in *Theological Studies, Philosophy and Theology, Louvain Studies, Logos, ACPA Quarterly*, and elsewhere. He holds a doctorate from Yale University and has served as President of the Jesuit Philosophical Association. Address: Theology Department, Georgetown University, Washington, DC, 20057, USA.

Gabriel Flynn is Lecturer in Ecumenism and Interreligious Dialogue at the Mater Dei Institute of Education, Dublin, a College of Dublin City University. He was formerly Lecturer in Theology and Head of the Department of Moral Theology at the Milltown Institute of Theology and Philosophy, Dublin, a Recognized College of the National University of Ireland. A priest of the Diocese of Meath, he is the author of *Yves Congar's Vision of the Church in a World of Unbelief* (Aldershot, Hampshire: Ashgate, 2004). His areas of specialization include ecclesiology and ecumenism, historical and political theology, and the great Catholic thinkers of the twentieth century. His articles on the theology of Congar have appeared in *Louvain Studies, New Blackfriars, La Vie spirituelle, Theology Digest* and elsewhere. He holds a doctorate from the University of Oxford and is presently writing a book on the ecclesiology of Yves Congar. Address: The school of Theology, Mater Dei Institute of Education, a College of Dublin City University, Clonliffe Road, Dublin 3, Ireland.

Jean-Pierre Jossua, OP, is a veteran of Congar's era and was a loyal disciple, friend and colleague during the long years of labour, study and struggle at Le Saulchoir, Paris. He is a theologian, but also a specialist in modern literature. He has contributed to the dialogue between church and culture, and religion and literature. He is author of the influential study *Le Père Congar: la théologie au service du peuple de Dieu* (Paris: Cerf, 1967). His other publications include *Le Salut: incarnation ou mystère pascal* (Paris: Cerf, 1968); *La Condition du témoin* (Paris: Cerf, 1984); and *Pour une histoire religieuse de l'expérience littéraire*, 4 vol. (Paris: Beauchesne, 1985-1998). Address: Couvent Saint Jacques, 20 Rue des Tanneries, F-75013 Paris, France.

Fergus Kerr, OP, is Honorary Senior Lecturer in Theology and Religious Studies at the University of Edinburgh, and formerly Regent of Blackfriars Hall, University of Oxford. He is editor of *New Blackfriars* and author of *Theology After Wittgenstein* (Oxford: Blackwell, 1986; 2nd ed., London: SPCK, 1997); *Immortal Longings: Versions of Transcending Humanity* (Notre Dame, IN:Notre Dame University Press, 1997); *After Aquinas: Versions of Thomism* (Oxford: Blackwell, 2002); and *Twentieth-Century Catholic Theologians: From Chenu to John Paul II* (Oxford: Blackwell, forthcoming). Address: Blackfriars, Oxford OX1 3LY, UK.

Karl Cardinal Lehmann is Bishop of Mainz, Germany. He was an assistant to Fr. Karl Rahner, SJ. In 1968, following studies in Freiburg/Br., Rome, Munich and Münster, he was appointed Professor of Theology at the Johannes-Gutenberg University in Mainz. From 1971 to 1983, he was Professor of Dogmatic and Ecumenical Theology at the Albert Ludwigs University in Freiburg/Br. He was appointed Bishop of Mainz in 1983, and in 1987 was elected President of the German Bishops' Conference, a position he held for three terms. In 2001, he was created a cardinal by Pope John Paul II. Cardinal Lehmann is a committed ecumenist and has engaged in dialogue with, among others, the main Lutheran Church organization in Germany. He is a member of the Ponticial Council for Promoting Christian Unity. A prolific author, his publications include *Glauben bezeugen – Gesellschaft gestalten: Reflexionen und Positionen*, 2Bde. (Freiburg iBr.: Herder, 1993); and *Frei vor Gott: Glauben in öffentlicher Verantwortung* (Freiburg iBr.: Herder, 2003). Address: Bischofsplatz 2a, 55116 Mainz, Germany.

Richard P. McBrien is Crowley-O'Brien Professor of Theology at the University of Notre Dame, Indiana. A priest of the Archdiocese of Hartford, Connecticut, he is an internationally recognised author and Catholic commentator. His books include *Catholicism*, new ed. (Francisco, CA: Harper, 1994); and *Lives of the Saints* (Francisco, CA: Harper, 2001). He was President of the Catholic Theological Society of America (1973-74), and winner of its John Courtney Murray Award in 1976. Address: Department of Theology, University of Notre Dame, 130 Malloy Hall, Notre Dame, IN 46556-4619, USA.

Alberto Melloni is Professor of History at the University of Modena-Reggio Emilia, Italy, and a member of the John XXIII Foundation of

Religious Science in Bologna. He is an internationally recognised authority on the Second Vatican Council, Pope John XXIII, and the thought of Yves Congar. He is a contributor to the *History of Vatican II*, directed by Giuseppe Alberigo, and editor of the Italian edition. Address: Via san Vitale 114, Bologna, Italy.

Terrence Merrigan is Professor of Dogmatic Theology at the Katholieke Universiteit Leuven, Belgium. He is Editor-in-Chief of *Louvain Studies*. He is an authority on the thought of John Henry Newman and on interreligious dialogue. He is the author of *Clear Heads and Holy Hearts: The Religious and Theological Ideal of John Henry Newman* (Leuven/Grand Rapids, MI: Peeters/Eerdmans, 1991), and the editor of *The Myriad Christ: Plurality and the Quest for Unity in Contemporary Christology* (Leuven: Peeters, 2000) and *Newman and Faith* (Leuven: Peeters, 2004). Address: Faculty of Theology, Katholieke Universiteit Leuven, Sint-Michielsstraat 6, B-3000, Leuven, Belgium.

John W. O'Malley, SJ, is Distinguished Professor of Church History at Weston Jesuit School of Theology, Cambridge, Massachusetts. He is an expert in medieval and early modern European history, notably, early modern Catholicism and Renaissance culture. His publications include *The First Jesuits* (Cambridge, MA: Harvard University Press, 1993); *Trent and All That: Renaming Catholicism in the Early Modern Era* (Cambridge, MA: Harvard University Press, 2000); and *Four Cultures of the West* (Cambridge, MA: Harvard University Press, 2004). Address: Weston Jesuit School of Theology, 3 Phillips Place, Cambridge, MA 02138, USA.

Thomas F. O'Meara, OP, is the William K. Warren Professor Emeritus of Theology at the University of Notre Dame, Indiana. His publications include *Thomas Aquinas: Theologian* (Notre Dame, IN: Notre Dame University Press, 1997); and *Erich Przywara, SJ: His Theology and His World* (Notre Dame, IN: Notre Dame University Press, 2002). Address: St Thomas Priory, 7200 West Division Street, River Forest, IL 60305-1294, USA.

Jonathan Robinson, is the founder of the Oratory of St Philip Neri, Toronto and was formerly a member of and for a time Chairman of the Department of Philosophy, McGill University, Montreal, Quebec.

His publications include *Duty and Hypocrisy in Hegel's Phenomenology of Mind* (Toronto: University of Toronto Press, 1977); *On the Lord's Appearing: An Essay on Prayer and Tradition* (Edingburgh: T&T Clark, 1997); *Spiritual Combat Revisited* (San Francisco, CA: Ignatius, 2003); and *The Mass and Modernity* (San Francisco, CA: Ignatius, 2005). Address: The Oratory of St Philip Neri, 1372 King Street West, Toronto, Ontario, Canada, M6K 1H3.

J. J. Scarrisbrick, is the Professor Emeritus of History at the University of Warwick. His publications include *Henry VIII* (London: Eyre & Spottiswoode, 1968); new ed. (New Haven, CT: Yale University Press, 1997) and *The Reformation and the English People* (Oxford: Blackwell, 1984). He was a member of the first Anglican Roman Catholic International Commission (ARCIC1), and is currently the national Chairman of LIFE (UK). Address: LIFE House, Newbold Terrace, Leamington Spa, Warwickshire CV32 4EA, UK.

John Webster is Professor of Systematic Theology at King's College, University of Aberdeen and sometime Lady Margaret Professor of Divinity in the University of Oxford. He is a founding editor of the *International Journal of Systematic Theology* and editor of *The Cambridge Companion to Karl Barth* (Cambridge: Cambridge University Press, 2000). His recent publications include *Holiness* (London: SCM Press, 2003); *Holy Scripture: A Dogmatic Sketch* (Cambridge: Cambridge University Press, 2003); and *Barth*, 2nd ed. (New York: Continuum, 2004). Address: King's College, University of Aberdeen, Aberdeen AB24 3UB, UK.

A. N. Williams is University Lecturer in Patristics and Fellow of Corpus Christi College, University of Cambridge. She previously taught at Yale University where she received her doctorate. She is author of *The Ground of Union: Deification in Aquinas and Palamas* (Oxford: Oxford University Press, 1999). Her research interests include patristic and medieval theology, and systematic and ecumenical theology. She is presently writing a book on the intellect in patristic theology. Address: Corpus Christi College, University of Cambridge, Cambridge CB2 1RH, UK.

INTRODUCTION

Gabriel FLYNN

Lecturer in Theology
Mater Dei Institute of Education, a College of Dublin City University

The greatest challenge for the Church at the dawn of the third millennium of Christianity is evangelisation. Faced with the de-Christianisation of Europe and of the Western world, evinced by the rise and widespread dissemination of modern atheism, unbelief, religious indifference, and an increasingly pervasive amorality, as well as a newly resurgent political hostility to religion extending from the nation states of Europe to the highest level of European parliamentary democracy, the only appropriate Church response is a new proclamation of the gospel of Jesus Christ. The cultural challenge posed by a renewed evangelisation of European society is gargantuan. In this regard, I do not think it is an exaggeration to say that the French are among the leaders in the field of evangelisation in the present generation, as they were in the renewal of ecclesiology and Church a generation ago — the brilliant generation of Cardinals Yves Congar, Henri de Lubac and Father Louis Bouyer, to mention just some of the most illustrious.

In one of his last works, *Entretiens d'automne* (Paris, 1987), Yves Congar offers an incisive analysis of the place of religion in European society: "Europe was made by Christianity. It is impossible to see modern Europe without Christianity... When Paul VI named St. Benedict the patron saint of Europe I think that he had a very profound intuition, since it was really monasticism, and in particular the Benedictine order, which deeply shaped Europe."

But Congar also identifies the Achilles heel of "Christian" Europe in precise terms: "This Christianity and this monasticism have been monopolised by the Church, and by a Church which became increasingly clerical and even ended up by being very theocratic and even hierocratic (theocracy being the domination of God and hierocracy the domination of priests). That was very serious because it provoked a reaction." To the extent that a clerical, hierocratic Church still prevails, it continues to engender a hostile reaction in Western secular society. Faced with the dual challenge of hostility from within old "Christian" Europe, now deeply marked by the present aggressive expansion of Islam, and certain inherent, recurrent problems associated with reform of ecclesial "structures," the Catholic Church and Christianity in Europe, and the West in general, must chart a new course. A church which dares to embrace accountability and transparency should respond urgently and effectively to the challenges of the post-conciliar era, notably, the ongoing application of the Second Vatican Council's vision for the laity and ecumenism; the formulation of a comprehensive response to the clerical sexual abuse scandals; and, while honouring the Church's teaching on orders, the recognition of the essential contribution of women in the Church's ministry of decision-making.

An undisputed "Master," honoured belatedly as an intellectual giant of his time, Cardinal Congar knew well the anguish that normally accompanies great thinkers. His plight in the period before the Second Vatican Council and following his dismissal as Professor of Fundamental Theology at the Saulchoir in 1954,[1] now fully

---

[1] See Marie-Dominique Chenu, *Une école de théologie: le Saulchoir* (Paris: Cerf, 1985). In 1937, the Saulchoir, with its two faculties of theology and philosophy, 22 professors and 125 students, was transferred from Kain-la-Tombe, near Tournai in Belgium, where it had been in exile owing to the anti-clerical legislation of the French Third Republic, to Étiolles, near Corbeil. Then, in 1971, it was moved to the Couvent St. Jacques in Paris, followed in 1972 by its important library.

documented in *Journal d'un théologien (1946-1956)*,[2] is aptly
described in that pertinent phrase of Albert Einstein, "Great spirits have always encountered violent opposition from mediocre
minds." Congar's theological edifice relates to the challenges of
the present-day Church and offers relevant insights into some of the
most controversial issues currently debated by theologians, philosophers and secular commentators. When Congar formulated a
renewed vision of the Church, a lifetime's work, he was concerned
to respond effectively to the burning questions of his time, in particular, the role of the laity, renewal in liturgy and mission theology, ecclesial reform and a new Church engagement with the modern world, following the centuries-old policy of defensive
isolationism. That Congar's vision eventually reached the highest
level of the Church's life at Vatican II is a remarkable achievement. Nonetheless, that vision has been realised only partially in the
post-conciliar period and therein lies a great opportunity for the
Church today.

At the dawn of the twenty-first century, leaders of the Christian
Churches have called for a new beginning. Pope John Paul II,
whose efforts at evangelisation through World Youth Day and other
initiatives in the course of his international pilgrimages are at once
effective and attractive to young people globally, shows that evangelisation, in order to be effective, must be personal and doctri-
nally based. By making evangelisation a priority for the Church,
Pope John Paul has made his papal ministry an evangelical one,
thereby providing an effective model of evangelisation for all
Christians, perhaps his greatest service to humanity. As he writes:
"To nourish ourselves with the word in order to be 'servants of the
word' in the work of evangelisation: this is surely a priority for

---

[2] Yves Congar, *Journal d'un théologien (1946-1956)*, ed. and annotated
Étienne Fouilloux and others, 2nd ed. (Paris: Cerf, 2001).

the Church at the dawn of the new millennium."[3] The realisation of this lofty goal calls for "costly grace," to borrow a phrase of Dietrich Bonhoeffer, the Lutheran Pastor who was executed by the Gestapo on 9 April 1945, now acclaimed for his moral courage in the face of the systematic brutality of the German Nazi regime. He writes: "Costly grace is the gospel which must be *sought* again and again, the gift which must be *asked* for, the door at which a man must *knock*. Such grace is costly because it calls us to follow *Jesus Christ*. It is costly because it costs a man his life."[4]

In this regard, a point to be noticed is that Cardinal Yves Congar viewed the twentieth century as an occasion of evangelic opportunity: "I know that it is a century of unbelief and religious indifference, that it is also the century of the expansion of Islam, but among the minority of faithful who truly believe, it is a really evangelistic century."[5] I have argued elsewhere[6] that the Church should engage in a reassessment of its educational apostolate in order to ensure the success of the enterprise of evangelisation for the new millennium, inspired by Pope John Paul II.[7] In executing the mission of evangelisation, the Church depends on its two richest resources, namely, a holy priesthood and an educated laity — and

[3] John Paul II, *Apostolic Letter: Novo Millennio Ineunte of His Holiness Pope John Paul II to the Bishops Clergy and Lay Faithful at the close of the Great Jubilee of the Year 2000* (London: Catholic Truth Society, 2001) par. 40.

[4] Dietrich Bonhoeffer, *The Cost of Discipleship*, trans. Chr. Kaiser, complete ed. 13th ed. (London: SCM, 1984) 37.

[5] Yves Congar, *Fifty Years of Catholic Theology: Conversations with Yves Congar*, ed. Bernard Lauret, trans. John Bowden (London: SCM, 1988) 66; also id., *Entretiens d'automne*, 2nd ed. (Paris: Cerf, 1987) 86.

[6] See Gabriel Flynn, *Yves Congar's Vision of the Church in a World of Unbelief* (Aldershot: Ashgate, 2004).

[7] John Paul II, *Tertio Millennio Adveniente: Apostolic Letter of His Holiness Pope John Paul II to the Bishops, Clergy and Lay Faithful on Preparation for the Jubilee of the Year 2000* (London: Catholic Truth Society, 1994) pars. 56-59. John Paul II, *Apostolic Letter: Novo Millennio Ineunte*, pars. 36, 39-41, 54-57.

never has the Catholic laity been so theologically literate and self-confident as it is today. The point I wish to make is that the presence of the priest, alongside his theologically educated and articulate lay friends in the educational apostolate, is more necessary than ever for the renewal of the Church. The Second Vatican Council affirms the teaching office of priests as co-workers with the bishops in the transmission of the apostolic faith in all its integrity.[8] Pope John Paul II has called for a renewed commitment on the part of all consecrated persons to the Church's mission of education. He highlights their indispensable contribution to the cause of evangelisation and education in his Post-Synodal Exhortation *Vita consecrata*, given in 1996:

> With respectful sensitivity and missionary boldness, consecrated men and women should show that faith in Jesus Christ enlightens the whole enterprise of education, never disparaging human values but rather confirming and elevating them. [...] Because of the importance that Catholic and ecclesiastical universities and faculties have in the field of education and evangelisation, Institutes which are responsible for their direction should be conscious of their responsibility.[9]

We may be inclined to reply that the widespread decline in vocations in the Western world does not permit the continued large-scale presence of priests in education there. But it is to be noted that

---

[8] "Decree on the Ministry and Life of Priests, *Presbyterorum Ordinis*, 7 December 1965," *Vatican Council II: The Conciliar and Post Conciliar Documents*, ed. Austin Flannery, 7th ed., 2 vols. (New York: Costello, 1984), I, pars. 2, 12. "Dogmatic Constitution on the Church: Vatican II, *Lumen Gentium*," 21 November 1964, par. 28.

[9] John Paul II, *Post-Synodal Apostolic Exhortation Vita Consecrata of the Holy Father John Paul II to the Bishops and Clergy Religious Orders and Congregations Societies of Apostolic Life Secular Institutes and All the Faithful on the Consecrated Life and Its Mission in the Church and in the World* (London: Catholic Truth Society, 1996) par. 97.

while John Paul II acknowledges the vocations crisis in *Vita con-secrata*, he also emphatically urges "consecrated persons to take up again, wherever possible, the mission of education in schools of every kind and level, and in Universities and Institutions of higher learning."[10] It may be suggested that if the current trend in dioceses continues whereby priests are systematically removed from education at all levels, the words of Pope John Paul II may be reduced to the level of rhetoric. I feel, therefore, no hesitation in asserting that the Pope's perception of education as the key to success in his grand plan for evangelisation is prophetic and timely.

The celebration of the centenary of the birth of Yves Congar (2004), along with the distinguished Jesuit theologians Bernard Lonergan (1904-84), Karl Rahner (1904-84), and John Courtney Murray (1904-67), all born in the same year, has moved theologians to look again at the work of an outstanding scholar in an outstanding generation. The primary aim of the present volume is to examine Congar's role as theologian of the church and assess the significance of his contribution. It reflects on important questions, the result of research undertaken in the course of the past decade, questions which are best considered in the context of interdisciplinary scholarship. The contributors to the volume, experts in the fields of theology, ecumenism, philosophy and history from nine countries, are in many respects representative of Congar's intellectual and ecumenical interests. As will be apparent, an attempt was made to put theological questions into a broader frame. One of the reasons for this is to help redress the deleterious process of polarisation in the Catholic intellectual community in the period since the Second Vatican Council.

The contributions to this symposium are divided into five parts. First, ecumenical prefaces by leaders of the churches with which Congar worked closely in the course of his long and distinguished

---

[10] *Ibid.*

ecumenical career. Cardinal Avery Dulles, SJ, Laurence J. McGinley Professor of Religion and Society at Fordham University, New York recognises Congar's greatness as ecumenist and reformer and gives a positive assessment of his immense contribution at Vatican II, which he says "could almost be called Congar's Council." Dr. Kallistos Ware, Bishop of Diokleia and Fellow of Pembroke College, Oxford, who kindly supported this project from its inception, enunciates an Orthodox position in favour of an old friend of his Church. Dr. Kenneth Stevenson, Anglican Bishop of Portsmouth, England, makes an important observation in the course of a gracious tribute: "Congar's theology is rooted in history, in historical theology ... No understanding of the Church can ignore historical realities." Dr. Marc Lienhard, Honorary Dean of the Protestant Faculty of Theology of Strasbourg and formerly President of the Directoire of the Church of the Confession of Augsburg of Alsace and Lorraine, points to the importance of "elaborating an ecumenical vocabulary together" that would help avoid "serious misunderstandings" concerning the same words used with different meanings by Catholics and Protestants. Echoing Congar's call for "ecumenical metanoīa" in 1983, he asks rather poignantly: "Are we going to remain deaf to such an appeal?"

The second part brings together diverse lines of reflection on the question: what sort of theologian is Yves Congar? Dr. John Webster, Professor of Divinity at King's College, University of Aberdeen, sometime Lady Margaret Professor of Divinity, Christ Church, Oxford and Editor of the *International Journal of Systematic Theology*, offers "evangelical reflections" on Congar's *La tradition et les traditions*, "a classic example of *ressourcement* theology." From his perspective as a "Protestant dogmatician," he shows that Congar was profoundly concerned with tradition and history. He argues that the challenge Congar and other *ressourcement* theologians present to Protestant theologians is "whether Protestant zeal for purity — in the doctrines of God, Christ, the church and elsewhere — leads to a segregation of the divine from the creaturely, which in turn inhibits grasp of the plenitude of God's self-communication." This article may be read as a Protestant "conversation" with Congar and his *ressourcement* friends. More important is its profoundly pastoral invitation to continue "the dialogue between Catholicism and Protestantism." If Professor Webster dares to entertain the hope that Protestant theology "can grow beyond its attachments to a culture of suspicion," then perhaps Congar's vision for reconciliation and unity may yet be cherished and lived, not only by Protestants, but by all Christians.

Dr. Fergus Kerr, OP, formerly Regent of Blackfriars Hall, Oxford, Honorary Senior Lecturer in Theology and Religious Studies, University of Edinburgh and Editor of *New Blackfriars*, depicts Congar as the great champion of *ressourcement* theology who remained ever a Thomist. As he comments: "For all his immense influence in making Catholic theology much more *historical*, in reopening tradition, in practising *ressourcement* and so on, Congar did not think of himself as departing from Thomas's theological methodology, conceived appropriately in a sapiential-ontological mode." Fr. Kerr's contribution illustrates how Congar's *A History of Theology*, overshadowed by other more major works, is "truly a masterpiece." It sheds light on complex and controversial questions in the history of twentieth-century Catholic theology, not least the "nouvelle théologie." In his conclusion, Kerr comments: "Soon after Vatican II, Congar is happy to allow a 'new theology' along the lines by then being followed by Karl Rahner. It is clear, however, that he favours the example of Michael Schmaus, which shows that 'a classical type of theology can *adapt* and absorb the new questions and develop the new aspects, which … refer to man and his existential experience'."

Dr. Gabriel Flynn, Lecturer in Theology at the Mater Dei Institute of Education, Dublin City University assesses Congar's role as reformer and argues that "his contribution in this field makes him an architect of the contemporary Church." If it is true that the principles for reform articulated in *Vraie et fausse réforme dans l'Église* (1950), arguably Congar's most important and original contribution to Christian theology, "help to provide an effective safeguard against division and schism in the Church," then his contribution as Church reformer deserves renewed attention. By means of a retrospective application of his principles for reform to the great historical ruptures of the Church in the eleventh and sixteenth centuries respectively, as well as to the crisis in the post-conciliar period engendered by Archbishop Marcel Lefebvre, it is argued that "the juxtaposition of reform and unity in Congar's theology gives rise to a transformative and creative dialectic, one that offers the richest hope for a renewed Church of the future." The paper concludes with a dual cultural/pastoral response to the present crisis of Christian proclamation, one that points to the continued relevance of Congar as reformer.

Dr. A. N. Williams, University Lecturer in Patristics, Corpus Christi College, University of Cambridge, considers Congar's theology of the laity, viewed as "genuinely theological and a contribution to ecclesiology." In her assessment of the development of Congar's theology, Dr. Williams notes the tensions and indeed ambivalence in his writing about laypeople, ranging from concerns regarding the Church's teaching authority to problems of terminology, problems that may be explained by reference to the French context: "The legacy of the French revolution... necessarily haunts Congar's treatment of the subject in a way that is scarcely imaginable to an English-speaking reader: it is not surprising that the French church should have been suspicious of the secular world, actively hostile as it was to any kind of religious commitment or organisation, and it was precisely this anti-clericalism that fuelled the fires of an unhelpful clericalism, so that the very word *laïc* came to designate someone who was not only anti-clerical, but even anti-Christian." Williams's largely positive assessment of Congar's theology of the laity points to his profound concern for a church engagement with the world and indicates a welcome capacity for self-critique: "Not only the juridical and bureaucratic language has been abandoned in the later works, but the subordination of these ideas to those native to the ancient tradition of the church is explicitly declared, inasmuch as Congar asserts the primacy of persons over structures." The assertion of the primacy of "persons over structures" is of fundamental importance for the Church; a lesson that must be learnt anew by successive generations of leaders.

Cardinal Karl Lehmann, Bishop of Mainz, Germany, portrays his one-time friend as "a man of the Church." Perhaps more than any of the great theologians of the era, Congar is deserving of this appellation. Dr. Lehmann notes his "rare" giftedness: "At a very early stage, he established himself as a thinker with an acute sensibility for both history and reality — a rare combination indeed." As for his contribution to the Vatican Council: "Yves Congar belongs right in the heart of the Second Vatican Council." Cardinal Lehmann holds that Congar's willingness to tackle difficult issues, his peaceableness and obedience were inspired by a profound love of the Church — "an intense passion." His conclusion: "Yves Congar will always remain a man of the Church."

Cardinal Congar is perhaps best known for his contribution to ecumenism. He played a pre-eminent role in dialogue with Protestants in the period before the Vatican Council and succeeded, where others had failed, in extending the hand of friendship across the ancient divisions of history to the world of Orthodoxy. In the third part of this centenary tribute, three commentators assess his momentous contribution to the ecumenical movement. Professor Jean-Pierre Jossua, OP, sometime colleague and life-long friend of Cardinal Congar states his goal in precise terms: "With the benefit of hindsight, I propose to say simply and succinctly what seems to me to be the essential, and, I venture to suggest, what we agreed on together concerning him, during those last years when we had so many occasions to talk about these things." He holds that by placing ecumenism "within the Church," Congar manifested a "crucial spiritual intuition" which determined the two related preoccupations of his entire career, namely, "the re-founding of ecclesiology, and thinking about unity." A master of the psychology of ecumenism, Congar knew that to engage in ecumenical dialogue, "it is necessary to know and to like the other side, to respect them, to honour their Christian values… The priority is to get to know and to like what these Christians were in the past." Fr. Jossua, perhaps without intending to, discloses an important element in Congar's character. "Yves Congar was also capable of recognising the value of positions different from his own, such as that of Fr. Couturier with his prayer for unity; he saw in it a spiritual complementarity with his own way." The paper concludes with an adumbration of the "the very significant evolution" in Congar's ecumenism, a theme developed elsewhere by Jossua.

The second contribution on ecumenism comes from Dr. Bruno Bürki, formerly Professor of Theology at the University of Fribourg and sometime Vice-President of the Council of the Swiss Federation of Protestant Churches. He recognises the challenge of Congar's ecclesiology without wishing to appropriate him. "Our wish, rather — at the heart of Protestantism — is to meet the challenges of Congar the Catholic theologian, on important points in ecclesiology and liturgy. Father Yves Congar, now deceased, still has things to tell us, both from his own point of view and in the

GABRIEL FLYNN

Church to which he belonged." Professor Bürki's reflections on
ecclesiology, liturgy and ecumenism are important and call for careful consideration in Catholic as well as Protestant and Reformed
circles. He articulates precisely the challenge for Protestant theologians and pastors: "I am convinced that worship in the
Reformed tradition, has an ecumenical calling to come into contact
with Catholic liturgy." The essay analyses Congar's contribution
to liturgy in the period after the Second Vatican Council but
"always in the context of the ecclesial celebration of the liturgy."
It points to a problem with liturgical reformers in the Catholic
Church, one that also extends to other confessions: "Père Congar
considered that the promoters of church reform in the liturgical
movement were over hasty and too exclusively preoccupied with
restoring and innovating liturgical forms, without sufficient consideration of the raison d'être or the 'original nature of Christian
worship'." While discussion of questions concerning liturgical
mediation, sacraments and the nature of Christ's presence in the
Eucharist inevitably engenders debate and division, the ultimate
challenge is, as Professor Bürki notes, "to make an act of faith in
the divine presence among us, and so give glory to the Father by
the Son in the Holy Spirit."

In the third contribution to our discussion of ecumenism, Gabriel
Flynn examines how Congar's ecumenical theology contributes to
the difficult process of reconciliation. It considers the objection that
his "vision of ecumenism has failed, while Christian unity remains
an unrealised goal." The proposal that ecumenism be viewed as
"an ethical imperative for all Christians" is a challenging one.
It seeks to turn past failures into triumphs, a course that requires
not only a renewed ecclesiology and an effective ecumenism, such
as Congar proposes, but also an indomitable fortitude. On the question of the evolution in Congar's ecumenical thought from
"Catholicity" to a qualified acceptance of "reconciled diversity,"

Flynn suggests that the cause of ecumenism "may be better served by respecting diversities, rather than attempting to reconcile them." Much doctrinal work remains to be done, therefore, since "unity in pluralism" is impossible without substantial agreement on fundamental truths, as the philosopher John Rawls has noted. To advance the "remarkable achievement of Congar's ecumenism" which is also the achievement of Vatican II, it is necessary for theologians to engage anew in painstaking dialogue on Church doctrines and structures, dialogue that will not succumb to old obstacles to unity or falter in the face of new difficulties that may emerge in the future.

We now turn to the question of Congar's contribution to the history of Catholic ecclesiology, the subject of the fourth part of the present volume. Dr. John O'Malley, SJ, Distinguished Professor of Church History at the Weston Jesuit School of Theology, Cambridge, Massachusetts assesses Congar's *L'Église: De saint Augustin à l'époque moderne* (1970) and the more circumscribed study, *L'Ecclésiologie du haut moyen âge: De saint Grégoire le Grand à la désunion entre Byzance et Rome* (1968). Fr. O'Malley's highly laudatory review of *L'Église* is clear recognition of Congar's brilliance as an historical theologian. "This is a work of synthesis of the first order. Nothing quite like it previously existed, and in many ways it has never been surpassed. That fact alone testifies to its extraordinary importance." Even with its "limitations" and "omissions," "*L'Église* remains impressive as a work of historical synthesis. While the erudition is almost breathtaking, in its detail, it never overwhelms the text." O'Malley praises Congar's generation for their efforts "to move theology in all its aspects out of the arena of timeless truths to an enterprise in which history, including so-called institutional and social history, conditioned all its expressions." It is with certain regret that he notes, among other omissions, that there is only one passing reference to painting.

Turning to *L'Ecclésiologie*, it is also viewed as "a work of synthesis." O'Malley refers to the review of this work by Ovidio Capitani, written in 1970, which was "highly critical of Congar's method ... the method was not historical — or at least not historical enough." While accepting that such criticism raises "important questions" and must be taken seriously, it does not, however, "substantially damage Congar's historical achievement in *L'Ecclésiologie* and even less in *L'Église*." In the final analysis, Congar's "historical works," seen also as "works of theology," are judged to be "almost as relevant now" as when they were first published.

The volume would be incomplete without an analysis of the controversial diary which Congar kept during the Second Vatican Council, published as *Mon journal du Concile* (2002). Dr. J. J. Scarisbrick, formerly Professor of History at the University of Warwick, assesses its substantive issues from the perspective of a "lay" historian. His judgement cannot safely be ignored by theologians and pastors. "The *Diary* which Yves Congar kept during the Second Vatican Council is of extraordinary importance to the historian not only of the Council itself but, in a sense, of the Church in the twentieth century." Professor Scarisbrick's paper provides an account of the key "battles" for a renewed ecclesiology which went on over months and in some cases for several years in the commissions and sub-commissions of the Council. He notes that the diary reveals the "stupendous amount of work" Congar undertook at the Council, as well as the extensive involvement of Popes John XXIII and Paul VI, "albeit often behind the scenes." On the diary's assessment of Pope Pius XII, Scarisbrick comments: "Congar was unfair to Pius XII. He was probably also unfair to the Curia, overestimating its power, villainy and rigid conservatism." Scarisbrick acknowledges that Vatican II was "an incomparable blessing," while also documenting the "wholly unexpected, unintended and lamentable events" in the "period of turbulence" that ensued. His assessment of "the catechetical failure of the post-conciliar Church" raises questions about the present process and programmes of catechesis used in schools, as well as the formation of catechists in Catholic faculties and universities. On the question of "dialogue with the world," a phrase beloved of Paul VI and of Congar, the article concludes: "Was Congar, then, like *Gaudium et Spes*, too optimistic? Insofar as his purpose was to help the Church to rediscover her full, authentic self-understanding, he could be described as a radical *conservative*."

Dr. Alberto Melloni, Professor of History at the University of Modena-Reggio Emilia and a member of the John XXIII Foundation of Religious Science in Bologna, reflects on what he describes as the antinomy of "the system" and "the truth" in Congar's diaries which like "true/false reform" and "Tradition/tradition" are important for a full knowledge of the period under consideration. He sees *Mon Journal du Concile* as "a document of primary importance for getting to know Vatican II and the role played by the Dominican ecumenist within the council." In like manner, *Journal d'un théologien 1946-1956* (2000), the main focus of the present article, is viewed as "an extraordinary source for understanding that period." In the latter, Professor Melloni identifies "the dialectic between two dimensions of the church ... on the one hand, the church of Tradition, sensitive to the unceasing relating of the needs of the time to the Gospel and vice versa ... and on the other hand, the church of the condemnations ... that Congar does not hesitate to define as a regime and uses very harsh expressions to describe it." By means of a careful analysis of the Roman Curia's authoritarian "system" during the pontificate of Pope Pius XII and of its principal "personages," Melloni presents a detailed case for a "tyrannical apparatus," a "police regime" whose "monopoly" ultimately failed to stifle the Congar of Vatican II, who at that Council "earned for himself that very cardinalate that at the end of his life would honour his service to the truth."

We next come to the question of pneumatology, an important element in Congar's thought, one which receives its definitive formulation only at the close of his theological career with the monumental three-volume *Je crois en l'Esprit Saint* (1979-80), his last major work. Dr. Richard P. McBrien, Crowley-O'Brien Professor of Theology at the University of Notre Dame, Indiana, assesses the role of pneumatology in Congar's thought and its significance in the history of Catholic ecclesiology. His purpose is "to reflect only schematically on how Congar's evolving understanding of the Holy Spirit impacted his understanding of the nature and mission of the Church. For Congar is-first, last, and always-an ecclesiologist." Deeply sympathetic to Congar, Fr. McBrien writes: "He was undoubtedly the greatest ecclesiologist not only of the 20th century but of the entire history of the Church as well." High praise indeed. In the context of "a full and relatively detailed synthesis and critical evaluation" of *Je crois en l'Esprit Saint*, McBrien, in common with Orthodox theologians, is careful to place the Holy Spirit "at the heart of Christian theology" as "the power through which the [gospel] proclamation is made and fulfilled." The essay concludes with a six-point summary of the principal pneumatological elements of Congar's ecclesiology and asserts that his most enduring legacy is in the domain of ecclesiology, rather than pneumatology.

Dr. Jonathan Robinson of the Toronto Oratory and formerly Lecturer in Philosophy at McGill University, Montreal, assesses Congar's theory of tradition, a critical element in the history of ecclesiology. His stated aim is "to examine Fr Congar's analysis of the function of tradition in the Church from the standpoint of the questions raised by Catholic life today." At the outset, he expresses the view that Congar's theory about tradition "cannot sustain his basically orthodox and sacramental view of Catholicism." In his opinion, Congar fails to demonstrate that "the active side of tradition is the essential, or the most important, aspect of tradition." He asks: "In the end, does not Congar necessarily lead us to some sort of process theology; the theory, that is, that God is developing?" with a concomitant failure to erect a bulwark "against historicism." He holds that Congar's attitude towards the visible Church left the "monuments of tradition" — including magisterium, liturgy and the sacred canons — vulnerable to reformulation, thus contributing to "a decrease in the importance of tradition in the life of the Church." Fr. Robinson applies his arguments about the weaknesses in Congar's analysis of tradition to the liturgy and sexuality. He claims that "the far-reaching changes in the liturgy imposed by the Magisterium after the Second Vatican Council" broke with the organic development of the liturgical life of the Church and resulted in the "the liturgy as a *monument* to tradition" being "somewhat effaced." And while not suggesting that Congar wished to lend support to the sexual revolution, Robinson asserts that his view of tradition as "essentially movement forward under the influence of the Holy Spirit ... leaves the way open for fundamental changes in the way Christians should live their lives and think about their destiny."

In an address to the Italian parliament in November 2002, Pope John Paul II, commenting on the distortion of the great religions by international terrorism, issues a call to religious leaders and theologians: "Precisely for this reason, the world's religions are challenged to show all their rich potential for peace by directing and as it were 'converting' towards mutual understanding the cultures and civilizations which draw inspiration from them." It is hoped that the contributions to the fifth and final part of this collection may contribute to that process of "mutual understanding." The first essay by Cardinal Georges Cottier, OP, Theologian of the Pontifical Household, provides a general introduction to the "Theology of Religions," based on the teaching of the Second Vatican Council.

He indicates the relevant sources: "The Declaration *Nostra Aetate* should be read in conjunction with the Dogmatic Constitution *Lumen Gentium* and the Decree *Ad Gentes.*" He asserts that the Church is bound to "examine its relationships with non-Christian religions" as it "promotes peace and unity between persons and among peoples". He notes that *Nostra Aetate* and *Lumen Gentium* provide a direction of utmost importance. "The religions are presented according to a certain order, which is that of their distance from or proximity to Christianity. In this way, they have treated of Hinduism, Buddhism, traditional religions, then Islam which is a monotheistic religion, and, finally of Judaism and the Jewish people." In light of the Council's teaching, he argues that "a theology of religions must begin with a theology of Israel or at least incorporate such a theology. To ignore this essential dimension is to lean towards a sort of neomarcionism." Without overlooking difficult questions concerning the status of the great religions *vis à vis* the fullness of salvation in Christ, Cardinal Cottier arrives at an important conclusion: "The theology of religions may not disregard its anthropological foundations. The religious dimension belongs to human nature. The human person is inclined towards the Absolute and, by his or her own strength, is capable of taking significant steps in its direction. These steps are the precious 'waiting stones' on the way to welcoming grace."

The second contribution, by Dr. Thomas F. O'Meara, OP, formerly William K. Warren Professor of Theology at the University of Notre Dame, Indiana, discusses Congar's views on "the issue of salvation outside of Christianity." Describing Congar as "a theologian inspired by historical variety, a historian of church forms taught by Biblical origins to pastoral movements," he assesses his contribution in the context of a review of *The Wide World My Parish: Salvation and its Problems*, originally published in French as *Vaste Monde, ma Paroisse* (Paris, 1959). The main theme of this book is salvation, "human salvation with historical and global contexts." Although Congar's remarks on "salvation and religion are a quite marginal topic in his career in ecclesiology," his contribution is not without importance, as Fr. O'Meara notes: "If today we associate the topic of salvation outside of Christianity with Karl Rahner or Raimundo Pannikar, we will be surprised to learn that Congar too has his theology of the vast numbers of men and women who through an accident of history live outside of the possibility of belief and baptism in Jesus Christ." In the 1960s, Congar maintained a "somewhat negative" evaluation of non-Christian or non-Biblical religions because "unfashionably he would not overlook aspects of religions that are destructive, false, or idolatrous." Congar, in fact, "said he wanted to steer a course down the middle between what he termed an 'optimistic and broad solution' (Rahner, Schlette, Gustave Thils, Hans Küng, Leonardo Boff) and a 'negative and strict solution' (Martin Luther, Ludwig Feuerbach, Karl Barth, Hendrik Kraemer, and Wolfgang Pannenberg). God's salvific will is universal, and his grace prior to the Incarnation is generous; grace lives outside the limits of the church, and the limits between church and religion are not clearly fixed." O'Meara concludes: "In the last analysis, it is not easy to see how Congar differs from the 'optimistic' theologians, for despite his reservations he did see religions as means or mediations of salvation."

In a wide ranging article, Dr. Stephen Fields, SJ, Associate Professor of Theology at Georgetown University, Washington DC, considers Congar's contribution to the debate on salvation and the non-Christian religions. He argues that among thinkers who view Christianity as "the absolute religion," Congar offers "some bold and refreshing insights that chart a middle path" between the "optimistic and broad inclusivism of the Catholic Karl Rahner … and the 'negative and strict' exclusivism of the Lutheran Karl Barth." Fr. Fields comments: "Congar's thought on salvation outside

the Church, taken as a whole, shows subtlety in balancing the problem's constitutive elements: personal conscience, culture, sinfulness and error, the necessity of the Church, and the inclusion of all
humanity in the Incarnation." He disagrees with Professor
O'Meara's conclusion that "finally Congar does not differ essentially from Rahner's optimistic school," a view he considers unsus-
tainable "in light of Congar's unapologetic diagnosis of idolatry
in non-Christian religions." He is concerned that O'Meara's treatment does not sufficiently appreciate the implications of the shift
in Congar's thought "from its early emphasis on the person as the
locus of salvation to its later crediting of culture as an essential
mediation of God's universal saving will." Fields holds that Congar's later thought, which offers a more nuanced view of conscience, constitutes an important advancement: "His later thought,
in suggesting that conscience itself is mediated by specific, determinate religious forms, represents a key advance. It implies that
these forms, despite their errors, can lay some claim to association
with the Body of Christ. Surely it can be no accident that so
schooled a Thomist as Congar would refer to non-Christian religions as 'habitually' a canal of grace." In an attempt to articulate
a fresh understanding of the relation between nature and grace, one
that supports any solution to the problem of salvation outside the
Church, Fields draws on the insights of *Gaudium et Spes* and the
work of Fr. Hans Urs von Balthasar, to construct a model that
"understands nature and grace, not as harmonious but separate principles, but as a unity-in-diversity [which] would ... better understand the reciprocity between conscience and culture and better
undergird the efficacy of non-Christian religions as the habitual
means of humanity's salvation." In a noteworthy conclusion, he
remarks: "Congar and Balthasar move the problem of salvation
outside the Church beyond personal conscience and beyond seeing
non-Christians religions merely as preparations for the Gospel ...

Together with *Gaudium et Spes*, they understand on the one hand the reciprocity between culture and conscience. On the other hand, they understand that all the authentically true, good, and beautiful symbols of human culture participate in the Word-Son-Wisdom. Finally, therefore, they not only carry us beyond St. Thomas. They tone down the optimism of the anonymous Christian by a frank account of sin, while still including all that is created within the divine economy."

The final contribution to this volume, by Dr. Terrence Merrigan, Professor of Dogmatic Theology at the Catholic University of Louvain, considers the appeal to Congar in the theology of religions articulated by Fr. Jacques Dupuis, the controversial Belgian Jesuit who died on 28 December 2004. Professor Merrigan notes that the conflict between the Congregation for the Doctrine of the Faith and Dupuis that followed the publication of his *Toward a Theology of Religious Pluralism* (1997) "provided the ecclesiastical authorities with the opportunity to identify what they regarded as the foundational principles of the Catholic theology of religions." In its responses to Dupuis and "even more forcefully" with the publication of *Dominus Iesus* (2000), the Congregation for the Doctrine of the Faith "demarcated the boundaries within which it felt the discussion of the Christian understanding of other religions must take place." The present essay is an enquiry into "where Congar stood (or perhaps, more accurately, would have stood) in relationship to those boundaries, at least as far as we can gather on the basis of his writings." His role in the debate is clearly acknowledged: "The theme of the relationship between Christianity and the world's religious traditions had, of course, been growing in importance since prior to Vatican Council II, and Congar's *The Wide World My Parish* was one of the books that anticipated the prominence this theme would assume in the years to come." As regards his consideration of a complex, controversial theme in Congar's thought, Professor Merrigan's article has the dual advantage of objectivity and clarity as it moves, by means of four steps, to examine: first, the official view on the Church's role in salvation history; second, Dupuis's appeal to Congar, in light of Dupuis' own position on the matter; third, to provide a critical assessment of Dupuis' references to Congar; fourth, to offer considered reflections on the broader theological significance of the divergence between Dupuis and Congar regarding the role played by the Church in the salvific economy. By way of conclusion, Merrigan points to the enduring value of Congar's contribution: "To separate the Church from Christ — even for a moment, so to speak — would be to rob it of its 'essential' significance as instrument of his salvific will. This is not to suggest that the Church can simply be equated with Christ, only that it makes present, albeit in a limited (because historical) fashion, his universal saving work. After all, while it is possible to distinguish the sacrament and the reality signified, these can never be divided. To suggest, therefore, that Christ is always 'implicated' in the salvation of all men and women, but that the Church is only implicated in the salvation of Christians, would be to violate the sacramental (or incarnational) principle on which the Church is founded. For that reason, it seems to me, Congar's (somewhat ambiguous) defense of the Church's universal mediatory role may well prove more lasting than Dupuis' more daring embrace of the non-Christian religions."

The idea that inspired this centenary volume is to render honour to the memory of Yves Congar, theologian of the Church. At the same time, it is hoped that the volume may also contribute to the Church. A renewed Church for today will not be possible without a renewed engagement with the Second Vatican Council. The success of such an engagement depends, in part, on the Council documents being presented in a more accessible manner, published either separately or in theme-related categories. If the present volume contributes to making the documents of the Council more accessible to the modern person and, therefore, more widely read and applied, it will have rendered fitting tribute to Cardinal Congar. *Requiescat in pace.*

PART I

ECUMENICAL PREFACES

PREFACE

Avery CARDINAL DULLES, SJ

Laurence J. McGinley Professor of Religion and Society
Fordham University, New York

No theologian of the twentieth century is more deserving of a commemorative volume than Yves Congar (1904-95). Born a hundred years ago, in the same year as the great Jesuit theologians Bernard Lonergan, Karl Rahner, and John Courtney Murray, this distinguished Dominican outlived all three of them. Hampered though he was by a progressive sclerosis that limited his mobility since the mid-sixties, he continued to write voluminously through the 1980s. As a former military chaplain, prisoner of war, and highly decorated veteran, he was entitled to spend his final years in the Hôpital des Invalides, Paris, where I last visited him in 1988.

As is well known, Congar's ideas, somewhat advanced for his day, provoked opposition from highly placed churchmen during the 1950s. During that decade his ecclesiastical superiors put severe restrictions on his ability to teach and publish, but he patiently accepted such reserves with the help of his spirituality of the Cross. His many friends assisted in the study, development, and propagation of his ideas. Thanks to Pope John XXIII, who recognized the importance of his work, he was able to play so great a part at Vatican II that it could almost be called Congar's council. After the council, he was personally honoured by Pope Paul VI and then by Pope John Paul II, who created him a cardinal in 1994.

Congar's work may be said to centre about ecumenism, but the pursuit of ecumenism led him into a number of areas, including revelation, the Holy Spirit, and the Church. His understanding of Scripture and Tradition had a manifest influence on the Dogmatic Constitution *Dei Verbum*. His theology of the Holy Spirit has been helpful for Catholic renewal and has facilitated mutual comprehension between the churches of East and West.

Congar's ecumenical ecclesiology permeates the Dogmatic Constitution on the Church *Lumen Gentium* and the Decree on Ecumenism *Unitatis Redintegratio*. Viewing the Church as a people called together in the Holy Spirit, Congar anticipated what is today called a "spirituality of communion." He was among the earliest champions of the idea that non-Catholic churches and communions could possess important elements of the true Church. He believed that Catholicism should take on different forms in different cultures, and that the catholicity of the Church would be enriched if the Greeks and Russians, Scandinavians and British, were in full communion with Roman Catholics.

Congar emphasized the dialectic between structure and life in the Church. He held that lay persons, even without holding any office, could enjoy the gifts of the Holy Spirit and participate in the prophetic, priestly, and regal ministries of Christ. Reacting against the centralism of the previous few centuries, he resuscitated the concept of the local church and envisaged the universal Church as a communion of particular churches — themes with which Protestant, Anglican, and Orthodox could resonate. Together with several colleagues in France and Belgium, he retrieved the ancient idea of collegiality among bishops. In his great work on *True and False Reform* he laid down principles for authentic Catholic reform, carefully distinguishing it from revolutionary proposals that are sometimes marketed under the banner of reform. Open though he was to new research, he firmly adhered to the dogmas and divinely given structures of the Church.

I have mentioned only a few of the many themes that may be culled from Congar's voluminous writings. Highly creative though he was, he modestly concealed his own originality, drawing as much as possible on the work of others. Like his contemporary Henri de Lubac, he possessed an almost incredible mastery of the patristic and medieval sources. He could always find reputable predecessors to support his proposals.

Ten years after Congar's death, it is now possible to assess his achievement in retrospect. The present symposium commends itself by the high quality of the multinational group of scholars contributing to it. I feel privileged in being asked to introduce this timely volume.

PREFACE

Kallistos WARE

Bishop of Diokleia (Ecumenical Patriarchate of Constantinople)
and Fellow of Pembroke College, Oxford

In a talk entitled "Reflections on being a Theologian," given in 1981, Fr Yves Congar described theology as "the unfolding, the defense, the deployment of the confession of the apostolic faith within a communion that is fully catholic."[1] These last words, "a communion that is fully catholic," exactly describe what I see as the distinctive spirit of Congar's standpoint as scholar, writer and teacher. He was *par excellence* a "catholic" theologian, whose thought was marked by wholeness and balance, by integration and depth. Faithful to what he termed "the classical age of the church's life"[2] — to the age of the Fathers, both Latin and Greek — he bore witness to the great tradition that unites together West and East, to the common roots that Catholics and Orthodox share with each other. At the same time this tradition was always for him a living tradition, related directly to the insights and problems of the present day.

I never met Congar face to face, but know him only through his books. My first encounter with him was on 2 September 1964 — I still remember the precise date! — when I sat down in the Reading Room of the British Museum in London and started to

---

[1] Yves Congar, "Reflections on being a Theologian," trans. Marcus Lefébure, *New Blackfriars* 62 (1981) 405-409, p. 406.

[2] Congar, "Letter from Father Yves Congar, O.P.," trans. Ronald John Zawilla, *Theology Digest* 32 (1985) 213-216, p. 214.

read *Lay People in the Church*. So compelling did I find his argument, and so fascinating the wide range of his sources, that for nine hours I remained glued to my seat, with scarcely a single moment's intermission. Lunch, tea and supper were forgotten. Emerging that evening from the Reading Room, I found that my understanding of the Church's nature and task had been altered for ever.

A second book of Congar's, short but comprehensive, to which I remain permanently indebted, is his essay on the schism between Rome and Orthodoxy, *After Nine Hundred Years*. This has not received the attention that it deserves. I always recommended it to my students, and I still consider it to be the best existing treatment of the topic: *non multa, sed multum*. Here, as so often, he goes swiftly and unerringly to the heart of the matter.

If I were to select from his many other writings a third work that I particularly value, it would be the three volumes of *I Believe in the Holy Spirit*. Any future discussion of the *Filioque* will need to take this as a basis. If we Orthodox wish to understand ourselves, we should read Congar. In his generosity but also his critical acumen, he was a true friend of Orthodoxy.

Fr Yves Congar used to say that he loved the truth in the way that one loves a person. He loved the truth, and he loved theology. That is why his writings, for all their weight of scholarship, remain so attractive and so accessible. He did not simply study the mysteries of the faith, he celebrated them. May his memory be eternal!

PREFACE

Kenneth STEVENSON

Anglican Bishop of Portsmouth, England

One of the excitements about being a teenager at the time of the Second Vatican Council stemmed from the fact that new ideas were teeming in the Roman Catholic Church, and spilling over into other Churches as well. I can remember going to Mass in French Cathedrals and experiencing the fruits of the Liturgical Movement at a time when many Church of England Cathedrals seemed locked in another era. Among the many names that surfaced at that time was a whole series of French scholars, principal among whom was Yves Congar, with his writings on the nature and renewal of the Church. No one could afford to ignore his significance. For Anglicans, and perhaps for others as well, two particular features stand out.

First of all, Congar's theology is rooted in history, in historical theology. He was steeped in the writings of the great Dominicans, but, like Thomas Aquinas himself, just as steeped in the writings of the Fathers. No understanding of the Church can ignore historical realities, especially when the corporate sense of the Church that shines out from those great preachers and expositors of antiquity begins to pose some serious question marks on how we order our lives in the present. Congar, of course, had at times to work circumspectly, and some of his conclusions might be pressed yet further today. But the "retour aux sources" which typified not only the liturgical renewal articulated by Vatican II but the Council's ecclesiology was so deep that its pervading questions still remain and they continue to place challenges before all the Churches. We are all organic parts of a dynamic tradition.

The other area to which Congar points is ecumenism. One cannot travel through history without encountering some Christians very different from oneself! As a prisoner of war in Colditz during the Second World War, he experienced something of the hostility and suspicion in which Roman Catholics were generally held by other Christians, and this left a lasting impression on him. Ecumenism is — at root — about Christian friendship, those grace-filled encounters whereby we become immeasurably enriched simply by meeting someone else at the level of faith. Congar's friendships across the ecclesiastical boundaries bear witness to precisely this truth: he knew people, enjoyed them, and did not waste what they could mean to him, and to his Church. All the rhetoric about "Koinōnia" rests on many different kinds of dynamisms, and that includes the sheer need for theologians to talk to each other across traditional boundaries, perhaps discovering in the process that the boundaries themselves are not so great after all. This was abundantly plain in his work as an active member of the Roman Catholic-Lutheran Commission set up in 1965.

Travelling through history and geography in the way that Congar did — and at a time when to do so questingly in his own Church was (initially at least) frowned upon — gave him an increasingly open sense of Christian identity. It is here that the traditional Anglican appeal to Scripture, Tradition and Reason has many lasting resonances. By "open" I do not mean vague or relativising, but rather the ability to relate to others from a perspective of sufficient security in one's own tradition, and to be enriched and challenged in the process. In our own day, when the fruits of such figures as Congar run the risk of being taken for granted, those enrichments and challenges remain on the agenda. When Congar was first ordained, separated Christians, if they included Roman

Catholics, were not even allowed to pray the Lord's Prayer together. Now we can do so very much more, and Congar's vision of a Spirit-filled Church is but one sign of that freedom for fresh encounters with God and each other.

PREFACE

Marc LIENHARD

Honorary Dean of the Protestant Faculty of Theology of Strasbourg
Formerly President of the Directoire of the Church of the Confession of
Augsburg of Alsace and Lorraine

A monumental work! This is the word that comes to mind as one surveys the list of Père Congar's publications, or delves into the volumes
of the *Unam Sanctam* collection: the richness and extent of output
of this eminent theologian who was also an historian of ideas, and a
Churchman in the best sense of the word, have truly amazed us.

I had the privilege of meeting him on several occasions in the
course of my own journey as theologian and ecumenist. I was a
member of the team organized by him in Strasbourg between 1964
and 1968, which worked on the elaboration of an *Ecumenical vocabulary* which — though remaining incomplete — appeared in 1970.

He impressed us with his numerous reference cards, his familiarity with history and his theological energy. He was indeed the
soul of the initiative, while all the time busy as we know, with the
many tasks associated with the Second Vatican Council.

His role in the latter event is well known, and several contributors to the present volume highlight this fact. I often heard Yves
Congar speak of this Council. In particular, I recall a meeting with
young people at Neuwiller-les-Saverne during which he gained the
attention of his listeners by explaining to them, simply and clearly,
but also with enthusiasm — reference cards close as usual —
what was at stake in this Council. Not only what was at stake

for the Catholic Church, but also for Christianity as a whole. The Protestants in his audience were surprised when he told them that Catholics today ought to ask themselves the question about Luther's role in the history of salvation.

Congar afterwards left Alsace which he had grown to like, all the while regretting, as he said to me one day, his desire to cultivate geraniums and to delight in a certain passivity and a certain conservatism.

As far as I was concerned, I was to continue my intellectual journey with Congar. On the recommendation of my thesis director, Professor Regin Prenter, I began research work on Luther's Christology, all the while in theological dialogue with Congar. According to him, Luther had devalued the role of Christ's humanity in the work of salvation, putting the unique emphasis on the action of his divine nature (*Alleinwirksamkeit*). My work came to other conclusions, but a fruitful dialogue had been established.

Continuing my research on Luther, I never once ceased to take note of Congar's views on Luther, the importance of which he had underlined ("he re-thought Christianity"). Relying on Joseph Lortz, who in the 20th century had inaugurated the Catholic rediscovery of Luther, Congar said during an interview with Jean Puyo in 1975: "It would appear that Luther is unable to accept anything which is not derived from his own experience." It was the famous thesis on Luther's subjectivism. There again, what a debate on a subject that was not mere history!

But how can we not underline Yves Congar's ecumenical energy! The division of the churches occupied his mind at its highest level, and the re-establishment of communion and unity was one of his major preoccupations as a theologian. Dedicating his whole being to this end, he knew that an understanding of the meaning of a word and its significance was paramount. As Protestants and Catholics, we did not always place the same meaning behind the same words, resulting in serious misunderstandings, as we saw for example, with the term "faith" which had a different connotation for Luther from what it had for Thomas Aquinas. Thus the urgency of elaborating an ecumenical vocabulary together. Generally speaking, Congar was very conscious of the weight of history. He was constantly inviting us to engage in a re-reading of history together, so as to understand the reasons for the division; to correct certain images we have of one another, as well as to curb certain evolutions which in the course of history, had deepened the trenches. He showed appreciation for the work I had undertaken on the doctrinal condemnations pronounced by the Lutherans against the Reformers and the Reformers against the Lutherans. He showed interest too in my re-reading of this historical problem. Indeed, though the historical background was very familiar to him, he was able to marry the historical approach to a theological reading of the signs of the times.

In the later years, Congar was particularly interested in models of unity. The concept of "reconciled diversity" excited him, as well as all the fruitful dialogue between Lutherans and Catholics that was to lead to the common Declaration on justification by faith.

Nevertheless, he was fully aware that ecumenical progress is not a question merely of the intellect nor of the institution, but of mentalities and their willingness to change. "We need an ecumenical metanoïa, he wrote in 1983, by which each Church allows itself to be guided along by the example and the questioning of the other, to take another look at its points of view, to reflect on what was held in common from the beginnings, and on the needs of the world to which it wishes to bring the Gospel." And he added, "Is such a metanoïa taking place today (too) slowly and (too) timidly?"

Are we going to remain deaf to such an appeal? Let us acknowledge again and again, the enormous debt we owe to Yves Congar.

I sincerely hope that the present volume will serve to underline the fecundity and the actuality of this great theologian's work in the history of the Churches of the 20th century and let us hope, of the 21st also.

* Trans. by Marie-Humbert Kennedy, OP

PART II

YVES CONGAR: THEOLOGIAN

PURITY AND PLENITUDE
EVANGELICAL REFLECTIONS
ON CONGAR'S *TRADITION AND TRADITIONS*

John WEBSTER

Professor of Systematic Theology
King's College, University of Aberdeen

I

More than forty years on, *Tradition and Traditions* remains a deeply impressive book.[1] Both in manner and content it is a classic example of *ressourcement* theology. There are the long walks through the patristic and mediaeval countryside; there is the characteristic lack of anxiety about *wissenschaftlich* criteria, and the trust in the adequacy of citation for rational persuasion; there is confidence that — though Western Christian history stumbled rather badly around the end of the thirteenth century — we can with care recover the losses and extricate ourselves from the dualisms which have trapped theology and the estranged confessions of the churches. More than

[1] Y. M.-J. Congar, *Tradition and Traditions: An Historical and a Theological Essay* (London: Burns and Oates, 1966) [originally *La Tradition et les Traditions. Essai historique* (Paris: Fayard, 1960); *La Tradition et les Traditions. Essai théologique* (Paris: Fayard, 1963).] Page references in parentheses are to the English translation. For a full account, see J. Bunnenberg, *Lebendige Treue zum Ursprung: Das Traditionsverständnis Yves Congars* (Mainz: Grünewald, 1989); see also J.-P. Jossua, *Yves Congar: Theology in the Service of God's People* (Chicago, IL: Priory Press, 1968) 109-116; C. MacDonald, *Church and World in the Plan of God* (Frankfurt: Lang, 1982) 118-143.

anything, it is a book animated by a sense that theology is rational worship in the church, and that the church is the realisation in time of the self-communication of the triune God.

It is not a clever or stylish book, nor in one sense is it especially original. But it is a very joyful piece of theology; Congar — now reinstated and about to begin his work preparing for Vatican II — writes with fluency and confidence at a point of particular vibrancy in his own life and in the life of the church: "By God's grace, we are today emerging from the seven years of famine" (397). The two parts of the book were originally published separately, the historical essay in 1960, and the theological essay (perhaps less vivid than the first part) three years later. There is a good deal of overlap between the two, however: as often with Congar, the argument is not so much sequential as cumulative (sometimes, indeed, associative). The book works simultaneously on a number of fronts (historical analysis, dogmatics, spiritual theology, ecumenics, polemics), the whole undertaken as an act of homage and an appeal. The appeal is in part to Roman Catholic theology to renew the apprehension of the gift with which it has been entrusted, and in part to the separated Protestant churches to grasp again the plenitude of the Christian faith from which they have in some measure become isolated.

Congar's account of tradition is magisterial on at least three counts. First, the book is suffused by a sense that tradition is a theological and spiritual reality and not simply a historical-social magnitude. More pointedly: in order to talk about tradition, one needs to talk about God, and to do so directly. There is an immediate lesson to be learned here. A good deal of recent theological work has sought to reinstate tradition through extensive appeal to, for example, theories of cultural practice, the social character of knowing or the hermeneutics of reception.[2]

---

[2] Examples from a large literature would include Delwin Brown, *Boundaries of our Habitations: Tradition and Theological Construction* (Albany, NY: State

Congar occasionally touches on non-theological matters, but he does not have any particular theory about them, and they remain ancillary, not foundational, to what he has to say. The book's real centre of gravity is the historical depiction of the place of the church in the economy of salvation. "What theology means by Tradition," he writes, "is something other than a mere human factor of moral inheritance or social cohesion" (234). Throughout the study, Congar resists an immanentist account of tradition (whether the idiom be juridical, as in some post-Tridentine Catholic theology, or that of Romantic ideas of a human "common spirit," a problem from which even Möhler is not entirely free). Tradition is an ecclesial, and therefore a Christological, and especially a pneumatological, concept, and its explication requires us to see that "unity of the subjects of Tradition" which "has for its inner principle the Holy Spirit" (313).

This leads to a second factor in the book's power: it exemplifies a way of speaking of the history of the church and its theology in which the notion of "church" has some real work to do. From the early nineteenth century, Protestant church history often went about its business rather determined to allow no explanatory power to theological teaching about, for example, providence or the work of the Holy Spirit. This assimilation of church history to its non-theological neighbour is, of course, an aspect of the more wide-scale decline of a specifically theological rationale for the theological sub-disciplines. In church history, it leads to the bracketing of talk of divine action; one of its more recent fruits is a certain fondness for analysis of the church's past in terms of the agonistics of power. Congar was, of course, no stranger to such matters, and had more reason than most to look at the church without illusions. This does not, however, betray him into writing a critical history of tradition

University of New York Press, 1994); David Brown, *Tradition and Imagination: Revelation and Change* (Oxford: Oxford University Press, 1999).

(one, that is, which isolates the human history of the church and uses it as a sufficient explanation for the reality of Christianity). He certainly exposes what he regards as deformities in the church's past, most of which involve the hypertrophy of law and office in the church. But for Congar, the work of the Spirit outbids human depravity, and so a critical history can never be exhaustive.

His encomium on the fathers in the second part of the book is a case in point. Why, he asks, are the fathers "such a unique and very precious *locus theologicus*" (436)? The answer he gives is in the end a matter of "Christian ontology" (436), one which entails "a certain view of the Church and its historical life" (436). In that ontology, certain creaturely realities are, without detriment to their creatureliness, instrumental in the divine self-communication. If this is the case, then the church historian is permitted to interpret the fathers not simply as contingent actors in a social and religious history, but as *"those who have contributed a decisive element to the Church's life"* (438). This is not naivety. "The tradition of the Fathers is a very human thing. It is not an epiphany of glory, but a work of God in frail human vessels, a work whose luminosity of outline is apparent only to the eye of faith" (440). Yet for Congar the history of the church may not be written as if it were not luminous in this way. Put somewhat sharply; "History is the science of mankind's past. Tradition is something else entirely" (455). More pacifically; the church "has a special and ongoing relation to history which is itself superior to history although the Church does live out its life within history's confines" (457). One of the major questions raised by Congar's book is thus the extent to which church history is just that: *church* history.

Third, therefore, Congar grasps that questions about tradition are in large part ecclesiological questions, and therefore questions about the manner of God's relation to the creation and the common life of God's creatures. *Tradition and Traditions* is in many ways an extended ecclesiological proposal, as important in its way as de Lubac's *Catholicism*.[3] As an essay in ecclesiology, it is also an essay on Christ and the Spirit — and not, it is worth adding, an essay in social or political anthropology. The book's title does not quite make the point, suggesting that the heart of the argument concerns the relation of Tradition to what Congar calls the "monuments" or "witnesses" of tradition. In fact, this is only a corollary of the deep theological conviction which underlies the argument in its entirety, namely that "Tradition is a theological reality which supposes an action of the Holy Spirit in a living subject, and this subject is the Church, the people of God and the Body of Christ" (452).

In what follows, I want to accomplish a couple of tasks: (1) to offer an analysis of the main proposals of *Tradition and Traditions*; (2) to suggest some lines of reflection from my perspective as a Protestant dogmatician who brings to the reading of the book a rather different arrangement of Christian doctrines from that which Congar himself expounds with such serenity and perceptiveness. No serious Protestant theologian reading Congar or any other *ressourcement* thinker should fail to register the challenge which this theology poses, and which continues to be pressed by de Lubac's rather mannered Anglo-American epigones. Briefly stated, the challenge is whether the Protestant zeal for purity — in the doctrines of God, Christ, the church and elsewhere — leads to a segregation of the divine from the creaturely, which in turn inhibits grasp of the plenitude of God's self-communication.

---

[3] More generally on Congar's ecclesiology, see Jospeh Famerée, *L'ecclésiologie d'Yves Congar avant Vatican II: Histoire et Église. Analyse et Reprise Critique* (Leuven: Leuven University Press, 1992); Gabriel Flynn, *Yves Congar's Vision of the Church in a World of Unbelief* (Aldershot: Ashgate, 2004); Jossua, *Yves Congar*, 87-126.

II

Congar's historical essay is in part a celebratory description of the abundance and spaciousness of the Christian tradition, and in part a pathology of modern Western divinity ("modern" in the rather loose sense of stemming from the Reformation and its antecedents). Before turning to the main lines of the historical presentation, three preliminary orientations about the general character of Congar's historical theology will be useful.

First, history serves theology. "My immediate aim ... is historical; but my ultimate intention remains strictly theological" (xix). This does not mean that Congar is in the business of historical apologetics: far from it. Tradition is not just a source book of evidences, unearthed by clever historians and then deployed in the service of polemic. Rather, history is inseparable from theology because a true conception of the history of the church sees it as the temporal process of God's saving revelation. Historicist attempts to study it as something else do just that: they study something other than the history of the church.

An immediate effect of this, second, is that Congar's history is strongly synthetic in character. "I have tried to draw out the key points of an overall history, with a logic and development of its own. Basically, my aim has been to outline a history of how the *problem* of tradition has been examined" (xix). The task, he says later, is one of gathering together "the general witness provided by the way [the fathers] prayed, lived and died" (353). Synthesis may cause the professional historian's heart to flutter; but it is worth pointing out that Congar's aim here is not to privilege the *grandes lignes* over the annoying counterfactuals, but rather to propose a different ontology: the history of Christianity *is* a unified reality; church history *is* (and is not just taken to be) the history of the church.

Third, however, if history is taken up into theology, theology is equally an intrinsically historical undertaking. This is because its object is the mystery of Christ as it takes form in human time. When Congar aligns himself with "the present threefold return to the biblical, liturgical and patristic sources" (64), he is directing attention to the historical realities which testify to the fact that the gospel is not available apart from its presence in history through forms of common life, thought and action. Part of Congar's genius is his resistance both to the naturalisation of the forms of the church and to their eclipse by a separate supernatural realm. To grasp Christian truth is to see it in its historical career and plenitude.

In substantive terms, Congar's account of the history of tradition is, at heart, a proposal that, until the period around the Gregorian Reform, tradition is envisaged as a salvation-historical reality, integrally related, on the one hand, to the divine self-communication and, on the other hand, to the corporate life of the people of God to which that self-communication gives rise, and in which it continues to bestow itself. The point is made initially with reference to the growth of the biblical tradition. The matrix and the interpretative milieu of the biblical materials are to be found in the church as the community of salvation. "Begotten in tradition, or even from tradition, the biblical writings come to us borne on a living religious reality — the community of God's chosen people, and this religious reality itself existed before these writings" (2). This enables positive theological use of the findings of *Formgeschichte* with respect to the biblical texts, precisely because "the *formgeschichtlich* school ... reinstated the spiritual bond uniting Scripture and Tradition, in the reality which embraces both of them: the Church" (6). In effect, Congar can de-secularise the critical history of the biblical tradition, allowing its findings but replacing its overemphasis on community creativity by talk of divine action in the acts of the church. The theological principle to which he appeals in giving an account of the growth of the biblical tradition is that "*the Lord himself* effects everything in his church" (12), and that there is, accordingly, "the coincidence of an historical transmission and a direct action of the Lord" (12).

This means, further, that tradition has both an historical and a charismatic character. Apostolic tradition properly concerns both origin and present effectiveness. "Historical in its origin and in the materiality of its content; pneumatic or charismatic in the power that is at work in it: power of perception, of faithful conservation, and of dynamic affirmation. The tradition of the apostles is simultaneously unchanging and timely, recollection of events and unfolding of their significance, conformity to what has been given or done once and for all, and the permanently present and dynamic reality of this thing given or done once and for all" (19). Put a little differently, tradition can be seen as both deposit and pattern (ὑποτύπ-ωσις). It refers to an accomplished reality, but not in such a way "that the Holy Spirit will cease to actualize and explain, in the course of history — of a *true history* — the meaning of inexhaustible treasure of the deposit of faith" (21). What is crucial to Congar's account here, we should note, is an ecclesiology in which the processes of the church's history, including its transmission of the apostolic heritage, are the temporal showing forth of the divine mystery, and as such intrinsic to that which they transmit. And so of the ante-Nicene period he says: "We are at the point where the concepts of Revelation, the Church and tradition overlap: what was hidden in God is manifested in time. This manifestation, as knowledge, is revelation and tradition; as a present mystery, it is the Church, salvation and again Tradition, *paradosis* being this content of saving knowledge and practice which the Church transmits and by which it lives" (25). Congar is quick to emphasise the sheer gratuity of what the church transmits: revelation is not simply identical with its ecclesial transmission. "The source whence springs the tradition of the Church descends, before flowing over the plain, like a cascade out of heaven, from God (the Father) who manifests

himself in human terms in sending Jesus Christ" (25). Nevertheless, revelation and church cannot be sundered, for "like the Church
itself, tradition is simply the manifestation, *in the time of human
history*, of the 'mystery' of salvation which, already announced,
outlined and launched under the old Dispensation, has now
appeared and been given to us in its fullness on Jesus Christ" (43).

As a reading of the history of the early church, this is a far cry
from the doctrinal criticism which exercised such a long fascina-
tion in patristic scholarship (especially British). It shows little interest in the philosophical environment of early Christian and patristic thought, and is largely silent about its political surroundings; it
is much more interested in liturgical and exegetical materials than
in either the history of religions or conciliar dogmatics. It is also
startlingly direct in its invocation of a number of theological themes
which Congar firmly believes to be crucial to making sense of the
material: apostolicity, for example, and above all that "supratem-
poral and supraterrestrial principle, the Holy Spirit" (37).

Like de Lubac, Congar identifies a distortion of this revelatory
and ecclesial conception of tradition in the late thirteenth and early
fourteenth centuries. In the early Middle Ages, his argument runs,
the authority of tradition was not tied to its apostolic genesis and
so to its capacity to function as historical warrant, but to the capacity of tradition to extend the communication of divine truth into
the present, a communication which "continues via the human
cooperation which is coextensive with the duration of the church"
(90). Put rather formally, "interest centred on the present reality of
transcendent causalities, rather than on the occasional causes at
some time in the past of the historical appearance of some idea or
institution" (89). This is fractured in the very early modern period.
Congar adduces a range of factors: the translation of an antique
notion of *auctoritas* into the idiom of theological criteriology and
institutional warrant; the immanentising of God's presence as an

ecclesial property rather than a spiritual movement; a shift from language of the mediation of the invisible through the visible to that of efficient causality; protest against the perceived expansion of the governing power of office in the church; the consequent deployment of apostolicity and Scripture as "anti-ecclesiastical" (98) realities. The synthesis of revelation, Scripture, tradition and church begins to disintegrate. Revelation becomes an act of origination; Scripture and church become "*two authorities forced into competition*" (98); the church becomes less the corporate manifestation of salvation than a juridical governed institution. The Reformation's assertion of *sola Scriptura* is simply the outworking of an earlier loss, namely of a sense that through the Spirit the divine acts of *revelatio* and *inspiratio* are permanent realities in the church.

From here, the historical presentation is wrapped up in fairly short order. There is a cautious reading of Trent's 1546 decree *de canonicis scripturis*, which suggests that in Trent's pneumatological ecclesiology it is not always as clear as it might be who is calling the shots, Spirit or institution. And this is followed by a more leisurely account of post-Tridentine developments to 1950, with some generous and finely-drawn portraits of Möhler, Franzelin, Newman, Scheeben and others.

The theological essay which follows gives a more schematic presentation of the materials which have emerged from the history. Three major themes can be identified: the coherence of revelation, tradition and church; the relation of Tradition and "traditions;" and the inseparability of Scripture from tradition.

(1) At the centre of Congar's proposal in *Tradition and Traditions* (and elsewhere in, for example, *The Mystery of the Temple*) is a conviction that God's saving self-manifestation is not punctilliar but a spacious, historically and socially extended reality, such that

"the total self-communication of God" (308) embraces both supernatural and natural agents and their relations in time. In terms of a
theology of tradition, this means that a primary task is "to deter-
mine the place of tradition ... in the whole complex of the plan
whereby God's mystery is made known to men" (237). A key element in the argument is Congar's description of what he calls "dis-
closure through created signs" (238) — a theology of mediation.
"God's plan," he writes, "is one of mission and tradition" (239):
"mission" in the sense of "the entrusting of a task to another by
one who has responsibility to see that the task is completed," and
"tradition" in the sense of "successive communication of one and
the same object to others" (240). There is, in other words, no *isolation* of revelation, but rather a cumulative temporal expansion of
its range through creaturely instrumentality. Consequently, the
church is not merely a kind of empty space into which revelation
intrudes; it is, rather, an historical process of receiving and extending onwards, of inheritance and transmission, and so at the same
time "an incorporation into a communion" (241). Divine self-
communication is thus of its essence generative of history, not self-
enclosed or segregated but diffusive; and what it brings about is
"a structure of relationships ... in the world" (258). This history may
fittingly be called "sacramental time, the time of the Church" (260).

   A crucial component of Congar's analysis is that this sacred history evoked by God's revelatory extension of himself in Christ and
Spirit is "both human and divine" (257). Because of this, the
church is what he calls "the subject of Tradition" (329; cf. 35): that
is, the agent through which God "communicates his revelation"
(327). Congar's insistence here (and elsewhere) that it is the church
in its totality which undertakes this task, and not just the magisterium, need not detain us here. What is most important for our
purposes is his attempt in a number of places to deploy the notion
of tradition in order to repair the breach between divine revelation

and the acts of the church in time. He can speak of "the history of the Church as the People or City of God, which unfolds at the heart of secular history as the gradual realisation of man's covenant relationship with God" (262f.). Or again: "The time of the Church is … the time of those responses that are stirred up in us, in the order of truth and love, by the 'divine missions' or visitations, of the God who is, who was, and who is to come, by which he brings this relationship, revealed and definitively established in Christ, to its final fulfilment" (264). Nevertheless, an adequate statement of tradition as "the continuing presence of the past in the present" (264) requires the transcendent reference afforded by Christological and pneumatological language: Christology, because tradition concerns "a finally established and supra-temporal deposit" (265); pneumatology, because it is by the Spirit that tradition is "interiorized and actualized in the faithful throughout the course of history" (265). The Christology remains oddly muted in the theological essay, perhaps because Congar is anxious to avoid the excessive emphasis on the Christological *ephapax* which he finds so problematic in Protestantism. The pneumatology, by contrast, does the lion's share of the work, precisely because only a thoroughly charismatic ecclesiology can escape the extrinsicism of those plodding controversialist manuals *de traditione*. "If spiritual men are thus bearers of Tradition, this tradition itself must be holy, *heilige Überlieferung*. That is holy which comes from God, who alone is holy, from his Spirit, who is the Holy Spirit. It is because the promptings of the Spirit are at the origin of the whole succession of genuine spiritual gnosis whose total aggregate, stored up and transmitted through the centuries, forms its basis, that we can justly term Tradition itself holy" (396).

(2) This expansion of the notion of tradition to become "the active presence of revelation in a living subject" (401) facilitates the

distinction between Tradition and traditions, or what he more happily calls the "monuments" or "witnesses" of Tradition. Because "[t]he monuments of Tradition are objective historical realities; but Tradition is a theological reality which supposes an action of the Holy Spirit," (452) then "Tradition is ... prior to its monuments, since they are only expressions of it" (425). This kind of distinction is, of course, a common modern strategy for avoiding some inherited historical embarrassments. In Congar's hands, it has anti-juridical and anti-historicist force, serving to recommend a more pneumatological and sacramental understanding of the relation between the theological reality of Tradition and its historical visibility. His account of the distinction may only be partially successful, largely because his understanding of the liturgy as efficacious representation tugs in rather different direction from the basic idea of traditions as witness. That being said, there is doubtless a certain liberation in disentangling tradition and traditions, since it at least makes possible a sense that the historical monuments of the church's past are contingent, and so not wholly beyond the possibility of revision.

(3) More weighty for our purposes here is what Congar has to say of the relation of Scripture and tradition. The basic shape of his treatment should by now be clear: "re-examination of the sources and of traditions prior to the divisions, polemics and separations of the modern period" (377) unearths an earlier tradition in which "Scripture, Tradition, the Church were three inseparable terms" (378). In telegraphic form, Congar's argument goes something like this: Scripture is materially sufficient (everything the church needs can be found in it) but formally insufficient because not perspicuous apart from the activity of the Holy Spirit in communicating the Word of God in the life of the church. Scripture and tradition cannot be separated because inspiration and illumination form a single trajectory of the Spirit's action in communicating divine truth

and generating a form of common life bound together in part by "an exegetical tradition" (399). Hence "Scripture is not, by itself, the word and message of God by which God purposes to give life to men" because "in order that its content may be rendered actual in a living mind, its meaning must be perceived in the present movement of such a mind, as a result of a new act of God" (400). More schematically, Scripture is a first stage of revelatory action ("the definitive formation of an objective deposit"), and tradition is a second stage, that of "the Gospel's flowering in a personal human subject" (401). The scriptural texts have their place in the communicative presence of God as it takes place in the church. Tradition is not an independent source of revelation so much as the ecclesial and historical environment in which Scripture is at work, towards which Scripture is directed, and by which its witness is expanded. Tradition is the amplification of the gospel communicated in Scripture, what Congar calls "the essential means" of ensuring the "fullness" of the apostolic heritage (416). None of this is intended as a rejection of the supremacy of Scripture; but supremacy is not isolation: "Scripture's sovereign character does not prevent it from being *just one component* of God's redemptive work, a work which demands in addition the Church and Tradition" (422).

It is just this that the Protestant tradition has failed to see. Throughout his exposition, Congar distinguishes his salvation-historical and ecclesial view of tradition from, on the one hand, the juridical strand of post-Gregorian Catholicism and, on the other hand, the tradition of the Reformation (both, of course, are versions of the same dysfunction). Of the two, the Reformation is handled more severely, and, it must be said, rather less knowledgeably: Congar read widely in modern Protestant materials on tradition, especially of the ecumenical variety (Leenhardt, von Allmen, and others), but was a good deal less secure in the literatures of the magisterial Reformation or the developing dogmatic tradition of Protestantism. Yet what he has to say is extraordinarily instructive, most of all because he perceives that the fundamental point at issue is not the relative authority of Bible and church tradition, but "the actual ideas of what constituted the spiritual relationship between God and man" (145).[4]

As Congar presents things, Protestantism is flawed by its isolation of Scripture from the total history of God's revelatory presence in the history of the people of God. The isolation results from making a gesture of defiance into an all-embracing principle: faced with the expansion of ecclesiastical power, the Reformation reacted by asserting the primacy of Scripture as a way of reaffirming the absolute, non-transferable rule of God in his Word. "It was with the intention of restoring the sovereignty of *God alone* that they presented that of Scripture as exclusive" (116). It is this *solus* which troubles Congar. If for Luther and Calvin "it is a question of restoring to God... the full determination of religious existence," the problem is not "God first" but "God alone" (141). "Alone" for Congar signals an ecclesiological deficiency and at the same time a drastically straitened conception of the economy of salvation, one which cuts it loose from its occurrence in the church's temporal existence. In effect, this means "[e]limination of the reality 'Church' as a constituent of the covenant relationship" (463). The cost of maintaining the revelatory *ephapax* is a purely vertical

---

[4] On the ecclesiological dimensions of Congar's critique of Protestantism, see M.-M. Wolff, *Gott und Mensch: Ein Beitrag Yves Congars zum ökumenischen Dialog* (Frankfurt: Knecht, 1990); Famerée, *L'ecclésiologie d'Yves Congar avant Vatican II*, 103-108; C. Meakin, *"The Same But Different" ? The Relationship between Unity and Diversity in the Theological Ecumenism of Yves Congar* (Lund: Lund University Press, 1995) 124-171. The ecclesiological critique of the Protestant tradition was already worked out by Congar in *Vraie et fausse réforme dans L'Église* (Paris: Cerf, 1950).

concept of revelation and thus "the concentration of all the means of grace, or of the realization of man's covenant relationship with God, solely in the Word of God, in practice identified with Scripture" (464).

Sola Scriptura is ecclesiologically ruinous. It leads to a fatally competitive picture which forces a choice between "the primacy of Scripture and the primacy of 'the Church'" (142). It reduces the history of the church's acts to the history of exegesis, failing to see that the lived tradition of the community of salvation cannot be given an exhaustive textual determination — that there is what Odo Casel called the element of *Nicht-schrift-sein* in the fullness of the church's life. It is inattentive to the *"public* order of faith, worship and salvation" (142). And, more than anything, in the notion of *sola Scriptura* there surfaces the sorry divide of natural and supernatural, the separation, the splitting of that "one single event of grace: a heavenly moment of the gift promised, and an earthly moment of the gift given" (147). Whether Congar is right to argue that Protestantism restricts the temporal presence of the supernatural to Scripture, individually interpreted, is a moot point. But what he wishes to secure is that for Catholicism "the *reality* of God's gift is transmitted in a far more complex and richer way than textual statement" (150). Hence his appeal to Protestant theology, "to draw the implications of the fact, witnessed to in the whole saving economy, that revelation has not an individual and private, but rather a social and public, nature," and "to take seriously the promise made to the Church of the presence and assistance of the Holy Spirit" (338). Otherwise, Protestants will simply "sacrifice the Church" (402).

III

What might a Protestant admirer of this book be moved to say by way of response? Three lines of reflection may be the beginnings of a conversation.

First, a comment on Congar's characteristically *ressourcement* way of proceeding, namely retrieving and putting to work a set of theological resources which antedate early modern problems and can help us circumvent them. The procedure enjoys almost unquestioned ecumenical prestige after its use in ARCIC ("almost", because unless one dismisses the worries of some substantial German Lutheran theologians about the *Common Declaration on Justification*, those worries constitute a significant disavowal of this style of ecumenical work[5]). But, whatever its historical merits and ecumenical utility, it ought not to go by default. Three comments might be made. (1) It "explains" Protestantism by presenting it as part of the larger malformation of Western Christianity after the Gregorian Reform. There is a truth here; but it ought not to be pressed in such a way as to deprive the reformation of any insight into the *permanent* character of Christianity. (2) The *ressourcement* method is heavily Catholic, insofar as it tends to assume that the emphasis on ecclesial visibility which it reconstructs out of patristic and early mediaeval materials is normatively Christian, and thus that Protestantism is a declension into spiritualism, transcendentalism, individualism and the like. Congar's own version of ecclesial visibility is, of course, immensely impressive and subtle, and resists any crude identification of the church with institutional regularity. But there are other ways of conceiving ecclesiology which deemphasise ecclesial "realization" of the saving mystery and are more heavily invested in the church's passivity, whose legitimacy tends to be excluded by Congar's way of proceeding.

[5] The worries are expressed with some force in E. Jüngel, *Justification: The Heart of the Christian Faith* (Edinburgh: T&T Clark, 2001).

ARCIC — Anglican-Roman Catholic International Commission, a joint Commission of the Roman Catholic Church and the whole Anglican Communion set up following the meeting between Archbishop M. Ramsey of Canterbury and Pope Paul VI in 1966.

(3) *Ressourcement* theologians commonly write the history of Christianity on the understanding that the distinction between "apostolic" and "post-apostolic" ought not to be pressed. Apostolicity is not primarily a matter of *backward* reference because, as Congar puts it, "the Church and her tradition were *the spiritual content* of what came from the apostles" (41). This is why he is heavily critical of, for example, Cullmann's account of the formation of the canon:[6] by interpreting the canon in terms of *sola Scriptura*, Cullmann bifurcates "apostolic tradition and Church tradition" (40). But part of what it means for the church to stand beneath apostolicity as a law of its existence is that there is a proper *retrospective* dynamic in the church. That is, the church is not only a Spirit-produced set of expressions of the mystery of salvation, but a company which looks back to the apostolic testimony set before it in Scripture and finds itself placed beneath its judgement. That testimony is properly segregated, discontinuous, intrusive in the busy processes of ecclesial invention. This is not to fall victim to those styles of Christian historiography (of which Protestantism has been lamentably fond) which regard the history of the church as simply one long decline from apostolic purity. Such a reading of the Christian past is a denial of *credo in Spiritum Sanctum*. But the creedal sequence is not without its ecclesiological significance: I believe in the Holy Spirit, the holy catholic church, the communion of saints, the remission of sins — the last is as ecclesiologically fundamental as what precedes it, and is therefore also a sign under which the church stands. Indeed, the remission of sins is constitutive of the holiness, catholicity and fellowship of the church. And at the very least this ought to alert us to the danger of assimilating the apostolic testimony too thoroughly into the life of the church, lest its summons to conversion be in some way muted.

[6] See O. Cullmann, *The Early Church* (London: SCM, 1956).

This leads to a second line of analysis, namely Congar's ecclesiology. Congar very acutely sees that in the confessional divergences over the relation of Scripture and tradition, the real issue is often "one of ecclesiology rather than of hermeneutics" (409). "It seems to me," he writes, "that Protestant thought separates Christ in too radical a manner from his Body, the Church. Failing to recognise sufficiently that by the sending of Christ and his Spirit God has truly entered into history, it isolates in an excessive manner the *ephapax* of Christ from its effects in humanity, which effects it plays down in order to exalt the sovereignty of the Lord" (409). By way of response: Congar speaks of "the absence in Protestant thought of a genuine ecclesiology" (422). But Protestant ecclesiology is not *absent*; it is just *different*. The difference can, I think, best be characterised by seeing it as a function of a deep sense of the perfection of Christ, that is the utter uniqueness, integrity and sufficiency of the Word made flesh. Protestant ecclesiology, especially in its Reformed strand, is undergirded by an affirmation of Christ's character as an ontological *perfectum*. Of course, as such he communicates himself; he is risen, alive, present, active. But what is present and active is one whose identity is in a real sense exclusive, because already fully achieved. His perfection includes his self-communication; but his communication of himself does not make him as it were porous or diffuse.

Consider what Congar says of Protestant accounts of the lordship of Christ. They view this lordship "too exclusively as an attribute of the glorified Christ and not enough as a *de jure* power residing already in Christ made man... It is this royal power of Christ which efficaciously inserts his priestly and prophetic functions into time, making him truly the Lord of time: and he is this not only in himself in heaven but also in his Church" (490). But what are we to make of the phrase "also in his church?" Congar is very far from wanting to reduce Christ to some immanent principle of ecclesial life. Yet Christ's royal power, his offices as priest and king, his lordship, are not in any way extensible. His lordship has its ecclesial sphere; but his presence there is always the presence of one who is infinitely superior, even as he gives himself in the most intimate fellowship — a point which in my judgement is not adequately built into the fabric of Congar's account of God's presence in *The Mystery of the Temple* (Congar's attraction to the temple motif — rather than to prophecy, for example — is telling, as is his presentation of the temple theme in terms of divine indwelling rather than the terrors of holy mercy).

My question to Congar is a sort of ecclesiological extension of the so-called *extra Calvinisticum*, namely the conviction that in the incarnate Word's relations *ad extra* he enjoys sovereign liberty. One way of broaching the issue would be to reflect on the term "covenant" with which Congar often describes the relation of Christ and the church. As he uses the term it has strong overtones of participation, functioning as a summary term for the way in which the history of the church is the temporal bodying forth of the Christological mystery of salvation. Congar is, of course, highly alert to the difference "between a hypostatic and a covenant union" (312).[7] But rather more is needed to secure the distinction: an emphasis that covenant is a term for differentiation and drastic inequality as much as of mutual encounter; it signals the astonishing *unitio* of God and the fallen creature, not ontological *unio*. To speak in such terms is not to repeat some principled separation of nature and supernature, but simply to indicate that the history of the covenant is about God's

---

[7] See here his article "Dogme christologique et ecclésiologie. Vérité et limites d'un parallèle," *Sainte Église: Études et approches ecclésiologiques* (Paris: Cerf, 1963) 69-104.

merciful *election*. The topic of election does not figure large in Congar's presentations of salvation-history, eclipsed by a Christological and pneumatological conception of the divine presence. But the inattention to election is not unproblematic. The force of "election" is to underscore that the sheer difference between creator and creature remains uncompromised even in the covenant fellowship between Christ and his people. Even as he gives himself, he remains the electing God, *solus*, unassimilated, his plenitude *in se*.

There is a pneumatological dimension here: does Congar compromise the transcendence of the Spirit by associating him so firmly with the processes of tradition? Again, the term "covenant" may offer a safeguard: "the Church and the Spirit," he writes, "are only united by a covenant link" (345). Nevertheless, Congar fears that with its apparently exclusive vertical reference Protestant ecclesiology does not take with sufficient seriousness "the promise of the Spirit" (345). Yet: what kind of promise? God's promises are about the inexhaustibility and infinite reliability of his grace, not about its availability as historical reality. They are about eschatological security as much as about the presence of a gift. Once again, this is not extrinsicism. It is, rather, a hesitation in following Congar when he affirms "the complete historicity of God's gift" (492).

Third, *sola Scriptura*. In one highly important sense, Congar is entirely correct to set Scripture in the larger context of the history of God's self-communication. For a variety of reasons, Protestant dogmatics often lost the plot at this point, relocating Scripture away from soteriology into criteriology, with rather disastrous results. But I am not fully persuaded that the resultant extrinsicism can be adequately dealt with by Congar's folding of Scripture into the larger stream of the church's life. This is because Scripture's task as prophetic and apostolic witness to the divine Word can only be accomplished if it is in some sense an alien element in the church.

Congar argues that Scripture is materially sufficient but formally insufficient. But without formal sufficiency, material sufficiency has no teeth. The sufficiency of Scripture (formal and material) does not, of course, mean that Scripture exists in abstraction from its presence to the church. But what kind of presence? Church and tradition, though they are the "space" in which Scripture is active as sanctified testimony to the *viva vox dei*, do not "fill out" Scripture or make good its insufficiency, any more than the servants of Jesus Christ fill out his lordship. *Sola Scriptura* does not extract Scripture from Christian history. But it does qualify that history as one which is addressed by an intrusive voice, the voice of the one who awakens the sleepers and raises the dead.

IV

By way of brief conclusion. "The dialogue between Catholicism and Protestantism," Congar remarks, "is not yet by any means over; perhaps it has scarcely begun, at least as an eirenical dialogue, carried on with the resources supplied by a biblical theology made transparent to the light of Truth at the price of much humility, prayer and love of God" (346). Just so! No Protestant theologian with any measure of spiritual or theological intelligence can fail to be moved by the appeal of Congar's work or of that refreshing work of the Spirit in the church of which it is part. But is it too much to hope — for ecumenical reasons! — that in this eirenical dialogue Protestant theology may not entirely forget some of what lies in its own traditions, may, indeed, look at them with more love than embarrassment, may even think of them as worth offering to the wider fellowship? If that is to happen, Protestant theologians could do worse than follow Congar's example in those grim years of exile, poring over the texts of the past, and doing so with expectancy, hopefulness and joy. Karl Barth — whose deep investment in historical theology is now only beginning to be appreciated with the publication of his lectures on the history of Reformed theology from the 1920s — thought of such theological work as obedience to the fifth commandment.[8] Whether Protestant theology can grow beyond its attachments to a culture of suspicion and listen to its own past, remains to be seen. If it does so, others will be in its debt.

---

[8] In theology's respect for and deference to the confessional tradition of the church, Barth argues, there is no question of bondage and constraint. It is merely that in the Church the same kind of obedience as, I hope, you pay to your father and mother, is demanded of you towards the Church's past, towards the "elders" of the Church. In obedience to the Church's past it is always possible to be a very *free* theologian. But it must be borne in mind that, as members of the Church, as belonging to the *congregatio fidelium*, one must not *speak* without having *heard*: Karl Barth, *Credo* (London: Hodder and Stoughton, 1936) 18.

YVES CONGAR AND THOMISM

Fergus KERR, OP

Formerly Regent of Blackfriars Hall, University of Oxford
Honorary Senior Lecturer in Theology and Religious Studies,
University of Edinburgh

I

In 1968 Hunter Guthrie brought out *A History of Theology*, an edited translation of Yves Congar's monograph-length entry "Théologie" in the *Dictionnaire de Théologie Catholique* written thirty years previously.[1] Congar, as he tells us in the Preface of *A History of Theology*, sent the manuscript of "Théologie" to the editor of the *DTC* at the beginning of September 1939, just as he was leaving Le Saulchoir for the general mobilisation prior to the German invasion of France.[2] Returning from captivity at the end of May 1945, he was surprised to find that the editor had discarded "about two-fifths of my text."[3] Sometimes "long heavy arguments" were replaced by "useful simplifications," changes that Congar says he accepted. On other occasions, however, deletions weakened the text and documentation, so he considered, and

---

[1] Yves M.-J. Congar, *A History of Theology*, trans. and ed. Hunter Guthrie, S.J. (Garden City, NY: Doubleday, 1968); "Théologie," *Dictionnaire de Théologie Catholique*, vol. 15, columns 341-502.

[2] *A History of Theology* [*HT*], 7.

[3] The editor, since 1922, was Mgr Emile Amann (1880-1948), who taught at Strasbourg for many years and made many important contributions to the *DTC*.

these passages and references he decided to restore. Thus, as he says, "the present text is more complete than that published in the *Dictionnaire*."

The text as we have it in Guthrie's translation may have been intended by Congar to be much closer to his original than the version in the *DTC*. In fact, however, the English version is not substantially longer than the *DTC* text. Comparison suggests that the lengthiest "restoration" is the paragraph comparing Cajetan's understanding of *sacra doctrina* as "supernatural teaching" with John of Saint Thomas's understanding of it as "theological science."[4] Moreover, while it is true that the English version shows that Congar sought to "update" it, "particularly in its historical section," this does not amount to much more than a few references to the texts of the Second Vatican Council. As regards the bibliography, on the other hand, far from being brought up to date — "Since 1939 there have been many books devoted to the object and method of theology" — Guthrie cuts out all the bibliographies included in the *DTC* while including nothing new.

According to Guthrie, in his Foreword, *A History of Theology* is "truly a masterpiece." This is for two reasons. In the first place, Congar offers a basic orientation course for students of theology, introducing them to all the great names in Catholic thought, together with their methods and conclusions. Guthrie is right about this, though there is, unhappily, little evidence that the work was ever much used as a textbook, even in Catholic seminaries, in the English-speaking world. Secondly, according to Guthrie, the book is also a great work of creative theological thinking, a landmark contribution precisely in the immediately post-Conciliar climate: "In this day of cloudy thinking it comes to grips with reality at every point that is important for man's relationship to himself and

---

[4] Compare *HT*, 34 with *DTC*, column 346.

to eternity." Here also, it may be doubted if it ever had the impact for which Guthrie hoped.

Overshadowed by his other major works, *A History of Theology* was soon forgotten even by readers familiar with Congar's bibliography. By 1968, particularly in the light of his immense contribution to the achievements of Vatican II, Congar was appreciated chiefly for his work on ecumenism, ecclesiology, and a richer understanding of the notion of tradition. Few then would have thought of him as interested in anything as abstract and abstruse as theological methodology and the history of its development.

In any case, a *history* of theology would not have seemed *theology*, either to the surviving (albeit somewhat beleaguered) partisans of "Post-Tridentine Scholasticism" (Congar's phrase), for whom Catholic theology properly conducted was a systematic exposition of the dogmatic beliefs of the Church independent of their historical provenance and genesis, or on the other hand to the new wave of post-Conciliar theologians, interested in a diversity of ways in re-creating theology in tune with contemporary questions, social and political as well as philosophical.

II

Congar prefaces Guthrie's edition with a reflection on the evolution of Catholic theology since 1939, in the light particularly of the "serious problems" that "have arisen from the pact that Catholic theology seemed to have had with medieval or post-Tridentine Scholasticism."[5]

Congar begins by stating the obvious, namely that the theological situation in 1968 had changed since 1939: in particular, however, he means that "even the idea of theological endeavour" had

---

[5] *HT*, 8.

changed. That is to say, in the years that had passed, new conceptions of what theologians are supposed to be doing had emerged.
At once he insists that "the continuities are more profound than
the differences." What has been called the "new theology," he
goes on to insist, "radical as it may seem," is in fact "more traditional than similar advances in other intellectual disciplines." Later,
in one of the new passages inserted into the text, he speaks of
"what has abusively been called 'the new theology'."[6]

As far as continuities are concerned, "research turns up traditional leads and data in the economy or history of salvation, in
eschatology, anthropology, etc." In effect, the so-called "new theology," Congar is suggesting, is, far from being novelty and inno-
vation, actually a retrieval of tradition, no doubt neglected and even
forgotten. Indeed, since 1939, there has been "an inspired and profound renewal of traditional Christian thought" — *ressourcement*
as we might say — which is not to say, however, Congar notes, that
problems have not emerged, specifically with what he here refers
to as "Scholasticism."

Congar then offers a quick survey of what has been happening
since 1939, to assess "where we are today."[7] He begins, as we
might expect, by mentioning *Sources chrétiennes* and *Théologie*,
the former initiated in 1942 and beginning by translating
Greek patristic literature, particularly works by Origen, the latter
offering studies by the Jesuits Henri Bouillard (*Conversion et
Grace chez Saint Thomas d'Aquin*, 1944) and Henri de Lubac
(*Corpus Mysticum*, 1944 and *Surnaturel*, 1946). "It was thought,"
he says, "that these publications were the beginning and first
expression of a 'new theology'." The "manifesto" of this "new
theology," so it "seemed," was "Les orientations présentes de la

---

[6] *HT*, 200: *la Nouvelle Théologie*.
[7] 1968, that is to say.

pensée religieuse," an article by Jean Daniélou, S.J., in *Études*, avril-juin 1946. Congar is obviously distancing himself from those (unnamed) theologians who regarded any of these texts as constituting a "new theology."

In addition to these retrievals of Catholic tradition, as he clearly believes they were, Congar allows that there had been "new thinking on the nature of theology itself": here he mentions the Dominicans Marie-Dominique Chenu and Louis Charlier, who both published books on theological method in 1938, both of which were placed on the Roman Index of Prohibited Books in 1942. He comments that Charlier's critique of the nature and validity of theological conclusions "never gained much support." Chenu's work, he notes with every appearance of neutrality, "examined the role of spiritual experience in the orientation of theology and also the value which the life of the Church has a *locus theologicus*." Clearly, he finds nothing misguided about this.

"The problem arose," he goes on to say, "when, in a very questionable manner, these ideas of a vitalist religious conception of theology were grouped together and published, each in its own perspective, by Fr. Th. Soiron, G. Koepgen, and Fr Hans Urs von Balthasar." What exactly Congar is up to in citing these three theologians is difficult to decide. There should have been no problem, presumably for partisans of Scholasticism, in the retrievals of tradition under the heading of *ressourcement*, "return to the sources." Charlier's essay on the misguidedness of *Konklusionstheologie* he seems largely to dismiss. Chenu's attempt to reconnect the practice of theology with liturgy, spirituality and life he seems tacitly to endorse — at least it only becomes a "problem" when it is pushed, "in a very questionable manner," to the extremes to be found in the publications of Soiron, Koepgen and Balthasar.

In effect, by implication, if it made any sense, from the perspective of 1960, to regard recent theological developments as constituting a "problem," then we have to look, not to the work of Bouillard, Daniélou, de Lubac, Charlier and Chenu, but to that of the three German-speaking authors whom Congar mentions. In fact, back in the *DTC* entry Congar had already identified Soiron and Koepgen as exponents of a movement within modern Catholic theology of which he clearly did not approve. Long before any putative influence of Chenu's idea of theology, that is to say, Congar had located a "tendency to fuse theology and life," to turn Catholic theology into *Lebenstheologie*.[8]

Thaddaeus Soiron (1881-1957), a Franciscan, was one of the most prolific and respected German theologians of the first half of the twentieth century. His many books and articles mostly deal with New Testament subjects. In 1935, however, he published *Heilige Theologie*, the book which Congar lists; it appeared in 1953 as *La condition du théologien* (Paris: Plon), which perhaps jogged Congar's memory of this "vitalist" theology. Soiron is probably best remembered now, if at all, as the author of *Die Verkündigung des Wortes Gottes: homiletische theologie*, published in 1942: something of a manifesto of what was then called "kerygmatic" theology, as distinct from, indeed even opposed to, Scholastic theology. Obviously, as a Preacher, Congar would not have wanted to separate theology from preaching; it would have been another matter, however, to equate expounding sacred doctrine with proclaiming the Word of God, or vice versa. Congar, in 1968 as in 1939, was always too much of a Thomist to countenance that equation. We might even say that, in criticizing the tendency he deplored in Soiron's theology Congar was revealing his Thomist commitments.

[8] *DTC*, column 447: "la tendance a fusionner théologie et vie."

Georg Koepgen (1898-1975) published very little. Congar lists *Die Gnosis der Christentums* (1939).[9] In fact, Koepgen's previous book, *Die Grundlagen der neuen kritischen Ontologie und die scholastische Methode* (1927), subtitled "a study of the significance of religious knowledge," might have been cited, more plausibly, as a somewhat anti-Scholastic work, to the extent at least that Koepgen was arguing for an alternative approach, itself already a problematic move for theologians who accepted the hegemony of Scholasticism. His only other book, *Lösungen und Erlösung: eine Theologie in Fragmenten* (1948), as the title perhaps indicates, evinces a certain unhappiness with the theological climate of the day.

Soiron and Koepgen are cited in the *DTC*, but in a cluster of authors whom Congar regards as propounding the theological "vitalism" which he deplores. Some of the others who are not mentioned in 1968 are much more eminent. The list is worth some attention.

Some of the evidence which Congar cites as symptomatic of the suspect vitalistic theology is somewhat flimsy. The first text is *Die Wertprobleme und ihre Behandlung in der katholischen Dogmatik*, the inaugural lecture at the University of Freiburg im Breisgau by Engelbert Krebs, delivered in 1917.[10] While it is clear that Krebs (1881-1950), one of the most prolific German theologians of the first half of the twentieth century, was primarily a medievalist, as most of his publications attest, he also had great pastoral concern to bring out the "life value," *der Lebenswert*, of Christian doctrine, and certainly appealed to the then fashionable *Wertphilosophie* (Max Scheler) in his more speculative writings. He was, incidentally, removed from teaching by the Nazis in 1938.

---

[9] *DTC*, column 447, misspelling the name as Koepken.
[10] 1917 was the year Krebs conducted the wedding of his friend Martin Heidegger to Elfride Petri.

Congar lists books by Arnold Rademacher (*Religion und Leben* 1928) and Linus Bopp (*Theologie als Lebens-und Volksdienst* 1935), the titles of which show interest in relating theology to "life," in the latter case in presenting theology in "the service of life and of people." Rademacher's book, published in English in 1961, belongs on the spirituality shelf. Presumably Congar was not aware, when he was composing the *DTC* entry, that Arnold Rademacher (1837-1939), who spent most of his life teaching theology in Bonn, was by far the most committed Catholic ecumenist in Germany, with several publications in the late 'thirties which went much further than Congar had done by then in advocating reform in the Catholic Church to open the possibility of Christian reunification. Linus Bopp (1887-1971), chiefly associated with Freiburg im Breisgau, very prolific, was concerned with pastoral and liturgical theology, which of course means that his book is, as the title suggests, directed towards making theology relevant to clergy and people. What Congar perhaps did not realize is that Bopp was among the Catholic theologians who, while never being members of the Party, sought to reconcile Nazism with Catholicism, in the early 'thirties — theology as *Volksdienst* was a project, in that context, with implications one would deplore, in retrospect.[11]

Congar refers to a 9-page article by Anselm Stolz, "Charismatische Theologie," and a 25-page essay by Karl Adam, "Von dem angeblichen Zirkel im katholischen Lehrsystem oder von dem

---

[11] As is well known, the hesitations about the expression "people of God," for many theologians including Cardinal Ratzinger, spring from memories of the Catholic and Nazi uses of the notion of *Volk* in the 1930s: it would also be possible to explore the vulnerability of some theologians in the Tübingen tradition, with its emphasis on *Lebenstheologie* to the allurements of Nazism; but then there were major exponents of Scholastic Thomism, particularly in France, who proved even more inclined to Fascism (see *Action Française*).

einem Weg der Theologie," published in 1938 and 1939 respectively, both in *Wissenschaft und Weisheit*, the review founded in 1934 by the German Franciscans, as Congar tells us, clearly regarding it as "en general" inclined to publish this deplorable *Lebenstheologie*.

Anselm Stolz (1900-42), a Benedictine who taught in Rome at San Anselmo from 1928 until his death, was among the many who sought to reconnect systematic theology with spirituality. It is a little ironic that Congar, whose last great work would consider the doctrine of the Holy Spirit, should have singled out this essay on "charismatic theology," probably the earliest by any Catholic theologian on the topic. It was a by product of Stolz's translation and commentary on the relevant questions in the *Summa Theologiae* in the standard German edition. His best known book, translated as *The Doctrine of Spiritual Perfection* (1938), could not fairly be regarded as promoting "vitalism."

It is perhaps a little odd, also, to classify and, by implication, castigate Karl Adam's article about the "circularity" in Catholicism between life and doctrine as a "questionable" *Lebenstheologie*; but here, in retrospect, if we consider one of his best known books, translated as *The Spirit of Catholicism* (1929), we have to agree that Karl Adam (1876-1966), another of the great German Catholic theologians of the first half of the twentieth century, had moved well away from the prevailing Scholastic theology. Like Bopp, Adam was at first attracted by the possibility of reconciling Catholic ideals of "organic community" with the "renewal" of the German "people." He was the most eminent representative of the Tübingen School.

Finally, in this cluster of theologians of whom Congar disapproves, we find the Belgian Jesuit Emile Mersch (1890-1940): here Congar refers us to the later discussion[12] where he attacks Mersch

---

[12] *DTC*, column 458.

for coming close to maintaining that the *subjectum* of theology is the *Christus totus*, citing essays in 1934 and 1936. At this point Congar is at his most explicitly "Thomist." He invites us to compare the work by J.-A. Jungmann, S.J., *Die Frohbotschaft und unsere Glaubensverkündigung* (1938), an example of "kerygmatic" theology. His objection is to theologians who want to make Christ the beginning and end of theology. Without mentioning it explicitly here he clearly has in mind the famous text where Thomas Aquinas contends that "everything in sacred doctrine is treated *sub ratione Dei*" — "*secundum ordinem ad Deum*" — ruling out specifically the possibility of framing the exposition of Christian doctrine in terms of *totus Christus caput et membra*.[13]

For a critique of this misguided *Lebenstheologie* Congar advises us to consult an article by his German Dominican confrère Mannes-D. Koster, and the entire issue of *Revue Thomiste*, the Toulouse Dominican journal, for July 1935: "Théologie et action." Thus Congar allies himself unmistakably with mainstream Thomism.

In the *DTC* this rejection of Mersch's radically Christocentric approach to sacred doctrine is preceded by a paragraph describing but obviously also deploring the theologians who, wanting to construe dogma as a "system," give way to "l'inspiration romantique du vital ou de l'organique": they take as "organizing principle" of their theological systems, not the mystery of God, but the notion of the Kingdom of God.[14] Here, in a lengthy catalogue, Congar lists "J.-S. Drey, J. Hirscher, B. Galura, Cardinal Katschthalter, etc.," without specifying any particular works by any of them. It is a fairly odd list. The major figures are obviously Johann Sebastian von Drey (1777-1853) and Johann Baptist Hirscher (1788-1865), co-founders in 1819 of the most venerable of all Catholic

---

[13] *Summa Theologiae* 1. 1. 7.
[14] *DTC*, column 458.

theological journals, *Theologische Quartalschrift*, and in the original generation of the Catholic "Tübingen School." Karl Adam, we should recall, was the most eminent representative of the Tübingen School in the 1930s.

Drey's vision of Christianity was governed by the idea of the drama of the Kingdom of God. His major work, *Die Apologetik als wissenschaftliche Nachweisung der Geschichtlichkeit des Christentums in seiner Erscheinung* (1838-47, three volumes), as the title, let alone the contents page, suffice to show, could not be more different from the *Summa Theologiae* of St Thomas Aquinas, not to mention the dozens of manuals of Thomistic philosophy and theology which began to appear in the later decades of the nineteenth century. Hirscher's major work, *Christliche Moral als Lehre von der Verwirklichung des göttlichen Reiches in der Menschheit* (1835), is just the kind of project which moral theologians weary of fifty years of Scholastic textbooks began to produce in the mid twentieth century!

Drey and Hirscher are of course significant theologians in the Tübingen tradition, as important as their colleague and friend Johann Adam Möhler (1796-1838), whose writings in the areas of ecclesiology and comparative symbolics Congar had studied and greatly appreciated. His dissertation at Le Saulchoir, directed by M.-D. Chenu, focused on the doctrine of the unity of the church in the thought precisely of Möhler. It might even be plausible to suggest that, during the years when he was writing the distinctly Thomist orientated *DTC* monograph, Congar was also being drawn out in the contrary direction, from Scholasticism towards a certain sympathy for the Tübingen School. In the *DTC* entry, however, Congar shows no sympathy whatsoever for their approach to theological methodology.

Citing Bernhard Galura (1764-1856) and Johannes Katschthalter (1832-1914) seems somewhat unfair: Galura became Bishop of

Brixen, Katschthalter became Cardinal Archbishop of Salzburg, the publications of both are mainly concerned with what we should now call pastoral theology, homiletics and catechetics. Neither was a theologian, nor is there any reason to regard Katschthalter as in any way indifferent or hostile to the Scholasticism which was of course well established in his later years. On the other hand, perhaps these two are cited as symptomatic, as indicating what happens in homiletics and catechetics when the Thomist paradigm of theological methodology is abandoned or (in the case of the Tübingen theologians) never accepted and practised in the first place. The idea, anyway, so Congar notes, has been taken up again in our time, by Linus Bopp, in the book mentioned above. "These ideas," however, "issue more from a descriptive point of view and from an empirical organization of the elements of dogmatic theology than from a truly formal point of view: *Attendentes ea quae tractantur in ista scientia, et non ad rationem secundum quam considerantur.*"

Interestingly, Krebs, Rademacher, Stolz, Bopp, Adam and Mersch do not figure in 1968, but the reference to Soiron and Koepgen indicates that Congar remains critical of theologians who (as he thinks anyway) seek to reconstruct Catholic doctrine in terms of living experience, spirituality, and so on. It looks now, however, as if the tendency to a "vitalist religious conception of theology" has lost the most celebrated of its alleged proponents.

The new name, in 1968, alongside Soiron and Koepgen, is, amazingly, that of Hans Urs von Balthasar, not yet regarded as one of the three or four greatest Catholic theologians of the twentieth century. By 1968 Hans Urs von Balthasar (1905-1988) had shown his interest in patristic *ressourcement* by translating Origen (1938), as well as his rage against much that he saw as defacing the Catholic Church, in such books as *Schleifung der Bastionen* (1952), and several of the essays collected as *Verbum Caro* (1960) and *Sponsa Verbi* (1961). Congar must have been familiar with

Balthasar's book on Karl Barth (1951). All but one of the volumes
of *Herrlichkeit* had appeared. This body of work was obviously,
even in 1968, by a far more significant theologian than either
Soiron or Koepgen. Plainly, however, in many places in these writings, Balthasar is openly critical and even scornful of Scholastic
theology ("sawdust Thomism"). It looks as if Congar's naming of
Balthasar here continues the Thomist hostility in the *DTC* entry to
anything that smacks of *Lebenstheologie*.

No doubt Balthasar's later denunciations of post-Conciliar trends,
and his adoption by neoconservative Catholics, have diverted attention from this, but his work in the 1950s and '60s offered a uniquely
challenging alternative to the Scholasticism he abhorred — not that
many professional theologians, secure in their academic positions,
were much inclined to take seriously the publications of the lone and
isolated figure of the Swiss freelance writer. It is also not unreason-
able to see Balthasar, with his literary and aesthetic interests, as an heir
to a certain German Romanticism and even metaphysical idealism.
His work, however, so far as one can see, owes nothing to the Tübingen School. His most provocative writings remained in the future,
obviously, in the "theo-dramatics," which clearly break completely
with anything like conventional Scholastic exposition of doctrine and
could plausibly be regarded as fusing theology and spirituality. The
problem, however, for Congar, with Balthasar as with Soiron and
Koepgen, not to mention all the others criticized in the *DTC* entry, is
surely just that they are not in any sense Thomists in the Scholastic
tradition. Moreover, it is difficult to believe that Congar really
believed that theologians like Soiron and Koepgen represented anything very significant in the way of "a vitalist religious conception of
theology," or that, in his view, they either were in fact, or might plausibly have been perceived as, more of a threat to the "pact" that
Catholic theology evidently had with Scholasticism than Bouillard, de
Lubac, Daniélou, Charlier and Chenu — or Hans Urs von Balthasar.

It might even seem disingenuous on Congar's part, as seems to happen in the preface to *A History of Theology*, to deny the existence of "*la Nouvelle Théologie*," let alone its being perceived as a "problem," while diverting our attention to the "*Lebenstheologie*," in theologians such as Soiron and Bopp — whom he was criticizing thirty years earlier, in the *DTC* entry, for their penchant for "life," "the vital and the organic," a critique that he obviously makes unapologetically, perhaps even unconsciously, from a distinctively Thomist perspective.

III

Congar gives no hint, in the preface to *A History of Theology*, as to why Balthasar should be associated with Soiron and Koepgen in creating a "problem" on account of "these ideas of a vitalist religious conception of theology." The Tübingen School theologians mentioned in 1939 in the *DTC* entry have disappeared, perhaps because Congar had come to have a better appreciation of their contribution to ecclesiology, in particular to ideas about tradition, people of God, and so on, which Congar, and for that matter Vatican II, had largely accepted.

He goes on to allow, however, that *Sources chrétiennes* looked like a project to favour typological, spiritual and allegorical exegesis of Scripture to the detriment of the literal sense. Next, he admits that, in "Du symbole à la dialectique," the famous chapter in *Corpus mysticum*, which greatly alarmed mainstream Thomists, Henri de Lubac sought to encourage a much richer hermeneutic than the conceptual analysis characteristic of Scholasticism — as if imagination was more productive than reasoning! More notoriously still, Congar cites Henri Bouillard's *boutade*: "A theology which is no longer in tune with its time is a false theology" — reminding us, however, of the preceding sentence — "When the spirit evolves, a truth remains immutable thanks only to a simultaneous and correlative evolution of all its ideas and to the fact that these preserve the same relation to each other." He clearly thinks that this — surely fairly obscure — sentence clarifies what Bouillard meant and should have saved him from criticism.

He allows, however, that Bouillard's remark, together with the introduction to the *Sources Chrétiennes* translation of one of the works of Origen, and de Lubac's chapter in *Corpus Mysticum*, "could be interpreted as a profession of historic and philosophic relativism" — but obviously he thinks this would have been a mistake; "for it would seem that the invariant dogma, which the faithful profess formally to respect, remained foreign to ideas, that is, foreign to the concepts in which theology had given them a workable expression at some given date" — but this too would have been a mistake, even if not without some plausibility in the circumstances.[15] In particular, Congar continues, "it was left open to question what was to become not only of St Thomas's theology but of theological science as he defined it." There is no doubt that this captures precisely the anxiety of many, indeed most, Thomists at the time. Bouillard and de Lubac, after all, were making claims specifically about how to interpret Aquinas. Moreover, above all, Aquinas's conception of theology as a "science" seemed to be under challenge — the Thomist conception of theological methodology, that is to say, which Congar takes as normative throughout the story he recounts in the *DTC* and which allows, or compels, him to be so hostile to manifestations of *Lebenstheologie*, whether in the Tübingen School or in the "kerygmatic" theology of some German Franciscans or finally in Balthasar.

---

[15] *HT*, 9.

Some "professional Thomists," Congar goes on to say, naming
Réginald Garrigou-Lagrange, "soon gave expression to their dis-
turbance and their questions." However, the Jesuit collaborators of
Sources chrétiennes and *Théologie* hit back, granting that, though
their position was "basically modernistic," it was "not necessarily
destructive."[16]

The two key points in the debate were as follows: (1) "a distinction ... between faith and belief, the latter being the ideological
structure in which faith finds expression"; and (2) "the conception
of the relation between dogmatic pronouncements and religious
realities as a relation of symbol to reality, not as an expression
proper (however inadequate) to reality."

Congar goes on to explain. To some extent the problem encountered by the Modernists had indeed reappeared, namely "the variations in the representations and the intellectual construction of
the affirmations of faith." Theologians now, however, were cop-
ing with this problem, Congar says, by distinguishing between
"an invariant of affirmations" on the one hand and, on the other,
"the variable usage of technical notions to translate essential truth
in historic contexts differing culturally and philosophically." For
them, however, "the *invariant* was a set of affirmations having a
real content of truth" — Congar's emphasis. In this way, he
thinks, theologians now avoided "the ruinous anti-intellectual-
ism" of the Modernists. Moreover, they did not succumb, as the
Modernists did, to "dogmatic relativism"; rather, "in the differing notional translations" (of the essential truth), these theologians acknowledged "an analogy of relations," or, if you will, "a
functional equivalence between the notions used to express that
truth."

---

[16] *HT*, 10

On the other hand, Congar allows, critics were right in suspecting that no serious philosophical analysis had been offered to clarify the concept, reasoning and systematisation of theology. Indeed, there had been no "philosophical reinterrogation regarding the place of the concept in our perception of the truth, its nature and value" — the concept of a concept in general, presumably he means.[17] Here, Congar refers us to "interesting reflections" by Edward Schillebeeckx, in his *Approches théologiques*, I: *Révélation et Théologie* (Brussels, 1965).

He makes one more concession to the critics: "the simplified teaching of the schools and manuals, and even the authority of St Thomas himself," had, in some degree, been "infringed." "Certain positions and formulations generally considered settled — and almost canonised — had been brought into question." In other words, but without offering examples, Congar admits that the thought of Thomas Aquinas, as expounded — "simplified" — in the manual tradition, was indeed threatened by the re-readings offered by the likes of Bouillard and de Lubac. Since in general perception the "authority" of Aquinas was not separable, or separated, from the textbooks expounding sacred doctrine *ad mentem sancti Thomae*, any challenge to them must seem a challenge to him as well. On the other hand, as Congar is surely implying, there was a way of studying Thomas Aquinas independently of the manual tradition. What is not so clear, however, is whether those who read Thomas Aquinas in the light of such commentators as Cajetan and John of St Thomas, were justified, to some extent at least, in their suspicions of the interpretations offered by such scholars as Bouillard and de Lubac.

The "anxiety" aroused in theological circles was, so Congar avers, "for the most part artificial." True, "a certain few" fashioned the "fantastic idea" of *une nouvelle théologie*, which they

---

[17] *HT*, 10, footnote 3. Perhaps one might say that the principal problem in Modernism was confusion between image (*Bild*) and concept (*Begriff*).

were in any case incapable of characterising with clarity — "as this author has learned from personal experience a good hundred times between 1946 and 1950."[18] Congar concedes that Pope Pius XII used the expression "new theology" in his discourse to the general Congregation of the Society of Jesus in September 1946; and, without using the phrase, addressed the same admonition to the general Chapter of the Dominicans that year. The dangers to orthodox Catholicism envisaged in the "novelties" were spelled out in the Pope's encyclical *Humani Generis* (1950): "excessive concessions made to modern philosophies, dialectical materialism, existentialism, historicism, or — as is very evident today — irenics." In retrospect, Congar seems to mean, from the vantage point of 1968, the Pope was right to highlight tendencies which "fostered a distrust of the use of reason in apologetics and theology, a weakening of speculative theology and of the value of dogmatic formulas, a neglect of the ordinary *magisterium*" — but also "a failure to return to scriptural and patristic sources." "Today the crisis has passed, if indeed there was ever really a crisis," so Congar contends here in 1968.

The experience undergone by Congar and many others, in the aftermath of the encyclical *Humani Generis*, from 1950 until the election of Pope John XXIII and the convoking of the Council in 1959, was surely, by any standards, a time of crisis, both personally for these individuals and in the institutions where they had taught, as well as in the wider context of the Catholic Church, in France above all.

The problems, however, remain, in the limited area of theological method, Congar goes on to contend. First of all, the remarkable return to sources, the *ressourcement*, endorsed in *Humani Generis*,

---

[18] *HT*, 11. The expression "la nouvelle théologie," if not coined by Garrigou-Lagrange, appears most famously in his essay in *Angelicum*, 1946.

as he says, raised many questions about the nature of theological work. If we now see that divine revelation takes place in the framework of an "economy," then it becomes questionable whether "a conceptual-deductive method and an ordered plan of study following merely the formal sequences" are apt to deal with the data.[19]

Many of the concepts borrowed by Thomas Aquinas from Aristotle, and deployed in Scholasticism, fail to engage with such central biblical notions as covenant, *agape*, flesh, *hesed*, justice, not to mention word, kingdom and truth. There simply is a "gap" between what we find in Scholastic textbooks and what we find in any decent lexikon of biblical theology.

The questions raised by the Modernists reappear: firstly, the very idea of divine revelation itself has long been regarded "as though it were a collection of theorems," "dealing with realities which almost entirely escape our experience." For the past sixty years or so (thus since 1908?) Catholic theologians have worked at a much better understanding of the economic structure of revelation and furthermore have come to understand better the essential purpose of the covenant, namely to establish an interpersonal relation between God and his people. The dogmatic constitution *Dei verbum* (1965) of Vatican II appropriated these values, Congar notes, without prejudice to the intellectual content. "This is very important for the future of Catholic theology," Congar concludes; "it solves many problems or at least renders them less problematic."

Secondly, while the majority of theologians have long produced their theology as though the world had not become indifferent to the Church and the affirmation of faith, some have now begun to link theological work as a reflection on faith to the Church's duty of preaching the faith in ways intelligible to people as they actually are today.

---

[19] Congar refers us to his important paper in *Mélanges M.-D. Chenu* (1966): "Le moment 'économique' et le moment 'ontologique' dans la Sacra Doctrina."

Thirdly, the most fruitful approaches in Catholic theology are linked with phenomenology and the philosophy of existence. We have to consider personhood and all that goes with this. Then we have to develop an intersubjective or interpersonal ontology. Fourthly we have to see the human condition as historical, under the aspect of the condition of a being of the world.

All this introduces "values for theological reflection" hitherto absent in Scholasticism. In short, "today we find differing manners of theologising" — "Scholasticism: conceptual, argumentative, or deductive, exhausts the datum of tradition, not only of an *intellectus fidei*, rationally established, but of an application to different times and cultures." On the other hand, Congar says, we find "the reflective manner," which "philosophizes on the whole of Christian reality, illuminated, if you will, by the existential experience of man"[20] — which sounds, one might think, remarkably like what was attempted by some at least of the theologians inclined to favour a certain *Lebenstheologie*.

As regards the former, Congar cites the *Dogmatik* of Michael Schmaus (1897-1993): "a renovation of the classic *De Deo* treatise, beginning with a study of the divine Persons, an insertion of theology into economy, a complete renovation of ecclesiology and eschatology, etc."[21] In the wake of Vatican II Schmaus rewrote his *Dogmatik* as *Der Glaube der Kirche* (1969-70), endeavouring to take into account the Council's insights and concerns. Obviously, however, Congar has in mind the *Katholische Dogmatik*, three volumes in 1938 but extending to eight by the sixth edition, with the ninth and final edition appearing in 1964. Trained as a medievalist, associated for most of his life with the University of Munich, Schmaus succeeded in expounding the theology of Scholasticism

[20] *HT*, 17.
[21] *HT*, 16.

while orientating the entire discussion towards a theology of inter-personal relations in the service of the proclamation of the Gospel.

In the same line of renewed Scholasticism, Congar cites the series *Le Mystère chrétien*, specifically the first volume, *La Foi et la Théologie,* which appeared in 1962 and was written by himself, as he forebears to say. The other type of theology is exemplified by the work of Karl Rahner: making "no extended search into the annals of tradition to sift out the elements of an answer to new problems," Rahner and his followers offer "a philosophical reflec-tion on the relation which the global affirmation of faith has with man." This is "a real theology," Congar insists, but "a theology more philosophical and critico-reflective in character than histori-cal." The rest of the preface to *A History of Theology* deals with what Congar thinks is "only a vague indication of the theological work of the future" offered by Vatican II.

In sum, soon after Vatican II, Congar is happy to allow a "new theology" along the lines by then being followed by Karl Rahner. It is clear, however, that he favours the example of Michael Schmaus, which shows that "a classical type of theology can *adapt* and absorb the new questions and develop the new aspects, which ... refer to man and his existential experience" (his empha-sis). His own book in *Le Mystère chrétien* series is another exam-ple of this kind of work.

IV

In 1974, Yves Congar gave the Aquinas Lecture at Blackfriars, Oxford, as part of the commemoration of the seventh centenary of the death of Saint Thomas.[22] Obviously, this was an invitation to

---

[22] "St Thomas Aquinas and the Spirit of Ecumenism," *New Blackfriars* 55 (1974) 196-209.

reflect on his position as regards the thought of Aquinas, if not
about Scholasticism. He chose to highlight "aspects of the theology of St Thomas which have ecumenical value"; but here again,
as we study it, we find his commitment to a certain Thomism pervading the whole lecture. He begins by considering two great obstacles in the way of taking Thomas as a model or patron or precur-
sor of ecumenism. In the first place, "there can only be ecumenism
if one accepts the other *as other*" — allowing, to be specific, "that
[the other] *also* has insights, that he has something to give." What
possibility could there have been, in an epoch of Christendom when
"heretics" were to be "exterminated," of anything prefiguring
"ecumenical dialogue," however sketchily?

To this Congar replies that, at least, Thomas would have *debated*
with those with whom he did not agree (*Summa Theologiae* 2-2. 10,
7). True, he composed a *Contra errores Graecorum* — but, Congar
notes, the title is not his, and in fact there is *nothing* in the text which
is fairly described as being *against* the doctrine of the Eastern
Church. Thomas refutes objections to the papal primacy and the *Filioque* but that, Congar suggests, does not amount to an attack on
Greek Orthodox doctrine as such — only a defence of Catholic doctrine against Orthodox misunderstandings. Thomas writes against
the erroneous understanding the Greeks have of Catholic doctrines
— which is not to say that the doctrines of the Greek Church are
themselves erroneous. Moreover, Thomas venerated the Greek
Fathers — indeed, Congar insists, this theologian "whom one represents as a man of pure speculation... passed a large part of his life
in searching out and reading new texts, in having new translations
made, in dialoguing or debating with every current of thought."

There, clearly, we have Congar, a theologian who never fails to
document every thesis that he proposes with an array of references
to the texts of relevant authorities, reminding us that Thomas's
practice, albeit never so massively footnoted as his own or anyone

else's in modern times, is nonetheless grounded in *reading*. Without saying so in so many words, Congar is surely indicating that history is as important as philosophy for theology, and that the speculative ingenuity of the metaphysician need not be preferred to the historian's skill in finding authoritative documents to cite in support of a thesis. In effect, this is Congar endorsing the approach of *l'école du Saulchoir* over against any version of Thomism which suspected "historicism" of being little different from "relativism" — over against the fears of such Thomists, Congar is insisting, Thomas himself sought to ground his positions in *texts*.

The second obstacle to envisaging Thomas as in any sense a model for ecumenical dialogue is this: we might think that, as inhabiting a hierarchical cosmological view of the world, Thomas would have been completely incapable of understanding the "drama," the "putting of everything into question," which is characteristic of modern times. Indeed, Congar says, "this is one reason for our difficulty in really understanding the Protestant theologies or that of Luther" — why so? — because "they start from an existential point of view," they are "personal," "dramatic," they speak "of concrete, historical situations and not of the nature of things, abstracted from their historical and existential conditions." Thomas considers sin and grace, for example, before speaking of Christ — an option unacceptable to Protestants; and before speaking of the sacraments — an option unacceptable to the Orthodox. This is a difficulty for any appeal to Thomas in connection with ecumenical dialogue, which, Congar insists, he does not wish to minimise. Moreover, this is the difficulty "at the heart of the sort of disaffection with regard to St Thomas which one encounters in Catholic theology today": "One is more at home with the Fathers, more personalist, more historical, more existential, less systematic, less analytical."

Congar allows himself two comments. Firstly, "Thomists have often treated history as an accident which does not modify reality."

"With them, there is frequently a contempt for the facts." This "abstraction" is "a heresy which, sadly, has never been condemned" — so Congar says, with heavy irony. Here, obviously, he is distancing himself from those "Thomists" who succeeded in having so much of his own theological work placed under suspicion. Thomas, he insists again, is not guilty of this "abstraction." When he presents things "from a formal point of view," as Thomists (then anyway) liked to say, and as we saw him do in the *DTC* entry, this need only mean that "one attains the total, concrete reality from a particular angle" — not that historical reality in its density disappears.

Secondly, in response to the problem that we are nowadays so marked by existential drama, Congar contends that Thomas had "an extremely vivid perception of the originality of the human subject, of his, in a certain sense, autocreative liberty." Some — no doubt including Thomists — will be astonished to hear this, so Congar thinks. Yet, he insists, this emphasis on the subject "even orders the plan of the *Summa*" — in the sense, that is to say, that Thomas "treats first of all the realities and structures prior to man's exercise of his liberty, and thus prior to history, and then of the conditions in which this liberty is exercised." That the whole project of the *Summa Theologiae* is shaped by this emphasis on human liberty becomes even more obvious in the *secunda pars* —"where 'man' is not treated as a 'nature', in the current sense of the word, but as the creator of that which he is called to be, by his virtuous acts and the *habitus*." In short, for Thomas, man "creates himself." The theological vision of the *Summa Theologiae* highlights this "most profound and vivid conception of liberty," "the condition of the Christian as free." In short, for Thomas, "personhood" is "the supreme realisation of created being."[23] None of this should be allowed to "transform

---

[23] See two famous texts: 4 *Contra Gentiles* 11; *Summa Theologiae* 1.29.3.

Thomas into a modern"; it should however allow us to recognize "that which renders him still readable and profitable for us today."

The best criterion of Thomas's ecumenical value, Congar says, resides in the work of several non-Catholic scholars: he supplies a brief bibliography. He then sets out the principles to be found in Thomas's work which would have been decisive if Thomas had had to compose a theology of "church." He returns, then, to consider in some detail how Thomas *argued* —"how he liked to start from unsatisfactory, if not erroneous, solutions to problems which bore on dogmatic affirmations, in order to integrate their valid insights into a more synthetic solution, or, again, how he took up certain formulations from other schools of thought and placed them in a context in which they could bear an acceptable meaning." In Thomas's own words: "We must love them both, those whose opinions we follow and those whose opinions we reject; for both have laboured to discover the truth, and have helped us in that task."[24] Admittedly, this principle is applied "only on secondary questions." Nevertheless, so the burden of Congar's lecture runs, this kind of respect for the other's opinion, practised by Thomas, adumbrates what we may call "the spirit of ecumenism."

But there are, or can be, much more intractable differences. Congar refers to "our difficulty in really understanding the Protestant theologies or that of Luther" — that "they start from an existential point of view," and so on, — but the question of interest to us here is who it is with whom he is aligning himself, in that "our"?

Who did Congar mean by "us," in this lecture at Oxford, in 1974, to what he knew would be an audience composed half of Catholics and half of Anglicans with about thirty of his fellow Dominicans among the former? Who is it who has this difficulty

---

[24] *Commentary on Metaphysics* lib. XII, lect 9 end.

in reaching any deep understanding of Protestant theologies or Luther's theology? It is those who can speak, in theology, "of the nature of things, abstracted from their historical and existential conditions." No doubt Congar was including Anglicans among those who find Lutheran theology quite difficult to approach — as he should have done, in the light of the distinction between Anglicanism and Protestantism mentioned in the Vatican II document on ecumenism. It is difficult, however, to believe that Anglicans were included among those who speak, in theology, "of the nature of things, abstracted from their historical and existential conditions."

These are, on the other hand, presumably not the Thomists whom Congar denounces for the "heresy" of "abstraction." Congar is aligning himself, and "us," with Catholic theologians who are surely not afflicted with quite that degree of incapacity to understand Protestantism. It is a good ecumenical gesture to approach others whose views one expects to have to reject with initial sympathy; but it seems unlikely that he is placing himself with the Thomists who, much to his shock and anger, got M.-Dominique Chenu's book put on the Index, in 1942. It becomes clear, from what he goes on to say about some "very profound, and sometimes very voluminous, studies" which had recently appeared in German (in the 1960s, that is to say)[25] that what Congar is thinking of — what he greatly likes — is the distinction, made by Otto Hermann Pesch, between Thomas's "sapiential theology" and Martin Luther's *"theologia crucis."* We are not concerned with "secondary issues." On the contrary, with this distinction, we have to do with "questions of theological anthropology and soteriology" — which is "just where one would expect to find the maximum

---

[25] Congar refers to the work of Ulrich Kühn and Hans Vorster, both Protestants, and that of Stephan Pfürtner and Otto Hermann Pesch, both Catholics, indeed both members of the Dominican Order at the time.

opposition between the ontological and sapiential point of view of Thomas and the existential-dramatic approach of Luther."

There is no way in which we can "superimpose" these two approaches on each other; they are incommensurable — which need not mean they are incompatible. On the contrary, we can see, from Pesch especially, that Thomas expresses "authentic evangelical insights," starting (it's true) not from the historical event of the Cross, but rather from the conviction "that the order of redemption encompasses the order of creation, and that they are both subject to the same Lord." As Congar goes on to say, this is the "profound conviction which is ... expressed in the theological use of the analogy of being" — and here Congar refers to the work of Eric Lionel Mascall.[26]

The approach to St Thomas which Congar recommends, then, in 1974, is exemplified by Pesch and Mascall. One wonders how recently, if indeed ever, Yves Congar read Mascall's *Existence and Analogy* — much closer to the readings of Thomas by Garrigou-Lagrange and Jacques Maritain than to the approach of Chenu. Mascall, as Congar must have known, was not a central or representative Anglican theologian. Congar, anyway, is principally recommending Pesch's approach to Aquinas. It was Otto Hermann Pesch who would translate Chenu's great book on Aquinas into German, the book that situates Thomas in the context of a certain Augustinian Platonism, quite removed from Mascall's preference for Thomas the Aristotelian.

In other words, here, in 1974, Congar is recommending to his audience in Oxford that the way to go, in commemorating Aquinas, is to approach his theology in the light of the work of M.-Dominique Chenu. Thomas's theology is sapiential and ontological — everything considered *sub ratione Dei* (*Summa*

---

[26] Then still at Oxford, the most eminent Anglican Thomist; I cannot remember if Mascall was present at Congar's lecture.

Theologiae 1.1.7); which is what makes it difficult to understand
a theology which is existential and dramatic, relating everything to
the redemptive sacrifice of Christ. So, far from regarding Thomas's
approach as issuing in the "abstraction" with which certain
Thomists are charged, Congar evidently sees it as exhibiting,
embodying, a sapiential-ontological theology. This is something
radically different from Protestant theologies, or anyway Luther.
Clearly, the approach to Aquinas to be found in the work of Chenu
and Pesch is one which Congar is happy to endorse.

Indeed, he goes on to mention the disaffection with Thomas
Aquinas in post-Conciliar Catholic theology, tracing this to a "more
personalist," "historical," "existentialist" approach — "less systematic, less analytical" — and here, I think, from the tone, which
is not one of lamentation, Congar is not deploring such trends in
post Conciliar Catholic theology, he is simply saying that the per-
sonalist/historical/existentialist way or ways of doing Catholic theology are not his.

No doubt, as the years went by, Congar became more unhappy
with trends in Catholic theology; but here at least, in 1974, it seems
to me he is simply noting a quite radical difference of approach. For
all his immense influence in making Catholic theology much more
historical, in reopening tradition, in practising *ressourcement* and
so on, Congar did not think of himself as departing from Thomas's
theological methodology, conceived appropriately in a sapiential-
ontological mode.

"An attentive reading of the works of the *Doctor Angelicus*,"
Congar quotes Karl Barth as saying, "permits one to verify in him
[Aquinas] certain lines of force which, even if they do not lead
directly to the Reformation, do not tend, any the more, towards
Jesuitical Romanism. Thus when one knows how to use intelli-
gently this immense compendium of the previous tradition which
constitutes the *Summa*, one remarks that its author is, on many

issues, an evangelical theologian useful to know."[27] In other words, by overlooking the relationship of Thomas's work to the witness of the primitive and medieval church, modern theologians (Catholic as well as Reformed, Barth no doubt means) allow Aquinas to become a "father of post-Tridentine Catholicism" — a fateful decision. Are we to read Thomas's theology as inaugurating post-Tridentine theology, post-Vatican I natural theology, and so on, or as the "compendium" of all previous tradition?

It is an option that divides Thomists, that divided Thomists back as far as Chenu's little book, as well as his practice — the approach to reading Aquinas which led to accusations of "historicism," "relativism," "modernism," and so on.

In a footnote, Congar refers us to the work of Marie-Joseph Le Guillou, *Théologie du Mystère: Le Christ et l'Église* (Paris, 1963), a massive attempt to re-read Aquinas in the light of his biblical commentaries, relating his theology to the patristic tradition of biblical exegesis, highlighting the centrality in the *Summa Theologiae* of the focus on *beatitude*, the mystery made accessible in Christ and in the Church, the communion by grace in the life of the Trinity promised to the creatures who are made in the image of God; and so on.

In short, for Congar, Thomas's work is not the prolegomenon to modern Catholic apologetics, the quarry for arguments for the existence of God, and so on; it's more, as Barth suggested, a compendium of traditional theology, Latin and Greek: taking the sapiential-ontological way, then, not building one's theology from the historical event of the incarnation, redemption and so on; beginning rather from the end, from the communion in divine beatitude promised to the saints, anticipated in the moral and sacramental realities of lives of faith, hope and charity; and so on.

---

[27] *Kirchliche Dogmatik* I/2, 686; *Church Dogmatics* I/2, 614.

V

There would be other ways of estimating Yves Congar's indebtedness and allegiance to Thomism. We could explore, firstly, his thesis about the turn to the person in Aquinas's theology or the idea of Aquinas's theological vision as focused on beatitude. The studies Yves Congar refers to, such as Johann Baptist Metz's book on the "anthropocentric turn" inaugurated by Aquinas, have perhaps come to little or nothing. Yet, what has happened, on the other hand, increasingly in the 1980s and 90s, certainly in the English speaking theological world, is the discovery of "virtue ethics," which includes a return to Thomas Aquinas, often by way of Aristotle, as the way between the Scylla of Kant (duty, the categorical imperative, etc.) and the Charybdis of John Stuart Mill (utilitarianism, consequentialism, etc.) — "virtue ethics," "agent-centred" as the jargon has it, is very much the "personalism" Congar highlights in the *Summa Theologiae*.

And secondly, in several recent books, in the English speaking world, what Yves Congar labels the sapiential approach, following Pesch, is well and truly on the agenda. Consider, for example, the wonderful article by A. N. Williams (now at Cambridge) on the "mystical theology" of Thomas Aquinas, replacing his theology in the patristic tradition of a spirituality of sanctification as divinization.[28] Williams refers us to *A History of Theology*: "Yves Congar notes that for both Maximus and Evagrius Ponticus, theology is the most elevated of degrees of life, being that perfect knowledge of God which is identified with the summit of prayer;" and, even more importantly for our theme here, she takes Congar as her authority that spirituality grew apart from theology in the late

[28] A. N. Williams, "Mystical Theology Redux: The Pattern of Aquinas's Summa Theologiae," *Modern Theology* 13 (1997) 53-74.

Middle Ages. It's true that she goes on to quote Chenu, a much greater influence on her work; yet, in this rediscovery of Thomas Aquinas as mystical theologian, the contribution of Yves Congar is not forgotten.

YVES CONGAR AND CATHOLIC CHURCH REFORM
A RENEWAL OF THE SPIRIT

Gabriel FLYNN

Lecturer in Theology
Mater Dei Institute of Education, a College of Dublin City University

I. INTRODUCTION: "RAZING THE BASTIONS"

Both high acclaim and sharp criticism underscore Yves Congar's contribution to Catholic theology. He is honoured as a pioneer of Church unity and a champion of the laity. At the same time it is true to say that, for many in the Catholic Church, his role as reformer is ambiguous and his theology remains obfuscated to the present day. This article attempts to articulate Congar's vision for true reform in the Church, in order to provoke renewed engagement with one of the great Christian thinkers of the twentieth century. I shall argue that his contribution in this field makes him an architect of the contemporary Church. Looking at the matter historically, Congar holds an eminent place in the history of Church reform. He is careful but effective in his approach to reform and his extensive involvement at Vatican II helped to make reform of the Church the order of the day in practically every domain. Congar, in fact, sees himself as a man of ideas,[1] but it is his idea of reform that dominates his entire *oeuvre*

---

[1] Yves Congar, "Loving Openness Toward Every Truth: A Letter from Thomas Aquinas to Karl Rahner," *Philosophy and Theology* 12, no. 1 (2000) 213-219, p. 215.

and, in my view, constitutes his most important and original contribution to Christian theology. In *Vraie et fausse réforme dans l'Église* (1950), his *magnum opus* on reform and one of his most influential works, he describes the conditions for a true reform of the Church, which he says can be reduced to four principles: (i) the primacy of charity and the pastoral; (ii) to remain within the communion of all; (iii) patience; respect for delays; (iv) a true renewal by a return to the principle of the Tradition.[2]

In this article, I consider Congar's principles for reform. And, by applying them to the great historical ruptures to the Christian Church in the eleventh and sixteenth centuries respectively, as well as to the crisis in the post-conciliar period engendered by Archbishop Marcel Lefebvre of Ecône, Switzerland, who styled himself as "the defender of the faith,"[3] I endeavour to show that these original principles of reform help to provide an effective safeguard against division and schism in the Church. Further, in an attempt to articulate elements of a new vision for the Church of the future, an important objective of this article, I hold that the inclusion of Congar's principles of reform is justified on the basis of their marked contribution to unity in the Church. It should be added that the proposals for a new vision of the Church have been inspired, in part, by Congar's view of reform and his notion of the "threshold Church" — a theologically rich and pastorally sensitive approach to the Church of the future, presented in an article first published in 1976. Finally, if it can be shown, as the title of this

---

[2] See Yves Congar, *Vraie et fausse réforme dans l'Église*, Unam Sanctam, 20 (Paris: Cerf, 1950) 229-352. Unless otherwise stated, translations from the French are mine throughout.

[3] Jean Guitton, "The Future of the Council," Appendix III in Congar, *Challenge to the Church: The Case of Archbishop Lefebvre*, trans. Paul Inwood (London/Dublin: Collins/Veritas, 1976) 82-87, p. 83; also id., *La Crise dans l'Église et Mgr Lefebvre* (Paris: Cerf, 1976).

article suggests, that his programme of Church reform is consonant with a renewal of the Spirit, I contend that a new horizon has dawned for Congar and that the clouds of suspicion that marred his academic career and tainted his theological legacy may at last be dispelled. To begin, I shall consider the role of reform in his theology, a role that reached its zenith at the Second Vatican Council (1962-65).

In the struggle of minds at Vatican II, his was one of the most influential, and his thought is enshrined in its pivotal documents.[4] Congar, in fact, viewed his theology as an integral part of that Council, a point he expresses succinctly as follows: "If there is a theology of Congar, that is where it is to be found."[5] He was a harbinger of reform in the Church during the pre-conciliar era, a period marked by the Church's hostility to the modern world and many of its youngest and most brilliant reforming theologians. Like his influential mentor and friend Marie-Dominique Chenu (1895-1990), sometime professor of the History of Christian Doctrine and Regent of *Le Saulchoir*, the house of studies of the Dominican province of France, situated at Kain-la-Tombe near Tournai in Belgium during the French Third Republic and subsequently at Étiolles and the Couvent Saint-Jacques in Paris,[6] Congar knew that the renewal of Catholic ecclesiology and the elusive goal of Church reform would not be possible without "razing the bastions."[7]

---

[4] Yves Congar, *Mon journal du Concile* (hereafter *Journal*) ed. and notes Éric Mahieu, 2 vols. (Paris: Cerf, 2002) II: 511 (7 December 1965). See also id., "Letter from Father Yves Congar, O.P.," trans. Ronald John Zawilla, *Theology Digest* 32 (1985) 213-216, p. 215.

[5] Congar, "Letter from Father Yves Congar, O.P.," 215.

[6] See Marie-Dominique Chenu, *Une école de théologie: le Saulchoir* (Paris: Cerf, 1985) 7.

[7] The idea is borrowed from Hans Urs von Balthasar. See his *Razing the Bastions: On the Church in This Age* (San Francisco, CA: Ignatius Press, Communio Books, 1993).

In other words, without a general Council of the Church — at which a fierce battle for a renewed ecclesiology was to be played out between conservatives and progressives at the highest level in the Catholic Church — the hoped for *aggiornamento* of Pope John XXIII would almost certainly have foundered. Of course, an important part of "razing the bastions," and a clear sign of the success of Pope John's *aggiornamento*, was a new freedom for Catholics to hear and to celebrate the Word of God at Mass.

Any study of the concept of ecclesial reform is inseparably connected with a study of the prevailing concept of the Church — a point clearly illustrated in Congar's contribution to Catholic Church reform. It was to transcend the juridical idea of the Church that had dominated the post-Tridentine period through the manuals of apologetics, that Congar, together with his colleagues Chenu and Henri-Marie Féret, embarked on an enterprise to eliminate "baroque theology,"[8] a term which they coined to describe the theology of the Counter-Reformation.[9] It is clear, however, that the most decisive battle for the renewal of ecclesiology and the concomitant reform of the Church in the twentieth century, in which Congar was one of the major players, was to take place, not in Paris, but in Rome. The Vatican Council provided the broadest possible forum for dialogue and reform. Its triumph was due in large measure to the popes of the Council. Pope John XXIII, whose innate acuity and evident diplomatic skills (as Nuncio in Paris during the difficult period of the Second World War, he handled the French government excellently as well as helping the Jews) contributed to the successful execution of an extensive programme of

[8] Jean Puyo, *Jean Puyo interroge le Père Congar: "une vie pour la vérité"* (Paris: Centurion, 1975) 45-46.

[9] See Congar, *Martin Luther sa foi, sa réforme: études de théologie historique*, Cogitatio Fidei, 119 (Paris: Cerf, 1983) 79.

aggiornamento, while Pope Paul VI's greatest feat was to bring the Council to an end within a reasonable time.[10] In saying this, however, I do not mean to take away from the role of the theologians, whose contribution to the success of the Council was immense. Congar's part in the process of renewal initiated there, as illustrated in his recently published diary *Mon journal du Concile*, a question I have considered elsewhere,[11] was indispensable. Everything points to the conclusion that he was one of the outstanding reformers of Vatican II. While it is not my intention to make the Council the subject of consideration here, I will comment briefly on Congar's part in its proceedings, in order to make his position clearer.

He played a decisive role in the drafting of texts during the preparatory phase and at the sessions of the Council itself.[12] It must also be borne in mind that, together with his powerful friends and allies from the Belgian delegation, whose influence pervaded the whole Council, he was forced to engage in a relentless battle for its success, as even a perfunctory reading of his conciliar diary reveals. If at the Council the previously dominant Roman Curia theologians were ultimately obliged to give way to the more progressive reforming theologians from the French- and German-speaking countries, it should be pointed out that Congar remained *sub nube*. As he comments rather plaintively in *Mon journal du Concile*: "Personally, I have never [...] emerged from the apprehensions of one, suspected, sanctioned, judged, discriminated

[10] See Owen Chadwick, *The Christian Church in the Cold War* (London: Penguin, 1992) 118.

[11] See Gabriel Flynn, "*Mon journal du Concile*: Yves Congar and the Battle for a Renewed Ecclesiology at the Second Vatican Council," *Louvain Studies* 28 (2003) 48-70.

[12] Congar, *Journal*, II: 511 (7 December 1965). See also Congar, "Letter from Father Yves Congar, O.P.", 215; id., *Fifty Years of Catholic Theology: Conversations with Yves Congar*, ed. Bernard Lauret, trans. John Bowden (London: SCM, 1988) 14; also id., *Entretiens d'automne*, 2nd ed. (Paris: Cerf, 1987) 22.

against."[13] While Congar's participation in the proceedings of Vatican II, notably, his close association with the Belgian theologians, indicates his obvious political adroitness,[14] we must ever bear in mind that it is primarily as a servant of the Church,[15] and of the bishops,[16] that he perceived his role there. In fact, his work at the Council was a part, albeit the most important part, of a vocation dedicated to the service of truth. As he explains:

> I was filled to overflowing. All the things to which I gave special attention issued in the Council: ecclesiology, ecumenism, reform of the Church, the lay state, mission, ministries, collegiality, return to the sources and Tradition ... I've consecrated my life to the service of truth. I've loved it and still love it in the way one loves a person. I've been like that from my very childhood, as if by some instinct and interior need. When I was a young Dominican, I took over the motto of St Hilary which St Thomas Aquinas had first made his own (*Contra Gentes* 1, 2) and which was reproduced on his statue, in the house of studies at Le Saulchoir: "Ego hoc vel praecipuum vitae meae officium debere me Deo conscius sum, ut eum omnis sermo meus et sensus loquatur" (De Trin. I, 37; PL 1, 48 C), "For my own part, I know that the chief duty of my life is that all that I say and all that I feel speaks God."[17]

It is important to note the role of affectivity in Congar's theology,[18] because of its relevance to the present discussion. The point to

---

[13] Congar, *Journal*, II: 56 (14 March 1964).

[14] *Ibid.*

[15] Congar, *Journal*, I: 177 (31 October 1962).

[16] See Congar, "Letter from Father Yves Congar, O.P.", 215. He comments: "We were at the service of the bishops."

[17] Congar, "Reflections on being a Theologian," trans. Marcus Lefébure, *New Blackfriars* 62 (1981) 405-409, pp. 405-406. See also id., "St. Thomas Aquinas and the Spirit of Ecumenism," *New Blackfriars* 55 (1974) 196-209; id., "Saint Thomas d'Aquin et l'esprit œcuménique," *Freiburger Zeitschrift für Philosophie und Theologie* 21 (1974) 331-346. Patrick Granfield, *Theologians at Work* (New York/London: Macmillan/Collier-Macmillan, 1967) 253.

[18] See Gabriel Flynn, "The Role of Affectivity in the Theology of Yves Congar," *New Blackfriars* 83 (2002) 347-364; also id., "Le rôle de l'affectivité dans

which I wish to draw attention is his assertion made in 1975: "I am of the Church. I love the Church."[19] Congar's love for the Church informed and inspired all his theological projects.[20] In every question regarding the Church, its mission in the world and its reform, the guiding principle is, so to speak, love. As he comments: "But this [reform] must be done in love, not in indifferent disinterestedness or in cold criticism [*critique froide*], nor in latent revolt [*fronde larvée*]."[21] The absence of love in the theologian, so astutely observed by Pope Paul VI in the case of the Swiss Hans Küng, detracts from his/her capacity to be a theological leader, in Pope Paul's view.[22] As regards Congar, though he is prepared to admit the need for a reform of the Church, he certainly did not write *Vraie et fausse réforme dans l'Église* as a negative appraisal of the Church. It is, rather, a work of "love and confidence. Above all, of total love and absolute confidence towards the Truth. [...] That is why there are no insinuations in this book."[23] Its aim, according to Congar, is not to propose a programme of reforms for the Church, but to study the place of reform in the life of the Church, the reasons that eventually make reform necessary, and most important, how to carry out a reform without injury to the unity of the Church.[24] "Reform *of* the Church," in his view, must

la théologie d'Yves Congar," trans. Jean Prignaud, *La Vie spirituelle* 157 (2003) 73-92.

[19] Puyo, *Jean Puyo interroge le Père Congar*, 185.

[20] M.-J. Le Guillou, "Yves Congar," *Bilan de la théologie du XXe siècle*, ed. Robert Vander Gucht and Herbert Vorgrimler, 2 vols. (Paris: Casterman, 1970) II: 791-805, p. 792.

[21] Congar, "Pourquoi j'aime l'Église," *Communion: Verbum Caro* 24 (1970) 23-30, p. 30.

[22] Congar, *Journal*, II: 336 (23 February 1965).

[23] Congar, *Vraie et fausse réforme dans l'Église*, 15.

[24] *Ibid.*, 8. See John W. O'Malley, *Giles of Viterbo on Church and Reform: A Study in Renaissance Thought*, ed., Heiko A. Oberman in cooperation with E. Jane Dempsey Douglass and others, Studies in Medieval and Reformation

then be "reform *in* the Church."[25] Congar had already shown in 1938 that a reform ceases to be authentic if it moves outside the Church.[26] A true reform of the Church, in fact, requires such a demanding form of fidelity that its essential reference point can only be love.[27]

The concrete form that affectivity took in his ecclesiology was a demanding search for the sources of authentic ecclesiology. He worked consistently for a reform of the Church that would proceed by way of a return to the sources (*ressourcement*). In his view, however, *ressourcement* could be accomplished only by way of a *recentrement* (a re-centring on Christ), thereby effecting "a return to the essential, to Jesus Christ, especially in the central mystery of Easter."[28] The point of adding these remarks is to show that Congar applied his own affective thinking about the Church to his theory of reform. In other words, I suggest that his role as Church reformer should not be viewed in isolation from his role as theologian of the Church that he loved (*Cette Église que j'aime*) and as servant of evangelical truth.

There is one further point that should be alluded to briefly at this stage because it illustrates an important element in Congar's vision

Thought, 5 (Leiden: Brill, 1968) 1. O'Malley lists *Vraie et fausse réforme dans l'Église*, among other studies, as "being more interested in examining reform thought than in describing practical reform programs."

[25] Puyo, *Jean Puyo interroge le Père Congar*, 117. See Congar, *Vraie et fausse réforme dans l'Église*, 192.

[26] Congar, *The Mystery of the Church: Studies by Yves Congar*, trans. A. V. Littledale, 2nd ed. rev. (London: Geoffrey Chapman, 1965) 104, footnote 1; also id., 2 vols.: *Esquisses du mystère de l'Église*, new ed., Unam Sanctam, 8 (Paris: Cerf, 1953) 126, footnote 2. *La Pentecote [sic]: Chartres 1956* (Paris: Cerf, 1956).

[27] Congar, "Renewal of the Spirit and Reform of the Institution," trans. John Griffiths, *Concilium* 3 (1972) 39-49, p. 47; also id., "Renouvellement de l'esprit et réforme de l'institution," *Concilium* 3 (1972) 37-45, p. 43.

[28] Congar, "Il faut construire l'Église en nous," *Témoignage Chrétien* 7 July 1950, p. 1.

of the Church. I refer to the dialectical principle of Catholic fidelity which is at the heart of the notion of reform, as articulated in *Vraie et fausse réforme dans l'Église*. Congar's notion of reform is, in fact, founded on the dialectical principle of Catholic fidelity (*fidélité catholique*), that is, a dual fidelity to the tradition and, by the eventual overtaking (*dépassement*) of certain concrete historical forms of its life, to the future realisation of the Church's "missionary function, its programme of Catholicity, of belief and of adaptation."[29] While there is tension between its two aspects, Congar asserts that there must also be "a communication, indeed a continuity, and thus a harmony."[30] The view of reform that Congar proposes is, as I mentioned earlier, defined in reference to a constant search of the deepest sources.[31] This approach facilitates an openness to change and development while exercising a profound fidelity to the tradition. From what has been said, it is evident that reform and tradition cannot be considered in isolation.[32] The precise relationship between these two concepts is pivotal in Congar's ecclesiology and shows an awareness of what has become an unfortunate consequence of reform in the post-conciliar period, namely, a certain polarisation within the Church between reformers and those who see themselves as defenders of tradition. Congar was fully cognisant of such difficulties,[33] the preservation and restoration of the Church's unity being the pre-eminent concern of his ecclesiology. I suggest that the complex problem of polarisation in

[29] Congar, *Vraie et fausse réforme dans l'Église*, 601.

[30] *Ibid.*, 599.

[31] *Ibid*, 602. See Yves Congar, "Vraie et fausse contestation dans l'Église," *Spiritus* 38 (1969) 125-132, p. 128.

[32] Congar, *Challenge to the Church*, 66-67; also id., *La Crise dans l'Église et Mgr Lefebvre*, 80-82.

[33] Congar, *The Church Peaceful* (Dublin: Veritas, 1977) 13; also id., *Au milieu des orages: l'Église affronte aujourd'hui son avenir* (Paris: Cerf, 1969) 13-14.

the Catholic intellectual community is a factor in the loss of credibility of the gospel, as indeed of the Church in secular society,
particularly among the educated laity. It is a problem that should
be discussed openly, discussion that could contribute to a possible
resolution of the present crisis in Christian proclamation — a crisis on which I shall comment in greater detail below.

Turning first to Congar's programme of reform, I consider
whether or not his proposed principles for true reform provide a
charter for Church renewal and a guarantee against violent
schism.[34] It should be noted at this point that I shall not, however,
be concerned with the history of the idea of reform; although highly
influential in the theology and practice of the Western Church, theological research in this sphere has, in any case, been undertaken
by others.[35] Furthermore, I shall not be concerned to present a
detailed account of the background to *Vraie et fausse réforme dans
l'Église*, except to draw attention to the following relevant points.
This work was part of an emerging ecclesiology in France in the
period after the Second World War and is strongly marked by the
hopes and aspirations of the epoch, including initiatives for the
reform of the liturgy; a return to the biblical and patristic sources;
the realisation of the Church's missionary task; the worker-priest
movement; the young Christian student and the young Christian
worker movements.[36] The post-war period in France was also

[34] See Congar, *L'Église une, sainte, catholique et apostolique*, Mysterium
Salutis, 15 (Paris: Cerf, 1970) 13-121.
[35] See O'Malley, *Trent and All That: Renaming Catholicism in the Early Modern Era*, 2nd ed. (Cambridge, MA: Harvard University Press, 2000) 119-143. See
further id., "Reform, Historical Consciousness, and Vatican II's Aggiornamento,"
Theological Studies 32 (1971) 573-601; id., "Developments, Reforms, and Two
Great Reformations: Towards a Historical Assessment of Vatican II," *Theological Studies* 44 (1983) 373-406.
[36] See Congar, *Vraie et fausse réforme dans l'Église*, 22-30; also id., *Dialogue
between Christians: Catholic Contributions to Ecumenism*, trans. Philip Loretz

characterised by a new concern for the poor and an urgent need to define the relationship between the Church and the modern world. In the introduction to *Vraie et fausse réforme dans l'Église*, Congar identifies this relationship as a key problem:

> One noticed that the pastoral activities of the Church no longer had influence on the great mass of people, in particular on the most hardened and the most dynamic. Certainly, because men are more easily carnal than spiritual; but also because of our own circumstances, both priests and laity: because we bring the things of Christ to men in forms inherited from an honourable past, but past nonetheless, in gestures and a formulation that are only "rites" insufficient to arouse or express life.[37]

When Christianity is reduced to mere ritualism, it changes nothing. Furthermore, when the Church fails to construct a positive relationship with the world, the inevitable result is the loss of its most dynamic element, notably young people. Congar responds to the demands of the world and of believers, who will accept the gospel only from a pure and irreproachable Church,[38] by proposing a reform of the Church.[39] I want now to indicate how he explains the dialectical tension between reform and unity that is at the heart of his theological treatise on reform.

II. REFORM AND UNITY IN THE CHURCH: A CREATIVE DIALECTIC

Whether we agree or not with Congar's analysis of reform, it is necessary to understand his point of view as a reformer, for it is

---

(London: Geoffrey Chapman, 1966) 32; id., *Chrétiens en dialogue: contributions catholiques à l'œcuménisme*, Unam Sanctam, 50 (Paris: Cerf, 1964) XLIII.

[37] Congar, *Vraie et fausse réforme dans l'Église*, 25.

[38] *Ibid.*, 54.

[39] *Ibid.*, 57-59.

plain, as the history of the Second Vatican Council shows,[40] that
his greatest achievement is to have formulated a theory of Church
reform that was successfully acted upon at that Council. In *Mon
journal du Concile*, he repeats the assertion that Pope John XXIII
read *Vraie et fausse réforme dans l'Église* in 1952.[41] The suggestion that he discovered there the intuition for a Council of the
Church, along with a vision for ecumenism, is a matter for historians. But it cannot be denied that the genius of Congar's plan
of action, as presented in *Vraie et fausse réforme dans l'Église*,
lay in the proposed dialectical relationship between unity and
reform in the Church, and so we are justified in speaking of its
ultimate success at Vatican II. In other words, his influence on
the reforms executed at the Council and, therefore, his influence
on the contemporary Church is immense. Within the compass of
this article I cannot, of course, offer a comprehensive explication of Congar's principles for true reform, something I have
undertaken elsewhere,[42] but rather by presenting the central elements of his vision for reform, I want to bring out some of its
implications for the Church today. For I am convinced that much
of what Congar has to say to the Church today cannot be satis-
factorily understood or applied except by reference to his theory
of reform.

It has been said above that reform in Congar's theology must be
viewed in relation to tradition and the other major themes of his
ecclesiology, including ecumenism, eschatology and the theology

---

[40] See Klaus Wittstadt, "On the Eve of the Second Vatican Council (July 1-
October 10, 1962)," *History of Vatican II: Announcing and Preparing Vatican
Council II*, ed. Giuseppe Alberigo. English version ed. Joseph A. Komonchak,
5 vols. (Maryknoll, NY/Louvain: Orbis/Peeters, 1995) I: 405-500, p. 457.

[41] Congar, *Journal*, II: 441-442 (19 October 1965).

[42] Gabriel Flynn, *Yves Congar's Vision of the Church in a World of Unbelief*
(Aldershot: Ashgate, 2004).

of ministry.[43] This interconnectedness may be sketched briefly at this stage. In order to execute a true reform of the Church, Congar calls for a return to the biblical and patristic sources. This is also, in his view, a means of overcoming unbelief (an aspect of his thought on which I have presented my findings).[44] This insight gave rise to *Vraie et fausse réforme dans l'Église* in which Congar presents a course for Church reform crucial to the success of his entire programme of ecclesiological renewal. It should be pointed out at once that Congar locates the issue of reform and tradition within the larger domain of ecclesiology. In the first place, he argues that the study of the fact of "reforms" must be established on a solidly constructed ecclesiology.[45] In his view, a good ecclesiology is one of the best guarantees of a good reform.[46] This point, as we shall see, is at the heart of Congar's fourth condition for a reform of the Church.[47] It also emphasises the distinction between structure and life in the Church. As Congar notes: "Nothing would be more dangerous than to work to reform something in the domain of the ecclesial *life* without being assured of a very solid ecclesiology, that is to say a theology of the *structure* of the Church."[48]

Without wishing to defend Congar's point of view, we should, however, ask why he gives such prominence to the notion of structure and life in his theory of reform. Although doubts have been

---

[43] See Congar, *Dialogue between Christians*, 21, 356-357; also id., *Chrétiens en dialogue*, XXXI, 434-435. See further id., *Vraie et fausse réforme dans l'Église*, 81, 84, 97.

[44] See Congar, "The Council in the Age of Dialogue," *Cross Currents* 12 (1962) 144-151, pp. 147-148; also id., "Vœux pour le concile: enquête parmi les chrétiens," *Esprit* 29 (1961) 691-700, pp. 695-696. See further Gabriel Flynn, "The Role of Unbelief in the Theology of Yves Congar," *New Blackfriars* (July, 2004).

[45] Congar, *Vraie et fausse réforme dans l'Église*, 10.

[46] *Ibid.*, 252.

[47] *Ibid.*, 333-352.

[48] *Ibid.*, 338.

raised about the validity of Congar's elucidation of the dialectic of structure and life,[49] an authentic reform of the Church is, in fact, possible only if there is clear acknowledgement of the irreformability of its structure which he defines by reference to the presence of the Spirit in the Church. By making the Holy Spirit the fundamental criterion for reform, Congar gives his most adequate statement of what is required for a legitimate Church reform. Still, his claim that the Church cannot err in its secular and general practice is remarkable. He declares:

> But regarding the Church itself in its basic structures of doctrine, sacramental life, and institutional offices, the tradition is closed. The Church can err neither in its basic structures nor in its secular and general practice. To claim the opposite would be to deny the presence of the Holy Spirit. At the Seventh Ecumenical Council (the second of Nicea 787), this was the answer given to the Iconoclasts. To want to reform the Church on this level would mean to rise up against the work of God and thus to place oneself outside the truth.[50]

Further, Congar distinguishes between the structure of the Church, that is, its dogma, sacraments and hierarchical constitution and the ecclesial structures (*au pluriel, de "structures ecclésiales"*),[51] that is, the organisation of parishes; catechesis; preaching and other such matters, all of which may be changed because they pertain to the life of the Church, rather than to its essential structure, which is always irreformable.[52] In short, the effective strength of his propositions for Church reform lies in his recognition of the need to redress structural as well as personal sin in the Church and the necessity for an

---

[49] Richard McBrien, "Church and Ministry: The Achievement of Yves Congar," *Theology Digest* 32 (1985) 203-211, pp. 209-210.

[50] Congar, "Church Reform and Luther's Reformation, 1517-1967," *Lutheran World* 14 (1967) 351-359, p. 353.

[51] Congar, *Vraie et fausse réforme dans l'Église*, 57, footnote 50.

[52] *Ibid.*, 57.

honest self-critique, which in turn facilitates a more credible proclamation of the gospel in the world. Combined with the place given
to the laity in his ecclesiology, the insistence on the one Church, and
the acknowledgement of the absolute necessity of God's grace,[53]
the notion of structure and life helps to ensure a true reform.

The foregoing outline of the idea of structure and life in Congar's
theology gives rise to a number of questions. I can comment, however, only briefly on a few selected questions. First, I wish to consider the complex issue of reform in a holy Church. Congar's
efforts to resolve the difficult questions arising from the presence
of sin and holiness in the Church are based on a Catholic understanding of the Church, which is also the foundation for his notion
of reform and repentance. In contrast to the Protestant view which
sees the pure Christ alone,[54] the Catholic position, especially following St Augustine and his idea of "Christus integer, Christus
totus; Christus et Ecclesia, unus homo,"[55] situates Christ with the
Church (*Sponsus et Sponsa, una caro*).[56] As Spouse (*Épouse*), the
Church is pure by virtue of its union with Christ its head (*chef*), yet
always in need of purification in its sinful members.[57] The public
or ecclesial dimension of repentance in the Church is, in Congar's

---

[53] *Ibid.*, 48, 84, 103-106.

[54] Congar, "Norms of Christian Allegiance and Identity in the History of the
Church," trans. John Griffiths, *Concilium* 3 (1973) 11-26, p. 21. See further
George Yule, "Luther's Understanding of Justification by Grace Alone in Terms
of Catholic Christology," *Luther: Theologian for Catholics and Protestants*, ed.
Yule (Edinburgh: T&T Clark, 1985) 87-111, p. 107.

[55] See Yves Congar, "Comment L'Église sainte doit se renouveler sans cesse,"
Irénikon 34 (1961) 322-345, p. 331.

[56] See Congar, *Divided Christendom: A Catholic Study of the Problem of
Reunion*, trans. M. A. Bousfield (London: Geoffrey Bles, 1939) 61-63; also id.,
Chrétiens désunis: principes d'un "oecuménisme" catholique, Unam Sanctam, 1
(Paris: Cerf, 1937) 74-77.

[57] See Congar, *Vraie et fausse réforme dans l'Église*, 101, 462.

view, clearly acknowledged in the recitation of the *Confiteor* at Mass.[58] The crux of the matter concerns what may and may not be reformed in the Church. For Catholic reformers, the institutional Church cannot be called into question in order to reform it.[59] Far from denying the presence of corrupt practices in the Church and the subsequent need for reform, Congar is in fact concerned with facilitating a true reform of the Church. This is why he proposes a distinction between structure and life in the Church. He identifies the life of the Church as the proper domain of reform: "The Church is penitential, the Church is called to constant reform, not in its structure, but in its life."[60]

The question of the sinfulness of the Church brings us to a moot point of great ecumenical significance. An often repeated complaint of Protestant theology is that Roman Catholic ecclesiology, by proceeding too much from above, constructs a *theologia gloriae* instead of a *theologia crucis*. The unequivocal acknowledgement by Congar in *Je crois en l'Esprit Saint* (1979-80), his *magnum opus* on the Holy Spirit, that the Church is sinful constitutes a clear and definite development in his thought which raises an obvious difficulty. It marks a departure from the carefully formulated theology of sin articulated in his earlier writings, where he defends the Church's holiness.[61] It seems that the dialectic between the holy and sinful Church in the later Congar owes too much to Luther's *simul justus et peccator*.[62] Echoes of a strong Lutheran influence

---

[58] *Ibid.*, 129.

[59] *Ibid.*, 462.

[60] *Ibid.*, 466.

[61] See Congar, *The Mystery of the* Church, 48-49; also id., *Esquisses du mystère de l'Église*, 52-53. See further id., *L'Église une, sainte, catholique et apostolique*, 129; id., *Vraie et fausse réforme dans l'Église*, 456.

[62] See *Luther's Works: Lectures on Romans*, ed. Hilton C. Oswald, 55 vols. (Saint Louis, MO: Concordia Publishing House, 1972) XXV: 262-263. Luther recognises the Church as a sinner.

can be seen in the presentation of Congar's altered position on the sinfulness of the Church.[63] He elucidates the matter in this way: "The Church itself is a sinner forestalled by free forgiveness and is converted when the Lord comes and takes up residence in it."[64] Ultimately, Congar places the question of the holiness of the Church in an eschatological perspective when he says that the Church will be perfectly and totally holy only when it has experienced its Passover (*Pâque*), "a death to the flesh and a resurrection according to the Spirit."[65] I wish now to comment briefly on a second question, that is, Congar's insistence on a Catholic understanding of the Church and reform, a point of fundamental importance.

In a paper published in 1967, concerned principally with the identification of conditions under which it is possible to initiate reform, Congar asserts that the Catholic Church cannot be its own norm or rule of faith because this would be to absolutise its history and to equate the Church with divine revelation, thereby robbing God of his sovereignty. What is required, in fact, is a norm that precedes and transcends the Church while judging it. This can be found only in the Word of God, which Congar adopts, though not independent of the Church or outside of it, for the Church is implied in the adoption of the canon and in the interpretation of Scripture. To the extent that certain errors had penetrated the Church without encountering sufficiently official, widespread and effective opposition, Congar says it is possible to speak of a "state of things"

---

[63] See Congar, "Ecumenical Experience and Conversion: A Personal Testimony," *The Sufficiency of God*, ed. Robert C. Mackie and Charles C. West (London: SCM, 1963) 71-87, p. 74; also Congar, "Expérience et Conversion Oecuméniques," in id., *Chrétiens en dialogue*, 123-139, p. 126. This essay is not available in the English translation of *Chrétiens en dialogue*.

[64] Yves Congar, *I Believe in the Holy Spirit*, trans. David Smith, 3 vols. (New York/London: Seabury/Geoffrey Chapman, 1983) II: 123; also id., *Je crois en l'Esprit Saint*, new ed., 3 vols. (Paris: Cerf, 1995) II: 162.

[65] Congar, *L'Église une, sainte, catholique et apostolique*, 140.

(*état des choses*) that, in his view, necessitates a reform but not a reformation.[66] These faults concern elements characteristic of the decline of the medieval period, including papacy, clergy, piety and theology. I leave aside for the moment our theoretical discussion of reform in order to draw attention to certain practical problems affecting the Church.

The problems confronting the Church at the present time are certainly not new. The basic problem today, as in the medieval period, concerns service (pope, clergy/religious, laity and theologians) and worship (liturgy and piety), as well as the concomitant moral and social difficulties which are a direct result of the abuse of power and privilege by some of those engaged in the Church's service. These difficulties are, of course, rendered more complex, more controversial, and more costly — in the broadest sense — by a manifestly painful burden of history and by a perceptible inadequacy in the Church's excessively circumspect approach to their resolution.[67] Further light will, I hope, be shed on the current situation of the

---

[66] Congar, "Church Reform and Luther's Reformation, 1517-1967," 356. See also id., *Vraie et fausse réforme dans l'Église*, 356-367.

[67] See Helen Goode, Hannah McGee and Ciarán O'Boyle, *Time to Listen: Confronting Child Sexual Abuse by Catholic Clergy in Ireland* (Dublin: The Liffey Press, 2003) 110, 191, 120. This independent survey assesses the impact of child sexual abuse on victims, on clergy and on their respective families. The first of its kind to be commissioned by the Catholic Church internationally, it was conducted by the Health Services Research Centre at the Department of Psychology, Royal College of Surgeons in Ireland, on behalf of the Irish Episcopal Conference. The "loss of confidence in Church leadership was reported as the most significant effect of child sexual abuse by clergy." Further, the survey reveals widespread dissatisfaction with church leaders: 77 per cent of respondents felt that the Church's response to child sexual abuse by clergy was inadequate, while 72 per cent felt that the Church was not dealing with the problem directly. It is perhaps noteworthy that the Royal College of Surgeons survey also shows that "the majority (72 per cent) of those surveyed felt that most clergy have been unfairly judged because of the emergence of child sexual abuse by clergy."

Church through a consideration of Congar's principles for true reform. While I shall not be discussing the different conceptions of the Church nor its proposed self-critique presented in *Vraie et fausse réforme dans l'Église*, I want at least to illustrate the value for the Church today of Congar's original programme of reform. In the rest of this article, I shall confine myself mainly to exposition and explanation of his principles for true reform, so as to attempt to articulate a vision of hope for the Church at a time of crisis in the world. But first, it is necessary to clarify why Congar rejects Luther's reform, since a correct understanding of his conditions for a reform without schism is possible only on the basis of a clear knowledge of his deprecatory appraisal of the Protestant Reformation.

While acknowledging that the reform proposed by Martin Luther (1483-1546) was motivated in large measure by pastoral motives,[68] Congar asserts that Luther, in wanting to reform the doctrinal system, actually transposed reform from the order of morals and the life of the Church to that of faith and of the Church's structure.[69] It is precisely for this reason that he sees Luther as "more and something other than a reformer: he is a revolutionary."[70] Not surprisingly, then, Congar issues a call for vigilance regarding doctrinal fidelity because heresy, though it originates in the domain of the life of the Church and ruptures its communion, also calls the Church's structure into question.[71] To make Congar's position clearer, it should be added that he considers the best milieu for reform, that is, one that avoids the tendency to deviation and schism,[72] to be a Council of the Church. In

---

[68] Congar, *Vraie et fausse réforme dans l'Église*, 358.
[69] *Ibid.*, 360-362.
[70] *Ibid.*, 363.
[71] *Ibid.*, 494.
[72] *Ibid.*, 231, 239.

an article that he wrote eight years after the close of Vatican II, Congar displays his consistent concern to achieve reform without schism: "History shows that a reform requires the commitment of all the forces of the Church. This is one of the main reasons why, historically, reforms and councils have so often been linked with one another."[73]

Turning to Congar's principles for reform, I am concerned with trying to show that the claim he makes for them is still relevant and that their application to the present situation of the Church is sound. In the first principle, "*the Primacy of Charity and of the Pastoral*," Congar insists on respect for the reality of the Church and on a willingness to work within it. While recognising the need for its purification, he upholds the integrity of the Church that in itself cannot be called into question by reformers.[74] This, in his view, is the central problem addressed in *Vraie et fausse réforme dans l'Église*. He believes that it can be resolved by his principle of dual fidelity, the overriding concern of which is the preservation of the unity of the Church without prohibiting necessary internal change. A reform separated from charity and holiness results in separation from the Church.[75]

The second principle of reform, "*to remain within the Communion of all*," is an elaboration on the idea of communion. The concern for communion with the whole is indispensable for a true reform. In order to prevent the most beautiful religious experiences and the most sincere truths from becoming heretical, a real danger, Congar attempts to bring them under the control of the life and faith of the whole Church.[76] To facilitate this goal and to prevent

---

[73] Congar, "Renewal of the Spirit and Reform of the Institution," 46; also id., "Renouvellement de l'esprit et réforme de l'institution," 42.

[74] Congar, *Vraie et fausse réforme dans l'Église*, 252.

[75] *Ibid.*, 252-253.

[76] *Ibid.*, 268-269.

rupture to the unity of the Church, he proposes that reform initiatives that come from the periphery must seek the recognition of the hierarchy.[77] In responding to the phenomenon of new groups and movements in the Church, in the context of which he also refers to the problem of sects,[78] Congar, in fact, proposes a practical application of his principle of unity between the centre and the periphery. He writes: "The institution saves the inspiration; the law protects the life; in the body of Christ, which is the Church, the spirit finds itself a body, and, in animating this body, it is conserved by it."[79] The second principle of reform constitutes a genuine contribution to Congar's proposed vision of the Church through its articulation of a harmonious relationship between the centre and the periphery.

In the third principle for reform, articulated by the appellation *"patience; respect for delays,"* Congar notes that movements of reform which do not have patience as a constitutive feature are a source of danger for the Church. The lack of patience, which he sees as a failure to respect the delays of God, the Church, and life, in fact contributes towards turning a reform into a schism.[80] Luther is identified as an example of an impatient reformer of which history offers various other examples. The problem with the impatient reformer is that he/she "unfortunately compromises the true with the false; and wishing to speed development, he succeeds in slowing it down."[81] Aware of the risks and dangers involved in the matter of reform, Congar concludes his presentation on patience with a finely balanced statement

---

[77] *Ibid.*, 272, 275-277.
[78] *Ibid.*, 288-292.
[79] *Ibid.*, 292.
[80] *Ibid.*, 306.
[81] *Ibid.*, 318.

offering a *modus vivendi* for reformers and leaders in the Church:

> One can call on reformers not to be too impatient only by also ask-
> ing the guardians of the tradition not to be too patient; to be sensi-
> tive to the demands that risk exploding one day, because of having
> been repressed for too long; to unite to the sentiment of delay that
> of the urgency of the needs.[82]

The fourth principle, "*a true renewal [renouvellement] by a return to the principle of the Tradition*," is an expression of his concern for the unity and Catholicity of the Church. In it, Congar proposes an examination of the tradition and a return to the sources as the cardinal rule for reform:

> The great law of a Catholic reform will then be to begin by a return
> to the principles of Catholicism. It is necessary firstly to ask ques-
> tions of the tradition, to immerse oneself in it again: understanding
> that "tradition" does not signify that which is "routine" or "past".
> Certainly, tradition comprises an aspect of the past; it is, in part, the
> treasury of texts and the realities of the past of the Church; but it is
> certainly more than that. It is essentially the continuity of develop-
> ment since the initial gift and the integration of all the forms that this
> development has taken and presents at the moment.[83]

For Congar, tradition consists of all that is precious in the sources: Scripture, the Fathers, faith, prayer, liturgy, piety, and doctrine. These elements, so charged with a sense of the Church, are seen as normative for Catholics. Congar indicates that the return to the prin- ciple of the tradition, by going beyond how the Church responded to particular problems in the past, enters the depths of the original inspiration so as to see what it would want to say to the Church today.[84]

---

[82] *Ibid.*, 332.
[83] *Ibid.*, 335-336.
[84] *Ibid.*, 337.

While recognising the continued validity of his four principles for reform, Congar, in a clear concern for *praxis*, accepts Louis Bouyer's proposal for a fifth, good sense (*bon sens*).[85] These conditions for true reform, clearly influenced by Congar's love for the Church, permit change that enhances both the unity of the Church and the integrity of its mission in the world. This is made possible by his unified approach to the tradition and by his concern to embrace the whole Church (*tout le corps de l'Église*). The realisation of unity and wholeness, indispensable features of his programme for renewal, depends in large part on a return to the sources, which is itself indispensable to the principles of reform. These principles manifest a concern for Catholicity understood in terms of an acceptance of diversity rather than a search for uniformity, and of ecumenism rather than confessionalism. This is also the view of Catholicity found in Vatican II.[86] It can be plainly seen that Congar's application of the note of Catholicity to the Church is part of his concern to show that the Catholic Church is the realisation of the messianic community willed by God. The Church realises its Catholicity by a universal evangelism. Without denying a relative value of Catholicity to the other Christian Churches, Congar still wishes to question their claims to Catholicity, as well as the conception of Catholicity that they propose.[87] Nonetheless, he admits that one can criticise effectively only by recognising the truth in the positions criticised, which is the essence of a Catholic apologetic. Thus, for him, "the true apologetic is, in fact, ecumenism."[88]

I conclude that the schema for Church reform expounded by Congar, at the centre of which stand his principles for reform without

---

[85] Congar, "Vraie et fausse contestation dans l'Église," 132.

[86] *Dogmatic Constitution on the Church: Lumen gentium*, 8, 28; *Decree on Ecumenism: Unitatis redintegratio*, 4.

[87] Congar, *L'Église une, sainte, catholique et apostolique*, 177-178.

[88] *Ibid.*, 179.

schism, helps to facilitate necessary structural changes without detriment to the truth or to the totality of the Christian tradition, thereby contributing to the restoration of the ideal of unity. Unlike the proposals formulated by Luther and the Protestant reformers in the sixteenth century, or by Johann Joseph Ignaz von Döllinger (1799-1890) and the Old Catholics in the nineteenth, it upholds "the idea of reform *within* the Church."[89] Our discussion, however, gives rise to a problem. The problem is that the world neither accepts nor respects ideals or theories, however laudatory, unless it can be shown that their stated goals are practicable. I have argued that the juxtaposition of reform and unity in Congar's theology gives rise to a transformative and creative dialectic, one that offers the richest hope for a renewed Church of the future. I propose to assess his theory of reform by applying it to the gravest divisions in the history of Christianity, controversies which have, in any case, been the subject of analysis by him.

I begin with the Protestant Reformation. Here the following points should be noted. First, on more than one occasion Congar said that he was prepared to give his life for his Protestant friends and for the cause of unity. Nonetheless, his negative assessment of the Reformation in the third part of *Vraie et fausse réforme dans l'Église* calls for further explanation. Congar acknowledges that this section was not written in the reformist atmosphere of the rest of the work, making a revision necessary. As he comments: "The third part of *Vraie et fausse réforme dans l'Église*, which speaks of these [Protestant] reforms, would need to be re-worked."[90] I suggest that the

---

[89] Congar, *Challenge to the Church*, 21; also id., *La Crise dans l'Église et Mgr Lefebvre*, 20.

[90] See Congar, "Forward," [*sic*] in Timothy I. MacDonald, *The Ecclesiology of Yves Congar: Foundational Themes* (Lanham, MD: University Press of America, 1984) xxii-xxiii, p. xxii. See further Congar, *Vraie et fausse réforme dans l'Église*, 12. Congar écrit que cette étude "a été rédigée, sauf la troisième partie, en 1946, dans l'atmosphère réformiste qu'évoque l'Introduction."

negative attitude to the Reformation presented here, far from constituting an anomaly in Congar's ecumenism, was largely determined by a concern not to offend Rome. In other words, his early ecumenical dialogue was subjected to strict scrutiny by powerful, normally hostile, extraneous elements. Of course, Congar's ecumenism did undergo significant development, and in a later work, *Martin Luther sa foi, sa réforme: études de théologie historique* (1983), he presents a more positive appreciation of Luther, his Christology and his ecclesiology. Second, although Congar held Luther in high esteem and wanted the Catholic world to understand him rather than to condemn him, it must be remembered that, in the final analysis, he criticises Luther as an impatient reformer and attributes to him a redoubtable responsibility for the rupture which ecumenism seeks to redeem.[91] But it must also be remembered that it is not only Luther who was subjected to censure; Congar held Catholic priests, and particularly the Roman Curia, accountable for the Reformation.[92] Now, it is clear that the great figures of the Reformation on both sides are criticised because they contravened charity, communion and patience — three of the four principles propounded by Congar for a true reform in the Church. I suggest that the application of these principles to the current debate surrounding such issues as the role of women in the Church,[93] the vocation to holy orders,[94]

---

[91] Congar, *Martin Luther sa foi, sa réforme*, 9; see further id., *Vraie et fausse réforme dans l'Église*, 310.

[92] Congar, *The Mystery of the* Church, 48-49. *Esquisses du mystère de l'Église*, 52-53. See further id., *L'Église une, sainte, catholique et apostolique*, 129; id., *Vraie et fausse réforme dans l'Église*, 456.

[93] See Sister Prudence Allen, *The Concept of Woman: The Aristotelian Revolution 750 BC–AD 1250* (Grand Rapids, MI: Eerdmans, 1985).

[94] See John Paul II, *Pastores Dabo Vobis: Post-Synodal Apostolic Exhortation of His Holiness John Paul II on the Formation of Priests in the Circumstances of the Present Day* (London: Catholic Truth Society, 1992); Joseph Ratzinger, *Ministers of Your Joy: Meditations on Priestly Spirituality* (Slough/New York: St Paul

and the evangelisation of modern culture,[95] would contribute to the preservation of unity.

Turning to the centuries-old estrangement of the Eastern and Western Churches, the subject of a short study by Congar entitled *Neuf cents ans après: notes sur le "Schisme oriental"* (1954),[96] we again find that his principles of reform offer hope of renewal, even in the difficult domain of Orthodox-Catholic ecumenical dialogue. Since Catholics and Orthodox are divided on only a few doctrinal issues, principally the role of the Bishop of Rome, a new rapprochement might be possible through reciprocal charity and mutual respect. But first a grace of healing is necessary so as to attempt to overcome ancient animosities, including the legacy of the medieval crusades and the painful memory of the sacking of Constantinople (*c.*1204). A profound respect for tradition, fundamental to Congar's theory of reform, is also necessary if there is to be hope of improvement in East-West relations. Education too has an important role to play in helping to remove the obstacle of ignorance, especially in

Publications/Crossroad Publishing, 1989); Thomas F. O'Meara, *Theology of Ministry*, rev. ed. (New York: Paulist Press, 1999); Donald B. Cozzens, *The Changing Face of the Priesthood: A Reflection on the Priest's Crisis of Soul* (Collegeville, MN: The Liturgical Press, 2000); id., *Sacred Silence: Denial and the Crisis in the Church* (Collegeville, MN: The Liturgical Press, 2004); Matthew Levering (ed.), *On the Priesthood: Classic and Contemporary Texts* (Lanham, MD: Rowman & Littlefield, 2003); Gerhard Ludwig Müller, *Priesthood and Diaconate: The Recipient of the Sacrament of Holy Orders from the Perspective of Creation Theolgy and Christology*, trans. Michael J. Miller (San Francisco, CA: Ignatius, 2002).

[95] See Aidan Nichols, *Christendom Awake: On Re-energising the Church in Culture* (Edinburgh: T&T Clark, 1999); Paul Ricœur, *The Hermeneutics of Action*, ed. Richard Kearney (London: Sage Publications, 1996).

[96] Congar, *Neuf cents ans après: notes sur le "Schisme oriental"* (Paris: Chevetogne, 1954); also id., *After Nine Hundred Years: The Background of the Schism between the Eastern and Western Churches* (New York: Fordham University Press, 1959).

the West, where the danger of an exclusively Western view of Catholicism would inevitably result in a narrowing of Catholicity. Pope John Paul II, profoundly aware of the value of education and always concerned to promote unity with Eastern Christians, calls on Western Christians "to deepen their knowledge of the spiritual traditions of the Fathers and doctors of the Christian East."[97] The Pope requests that specialist institutions would train theologians, liturgists, historians and canonists for the Christian East, who in turn could spread knowledge of the Eastern Churches. The most effective means for the realisation of this goal, exemplified in Congar's lifelong work for unity, is through personal contact and friendship. The Second Vatican Council urges Catholics to make the first approaches towards their separated brethren, an important step in the restoration of unity — one of the principal concerns of the Council.[98] While mutual respect and reciprocal charity are insufficient in themselves for the restoration of unity and must be augmented by theological dialogue, nonetheless, without the profound bond of humanity, all theology remains ineffectual.

Finally, we come to the difficult issue of the division associated with a tragic figure of the post-conciliar period, namely, Archbishop Marcel Lefebvre. He died, excommunicated, in 1991. French by birth, Lefebvre had retired as archbishop of Dakar in West Africa and had formerly been bishop of Tulle in France. He enjoyed a wide body of support, principally in France and Switzerland, among lovers of the old liturgy who were disaffected as a result of the dropping of Latin from prayer and worship. On 21 November 1974, he issued a rather odd "Profession of Faith"

[97] John Paul II, *Orientale Lumen: Apostolic Letter of the Supreme Pontiff John Paul II to the Bishops, Clergy and Faithful to Mark the Centenary of Orientalium Dignitas of Pope Leo XIII* (London: Catholic Truth Society, 1995) 24.
[98] *Unitatis redintegratio*, 1, 4.

in which he announced to the world his tenacious adherence to "Catholic Rome," while also rejecting what he perceived as the neo-modernist and neo-Protestant tendencies of Vatican II and the reforms that issued from it. Briefly, the important dates in Lefebvre's estrangement from Rome include the foundation of a seminary at Ecône, Switzerland in 1974 to train priests "as before the Council"; the ordination of 13 priests and 13 deacons in 1976, and of a further 14 priests in 1977. He made the schism worse in 1988 when he performed an episcopal ordination of four priests without pontifical mandate and contrary to the will of Pope John Paul II. On 1 July 1988, Monsignor Lefebvre, along with the four priests whom he had raised to the episcopate as well as the bishop who had assisted him directly, Monsignor Antonio de Castro Mayer, incurred *ipso facto* excommunication *latae sententiae* reserved to the Apostolic See.

There are some important relevant lessons from this sad, largely forgotten, episode. The principal lesson, one associated with all situations of conflict, is that the institution, in this instance the Church, should listen more carefully and more expeditiously to the sometimes disenchanted voices of its members. A rhetorical question posed by the distinguished French philosopher Jean Guitton sheds some light on the Ecône affair. He asks: "How could one admit to the simple and the wise of this rational country [France] that the only Mass celebrated by the Fathers of the Council would become the only one to be forbidden?"[99] He argues that a reform requires a process of maturation and patience. It cannot be denied, however, that the liturgical reforms of Vatican II were sometimes executed in an entirely autocratic manner. Even Congar admits that he knew "of cases where the liturgical reforms were announced brutally, as a *fait accompli*, in force from that point in time

---

[99] Guitton, "The Future of the Council," 85.

onwards, to which it was necessary to submit — all without people's minds being prepared or any explanation being given."[100]
At the Council, Pope Paul VI was profoundly concerned to honour
the wishes of the minority.[101] But there can be little doubt that the
inability or unwillingness of the majority to understand or accept
the position of the minority contributed to the crisis at Ecône. It is
hardly surprising, therefore, that some among the minority failed to
accept Pope Paul's concomitant call to obedience. By closer adherence to the principle of the tradition, the central element of Congar's fourth condition for a true reform, the suffering and division
of Ecône could perhaps have been avoided. The peculiar difficulties of the Lefebvre debacle notwithstanding, it is clear that a more
enlightened and liberal policy now prevails towards the defenders
of a vital element of what is best in the tradition, that is, beauty in
the liturgy. Without intending to perhaps, it seems that Congar's
principles of reform, by honouring that which is most ancient and
noble in the Church — but clearly not uncritically — offer protec-
tion against schism executed in the name of Catholic liturgy.

   But Congar's notion of reform, clearly open to developments in
the Church and the world, is also concerned to accomplish other
exact goals. Essentially, what is proposed is a renewal of vision
that would effect a fundamental transformation of the pastoral life
of the Church.[102] This leads to an important concern of the present
article, that is, an attempt to articulate a new vision for the Church
of the future that would be a vision of hope for the world. It has

----

[100] Congar, *Challenge to the Church*, 70; also id., *La Crise dans l'Église et
Mgr Lefebvre*, 85.
   [101] Pierre-Marie Gy, *The Reception of Vatican II: Liturgical Reforms in the
Life of the Church* (Milwaukee, WI: Marquette University Press, 2003) 15-16.
   [102] Yves Congar, "Preface," in Karl Delahaye, *Ecclesia mater chez les Pères
des trois premiers siècles*, trans. P. Vergriete and É. Bouis, Unam Sanctam, 46
(Paris: Cerf, 1964) 7-32, p. 15.

already been stated that Congar's view of reform and his notion of
the "threshold Church" have contributed to that vision. In the next
section of this article, I propose to discuss the constituent elements
of a new vision for the Church. Turning first to Congar's view of
the relationship between the Church and the world, we find that he
places them in a relationship of mutual service. A defining feature
of his theology of the Church, in fact, is its orientation towards the
world.[103] His ecclesiology, far from being ecclesio-centric, is for the
world and at the service of all.[104] Congar's was a prophetic voice
speaking as much for the benefit of the world and humanity as for
that of the Church:

> At bottom, the Church and the world need one another. The Church
> means salvation for the world, but the world means health for the
> Church: without the world there would be danger of her becoming
> wrapped up in her own sacredness and uniqueness.[105]

III. The "Threshold Church":
A Vision of Hope for a World in Crisis

The present crisis in the Church is, of course, a crisis of faith. But
a crisis of faith on the scale currently affecting Europe, a continent
whose culture and life are deeply rooted in Christianity and the
Catholic Church, points to an even deeper crisis of culture. The

---

[103] Yves Congar, "Where Are We in the Expression of the Faith?," trans.
Dinah Livingstone, *Concilium* 170 (1983) 85-87, p. 86.

[104] Yves Congar, *Called to Life* (Slough/New York: St Paul Publications/
Crossroad Publishing, 1988) 88; also id., *Appelés à la vie* (Paris: Cerf, 1985) 95.

[105] Congar, *The Wide World My Parish: Salvation and its Problems*, trans.
Donald Attwater (London: Darton, Longman & Todd, 1961) 23; also id., *Vaste
monde ma paroisse: vérité et dimensions du salut* (Paris: Témoignage Chrétien,
1959) 34.

crisis of culture is well known and may be described as the loss of
the sense of belonging. The loss of the sense of belonging is a widespread phenomenon in European society and the West in general.
It affects individuals and families, the community and the Church,
as well as the state. A society deprived of the means of social and
religious cohesion quickly degenerates into various forms of isolation, individualism and cultural desolation. It would also be true to
say that such a society lacks peace and easily becomes prey to powerful forces of lawlessness and violence. Confining ourselves to
Western Europe, Ireland stands out as a classic example of a rapidly
changing society that mirrors almost exactly the deleterious trends
described above. The challenge facing the Church in Ireland, as
elsewhere in the West, is to overcome its own evidently "disfigured
visage" — largely a result of the abuse of power in the domain of
service, ranging from unrestrained clericalism to clerical pae-
dophilia — and a principal cause of that Church's alienation from
the prevailing culture. Failure to face the obvious problems of culture would mean that the most carefully laid Church plans for catechesis, gospel proclamation and evangelisation are deprived of
any real chance of success.

Looking at Western Europe as a whole, where the crisis of faith
has its roots in the eighteenth-century Enlightenment, it is important to bear in mind the following relevant points. First, present-day
objections to the claims of Christianity have, in large measure,
given rise to a crisis of proclamation. For its part, the Church
acknowledges that the manner of mediating Christian revelation
must become more explicitly a patient and respectful dialogue with
indifferent unbelievers.[106] Now, in this dialogue, the Church is concerned to avoid the twin temptations of sacrificing or devaluing the

---

[106] *Declaration on the Relation of the Church to Non-Christian Religions:
Nostra aetate*, 2.

truths of Christian doctrine and of succumbing to the old temptation of self-assured superiority. Second, the Church in Europe has
become a Church deprived of people — a large-scale survey of
32 countries in Western, Central, and Eastern Europe carried out in
1999/2000 indicates that 20.9% of Europeans consider religion to
be very important in their lives (but only 15.1% of those surveyed
attend Church every week), whereas the figures for work and the
family stand at 57.6% and 84.4% respectively.[107]

In response to the dual crisis of Christian proclamation and a
Church deprived of people, most notably young people, I propose
a two-fold cultural and pastoral/theological strategy. As I have indicated in the introduction, my approach has been inspired, in part,
by Congar's proposals for a "threshold Church." His obvious sensitivity to the needs of young people makes his argument worthy
of close scrutiny and so something more needs to be said about it.

In a percipient and realistic analysis, Congar acknowledges that
the Second Vatican Council contributed to the loss of a certain sim-
plicity in matters of faith, while doctrine and institution are under-
valued or discarded.[108] The implications of these changes, which
weaken the Church by making it a value only insofar as it is one
for the human person, are presented by him in the following terms:

> The Church is as it were dispossessed of Christianity in favour of
> what in Christianity appeals to men, dispossessed of the person of
> Jesus. Christianity, taken as a value for one's life, is removed from
> the structures and mediations of the Church. In theological categories,

[107] Loek Halman, *The European Values Study: A Third Wave. Source Book of the 1999/2000 European Values Study Surveys* (Tilburg: Tilburg University, 2001) 12, 35, 7-8.

[108] Congar, "What belonging to the Church has come to mean," trans. Frances M. Chew, *Communio* 4 (1977) 146-160, p. 152; also id., "Sur la transformation du sens de l'appartenance à l'Église," *Cardinal Yves Congar, O.P.: écrits réfor-mateurs*, ed. Jean-Pierre Jossua (Paris: Cerf, 1995) 235-247, p. 240.

we would say that this means remaining attached to the *res*, but without the *sacramentum*.[109]

Furthermore, Congar accepts that young people occupy a sort of no man's land and are neither inside nor outside the Church. He nonetheless presents a positive outlook for the Church of the future. Refusing to accept either an ever-decreasing ghettoised Church or the *status quo* based on religious observance but without much emphasis on personalised faith, Congar contends that the Church is forced towards a third solution which, in his view, is the only possible response to the burning questions of today, namely, a threshold Church that can support those who are outside the sacramental life of the Church, for whatever reason. As he explains:

> To accept and even encourage the existence of two *regimes* [a threshold Church and the Church as sacrament], making a distinction between a link with Christ, even with the Church, and the *Sacrament*. In any case, to provide areas which would represent a kind of threshold Church, a Church for catechumens, in order to support the spiritual life of those whose faith is unsure and, above all, of those who are unable to participate fully in the sacramental life.[110]

But it should be pointed out that Congar makes a clear-cut distinction between the proposed threshold structures and the Church in its fullness. The legitimacy of the former cannot be determined except by reference to the latter. This point brings out the fact that his proposed Church for catechumens is essentially transitional. Thus, while the Church is the gathering of catechumens before being a sacramental assembly, Congar, nonetheless, considers that the Church itself is fully realised only in "the fullness of communion [*plénitude de communion*] with the fullness of the gifts God

---

[109] *Ibid.*, 155-156 (243).
[110] *Ibid.*, 158 (245-246).

gives through Christ and in the Spirit."[111] By way of conclusion, I wish to draw attention to the urgent need to effect a transmutation of theory to practice. Without positive interaction between theology and the prevailing culture, there will be little chance of a successful proclamation of the Christian gospel. While accepting Congar's proposals for a "threshold Church," I hold that something more is needed for a successful dialogue between gospel and culture.

First, the Church needs actively to pursue a more person-centred approach in its pastoral mission to the world, in order to gain access to a rich, normally dormant resource, a whole stratum of people, men and women, naturally gifted communicators and evangelists who, after appropriate training, would apply the Vatican Council and help to make its ideals a reality. The success of such a profoundly personal strategy by the Legion of Mary in its mission of evangelisation in major European cities and elsewhere in the world is a case in point. Second, the ministry of healing, encompassing a listening Church and the sacraments of healing, so dependent on trust, contributes to effective gospel proclamation.[112] The success of such a person-centred, affective approach to ministry requires human skills to effect the co-operation of Church volunteers, secular and religious educators, chaplains, as well as the goodwill of the institutions of family and state. Third, the realisation of my proposed strategy depends on the creation of a profound sense of belonging, one that makes the Christian community — parish or chaplaincy — into a family. Such an ideal of belonging can best be achieved by adherence to the model of the Church as servant in which the priest and all others engaged in Church ministries are perceived as friends and fellows, in their respective

---

[111] *Ibid.*, 160 (247).

[112] See Paul VI, *Ecclesiam Suam: The Paths of the Church* (New York: America Press, 1964) 90. Pope Paul VI writes: "And before speaking, it is necessary to listen, not only to a man's voice, but to his heart."

domains of influence. In the case of the priest, however, his role as pastor and teacher must not be compromised or diminished in pursuance of other objectives, however laudatory. Fourth, a strongly affective approach to ministry is called for in order to bring the person of Christ and the human person into relationship, a process subject to the same tensions as all other relationships. It is important to recognise that the presence of tension and opposition in the dialectic of gospel and human experience, far from being negative or deleterious, is necessary and even expedient to Christian proclamation. Further, the absoluteness of the gospel message is best preserved by reference to the absoluteness of Christ.

IV. CONCLUSION

The foregoing remarks do not claim to present a comprehensive view of Church reform. Nor do they constitute a proof of the truth of Congar's position. Their purpose is simply to outline his view on reform and to illustrate its relevance for the Church today. As for demonstrating the validity of the claim that his programme of Church reform is consonant with a renewal of the Spirit, we need look no further than his influence at Vatican II, study of which clearly favours such a position. In the final analysis, the significance I have attributed to Congar's view of Church reform can be adequately demonstrated only by those engaged directly in the Church's mission and apostolate.[113]

---

[113] I would like to thank Father Jean-Pierre Jossua, of Le Saulchoir, Paris, for his valuable comments on this article. In a personal letter, 18 January 2004, he writes: "Your study is irrefutable. And it is true that the notion of reform, which makes the connection between the concern for unity and the passion for a Church that is true to the Gospel could be seen again as central in his *oeuvre*, even if it does not command in itself all its aspects. In any case, I agree with you that *Vraie et fausse réforme dans l'Église* is his most original book and the most important."

CONGAR'S THEOLOGY OF THE LAITY

A. N. WILLIAMS

University Lecturer in Patristics
Corpus Christi College,University of Cambridge

Yves Congar was one of the few professional theologians not
only to address the question of the role of the laity in the church,
but to return to the theme repeatedly throughout his career. More
significantly still, his reflections on the subject push beyond the
pedestrian level, the sheer positioning of the laity within an ecclesial hierarchy, towards reflection that is genuinely theological
and a contribution to ecclesiology. However Congar's thinking on
the subject developed considerably over time, providing almost
a map of developments in twentieth-century theology, the life
of the church, and the position of Christianity in modern Western society. Arguably, though, the changes in the church and
the world in the half century following the end of the Second
World War did not so much shape Congar's thinking by mould-
ing it in the direction of greater worldliness, as allow a context
in which his reflections on the laity could become more
profoundly theological and more fully integrated into his ecclesiology.

We might begin by noting a certain oddity in the recurrent attention of a vowed religious to the question of the lay state. Congar himself queried the propriety of the ordained being the ones who articulate the nature of the lay vocation when he ruefully noted the absence
of lay representation on the commission that informed the drafting of

Vatican II's documents on the subject.[1] Congar's repeated returning
to the issue, therefore, reflects not merely yet another form of clericalism, but his deep awareness of the dignity of the lay vocation.

The work that might be taken as his central contribution to the
subject belongs to the earlier years of his career and although subsequently revised, does not necessarily provide the fullest guide to
his thought on the issue. Congar would later point to the tentative,
provisional nature of his early thought by citing the title of this first
work on the subject, *Jalons pour une théologie du laïcat* — a preliminary study for a theology of the laity (translated into English
as *Laypeople in the Church*). Nevertheless, *Laypeople in the
Church* sometimes reads not so much like a set of tentative first
thoughts as an authoritative pronouncement that is as concerned to
define what laypeople may not do as define what they can do.
Later, Congar would bewail the error of defining the role of the
laity negatively, solely in relation to the clergy and the ecclesiastical hierarchy, yet the theology of *Laypeople in the Church* often
does precisely this. He begins from a division of the Christian and
ecclesial estate into priests, monks and laity,[2] a division that is odd
inasmuch as its categories are not mutually exclusive: a monk may
be either a priest or a layperson, indeed, must be either ordained or
not ordained. Then again, this classification seems ecclesiologically questionable, inasmuch as bishops are apparently being
defined simply as priests, their distinctive and central role in the
church seemingly being elided. Congar identified the rationale for
his categories as reflecting a distinction of both function and state:

---

[1] *Priest and Layman*, trans. P. J. Hepburne-Scott (London: Darton, Longman
and Todd, 1967) 248.

[2] *Laypeople in the Church: A Study for a Theology of the Laity*, trans. Donald Attwater, rev. ed. (London: Geoffrey Chapman, 1985) 6. See *Priest and Layman*, 289 and *Faith and Spiritual Life*, trans. A. Manson and L. C. Sheppard (London: Darton, Longman and Todd, 1969) 137.

clerics are distinguished by their function (as ministers of the church), monks by their state of life.[3] Both were distinguished from the layperson by their dedication to the things of God; laypeople, by their very state, are dedicated to human things.[4] The question raised by this element of Congar's taxonomy is theologically more serious than the lack of mutual exclusivity of its constituent categories, because at first glance, the opposition of these realms of activity seems prejudicial to any positive view of the laity inasmuch as it appears to stipulate that laypeople are *ipso facto* not dedicated to the things of God.

Yet even in *Laypeople in the Church*, Congar was critical of those elements of the tradition which defined the lay state as a concession to human weakness, even as he agreed that this idea was itself in conformity with Christian tradition and "in the last resort, with the nature of things."[5] This monastic view, dominated too exclusively by the notions of renunciation and worldly wickedness,[6] Congar deemed unsatisfactory, even as he agreed that laypeople do not live exclusively for heavenly things and therefore have only limited competence in relation to the properly ecclesial means to life in Christ.[7] Later on, Congar would write in terms that are almost the reverse, seeing the concession being made to priests and monks, who are dispensed from family, professional and political life in a way that the laity cannot be.[8] While this latter way of defining the issue puts lay engagement with the world in a less negative

[3] *Laypeople in the Church*, 7.

[4] *Ibid.*, 11.

[5] *Ibid.*, 12.

[6] *Ibid.*, 12.

[7] *Ibid.*, 18. He does here also acknowledge that it would be inaccurate to say that clerics and monks are exclusively ordered to heavenly things and laypeople exclusively to earthly things.

[8] *Faith and Spiritual Life*, 137. Here, too, though Congar views the dispensation as 'profitable'.

light, it does not escape from the fundamental dichotomy, in virtue of which layfolk are viewed as not-priests and not-monks. This was precisely what Congar wanted to move beyond, namely classifying laypeople solely in relation to clerics,[9] a classification which he regarded as owing more to canon law than to theology.[10]

The tensions in Congar's thought in *Laypeople in the Church* manifest themselves more broadly than in the opposition of clerical and monastic states with the lay one, moreover. Congar wanted to deem laypeople fully of the church,[11] and not merely passive recipients of its ministry,[12] yet insisted that their role must and always will be secondary or subordinate.[13] Overwhelmingly, Congar's prime concern in insisting on this secondary status often relates to teaching authority. If the laity are to echo "the fatherly and fertilising voice of apostolic authority," they are not merely to repeat the dicta of the magisterium mechanically, but to amplify it and carry it further;[14] although at this stage in his thought no provision is made for laypeople to challenge or question the church's teaching, Congar sees in these activities of amplification and extension the possibility that the lay contribution may exceed that of the magisterium in depth.[15]

---

[9] *Laypeople in the Church*, 25.

[10] *Ibid.*, 24.

[11] *Ibid.*, xii.

[12] *Ibid.*, xiii.

[13] *Ibid.*, xi and 298.

[14] *Ibid.*, 294.

[15] *Ibid.*, 298. Congar conceded — albeit very cautiously — that laypeople might function as theologians (*ibid.*, 308) but preferred to view lay 'doctors' as functioning beyond the bounds of dogmatic theology, the latter being properly the domain of the clergy (*ibid.*, 310-311). Congar's views of these matters cannot be seen simply as reflecting the understandable caution of one who had been officially reprimanded and silenced by the Vatican for an earlier work (*Vraie et fausse réforme dans l'Église*), because the manuscript of *Laypeople in the Church* had already been sent to the publisher before the official censure was announced,

Congar's earlier works are also marked by preoccupation with Catholic Action as the focus of lay Christian activity that now seems exaggerated. His early writings give the impression that one need look no further than this one movement to see and conceive of faithful engagement with the world on the part of laypeople: a full chapter of *Laypeople in the Church* is devoted to it. If Congar does seem to overstate the significance of the movement, he reflects his time and place in doing so: it loomed larger in France than it ever did in the Anglophone world (for example), and Congar himself admitted that its heyday was in the first half of the twentieth century, now long past (specifically, 1925-39).[16] Moreover, while he essentially approves the views of Pius XI and Pius XII, who saw Catholic Action as *the* solution to what they called "the plague of laicism,"[17] Congar distances himself from the notion of laicism as a plague (even though the connotations of the term *laïcisme* in French are not what they are in English), and recognises that the question turns not so much on whether this or that movement is beneficial, or even vital (which is after all only the substitution of one from of institution for another) as on the possibility of action in the world. That action, he acknowledged, might take place through a formal movement such as Catholic Action, but could equally well be furthered in other ways.

The French context explains, up to a point, some of the ambivalence that comes through in his writing about laypeople, for as we have noted, some of the terms denoting the laity in French have

---

but the issue has in any case been rendered all but moot, given the predominance of lay 'doctors' in university theology faculties: there simply are not enough priests, or even religious, to staff all of them.

[16] *Faith and Spiritual Life*, 192.

[17] *Priest and Layman*, 374.

overtones they do not have in English. Congar himself points to this problem of vocabulary in his native language, remarking upon the specific connotations of *laïcisme* and *laïcité*, for example: the former denoting secularism and the latter, the religious neutrality of state education.[18] The legacy of the French revolution, including the proscription of religious orders in the name of freedom, necessarily haunts Congar's treatment of the subject in a way that is scarcely imaginable to an English-speaking reader: it is not surprising that the French church should have been suspicious of the secular world, actively hostile as it was to any kind of religious commitment or organisation, and it was precisely this anti-clericalism that fuelled the fires of an unhelpful clericalism,[19] so that the very word *laïc* came to designate someone who was not only anti-clerical, but even anti-Christian.[20] In light of that background, it is less surprising that there should be traces of clericalism in Congar's early writings on the laity than that he should have felt prompted to treat the subject at all.

Thus far, we have largely considered the more problematic side of Congar's view of the laity, a theology developed in the context of the France of his youth and early adulthood, rooted in a church used to defining itself sharply over against a frequently inhospitable secular culture, but whose Christianity was largely untroubled by the need to respond to the challenges of that world, a church whose masses were attended, whose parishes were adequately staffed by priests, and whose religious orders were not lacking for vocations, a world above all in which the traditional understanding of the role and authority of the clergy had changed little over the centuries.

[18] *Ibid.*, 413; see *Église catholique et France moderne* ([n.p.]: Hachette, 1978) 53.
[19] *Faith and Spiritual Life*, 189.
[20] *Priest and Layman*, 289.

Against that backdrop, the emphasis even in Congar's earliest writings on the laity's vocation to engage with secular society, constitutes less a refusal to envisage any active role for laypeople in the church, as an insistence that the church attend to the world: "If the world is not taken seriously, neither is the laity," Congar wrote,[21] though he might on his own principles equally have written the reverse. Thus, while at times it might seem as though the world is being consigned to lay hands because priests and religious are above dealing with it, Congar in fact saw the laity at the forefront of the church's apostolate: the laity are called to do God's work in the world.[22] The church is not able fully to accomplish its mission without the laity. If, as "an organism of grace," the church needs only its bishops,[23] nevertheless the church exists, not for its own sake, but for the sake of the world.[24] There is therefore a mutuality in the relation of clergy and laity: laypeople cannot perfect the church, for that perfection requires the sacraments; yet even if priests and religious play a large role in society (what Congar calls "cultural creation"), they do so, in his view, qua laypeople,[25] and it is still through the lay faithful that the world is drawn towards the church.[26] However the laity's role, even in this missionary aspect, does not consist solely in the expansion of the membership of the church, but in the sheerly doxological function of glorifying

---

[21] *Ibid.*, 261.

[22] *Laypeople in the Church*, 18.

[23] *Priest and Layman*, 290. This statement is hard to reconcile with the taxonomy of *Laypeople in the Church*, which, as noted, seems tacitly to subsume the role of the bishop under that of the priest as the archetypal ordained person, and perhaps even as the key order of the church.

[24] *Un peuple messianique: L'Église, sacrement du salut et libération*, Cogitatio Fidei, 85 (Paris: Cerf, 1975) 20.

[25] *Priest and Layman*, 291.

[26] *Laypeople in the Church*, 118.

God, in this instance, in and through one's daily work.[27] Although Congar viewed the constitution of the church as "essentially apostolic,"[28] inasmuch as it was "clearly sacramental," even in its apostolic dimension, it must be about the business of glorifying the Father, from whom its mission originates. This church is the fruitfulness *ad extra* of the Trinitarian missions, and it is for this reason it is "an organism of knowledge and love."[29]

Despite his insistence upon the proper calling of the laity as lying in engagement with the things of the world — specifically, in marriage and the professions — Congar sought to construct his theology of the laity systematically, especially in relation to both ecclesiology and theological anthropology.[30] In *Laypeople in the Church*, he may have been more successful in expressing the wish that this be so than in bringing his intuition to fruition. The focus of the earlier works tends to locate laypeople, not only too one-sidedly in relation to clergy and monks but more generally in relation to the hierarchy of the church, in a way that often seems more juridical than theological. In *Laypeople in the Church*, this forensic element seems not only to dominate, but even threatens to drown out every other: "[Laypeople] have to pronounce Amen to the decisions of the Church and her hierarchical government, as they do to her liturgical action, which also is hierarchical, but has its complement in their assent. In neither case is this Amen 'totalitarian'...; it does not bring about the validity of the hierarchical action."[31] Much of what Congar says of the hierarchy could be taken in the most narrowly

[27] *Ibid.*, 391.

[28] *The Mystery of the Church*, trans. A. V. Littledale, 2nd ed. rev. (London: Geoffrey Chapman, 1965) 39.

[29] *I Believe in the Holy Spirit*, vol. II: *'He Is the Lord and Giver of Life'*, trans. David Smith (New York: Seabury, 1983) 8.

[30] *Laypeople in the Church*, xvii.

[31] *Ibid.*, 250.

institutional and authoritarian sense, as when he concludes his study of the laity, "The laity ... are not the subject of the acts by which the Church receives her structure as institution of salvation, which involve the exercise of apostolical powers; they are not the subject of the juridical mission constitutive of apostleship."[32] Nevertheless, the laity are not remote from the apostolicity of the church, any more than they are from its unity, holiness or catholicity; the liturgy and theology of confirmation, as Congar notes, are redolent of an apostolic and pentecostal atmosphere.[33] If Congar here forbears to join in the chorus of those who readily refer to confirmation as a "lay ordination" (an estimation which may be subject to precisely the clericalist traps it seeks to avoid), that may only be a testament to his deep conviction of the genuine worth and distinctiveness of the lay vocation, even as it is contiguous with the mission of the church. Congar would extend these insights still further in an essay on the significance of reception in the church (the fact that it begins with the words "Thème dangereux?" is an indication of the fact that Congar was still willing to risk tackling controversial issues). In this essay, he distinguishes between power and authority, noting that power is juridical and pertains to the realm of law; authority, in contrast, is spiritual and moral. Congar notes repeatedly that there cannot be power without authority and that what reception by the whole body of the faithful adds to a dogmatic or moral decision, which is in itself legitimate without reception, can therefore be parsed as "credibility."[34]

Moreover, even in the early work, there are hints that the talk of hierarchy might have been intended in terms other than the purely bureaucratic or juridical. When, for example, he writes that the

[32] *Ibid.*, 452.

[33] *The Mystery of the Church*, 192.

[34] See "La 'Réception' comme réalité ecclésiologique," *Droit ancien et structures ecclésiales* (London: Variorum Reprints, 1982) 401.

hierarchy alone is "the subject of the messianic energies communicated to the church in the form of *powers*,"[35] he is directly employing categories native to Eastern theology, and one might therefore speculate whether there is not an Eastern antecedent for his talk of hierarchy — specifically, the celestial and ecclesiastical hierarchies in the work of the Pseudo-Denys, which have nothing to do with ecclesiastical bureaucracy and everything to do with the communication of grace through a structure, which, qua ordered, is able to act as the medium of divine intention to vivify and sanctify all creation.[36] If on the Dionysian account ecclesial structure is in the first instance a form of communicative order rather than a means of imposing power and controlling or subjecting the lesser ranks, then one can see how Congar can maintain, as he also does at the end of *Laypeople in the Church*, that the church's hierarchical principle is necessarily accompanied by a communal principle, and that these are in no way opposed:[37] it is not a matter of a vertical axis which necessarily exists in tension with a horizontal one, but two means by which grace is mediated to the church, and through the church to the world, means which are ecclesiologically parallel.

In later works, Congar would extend the notion of the complementarity of the hierarchical and communal principles, seeing the collaboration of clergy and laity as that of a couple: he was still willing to invoke hierarchy in this context, but he views the "couple" additionally as a friendship, a diversity and a mutual completion.[38] The trajectory reaches its theologically richest form in the

[35] *Laypeople in the Church*, 375.

[36] Perhaps to a modern reader, the Pseudo-Denys might seem an unlikely source on which to draw, but his treatises are among those most frequently cited by Aquinas, whose work was of course a natural home to a Dominican.

[37] *Laypeople in the Church*, 452.

[38] *Priest and Layman*, 255.

second volume of his trilogy on the Spirit, where he again appeals
to the Thomistic notion of friendship, thinking through these ideas
in the context of a theology of personhood: it is because the Church
is a fraternal communion that in it a personal principle and a principle of unity come together, two principles brought into harmony
by the Holy Spirit. Persons, Congar adds, are "the great wealth of
the church."[39] Not only the juridical and bureaucratic language has
been abandoned in the later works, but the subordination of these
ideas to those native to the ancient tradition of the church is explicitly declared, inasmuch as Congar asserts the primacy of persons
over structures.[40] Indeed, the notion of a hierarchical and a communitarian principle which balance one another seems to have been
subjected to an internal critique and not so much revised, as abandoned in favour of categories rooted at the very heart of theology,
in the doctrine of God: the monarchical or pyramidal model of the
church, in virtue of which all is determined by a vertical line that
finally reaches a base, which is merely passive, is now deemed,
not only inappropriately masculine, but monotheistic in a pre-Trinitarian way.[41] There are hints that the reciprocity and mutuality
of a Trinitarian model informed Congar's thought in other respects,
as well. In *Priest and Layman*, he cited a youth worker, who

---

[39] *I Believe in the Holy Spirit*, II: 16.

[40] *Un peuple messianique*, 85.

[41] *Ibid.*, 89. Before *Laypeople in the Church*, however, Congar had already
tried to find conceptualities with which to express both dimensions of the church.
In *Vraie et fausse réforme dans l'Église*, Unam Sanctam, 72, 2nd ed. rev. (Paris:
Cerf, 1968) 91 (he speaks on the one hand, of the church as both institution and
community and — perhaps more fruitfully still — as the institution which both
comes from God and is "le peuple des chrétiennes" (99 and 102). In *Laity, Church
and World: Three Addresses*, trans. Donald Attwater (London: Geoffrey Chapman, 1960) 58, trinitarian theology grounds the reciprocity of the principles of
fatherhood and brotherhood — a hierarchy of origin grounds the oneness of broth-
erly fellowship.

commented after a meeting with a bishop "[we were] disappointed that we had been treated like children ... 'the bishop has everything to give, nothing to receive'."[42] While Congar considered that the problem of which this case was symptomatic was two-sided — laity who did not grasp the full weight of tradition and clergy who could not see the urgency of the church's contemporary problems — the fact that he could see the possible legitimacy of viewing the bishop as a recipient and not solely a giver is still highly telling.[43]

This sensibility, which at some points in Congar's work is only hinted at, reaches its fullest theological expression in his notion of the church as sacrament and the people of God as sacrament. While calling the church itself a sacrament or sacramental,[44] is still perhaps to focus on the institution, inasmuch as it is being viewed as a *sacrament*, there is necessarily a movement away from a merely bureaucratic ecclesiology.[45] Congar's sense of sacramentality is rooted in Old Testament conceptualities as well as those of the New Testament, of the Gospel of John and the epistle to the Hebrews, as *Le Mystère du temple* shows. There Congar reminds us that the

[42] *Priest and Layman*, 247. The necessity of such reciprocity in Congar's view is illustrated also by his approving quotation of Roger Schutz, the founder and first prior of the Taizé community, to the effect that partners in ecumenical dialogue need to receive from one another (see *I Believe in the Holy Spirit*, II: 208-209).

[43] Contrast the earlier verdict, in *Vraie et fausse réforme dans l'Église*, 45, that although the bishop should take advice from diocesan clergy, he remains the sole judge and legislator.

[44] *I Believe in the Holy Spirit*, III: 271 and *The Mystery of the Church*, 35. In the second volume of the pneumatology, he called the church a person (p. 19) and however odd (indeed perhaps even categorically confused) this idea might seem, it is a sign of the fundamentally non-, and even anti-, bureaucratic strand of Congar's ecclesiology.

[45] In *Christ, Our Lady and the Church: A Study in Eirenic Theology*, trans. Henry St John (Westminster, MD: Newman, [1957]), 39 Congar acknowledged the error of some ecclesiologies, of treating the church too exclusively as an institution, noting that this is not the usage of tradition and the liturgy.

church is not only body, but also temple, the very tabernacle of the Most High, which is built of the living stones of the faithful.[46] Thus, it is the people of God that is the sacrament of salvation.[47] If in the early works it seems as though the church can be the church without the laity as long as there are priests to offer the eucharist, by the time of *Priest and Layman*, the paradigm had shifted significantly: "[Christ] is priest and sacrifice, but the faithful are priests and sacrifices with him."[48] On this point, Congar becomes critical of Rahner, the force of whose criticisms of his own thought he often generously acknowledged, for locating the laity too far outside the church's "sacral order."[49] While Congar became more insistent on the dimension of the laity's role in the church in the years after Vatican II, however, it was never entirely absent from his thought; as early as *Laypeople in the Church*, he wanted to see Christian priesthood as extending beyond an exclusive reference to the power to consecrate the eucharist[50] and spoke of the priesthood of the faithful as "a reality so rich in content that no single aspect or statement exhausts it."[51] That richness is perhaps related to the very wealth of the church itself. For Congar, the sacramentality of the church is a consequence of its sociality.[52] The renunciation of the world, of which Congar sometimes spoke, is never a renunciation of "les autres," never individualistic. Union with Christ,

---

[46] *Le Mystère du temple ou l'Économie de la présence de Dieu à sa créature de la Genèse à l'Apocalypse*, Lectio Divina, 22 (Paris: Cerf, 1958) 7. He claims this is a leading idea in *Laypeople in the Church* (see footnote 1), but the reader of the latter might well be forgiven for having missed the theme there, yet no less grateful for being reminded of it in the later work.

[47] *Un peuple messianique*, 98.

[48] *Priest and Layman*, 75.

[49] *Ibid.*, 317.

[50] *Laypeople in the Church*, 178.

[51] *Ibid.*, 138.

[52] *The Mystery of the Church*, 41.

traditionally regarded as the peak of mystical experience, and for the sceptic (whether Christian or not) the peak of navel-gazing pre-occupation with one's own salvation and sanctification, is, on the contrary, for Congar a state which is acquired only socially and within the church.[53]

The sacramental dimension of the laity's life emerges also in Congar's conception of lay vocation. As the dominant tendency of the earlier works is to see the laity's purpose as mission to an unbe-lieving world, so is the conception of lay vocation in those works: "Every Christian is called to the apostolate in the wide sense: he has not to wait for any other vocation than his vocation to a Chris-tian life; no other mission than that of a Christian life, lived in the concrete conditions of his profession and of the circumstances and personal contacts of his life. For us, all this is not merely secular: it is an application to us of the will of God, who has given us a place in his plan of salvation."[54] This vocation, although often seemingly lesser than that of the priest and monk is actually more arduous: "the layman works for the kingdom of God through mar-riage and the professions. He does not take the shortcut taken by the priest or the religious — he follows a road which is longer and more difficult, but it is his own, his vocation."[55] This road is not simply an arduous way, a grim endurance test existing for its own sake, however; it is the way of the Mystical Body, that gathers up into itself the whole variety of human activity,[56] and in offering it to God, so allows the Spirit to sanctify and transform it.

The Christian calling is most fundamentally not to serve the world, to do something for it, but simply to give oneself to it.

[53] *Ibid.*, 44.
[54] *Priest and Layman*, 12.
[55] *Ibid.*, 290.
[56] *The Mystery of the Church*, 94.

The faithful offer the eucharist through the priest, but they also
offer Christian sacrifice directly, by offering the oblata and giving
themselves.[57] This sacrifice has therefore not simply to be offered,
but to be lived: "For each of us, according to the duties of our state
in life, according to the opportunities offered us, there is this essentially sacrificial life to be brought into existence every day."[58] This
offering of the spiritual life makes every call in the Body of Christ
a priestly one, made so by the animation of Christ the High Priest.[59]
It is the role of those who are priests in the sense of actually offering the mass to bind together these other offered sacrifices to the
great sacrifice of Christ,[60] so that the offering of the eucharist, while
in an important sense still primary, is so partly in virtue of its unitive value in gathering together all the offerings of the people of
God. Congar's strong sense of the High Priesthood of Christ also
exerts a nuancing force on his conception of authority. While real
jurisdictional power does exist in the church, it is a power received
solely from Christ and exists only within the structure of the fundamentally religious relationship of the gospel, so it can never be
merely a relation of subordination or superiority, but only a loving
obedience to Christ.[61] More fundamentally, Christ is not only the
unifier of all priestly offerings, but is the *only* priest of the new
covenant.[62] In pointing to the unique quality of Christ's priesthood,
Congar effectively mitigates the sharp clerical-lay dichotomy characteristic of his earlier work, not by "elevating" the laity to a position of equality with the clergy, and certainly not by denying the
unique character of the priesthood of the ordained, but by placing

[57] *Laypeople in the Church*, 220.
[58] *Faith and Spiritual Life*, 186.
[59] *Priest and Layman*, 96.
[60] *Ibid.*, 97; see *Faith and Spiritual Life*, 192.
[61] *Power and Poverty in the Church*, 98.
[62] *I Believe in the Holy Spirit*, vol. II, 113.

both around the table in the Upper Room. Here we see the broader trajectory of Congar's ecclesiology: from a preoccupation with intellectual and juridical structures, to doxology.[63]

This doxological trajectory manifests itself in the breadth of relation between priesthood and sacrifice as envisaged in Congar's theology. Sacrifice and priesthood exactly correspond, but this does not mean that only the one who offers the sacrifice of the eucharist is a priest, but that there are a variety of forms of priesthood as there are a variety of forms of sacrifice. Thus, a liturgical and sacramental sacrifice requires a liturgical and sacramental priesthood, and an interior, spiritual and personal sacrifice requires an interior, spiritual and personal priesthood.[64] The breadth of Congar's conception of sacrifice emerges clearly in his reflections in *Sainte Église*: certainly, he is thinking of the eucharist, but by no means exclusively. He rejects the popular notion of sacrifice as "that which costs,"[65] preferring instead to define sacrifice as that which comes from the whole of what we are and have, and totality of our being, our activity and what we possess.[66] More broadly still, the spirit of sacrifice (as opposed to its matter) is the free and loving acceptance of our reference to God, our absolute dependence on

---

[63] There is a suggestion of inclination in this direction as early as *Vraie et fausse réforme dans l'Église*, 67, where Congar points to the wearisome nature of a contemporary notion of sanctity, that saints are those who are useful to their neighbours. By 1964, Congar even wrote of "the invasion of legalism" and deplored its rise in ecclesiology (which he dated from the end of the sixteenth century to the present); see the chapter of this title in *Power and Poverty in the Church*, trans. Jennifer Nicholson, (London: Geoffrey Chapman, 1964), 103-110. Likewise, in *Laity, Church and World*, 31, he blamed the rise of legalism on a collective forgetting of the relationship of service and subordination.

[64] *Priest and Layman*, 93.

[65] *Sainte Église: Études et approches écclesiologiques*, Unam Sanctam, 41, (Paris: Cerf, 1963) 241.

[66] *Sainte Église*, 242.

him.[67] What a Christian does as a Christian is an act of Christ,[68] so that all the activity of the baptised in some sense partakes of the character of his high priesthood. "What every Christian does" should not be construed in a merely bland sense, however. Although Congar certainly leaves open the possibility that all genuinely Christian activity by definition partakes of Christ, his eucharistic sensibility is also reflected in his emphasis on the sacrificial centre of that life: for every one of us, he writes, there is an essentially sacrificial life.[69]

It is in this specifically sacrificial sense that the laity partake of Christ's priesthood, by offering the whole of their lives, as Christ offered his. It is in this sacramental and eucharistic context that Congar's avowed denial of the world is best understood. "A Christian," he writes, "really is withdrawn from the world, dead to the world … In every authentic Christian life there is a kind of devaluation and dismissal of the things of this world."[70] How Congar could maintain such a position at the same time as counselling "Let us not be dualists, dividing the world into a zone of light wherein God dwells, and a zone of darkness"[71] would itself be a mystery, were it not for his emphasis on sacrifice. Renunciation of the world — which is construed as the responsibility of Christians generally, and not just of vowed religious — is rooted not so much in disdain for the world because it is the way it is, as rooted in the one who renounces, who by so doing, joins in Christ's "yes" to life that is the creative and love-filled response to the world's harsh "no" in the cruelty of the Passion. Here Congar overcomes two powerful dichotomies of the earlier *Laypeople in the Church*. First, the sharp

[67] *Ibid.*, 242.
[68] *The Mystery of the Church*, 26-27.
[69] *Faith and Spiritual Life*, 186.
[70] *Ibid.*, 138.
[71] *Ibid.*, 180.

distinction of priest and layperson, in terms of which laypeople are not-priests, has been modified so that the clergy and faithful are now understood as both standing before God with the uplifted hands of those who offer and pray, each kind of proffered gift having its value and place. Second, the sharp distinction of church and world seems to have become more nuanced, so that those whose apostolate is to be active in the world are now seen as equally having a role in the church's life of prayer, their work comprising both the exterior activities of secular profession and mission and the interior acts of worship and prayer.

This shift is one of the most important in Congar's theology of the laity, for there are strains in his thought which seem curiously to downplay the role of the laity in the church's life of prayer. For example, Congar once faulted an (unnamed) archbishop of Rouen for "conceding" to the laity the task of prayer and asks whether there is not something else which might be seen as their contribution.[72] Although he acknowledged that prayer is "no small thing," there seems to be here a downplaying of the significance of the laity's prayer in a way that correlates with the earlier distinction of worldly-minded laypeople from godly-minded monks, yet with the added irony that the very activity which constitutes the heart of the monastic vocation seems relativised when considered as part of the life of the laity. Something of this sensibility lingers in the later works. In *Église catholique et France moderne*, for instance, there is no mention of the participation of the laity in an extended, and quite beautiful, meditation on the liturgy,[73] and Congar speaks of the divine office of "priests, monks and religious sisters," as if it were unheard of that laypeople might also pray the office.[74] His

[72] *Priest and Layman*, 248.
[73] *Église catholique et France moderne*, 114.
[74] *Ibid.*, 115.

hesitancy in this regard may however have less to do with any disinclination to allow for lay contribution to the church's liturgical
offering, as a concern that prayer not be defined too narrowly, too
exclusively as liturgical; in addition to prayer in the narrowest
sense, Congar stressed, there is also the prayer diffused throughout a working day, the whole of which is offered to God, and the
prayer of action and encounter with one's fellow human beings.[75]
If he expressed distrust of the notion that the church exists *solely*
for the purpose of doxology, and not also for the world and its conversion,[76] he is equally clear that a Christian is in the first instance
one who prays,[77] and prayer is the essential, and fundamental, act
of Christian living,[78] as religion essentially consists in worship.[79]
Because it is fundamental, it encompasses all of life, rising from
the ground-level of human existence, a shaft of praise terminating
only in God. Because prayer means, in the first instance, entering
into communion with the will of God,[80] the laity of necessity enter
into its work as fully as contemplative religious, even though the
lives of the latter are of course more focused on prayer in the narrower sense.

The apparent contradictions of Congar's theology of the laity
can perhaps best be understood by looking at two pairs of terms in
which he proposes to view the Christian approach to life before
God and life in the world: duty and grace, and gift and task.
In *The Mystery of the Church*, he points to the paradoxical truth that
while all is fulfilled in Christ, yet we still have to bring Christ to
fulfilment and build up his body. This twofold truth he describes

[75] *Ibid.*, 115.
[76] *Un peuple messianique*, 20.
[77] *Priest and Layman*, 93.
[78] *Faith and Spiritual Life*, 187.
[79] *Ibid.*, 189.
[80] *Ibid.*, 187.

as "a dialectic of gift and task."[81] In the slightly later collection of essays, *Faith and the Spiritual Life*, he speaks of a successive movement, first of devaluing and dismissing the worldly things, but second, a restoration of these very things to us as "a duty and a grace"; this two-phase movement he calls the two arms of an antinomy.[82] While he is not here speaking specifically of the question of the nature of lay involvement in the church and the world, or the relation of laypeople to the clergy or vowed religious, his appeal to the categories of dialectic and antinomy may help to explain why he seems little concerned directly to address and resolve the apparent shifts in his thought. In holding together laity and clergy, hierarchy and community, church and world, Congar eschews any notion of synthesis which would obliterate the fundamental — indeed fruitful — differences between them and create a tertium quid which is authentically neither. The notion of antinomy is perhaps most helpful in exploring exactly how the two poles of each pair might co-exist. Here again, Congar seems to be leaning on the Eastern theological tradition, from which he learnt so much and which he loved so deeply. The practice of antinomy (if we may call it that) entails holding together contrasting — or even opposing, principles — not out of vacillation or an intellectually sloppy disinclination to investigate them and recognise the full weight of their difference, but because both are true and to abandon either would be to move away from the truth.[83] Antinomy differs from dialectic in that it does not suppose the truth is so much to be found in movement between the two poles which ultimately produces a synthesis, as in holding them together simultaneously,

[81] *The Mystery of the Church*, 27.

[82] *Faith and Spiritual Life*, 138.

[83] For an account of how antinomy works in Eastern theology, see A. N. Williams, "The Logic of Genre: Theological Method in East and West," *Theological Studies* 60 (1999) 679-707.

which is precisely what Congar does in his theology of the laity. In another way, Congar found resources to overcome the polarities of his early work by articulating multiple sets of vertical relationships: "the relationships which weave the fabric of our life on the horizontal plane of this world, are repeated or assumed into the vertical relationship of love which runs from God to us, and the vertical relationship of faith which runs from us to him ... But if this human relationship is lived 'in the Lord', and so stems from him and is lived according to him, it ceases to be the natural relationship recognized by the civil code ... It changes direction radically. It is no longer a relationship in two terms on the horizontal plane, one term opposed to the other, but in three terms, situated vertically ... Everyone, according to his place in the earthly organism ... bears the duty of care (*cura*) which God himself and his Christ have for their own."[84] The unifying principle of clergy and laity within the church, or of church and world, or the vertical axis of hierarchy and the horizontal one of community, or of action and prayer, is not to be found in any fusion or triumphing of one principle over the other, but in what lies beyond them all and yet animates them all: the Holy Spirit.

Pneumatology was not simply the focus of what is arguably Congar's most important contribution to theology, the trilogy *I Believe in the Holy Spirit*, but is also in a real sense the wellspring of all his work and it is for this reason that, in addition to making use of antinomy and dialectic, Congar was also able simply to acknowledge the need for development. He had reflected at length on this principle in his large work on tradition (*Tradition and Traditions*), but it is far easier to trace and approve shifts in communal thought as a tradition develops over time than to admit that one's own thought might stand in need of revision. In the book which records

---

[84] *Power and Poverty in the Church*, 89-90.

conversations with Congar late in his life, *Fifty Years of Catholic Theology*, he does just that, pointing not only to his earlier mistake of defining the laity too much in relation to the clergy,[85] but also embracing changes in society and the church and taking account of these theologically. The dynamic, essentially hopeful character of his thought is well illustrated by his reflections on the state of parish life in France towards the close of the twentieth century. While he naturally regretted the dire shortage of priests in France by this time (1987), he was able to see even in this essentially sad state of affairs an opportunity. The fact that Sunday worship in some communities had to be conducted without priests meant that a space developed in which laypeople could work in ways that Congar viewed not merely as emergency measures during hard times, but which represented a genuine opportunity for the church: such assemblies, Congar maintained, could be "magnificent,"[86] an estimation all the more significant in virtue of the recurrent, deeply eucharistic strand of his theology. If in his earlier work there were traces of an almost defensive authoritarianism, in these last conversations Congar quietly deplores the clericalism which he could still see still prevailing in the church.[87] If earlier it seemed that the teaching authority of the church and its clergy was such that laypeople could only assent and never question, now Congar was willing to say that one could disagree, indeed one had a duty to do so, in the name of a recognised truth.[88] His position does not license an individualistic, let alone petulant, stance, in terms of which any theology is deemed acceptable because someone finds it congenial

---

[85] *Fifty Years of Catholic Theology: Conversations with Yves Congar*, ed. Bernard Lauret, trans. John Bowden (London: SCM, 1988) 65.

[86] *Fifty Years of Catholic Theology*, 48.

[87] *Ibid.*, 67.

[88] *Ibid.*, 76.

(or indeed, unacceptable because one does not care for its implications), but it does allow for the at least theoretical possibility of
dialogue — of a conversation which is not simply a series of magisterial pronouncements punctuated by the predictable antiphon of
a lay "Amen."

There are hints in the later work that some of the shifts in Congar's view of the laity correlated with, and were perhaps even
shaped by, his growing awareness of the questions raised by altered
attitudes towards women. One may speculate whether some remarks
do not subtly show sympathy for the ordination of women,[89] but
whether or not that is the case, he certainly became aware that any
Roman Catholic theology of the laity must take account of the fact
that ordination is not an option for half the members of the church:
any relegation of the laypeople to the status of second class citizens
necessarily relegates women to that status as well. Characteristically, Congar saw the issue not only in terms of the value placed
upon a particular group within the church, but as one affecting the
whole church and its ecclesiology. Thus, he acknowledged that the
church needs both a masculine and a feminine dimension.[90]

The position Congar had reached by the end of his life highlights not merely a willingness to see one's own theology as cor-
rigible, but to listen to the winds of change in society and the
church, and above all, to listen to persons. Congar once pointed to
the distinction between priests who minister to people and those
whose work is less focused on the pastoral.[91] The distinction here

[89] *Église catholique et France moderne*, 89.

[90] *Ibid.*, 89.

[91] *Priest and Layman*, 189; see also *Vraie et fausse réforme dans l'Église*, 30,
where pastoral considerations are presented as exerting an additional constraint on
clergy, who cannot be as radical as laypeople in the way they express themselves,
because they must be ever-vigilant that their speech does no harm; the constraint,
note, is not fear of magisterial sanction. In *Laity, Church and World*, 84, he

surely devolves on which clergy are in a position where they frequently *listen* to laypeople — that is, who are in a position where
they have something to receive and not only to give. The desire
Congar recognised in all people to be free and responsible subjects,
and not merely objects,[92] reflects a recognition of the dialogical
character of the relation of clergy and laity, church and world, when
these relations are authentic and fruitful.

Congar's theology of the laity shows a broad movement from a
view of laypeople apparently largely marked, despite Congar's own
best intentions, by its concern to define their role in relation to that
of priests and vowed religious, to guard ecclesiastical authority,
and to keep the work of the laity firmly within the world, rather
than the church. Such an estimation does not hold entirely true even
of Congar's early thought, but by the end of his life, there was no
longer any hint of such tendencies. While it could be maintained
that the more consistently generous estimation of the laity in the
later work reflects no more than the intellectual largesse made possible in the wake of Vatican II, there are signs throughout Congar's work that from the beginning he was thinking in quite different terms, probing and altering his own paradigms even as he
proposed them. The mutuality of clergy and laity, originally parsed
as a division of labour between church and world, transformed in
the later work into a distinction between two kinds of priesthood
and sacramental life, both radically dependent on the High Priesthood of Christ and the power of the Spirit for their diffusion in the

pointed to the distinguishing quality of outstanding priests: they were all people
who lived close contact with the laity, in dialogue with them, always welcoming
their questions.

[92] *Fifty Years of Catholic Theology*, 67. He made essentially the same
point, explicitly in relation to the laity in *Laity, Church and World*, 22, although
the fact it is necessary to add that they are "personal subordinate subjects." See
also p. 40.

world. Without minimising the differences between the pastoral, monastic and lay vocations, and thus reducing the possibility of creative tension and interaction between them, Congar was able to articulate the value of each kind of vocation and state of life in its distinctiveness, as well as the dual end to which each one is directed: that the world be "charged with the grandeur of God" and that the Trinity of divine Persons from whom all holiness flows be glorified in the human response of self-offering and prayer.

CARDINAL YVES CONGAR: A MAN OF THE CHURCH

Karl Cardinal LEHMANN

Bishop of Mainz, Germany

It is interesting to note the surprising number of great men of the Church who would have celebrated their hundredth birthday around this time. One need only mention the names of Karl Rahner, Cardinal Hermann Volk, Father Hans Urs von Balthasar and, of course, Cardinal Yves Congar, with others such as Cardinal Henri de Lubac and Marie-Dominique Chenu also high up on the list. We are constantly given the impression that we are "standing on the shoulders" of these great men, as it were, that they are the pioneers for many developments in recent decades. Above all, without being aware of it at the time, they also provided the groundwork for the Second Vatican Council. As well as this, they have overseen the transition to a new era of the Church in many different ways, providing guidance all the way to the end of the millennium.

Yves Congar (1904-95) is one of these men of the Church who are endowed with extraordinary charisms. As Professor of Fundamental Theology and Dogmatics, he taught at the renowned Dominican educational institution *Le Saulchoir* between 1931 and 1954 (excluding the war years). Although he spent a carefree childhood in Sedan in the Ardennes region, he was later to experience not only the aftereffects of the First World War, but also the plight of the Second World War, during which he was interned as a prisoner of war.

At an early age, Congar noted the inner conflict which existed in the Church, and spent a lifetime channelling his extraordinary passion and energy into renewing it. In 1937, at the age of just 33, he produced the major work *Chrétiens désunis*, which remains one of the milestones in the history of the ecumenical movement within the Catholic denomination. Furthermore, he did not allow himself to be discouraged by restrictions placed upon his teaching activities from 1954 onwards. With his major work on true and false reform in the Church — which was published in Paris in 1950 as part of the *Unam Sanctam* series, which he established himself and which continues to be of great significance today — he set a positive course by constantly drawing attention to the essence of the Church, its vital elements, structures and life as well as on the diversity and unity which co-exist therein. At a very early stage, he established himself as a thinker with an acute sensibility for both history and reality — a rare combination indeed.

In his work, which he pursued constantly through a life plagued by ill-health, he explored the various theological pronouncements and dimensions of life within the Church, in order to demonstrate continually and convincingly the high degree of unity which is found in the varied components of ecclesiastical life: when one looks back at the entire history and tradition of the Church, it is far richer and more extensive than it often realises itself. It is for this reason that so many of Congar's historical studies are of a wholly liberating nature.

The Church of the twentieth century can consider itself extremely fortunate to have been blessed with a theologian such as Yves Congar who, by means of these revelations, was capable of providing the Church with an optimal preparation for the Second Vatican Council, thus opening it up for internal and external dialogue. In this way, it was also possible for the Eastern and Western Churches, to which Congar afforded equal attention, to find a new impetus to seek reunion. Inspired by J. A. Möhler, Congar rediscovered the Church through his in-depth knowledge of theological sources. This was achieved above all with the help of the two categories of People of God and Communion, which we almost take for granted today.

Standing out among the myriad issues and publications were a number of pillars which Yves Congar perceived as being particularly necessary for the renewal of the Church. These questions were dealt with resolutely in his major publications over the following decades: *Lay People in the Church* (1953), *Tradition and Traditions* (1960/1963), *I believe in the Holy Spirit* (1979/1980). These are joined by countless other publications, some fundamental in nature (such as the ecclesiology in the Textbook of Dogmatic History, 1968, *Mysterium salutis*, IV/I: 1972, and "Heilige Kirche" (*Holy Church*) (1966), others more parenthetical but no less stirring (Außer der Kirche kein Heil, Wege des lebendigen Gottes, Für eine dienende und arme Kirche, Im Geist und im Feuer) (*No Salvation Outside the Church, Paths of the Living God, Power and Poverty in the Church, In Spirit and in Fire*). There is no doubt that the work of this man of the Church draws on the central truths but also that he knows how these must be enhanced and implemented today. In this respect, his instinct is nothing short of miraculous.

Although no-one could have foreseen it, Yves Congar belongs right in the heart of the Second Vatican Council. To a very great extent, he has paved the way for this through numerous earlier studies, and supported it with unwavering commitment and extraordinary selflessness. He worked untiringly to develop interpretations as well as painstakingly contemplating and analysing thousands of submissions to the Council (*modi*). However, he was never merely concerned with "his" own ideas. He invariably saw himself, not as an ecclesiastical politician or *soi-disant* reformer, but as a witness for the tradition and spiritual life of the Church, one who brought to bear aspects which had long since been lost or forgotten. This may well explain his extraordinary ability to show such courage, determination and patience in the face of suffering. In view of his willingness to tackle issues, his peaceableness (provided that this did not merely constitute a lazy compromise!) and his obedience — which many modern-day observers fail to understand and which was fuelled by an intense passion — Yves Congar will always remain a man of the Church.

I myself had the good fortune not only to spend years studying his works in detail, but also to make his acquaintance in person during the Second Vatican Council. In the International Theological Commission at the Holy See, I had the opportunity to work closely together with him over a number of years (1974-84), particularly in the small working groups which prepared the texts. In the end, he entrusted me with the German version of the small, informative book "Der Fall Lefebvre. Schisma in der Kirche" (*The Lefebvre Affair, Schism in the Church*, Freiburg, 1977).

Even after his death, he left us a veritable treasure trove in the form of two unforgettable books, namely his childhood war diary (1914-18) complete with numerous illustrations (1997) and the two-volume diary of the Second Vatican Council (2002). Both of these were, particularly in German-speaking countries, no longer given the attention they deserved.

Yves Congar remains one of the greatest theologians of the twentieth century, and deserves to be in our thoughts on the hundredth anniversary of his birth. If we do not at least do him honour at this late stage, we will not only be failing to appreciate the magnitude of his contribution to our Church, but will also be depriving ourselves, since far too much of his work has already gone unnoticed.

* Trans. by Elke Wertz

PART III

YVES CONGAR: ECUMENIST

IN HOPE OF UNITY

Jean-Pierre JOSSUA, OP

Le Saulchoir, Paris

I would prefer not to devote these pages to yet another profound and well documented analysis of the ecumenical work and standpoint of Yves Congar. That has already been done sufficiently often and sufficiently well for there to be little point in repetition. With the benefit of hindsight, I propose to say simply and succinctly what seems to me to be the essential, and, I venture to suggest, what we agreed on together concerning him, during those last years when we had so many occasions to talk about these things.

CALL AND COMMITMENT

As I said in my book of 1967 (*Le Père Congar: la théologie au service du peuple de Dieu*), which I have to admit was largely dictated by him in Strasburg between 1963 and 1965, his commitment to the cause of unity seems always to have been linked to a call. But, he added, there can be no vocation without preparation through human circumstances that can often be traced back a long way. Sedan, where he was born, had been a great centre of Protestantism in the 16th and 17th centuries, and was still a region of mixed religion when he was a child, enjoying close relationships between the Christian denominations as well as with Jews. Yet there was a crucial moment of *kairos*. If the young religious's attention had been drawn towards the separated brethren by the

Russian seminary run by the Dominicans at Lille, and by certain
lectures given by the broadminded Father Chenu at the Saulchoir
on the subject of Faith and Constitution, it was during the retreat
he made in preparation for his ordination as a priest in 1930 that
he was particularly enlightened on this point. "It was whilst med-
itating on Chapter 17 of St John that I perceived a definitive call
to labour in order that all who believe in Jesus Christ might be
one." Later on, when the Council was on the point of coming down
in favour of dialogue, in a way that would have been unthinkable
a few years earlier, he would say: "Who planted this seed? And
who sowed it in me thirty-five years ago? But who makes the dawn
always follow on from night? And spring from winter?" The
metaphors of night and winter are not just for decoration, they refer
to the very real and bitter experiences of the end of the pontificate
of Pius XII.

   This feeling of having been set in motion by a call, this notion
of charism, in the theological sense of the term, meaning a gift of
the Spirit made to a Christian with a view to the service of his
brethren, is an essential key for understanding a man, a theologian,
for whom a spiritual or ethical call was always, by his own admission, to be more important than strictly intellectual intuitions. Even
if the latter, together with a good measure of hard work — especially historical, in the style that was proper to the Saulchoir school
— must necessarily be placed at the service of the former. This
was what fuelled his activity and his labours in those happy 1930s.
This was also how, in the post-war years, having been distanced
from the ecumenical domain by the wariness of the authorities, he
undertook a great programme of research, although it was an
unusual way to set about such research, as well as being against his
own nature. The orientation of this research would reveal an amaz-
ing premonition concerning everything that was to be decisive for
the life of the Church and the issues at stake at Vatican II: Church

reform and tradition, revelation, the role of the laity, links between Church and society, the renewal of ministries...

For from the very moment he chose to orient his life and work towards Unity, and while his masters and friends feared that he was locking himself inside too narrow a specialisation, he had grasped that ecumenism is not a speciality or a theme for study, but veritably an "all embracing dimension within the Church." Indeed "in her the *essential nature* cannot be separated from what she contains *for other people*." This is a crucial spiritual intuition, and in order to understand it, it is necessary to trace back the fundamental religious attitudes of the theologian. God himself, in Jesus Christ, demonstrates that he is *for other people*, and he cannot be known, unless he is welcomed in this movement of giving, accomplished through his inexhaustible generosity.

ECUMENISM AND CHURCH

It seems to me to be something of a waste of time to ask oneself what comes first in Yves Congar's commitment and research: whether it is the Church or the cause of unity. What I have already said will have enabled the reader to guess as much. Historically speaking, a passion for the Church came first: he was to say that he had experienced an early awakening of "a very deep sense of the Church." Yet, once the concern for unity appeared to him as stemming from a personal call, it would move into the centre of his perspective, and would soon culminate in his major work *Divided Christendom*. Bearing in mind that at the Saulchoir, Father Congar had to teach the "treatise on the Church" which at the time came under the banner of "apologetics," we should not *oversimplify*. In particular there co-existed two preoccupations: that of re-founding ecclesiology, and thinking about unity, which would lead him to study the structures of the Church, and to remain vigilant concerning various aspects of her life. In particular he discovered the scale of contemporary "unbelief," on the subject of which he published in 1935 an article that was to become a landmark. After the war, he would write as he recalled those years: "I had at that time become conscious of an ecumenical vocation, which was in the same dynamic as an ecclesiological vocation." From the 1930's onwards, he believed that if one wanted to be active in ecumenism, it was the state and concept of the Church that needed to be tackled, and the very fact of listening to others constitutes a challenge for her. This was true just as much of the quest for a return to sources, as for an opening up, that would be more truly Catholic, in the sense of universal, rather than denominational. Moreover, the big questions carry with them their own weightiness of meaning, and it would be simplistic to tie down to any one cause the interest that Yves Congar showed for the creation of an ecclesiology of communion and mystery, rather than one that was social and institutional. This very desire for a return to the purity of "the beginnings," for a rejuvenation of the Church, was to intensify after the war in a climate of intense fermentation of ideas. Father Congar was to speak of it later with such emotion and not a little nostalgia, for it was not only ecumenical, but quite simply evangelical.

After his imprisonment in Germany and his return to the Saulchoir, Father Congar, who before the war had established so many ecumenical contacts amongst both Catholics and Protestants, and repeatedly spoken of the need to open minds to the cause of unity, saw himself being progressively excluded. As I have said, this subject was itself laid to rest between 1946 and 1948; and Congar was to be distanced from it and even labelled "suspect, irredeemably suspect." And so he transferred all his energy to ecclesiology. In fact he came to understand better than ever before that only a profound reform of the Church would render possible a fearless confrontation with the question of union and prepare the way for it ("The most profitable ecumenical work is that which each accomplishes for himself and follows through in his own Church." "My God, who helped me to understand as early as 1929-30 that if the Church were to change her face, or rather if she simply put on her true face, if she were simply to be the Church, then everything would become possible on the road to unity [...].") At the same time, he hoped that the quality of the great works he was writing, with the specific aim of fostering the cause of unity (*True and False Reform in the Church*, *Lay People in the Church*, etc.) would bring credibility to the cause that remained dear to him. "Through serious academic studies of incontrovertible worth, I wished to build up sufficient credit to cover and support my position in ecumenical work," but, it must be stressed that this was by no means seen simply as a means to an end.

To the extent that Yves Congar was never to be in the front line on the Catholic side in ecumenism, even at the time when John XXIII reversed many trends and invited him to the Council, showing the theologian the confidence he had in him, nothing was to change as far as his work was concerned. Even at the Council, he was not much called upon to collaborate in the preparation of the declarations on Christian unity, except belatedly, for contributions requested during the preparation of the texts on unity and religious freedom. Why was this? Because he was too much in demand for the texts dealing with ecclesiology; because a new generation of ecumenists was at hand, around Cardinal Bea; perhaps also, he was to tell me, because something inside him had been broken, that it was obvious to others, and that it could not be mended... Here again a nuance of meaning must be added: if his work during these years is centred on the Church in her various aspects, the publication during the Council and later of books such as *Dialogue between Christians* and *Diversity and Communion*, reveals, as we shall see, a significant evolution in his ecumenical thinking. These works bear witness to the enduring interest and hope of a believer still striving for the desired goal of unity.

KNOWING AND LOVING OTHERS

One of Yves Congar's essential convictions, reiterated many times, was that if one wishes to engage in ecumenical dialogue, it is necessary to know and to like the other side, to respect them, to honour their Christian values, some of which may be less in evidence in Catholicism, but more so in their case, sometimes in proportion to a certain unilateralism on their part. The priority is to get to know and to like what these Christians were in the past. What kind of man was the German Lutheran in the 16th century, and above all, Luther himself? Early on, Father Congar went to visit the memorable places associated with him, and found him to be one of the greatest religious geniuses of all time, endowed with an extraordinary spiritual instinct and quite purely biblical. A significant evolution in his judgement of the theology of Luther is to be noted between *True and False Reform in the Church* (1950) and the book he wrote in 1983 on *Martin Luther, his Faith, his Reformation*, which concentrates not only on the intense affirmation of the essential ideas to be found in him, but also on the positive aspects of his Christology and his ecclesiology, noting even that at the end of his life, Luther adopted a reductionist perspective, used oppositions that were too categorical, upsetting certain necessary balances. Neither did he neglect those who first adhered to the Reformation in France. In fact he speaks less about Calvin, simply alluding when appropriate to his admirable use of language and the influence of his *Institutions*, sketching a phenomenology of Reformation sensibility, to make it known to the readers of *La Vie intellectuelle* in

1938. He enjoyed a fellow feeling with them all, entering into "their Christian effort," into their founding intuitions. In his preliminary report to the Council, Father Congar said that he was prepared to give his life to justify his love for the first generation of Protestants, revealing his respect for witnesses who remind us that the human person is not a reservoir in which an objectified form of grace accumulates, but that he/she must remain ever attentive to God, who is always committed personally as a source of initiatives in our relationship with him, always active and immediately present.

Then he had to discover and understand those who had laboured before him in this field, German Lutherans such as Heiler who strove for a more "Catholic" renewal, as well as his precursors in ecumenism on the Catholic side: those who took part in the Malines conversations, Father Portal, theologians close to Orthodoxy, some of whom, such as Dom Lambert Beauduin and Fr Gratieux, were treated with suspicion. All of this with patience, docility, respect, but also an enthusiasm and a capacity for initiative that worried some people who became overheated by these matters, until they were able to discern the fruits of his efficacy and the soundness of his judgements; this is true at least of the general public and the theologians. Yves Congar was also capable of recognising the value of positions different from his own, such as that of Fr Couturier with his prayer for unity; he saw in it a spiritual complementarity with his own way. He even attributed to him his own discovery of the fact that the movement undertaken in common is at one and the same time a step towards unanimity and already an expression of it. At the same time, he established innumerable contacts, especially on the Protestant side, as he followed courses at the boulevard Arago, where he listened to the masters and met their disciples at the time the sources of the Reformation beyond liberalism were being rediscovered. On the Orthodox side too, thanks to Berdiaeffs' Franco-Russian circle, frequented also by Maritain, Mounier and Father Lev Gillet. So many theologians found this young Dominican on their doorstep, sometimes in amusing circumstances, such as those recounted by Oscar Cullmann: his elderly maid, who came from an exclusively Protestant village in Alsace, was terrified by this "monk" and concerned for the danger he might represent for her master!

As I was saying, Father Congar was subsequently responsible for some remarkable initiatives, such as setting up encounters that were rare in the early 1930's, like the one sponsored by *La Vie intellectuelle* around Karl Barth in 1934, then those at Bièvre and Le Saulchoir. Immediately afterwards, he began to produce a regular column on Protestantism and ecumenism in that same journal (he was later to reproach himself with not having invited the other side to write directly for this column), and he undertook various collaborative ventures. In particular he launched the collection *Unam sanctam*, which John XXIII and Paul VI recognised as valuable in preparing the way for the Council. I realise that so far I have not mentioned Anglicanism, which was the motive behind his trip to England in 1936; *Divided Christendom* reveals great affinities with the Anglican Church, and it is perhaps this part of the book that has dated the least, and of which Yves Congar was to say subsequently: "I love the Anglican Church for its great heritage, its worship, its ethos which is both religious and humanist, respectful and free." All of these activities and, above all, a great amount of work shot through with the conviction that there are positive things to be found on the other side. All his effort was imbued with a total confidence in the truth, the conviction that truths will achieve harmony one with the other, even if their meeting point cannot as yet be discerned, this being the opposite of Catholic apologetics which sees only contradictions on one side and exclusive possession of the truth on the other. In his eyes, the desire for justice did not hinder critical freedom in respect of scriptural elements or things from the ancient tradition of the Church that had been discarded or used clumsily. At the same time, he steered a clear course away from incompetence and incomprehension. He also thought that the academic solidity of his work would enable him to rise above the internal suspicions of the Catholic Church; in this he was sorely deluded, as he was to discover only too soon.

As for the reception of this great work by his partners, it will suffice to recall the friendly homage paid to him at Strasburg in December 1963 by theologians of all denominations and all countries. Amongst them, Oscar Cullmann recognised in him a "prophet" within Catholicism, capable of stirring believers of other Churches. Jean-Jacques von Allmen affirmed that through his challenges that were frank but lovingly made, by taking their questions seriously and handing them on to his Church, Yves Congar succeeded in dispelling the myth by which Protestants considered themselves to be virtually the only ones paying careful attention to the Word, thus freeing them from a spirit of pride and opening them up to unity. Leo Zander, a lay theologian teaching at Saint-Serge, rejoiced in the encounter with people like him who, through a kind of personal aura, communicate something of the richness of their own Church, breaking down barriers and becoming as it were "icons" of the saints — in this case St Dominic — who was himself an icon of his Church.

PROTESTANTISM AND ORTHODOXY

I would like to pause for a moment to consider the two great Christian denominations to which Father Congar devoted his greatest efforts. Unquestionably, through circumstances and affinities that were perhaps more cultural than religious, it was to Protestantism that he turned first. "Although I gain much from the Orthodox tradition, which was revealed to me through the liturgy of the

oriental rite, through friendships and study, through reading Dostoyevsky, my attention remained largely devoted to Protestantism." I think I can see what attracted him as a theologian more
than anything else in Protestantism and Orthodoxy: the particular
importance attached to the Holy Spirit, largely absent from
Catholic theology and spirituality, but operating on a different
scale of values in each case. In the one it was the Spirit present
and living within the depths of the community, source of communion in an all-enveloping love. In the other, the Spirit represented above all supreme freedom and the immediacy of God's
presence to each individual (through the event of Grace) and to all
(through the charisms).

I will not dwell long on the Protestant Reformation, as I have
already mentioned it several times in what has preceded. In Yves
Congar's view, there is another regrettable side to this immediacy,
or, as he expressed it with reference to Karl Barth, this verticality
of divine action, compounded by reluctance to overestimate institutional mediation and individual merit in the late Middle Ages.
It would amount to something like a lack of a sense of the collaboration of the human person in the work of his/her own salvation,
a participation to which God invites us, and which for Augustine
was by no means detrimental, as the two things operate on different levels, he who by no means belittled the notion of grace as
freely given. The glory of God is in no way lessened by the greatness of the human person. "After all the critical point seems to me
to be a certain impotence on the part of the Protestant mind to grasp
the true status of transcendence and immanence [...]. They do not
perceive that something can be *within us*, and thus our own, whilst
still being of God." This value of immediacy, with God himself still
instrumental in salvation, and this lack of trust in the human part
in it, are I believe, at the heart of the evaluation of Protestantism
arrived at by this theologian. This holds true, even if the writings

of his last years brought nuances to these judgements, putting particular emphasis on the positive and on the closeness of the Reformation to the spirit of the modern period, with which it is contemporaneous through the dating of its origins. This can be seen as
both advantageous and risky. "The Reformation had a sense of the
subject, it formulated the religious dimension in less antiquated terminology, more personalised, more dialectical [...]; the Reformation made way for historical and biblical criticism."

It is not impossible that in his relationship with Orthodoxy, Yves
Congar was hindered by an "idealist" vision, which was often that
of Russian theologians in exile. Why always contrast the reality of
Catholicism with the ideal of the Orthodox Church, he would say
to me sometimes. But he greatly admired in her a 'monastic' spirituality — which has tended at times to become coextensive with
Russian Orthodoxy — escaping what he called western "monastic
ideology," with its tendency to despise the world, in order to seek
loving refuge in Orthodox monasticism's insistence on the cosmic
dimension of the paschal message, for this enabled him to renew
his own equilibrium. It did not escape his notice that this openness
did not go as far as taking into account the concrete realities of history ... In the same sense, the role accorded to symbol and the
whole of Christian experience seemed to him a precious antidote
to Latin-rite conceptualism. Why, despite the closeness on the dogmatic level between Orthodoxy and Catholicism, were *émigré*
Russian theologians more in tune with Protestantism? Doubtless,
thought Father Congar, because they have recognised in it a way
of tackling issues closest to their own, a certain fellow feeling in
the domain of Christian freedom and openness to others. Today
renewal of the Catholic Church should revive an awareness of the
enormous common heritage, and permit a drawing closer, enabling
Orthodoxy to teach us its very profound sense of tradition, the way
everything is always referred back to the Trinitarian essential.

Whereas the renewal and re-orientations adopted by the Council itself paradoxically had the effect of drawing Catholics closer to the Protestants than to the Orthodox, who, according to Father Congar, took fright at this apparent "Protestantisation" of Catholicism. It is and it isn't, he used to say, and this is not the place to go into the discernment he arrived at on this particular point. But cannot the Orientals also be reproached with their "immobility," their lack of interest in other people — what he called their lack of curiosity, their refusal of all that might be gained from dialogue, and above all to be challenged in their conviction that they are Church in all its fullness. These characteristics certainly do not favour a *rapprochement* as our theologian would say, but the obstacles must be overcome. We would discover that the essential is at one and the same time the same and different: variations in identity at the very deepest level, affecting modes of representation and actualisation, but which all may be invited to "receive" in reciprocity, and in the full ecclesiological sense of the term. Father Congar did so much to restore awareness of these matters at the heart of consciousness and practice in the ancient Church.

A Very Significant Evolution

Before concluding, it seems to me capital to evaluate in a more rigorous manner, the evolution of the problematic of Christian unity between *Divided Christendom* (1937) and *Diversity and Communion* (1982), not forgetting on the way *Dialogue between Christians* (1964 and 1973). Their very titles, plus a certain number of changes or self-criticisms, revealed a shift of emphasis existing already between the two earlier works. But the deepening process did not stop there, and it is the book written by the seventy-eight year old theologian that must be taken into account if the transformations, or rather about-turns that took place in his thinking during forty-five years of intense work, experiment and progress, are to be understood. I believe it is possible to present them under three headings.

In Father Congar's thinking, there is first and foremost a fundamental and constant polarity between the idea of oneness and the notion of an internal richness of diversity within the Church. But the second concept, acting in articulation with unity, varied in a very characteristic manner over this half-century. In 1937, it was *Catholicity*: "The Catholicity of the Church is its universal capacity for unity." In 1982, it was to be *diversity* or pluralism: "Pluralism as an internal value in unity." An all embracing model, or an image of unfolding, is followed by one of openness, a figure of the tensions existing between two terms. One was doctrinal — and ideological, that is to say justifying a certain state of affairs — the other historical, factual. At the same time, the ecumenical task appears henceforward to be, as it were, less exclusively doctrinal and more attentive to facts of life, to common projects. He had already said à propos of his earlier writings: "I had not seen the profound truth that emerges from concerted action" (Preface to *Dialogue between Christians*).

Secondly, unity was defined in earlier times as structural obedience to a double logic as in systematic theology. A divine logic offered in the uniqueness of Christ (the Church emanating from the Trinity, the Church in Christ); a human logic, because men have need of unified social structures (Church emanating from humanity). The danger was to identify the Church as mystery and the Church as society, this latter being the Catholic Church in concrete terms, whilst not failing to mention its weaknesses and shadows. Certainly the Church appears as being more vast than what is visible of her, but all Christians who are saved belong in reality to the one Church. In 1982, we find again a double orientation of theological and human thinking, but it has greatly changed in nature.

On the one hand, the Church is still defined mystically — although less abstractly — but from its roots as a *communion* of persons or of Churches, with a pneumatological and not only Christological note. This reference to the Holy Spirit points to harmonious diversity, liberty, the unforeseen. What the theologian referred to as western "Christomonism" linked with institutionalism and centralisation is thus averted. Henceforward more emphasis is laid on the transcendent nature of Mystery — ever inaccessible and never possessed. On the other hand, the anthropological dimension is now much less rooted in the "social order" model, than in that of human historicity, a source of differences rather than of uniformity.

Finally, as far as the search for unity is concerned, this seemed in 1937 to be represented by the "Roman" Catholic Church, to which separated Christians are invited to return, with all due respect, without being required to renounce anything positive, and even with the idea that the one true Church could better demonstrate Catholicity. In 1982, unity appears rather as something for the future, something to be searched for by all Christians together, even if all do not share the same position concerning it. To a considerable extent, they can remain different, within the bosom of a new-found unity, pluralism having been discovered in this work to be not a defect but rather a source of richness, not only between individual Churches, but also between separated Churches. The ecumenical movement, formerly viewed with reticence — less so, certainly, by Yves Congar than by others — is now seen as a "sign of the times." This view of accepted differences is reinforced by another principle that comes into play in *Diversities and Communion*, that of a "hierarchy of truths" (officially accepted at Vatican II). All is not of the same importance or to be considered on the same level, so that we can be united in the essentials, the heart of faith — even if it is expressed in different ways — whilst remaining different, disagreeing even over other points.

As I read this work, studying it in order to present it to readers, I used to wonder how deep this evolution went and why it seemed to come to a halt where it did. I was tempted to extend, wonderingly at least, the curve that emerged in the 1982 work, after a journey marked by seriousness, loyalty and intelligence. Is not this plural unity of which the theologian speaks, founded as it is on the heart of the confession of faith, already on offer to those whose vision is wide enough to grasp it, to receive it from Christ? Does not all that constitutes an obstacle in theological discussions, in ecclesiastical positionings, and in popular reactions, stem principally from particular traditions? Sometimes these are venerable — and which no-one would be obliged to abandon in a scheme of accepted diversity — but sometimes they are also abusive. Do these justify holding up a Eucharistic communion, founded on unanimity of faith as far as the essential is concerned, whilst respecting different interpretations? In refusing this do we not demonstrate our inability to reaffirm in depth our adherence to the fundamental message, to relativise various "truths" emanating from history, and which could profitably remain in the past? Or might we lose some power in the process? As I explained all these questionings to Father Congar while he was living in the Invalides hospital, my surprise was to hear him tell me that he was in agreement, but that he feared that such positions would not be accepted for a long time, and that it would thus be risky to anticipate them individually. So much distance travelled, following the little star of hope!

* Trans. by Barbara Estelle Beaumont, OP

THE CHURCH'S SACRAMENTAL CELEBRATION OF THE EASTER MYSTERY YVES M. J. CONGAR AND ECUMENICAL LITURGICAL PERSPECTIVES

Bruno Bürki

Formerly Professor of Theology
University of Fribourg, Switzerland

I. INTRODUCTION

It is unthinkable that a commemoration of Père Congar be made, without hearing a Protestant voice, and likewise a voice from the Reformed and Calvinist traditions. Congar's fundamental ecclesiological viewpoint — as articulated in *Jalons pour une théologie du laïcat*[1] — is so challenging for the reformed concept of the Church, that comparisons must be made, without however, neglecting discussion about differences. Congar's personal destiny in the institutional context of his own Church was very similar to that lived by several Fathers of the Protestant Reformation, so sympathy was spontaneous. There is no question however, of our appropriating Yves Congar — Protestants that we are. Our wish, rather — at the heart of Protestantism — is to meet the challenges of Congar the Catholic theologian, on important points in ecclesiology

---

[1] Yves Congar, *Jalons pour une théologie du laïcat*, Unam Sanctam, 23 (Paris: Cerf, 1953). See 3rd ed., rev. with additions and corrections, 1964. Translated into several languages.

and liturgy. Father Yves Congar, now deceased, still has things to tell us, both from his own point of view and in the Church to which he belonged.

Having been one of Congar's students (at least for a few weeks) at the Lutheran Centre of Ecumenical Studies in Strasbourg,[2] just after the Second Vatican Council, I feel today invited to lend my ear to what he has to say. As a student of liturgy and ecumenism at the time, I had available to me the most recent Council documents, especially those on the liturgy and on the Church, *Sacrosanctum concilium* and *Lumen gentium*, together with Aimé-Georges Martimort's manual *L'Église en prière* in its post-conciliar edition.[3] The personality of Congar fascinated me at the time, as indeed did that of many others. His teaching was an inspiration, as was that of several non-Catholic observers participating in the Council, in particular the Danish Lutheran Kristen Ejner Skydsgaard and Oscar Cullmann.

I am still convinced that Yves Congar's ecclesiological questionings can and, may I say, ought to contribute to the reform of worship, Protestant or Reformed, so that it may bear fruit. I intend in fact, to highlight the importance of Congar's theology with regard to liturgy and in an ecumenical perspective — given the impossibility of dealing with his treatment of ecumenism as a

---

[2] An article by Congar was published in the first annals of the Centre: "Composantes et idée de la Succession Apostolique," *Oecumenica*, ed. F. W. Kantzenbach and V. Vajta (Gütersloh: G. Mohn, 1966). See "Protestants et catholiques s'interrogent: Réponse du P. Y. Congar au Pasteur J. L. Leuba," *Le courage des lendemains* (Paris: Centurion, 1966) 98-113. In 1964, Congar wrote in the golden book of our Institute at Fribourg in Switzerland: "Happy to have been able to visit the Institute of ecumenical studies of the University of Fribourg ... I believe in theology. I believe in ecumenism. I believe in a living relationship between the two."

[3] Aimé-Georges Martimort, *L'Église en prière: principes de la liturgie*, 3rd ed. (Paris/Tournai: Desclée, 1965), ed. rev. and corrected by Martimort and the French promoters of the Catholic liturgical reform.

whole. It will be our method of reviving or deepening the ecumenical perspective, which many claim to be stagnant. I think that
ecumenism needs to address the broader issues of principle which
divide — or rather — unite Christians. This is what I want to illustrate, taking the liturgy as an example. I am convinced that worship
in the Reformed tradition, has an ecumenical calling to come into
contact with Catholic liturgy.

We know that Père Congar was not a professional liturgist. His
field was ecclesiology and ecumenism based on a new vision of the
Church. In this context however, the Catholic theologian could not
avoid treating of the liturgy of the Church.[4] In the period following Vatican II, he was led to speak more emphatically about it, and
it is this fundamental contribution that I wish to analyse, always in
the context of the ecclesial celebration of the liturgy. This celebration is of necessity sacramental, carried along by the Word and
sacramental signs, signifying Christ who died and rose again for the
salvation of the world. The liturgical celebration includes all the
faithful. Congar's contribution was heard in the Catholic Church as
it was in ecumenical dialogue. I am thinking here more explicitly
of the dialogue between Catholics and Protestants, Reformed or of
Calvinistic origin in Western Europe.

II. For an Ecclesial Foundation to Worship

In the important work *La liturgie après Vatican II* which Père Congar edited (with his *confrère* J. P. Jossua), the introduction claims

[4] Thus, "singing" for "the divine liturgy as an expression of the Church" in
Congar, *La Tradition et les traditions: Essai théologique* (Paris: Fayard, 1963)
183-191. The liturgy celebrates and communicates the God-human person relationship "biblically, Christologically and universally" (187). In the 2000 or so
titles of his bibliography, there are certainly explicit liturgical subjects, but these
are rare and for the most part, occasional.

that liturgy is as it were, "a manifestation of the Church."[5] Consequently, it would be impossible to treat of the liturgy, without taking into consideration its ecclesial foundations, bringing us right into ecumenical theology. To follow the intuitions of Père Congar implies in fact, in each ecclesial community and for all the Churches together, in a concrete ecumenical effort, the consideration of the nature and purpose of worship, which is founded on the very essence of the Church.

Père Congar considered that the promoters of church reform in the liturgical movement were over hasty and too exclusively preoccupied with restoring and innovating liturgical forms, without sufficient consideration of the raison d'être or the "original nature of Christian worship."[6] This applies to all the other confessions as it does to the Catholic Church which was Congar's prior concern. He placed special emphasis on the second half of the 20th century. At a period in a hurry for concrete realizations — though conscious at the same time of the urgency of reforms and modernizations — a time particularly anxious to be seen as efficacious, renovations and reforms were introduced without sufficient thought being given to the whole purpose of the Church's liturgy. What was missing and what is still missing in the different churches, meeting as far as possible in a common ecumenical endeavour, is a theology of liturgy which has both an ecclesial foundation and liturgical inspiration. It means in effect, to take up Congar's expression, articulating the liturgy as manifestation of the Church of Jesus Christ. What is it that makes our worship that of the Church of Christ, not

---

[5] Yves Congar, "Introduction," *La liturgie après Vatican II: Bilans, études prospective*, ed. Yves Congar and Jean-Pierre Jossua, Unam Sanctam, 66 (Paris: Cerf, 1967) 11-15. Our quotation 11. See id., "L'Eucharistie et l'Église de la Nouvelle Alliance," *Vie Spirituelle* 82 (1950) 347-372.

[6] Congar, "Introduction," *La liturgie après Vatican II*, 15.

only a community assembly, religious in the broad sense, multi-
functional or reaching out in many directions, but in truth the very
essence of the Church of Christ who died and rose from the dead?
As faithful followers, or simply as students of Congar, let us try
then, to examine the foundations of an ecclesial theology of the
liturgy, before launching into a critique of its ever-changing rituals, often arbitrary and too often pure fantasy.

Congar acknowledges that the early promoters of the liturgical
movement — and we think here of Romano Guardini or Odo Casel,
but also of the French language promoters, Dom Lambert Beauduin
and Fr Bernard Botte — had this fundamental unease.[7] With these
we might mention the German Lutheran Peter Brunner, who in the
fifties elaborated "the doctrine of worship by the assembly united
in the name of Jesus."[8] With reference to the Constitution on the
Liturgy of Vatican II, Congar judges that it "supposes resolved
rather than in need of being addressed," this question at the very
heart of Christian worship.[9] The supposition was however evident
by reason of the liturgy's grounding in the Paschal Mystery of
Christ which the liturgy is called upon to actualise. But perhaps
the effective statements or principles expounded in the first chapter of *Sacrosanctum concilium* were insufficiently measured. The
document's aim was to arrive as soon as possible at the "practical
norms" in order to renew and restore the liturgy.

With regard to Congar himself, I think that the bulk of his reflection on the Church provides a solid foundation for a theological

---

[7] Their studies comprise the centre of the collection *Lex Orandi* and of the
review *La Maison-Dieu* (see the *Tables générales*, no. 200) since 1945.

[8] *Zur Lehre vom Gottesdienst der im Namen Jesu versammelten Gemeinde* the
title of his fundamental contribution to *Leiturgia: Handbuch des evangelischen
Gottesdienstes*, vol. I, ed. Karl Ferdinand Müller and Walter Blankenburg (Kas-
sel: Stauda, 1954) 83-364.

[9] Congar, "Introduction," *La liturgie après Vatican II*, 15.

grounding as to what liturgy really is. The nature of the Church prefigures its liturgy, which is far from being an accessory activity, destined to please or be modified according to what the actors of the moment deem appropriate. This fundamentally Catholic conviction of Congar corresponds in a striking manner to the original understanding of worship in the Reformation Churches, Calvinist or reformed as well as Lutheran for which worship is of divine institution in the Church of Christ. The creeds as well as the catechisms of the Reformation Churches are all at one on this matter.[10] Congar is both witness and herald for the rooting of this approach to worship in the theological depths of Revelation. It is not in the external and accidental forms of worship that Christians are invited to meet and found their unity, but above all in worship which is a gift from God, with the Church, and in the body of Christ. The Christian Church neither imagines nor improvises the modes of worship which its ceremonial may assume today or tomorrow. Rather it enters liturgically into the manifestation of its very essence, which is that of Christ's Body. If we affirm today — what was already thought in Congar's time — that liturgy or worship are a *Gestaltungsaufgabe* for ministers and the faithful in celebration, one ought not to imagine that this celebration would degenerate into *freihändig* action, hands aloft or without basic tenets.[11]

---

[10] See *Confessions et catéchismes de la foi réformée*, ed. Olivier Fatio with Introduction by Gabriel Widmer (Geneva: Labor et Fides, 1986). See, for example, article 28 of *La Confession de foi des Églises réformées de France, Known as La Rochelle* (1559), *ibidem*, 124. See *Confessiona Augustana*, art. 7 *Die Bekenntnisschriften der evangelisch-lutherischen Kirche*, 2nd ed. (1952) 61; *La foi des Églises luthériennes*, ed. Andre Birmele and Marc Lienhard (Paris: Geneva: Cerf/Labor et Fides, 1991) 46-47.

[11] On the Protestant side, see Alfred Ehrensperger, "Die Gottesdienstreform der evangelisch-reformierten Zürcher Kirche von 1960-1970 und ihre Wirkungsgeschichte," *Liturgie in Bewegung/Liturgie en mouvement*, ed. Bruno Bürki and Martin Klöckener (Fribourg/Geneva: Universitätsverlag/Labor et Fides, 2000)

It has its foundation on what has been given to the Church in its very being which is Christ's Body. This indeed is what implies the affirmation that a liturgy which is the manifestation of the Church's essence — an essence which is a gift of God and eschatological vocation, not merely traditional or institutional property. The Church belongs to the Lord explicitly in its celebration of the mystery of the Lord Jesus Christ, and not to itself, nor to the men and women who compose the People of God.

It is not without importance that Père Congar — in his Introduction and in the idea of the book on the liturgy after Vatican II which he edited — was equally attentive to the anthropological suppositions of the liturgy as he was to its grounding in ecclesiology.[12] One section of the book is entitled "L'homme de la liturgie" and includes an important chapter written by M. D. Chenu on liturgical anthropology. In this context, Congar mentions the role of signs in liturgical celebration, and these include gestures and symbols as well as signs that are verbal. The rooting of liturgy in the human condition is just as important as its rooting in the Church. To celebrate the mystery of Christ Son of God become man in order to reassemble in his body the children of God, there is no question here of an alternative, but of indispensable complementarity. On the ecumenical front, there is an important dialogue to be entered into between Catholics and Protestants, on the role and

192-205. Then the recent *Agende* of the Lutheran and United churches of Germany *Evangelisches Gottesdienstbuch* (Berlin: Evangelische Haupt-Bibelgesellschaft/von Cansteinsche Bibelanstalt, 1999) with *Grundformen* models and a chapter *Gottesdienstgestaltung in offener Form*, 204-238.

[12] Congar, "Introduction," *La liturgie après Vatican II*, 12f. followed by all Part 3 of the work, "L'homme de la liturgie," 157-238. See Jean-Pierre Jossua, *Le Père Congar: la théologie au service du peuple de Dieu*, Chrétiens de tous les temps, 20 (Paris: Cerf, 1967) 143-157 on Congar's "great theological options" among which "Theology for the human person and anthropology for God."

place of signs and of human realities in the liturgical life of the Church. Père Congar rightly mentions this in his Introduction.

The Protestant coming from the Calvinist tradition would like to ask another question of Père Congar: what is the role of the Holy Spirit in this context of the basis of liturgy? The question is posed to the master of a theological and especially ecclesiological work where the Holy Spirit plays a major role.[13] In the document on the liturgy of Vatican II, pneumatology does not appear to be conspicuous. On the contrary, we know how pride of place was accorded to the Spirit in the theology of the Eastern Fathers, and after them to all Oriental theology.[14] Since the post-Vatican liturgical reform and the corresponding liturgical movement in the Protestant world, the epiclesis prayer for the descent of the Holy Spirit on the liturgy and on those who are present, has become an important element in all the Churches. Père Congar himself underlines — in a preface to the collection for his colleague in the Reformed Church, Jean-Jacques Von Allmen — that there should be no distance between the Christological and the pneumatological reality in the liturgy.[15] Furthermore, the charismatic dynamic plays its role in contemporary liturgy in many of the Churches

[13] See in particular "Le Saint-Esprit et le Corps apostolique, réalisateurs de l'œuvre du Christ," *Revue des sciences philosophiques et théologiques* 36 (1952) 613-625 and 37 (1953) 24-48. "L'Esprit-Saint dans l'Église," *Lumière et vie* 10 (1953) 51-74. *Je crois en l'Esprit Saint*, 3 vols. (Paris: Cerf, 1979-80). See also *Initiation à la pratique de la théologie*, ed. B. Lauret and F. Refoule (Paris: Cerf, 1982), II: 493-510 on "eschatological pneumatology" and "The Spirit ... breath of the Word." See further the contribution of Richard McBrien to this volume.

[14] Théodore Strotmann, "Pneumatologie et liturgie," *La liturgie après Vatican II*, 289-314. And Georges Wagner, *La liturgie, expérience de l'Église: Études liturgiques*, Analecta Sergiana, 1 (Paris: Presses Saint-Serge, 2003) 57-66, in a text entitled "Le Saint Esprit, force de révélation et d'accomplissement" (original German: *Erfahrung und Theologie des Heiligen Geistes*, 1974).

[15] Congar in the "Prologue" to *Communio sanctorum: Mélanges J. J. von Allmen* (Geneva: Labor et Fides, 1982) 23f. He alluded to Von Allmen's inaugural

which we represent.[16] The Reformer that I am is thinking of the role which the Holy Spirit has played both as mediator and presence in Calvinist theology from its beginnings, and to which we alluded in our second paragraph.[17] Must we remain anchored in differing appreciations, or may we not call for a common theology of the liturgy which will be completely Trinitarian and consequently pneumatological?

III. HOLY AND LITURGICAL MEDIATION IN JESUS CHRIST

I am now going to refer to Congar's masterly study at the end of the volume on *La liturgie après Vatican II* which he entitled: "Situation du sacré en régime chrétien."[18] In our ecumenical context, we suggest placing beside these pages the Preface written by Père Congar for the volume dedicated to his colleague, our professor of ecclesiology and liturgy, the Reformed pastor Jean-Jacques von Allmen, to whom I have already made reference. It is a question of understanding what is meant by: Christ is given (or transmitted), handed over (if we dare use the term employed by St. Paul in Romans 8:32) in the dual form of Word and sacrament. What is the mediation between God and men or women in the body of Christ that constitutes the Church?[19]

In "Situation du sacré en régime chrétien," Congar reminds us first of all — with citations from biblical texts from the Old and the

talk at Neuchâtel on "The Holy Spirit and Worship," in his collection of studies *Prophétisme sacramental* (Neuchâtel: Delachaux & Niestlé 1964) 287-311.

[16] See Jürgen Moltmann, *Kirche in der Kraft des Geistes* (Munich: Kaiser, 1975) 287-302. In French: *L'Église dans la force de l'Esprit* (Paris: Cerf, 1980) 389-361 on "worship as messianic feast."

[17] Jean Cadier, "La doctrine calviniste de la sainte cène," in *Études théologiques et religieuses* 25 (1951) 52-66.

[18] Congar, *La liturgie après Vatican II*, 385-403.

[19] *Communio sanctorum* (quoted footnote 15), 19-24.

New Testaments — that Revelation had rendered obsolete what was held in the world of religions, between what is sacred — reserved to the divinity and to relations with it — and what is profane, or remaining outside of this relationship. Already for the Septuagint and a fortiori for the New Testament, everything is consecrated to God. According to the Gospel, the entire life of the Christian is sacred, with the exception of sin which would profane it anew. This new statute is inscribed however, in the living out of salvation history: Christ has already redeemed the world, but the world still awaits the eschatological fulfilment of the already definitive redemption. In this time of the "economy of grace," we discern by faith the new reality of the body of Christ according to its three modes which in the New Testament are: "the personal body of Jesus henceforth glorified in heaven," the "eucharistic body" and "the ecclesial body, at once identifiable and partially unknown."[20] It is precisely in this economy of grace that liturgical mediation functions, using the signs or symbols confided to believers. By signs, that is, the Word and the sacraments we touch Christ's transforming presence, enabling us to live the new reality, the final accomplishment, the eschatology of salvation. In the words of Congar: "The Eucharist is here the supreme case: in it, a little wheat transformed into bread and a few grapes become wine through the work of human hands, are assumed not only functionally, but substantially."[21] In Christ there is communion between God and humankind. The body of Christ becomes present in this world as it is in its transcendence before God.

Père Congar is highly critical here of the intransigence or radical stance of the "Calvinist or neo-Calvinist" position which maintains a dualism between faith and the world, deeming impossible

[20] Congar, *La liturgie après Vatican II*, 396ff.
[21] *Ibid.*, 398.

any real mediation. The body of Christ is never truly present, neither on the altar nor in the structure of the Church, but always in
the act of becoming. The essence of the Church is its mission. From
this point of view, the idea of happening or "functionalism" is in
danger of restricting us to the "unveiling of the meaning of this
present world," whereas we are called upon to lay hold of the grace
of the world to come.[22]

Previously, in a biblical study of the history of theology in the
context of inter-confessional dialogue, Père Congar had already set
about pointing out the concordance between faith and presence or
sacramental communication.[23] This text was composed in 1962 or
a short time beforehand, and thus at a time when the Council's
Constitution on the Liturgy had not as yet been finalized. The starting point was the chapter in St. John's gospel on the Bread of Life
(John 6). Congar's study concluded with the theme of the two
tables of Scripture and the Eucharist, formulated by Thomas à
Kempis in *The Imitation of Christ*, on the basis of patristic and
scholastic theology, and which are now accorded the familiar role

[22] *Ibid.*, 396f. It is obviously important to distinguish Calvin's teaching on the
Last Supper in its original form (expressed chiefly in *Institutio christianae reli-
gionis*, IV, 17 and in the *Petit traité de la sainte cène*, *Opera selecta*, I, ed. Petrus
Barth, et al. (Munich: Kaiser, 1926) 499-530 from Congar's appreciation of
Calvinism. The Eucharist is for Calvin the act of personal communion between
Christ raised in glory, and the faithful living by faith which is a gift of God, with
the Holy Spirit bridging the distance. The sacrament is a real and efficient sign,
according to the teaching of Saint Augustine. Christ's presence is the work of the
Holy Spirit. Besides Jean Cadier's study mentioned above, see the article
"Eucharist" by B. A. Gerrish in *The Oxford Encyclopedia of the Reformation*, ed.
Hans J. Hillerbrand (New York/Oxford: Oxford University Press, 1996) II: 71-
81.
[23] "Les deux formes du pain de vie dans l'Évangile et dans la tradition,"
Parole de Dieu et Sacerdoce: Études pour Mgr. Weber (Paris: Desclée, 1962),
reproduced in Yves Congar, *Sacerdoce et laïcat devant leurs tâches d'évangélisation et de civilisation* (Paris: Cerf, 1962) 123-159.

in *The Constitution on the Sacred Liturgy*, and in Catholic liturgy since its post-conciliar reform. In opposition to a Protestant tradition, and more especially that of the Reformed, tending as it does to isolate faith from the support of the sacrament, and making communication between God and men or women wholly dependant on the Word, Congar's aim was to show that since God's revelation in the incarnation of the Son of God, faith causes us to "touch God efficaciously."[24] The sacraments are thus a continuation of the presence of the incarnate Word. According to Catholic belief and to Eastern tradition, but also in the thinking of several modern Protestant theologians, (he makes particular mention of the Scottish Presbyterian, then Indian Leslie Newbigin[25] and of the Franco-Swiss Reformed Franz-J. Leenhardt[26]), the sacrament brings an added element "to the actuality of the Word and of the faith," given that Word and faith are also part of the sacrament.[27]

Where do we stand today in this regard? And in particular, what is our position with regard to liturgical mediation as conceived in Protestantism, whether it is in the Reformed or Presbyterian Churches? I imagine that Père Congar in his declining years would have been happy to see integrated the celebration of reformed eucharist into a memorial of salvation history. The actuality is that of newly-reformed liturgies, especially that proposed to the Reformed churches of French-speaking Switzerland.[28] Here there

[24] *Ibid.*, 131.

[25] Leslie Newbigin, *The Household of God* (London: SCM, 1953).

[26] Franz-J. Leenhardt, *Ceci est mon corps* (Neuchâtel/Paris: Delachaux & Niestlé, 1955).

[27] "Les deux formes du pain de vie dans l'Évangile et dans la tradition," 143.

[28] *Liturgie à l'usage des Églises réformées de la Suisse romande: Communauté de travail des Commissions romandes de liturgie*, 2 vols. ([NP]: 1979-1986). For the Eucharistic Prayer, vol. II (*Liturgie du dimanche pour le temps ordinaire*), 222-239. See also, *Liturgie: Église réformée de France* (Paris, 1963) 36-42. As back-up, the report presented for "Foi et Constitution (*Faith and*

is clearly more than a rather formal flashback to Christ's institution of the eucharist as if it were to the action of some distant founder, and the request for fruitful communion of the faithful assembled for worship that is occasionally sacramental, and not exclusively a service of the Word. In the newly-reformed liturgy, there is at the heart of the celebration, both eucharistic prayer and sacramental communion by the body of the faithful. In the liturgical anamnesis, today's Church becomes contemporaneous with and participates in the saving and redemptive action of the Pasch of Jesus Christ. In the epiclesis or invocation of the Holy Spirit on the faithful with their gifts of bread and wine, God is petitioned to actualize salvation already bestowed here and now. Christ is present in his body. The "perpetual memorial" is accomplished while awaiting "the day when he will come in his glory." As in the Catholic Mass, the holy eucharist is a celebration of the mystery of Christ, a celebration that is truly actual and not merely commemorative words on the cross. A recalling of the institution of the memorial, and a waiting for the world-to-come, address each other in the Church's celebration. The rediscovery in contemporary theology of the depth and dynamism of the anamnesis/memorial at the heart of the biblical tradition, has helped to pass beyond a purely formal or functional symbolism found among the Moderns.[29] It is not a mere elevation of the hearts of believers to the one who is forever with the Father in glory, but Christ is really present in the Church.

Order)" of the Ecumenical Council of the Churches by Jean-Jacques von Allmen, *Essai sur le Repas du Seigneur* (Neuchâtel: Delachaux et Niestlé, 1966).

[29] Here we would like to acknowledge with gratitude, the pioneering and prophetic work furnished by Max Thurian's study of biblical and liturgical theology: *L'Eucharistie, Mémorial du Seigneur: Sacrifice d'action de grâce et d'intercession* (Neuchâtel/Paris: Delachaux & Niestlé, 1959). On its publication Père Congar paid homage to it, honouring it with critical appreciation in the extract entitled: "Un théologien réformé traite de l'eucharistie," *Chrétiens en dialogue* (Paris: Cerf, 1964), 519-526.

The sacrament is a celebration of communion in the body of Christ — an act of thanksgiving for all that has been accomplished in Christ is equally important in this regard, as is the final coming of the Saviour. Each eucharistic celebration is an ecclesial celebration of the history of salvation, history of the Triune God with the men and women he has chosen to be children of God, bearers of salvation and of grace.

The Reformed Genevan theologian, Henry Mottu — ecumenically inspired by the prophetic Lutheran Dietrich Bonhoeffer — has recently written an essay on how a Protestant might celebrate the sacraments. His essay was entitled "Le geste prophétique."[30] Mottu is aware of the weakness in sacramental theology which weighs on his church of the Reformed tradition. On this subject, he is at one with Père Congar. The Reformation Churches have an urgent need to re-establish communication by gestures and symbols, and this in order to help our contemporaries from being won over easily by the ambiguities of a diffuse religiosity and a return to a vague sort of religion. Christians cannot do without religious expressions. At the same time, the mature person must not revert to superstitious gestures which belong to pagans or non-believers. Sacramental practice must correspond to the grace of God which is a costly grace. "The presence of Christ at the eucharist is an efficacious actual presence which manifests itself *in the very accomplishment of the action.*" The sacraments have a community function, and their continuity is especially ethical — here we note the influence of a witness such as Dietrich Bonhoeffer. "The sacraments are the sacraments *of God*, not of the Church, for humanity."[31] And for Mottu, it is vital that the sacraments be placed in an eschatological perspective which characterizes the Christian life.

---

[30] *Le geste prophétique: Pour une pratique protestante des sacraments* (Geneva: Labor et Fides, 1998).

[31] Both quotations from Mottu, *Le geste prophétique*, 248 and 249.

Mottu speaks of a "ritual of waiting" and of "prophetic ritual." He is conscious of what he is saying when he writes: "For we *do not know* where the sacraments are leading us."[32]

All of this can rightly be placed within the liturgical perspective which we have outlined, and which Père Congar would have rejoiced to see shared more and more by the whole Church. As proof of this, I have a text written by Congar when in the nineteen forties he was a prisoner of war in Germany, on preaching and a liturgy which would be "real." He thought about and wished for "a liturgy that would really be consumed into the human heart."[33]

Nevertheless, in Mottu's thinking, there is an insistence on and a shifting of emphasis towards actualization, essentially an ethical consideration, which Congar would have been at pains to follow without reserve. For Congar, at the heart of the liturgical celebration, there is fully and explicitly, confession of the unique mystery whose founder is Jesus Christ. As for the Constitution on the Sacred Liturgy of the Second Vatican Council, the liturgy is the realization of the work of redemption of humankind and the glorification of God, grafted on to the Paschal Mystery of Christ.[34] Thus at the heart of the liturgy, there is baptism in the name of Jesus together with the celebration of the Church's eucharist. For Mottu, in the research of gestures for humanity of today and tomorrow, things are much more open "Jesus is present ... *by the action which makes him present*, at the very moment and for the future ... *we cannot lay hold of the real presence of Christ outside of this gestation.*"[35]

---

[32] *Ibid.*, 256.

[33] "Pour une liturgie et une prédication 'réelles'," *La Maison-Dieu* no 16 (1948) 75-87, reprinted in *Sacerdoce et laïcat devant leurs tâches d'évangélisation et de civilisation* (Paris: Cerf, 1962) 161-173. The reference in this collection, 166.

[34] *Sacrosanctum concilium*, paras. 5-8.

[35] Mottu, *Le geste prophétique*, 118f.

In a definition which Mottu wishes to underline, the prophetic gesture is clearly determined by "*the humanity of God in Christ Jesus*"[36] — I presume that Congar would have wished for a more explicit Christological expression. As for Mottu, he employs the term utopia in connection with the sacrament. And he explicitly affirms, I mean of course in relation to the Roman Catholic eucharistic liturgy (at the moment when the eucharistic gifts are being prepared): "The holy eucharist does not celebrate 'the sacrifice of the whole Church'; it announces the Kingdom which has yet to come."[37] The alternative would be a problem for Catholic theology which conceives of — as does Congar — a liturgical celebration which is more comprehensive or global, in short, more Catholic. A certain distrust about what the Church believes and accomplishes here and now in the actual liturgical celebration separates a form of Protestantism held by Mottu and the Catholic vision of things, the liturgy in particular.

Thus we constantly remain in a certain opposition between being and becoming, between the ecclesiastical institution and the prophetic project, between the Church as institution and a community on the march. The question I would wish to ask of the one and the other is: will the ideas and new theological and ecumenical instruments be able to free us one day from the impasse or "confessional" alternative? Père Congar is no longer here to answer that, so the question must be put to all of us.

IV. CELEBRATION BY ALL THE FAITHFUL

Père Congar's title on "la communauté chrétienne, sujet intégral de l'action liturgique" echoes like the sound of a trumpet. At the end

---

[36] *Ibid.*, 164.
[37] *Ibid.*, 255.

of this chapter of prime importance for *La liturgie après Vatican II*, Congar cleverly translates "sujet intégral" by the Greek term "plérôme."[38] He assumes of course the demand for the full and active participation of the faithful in the liturgy which was one of the principal objectives of the Constitution on the Liturgy of Vatican II. But Congar is anxious for a theological deepening of the demand which at first seems to belong to the pastoral or functional order, but which is in reality a basic principle of the Church's liturgical celebration of the *Ecclesia*, as Congar liked to term it. On this level, the Catholic theologian of Vatican II refers to the idea of the Protestant Reformation, which Martin Luther in particular articulated, in speaking of the common priesthood of all the baptized.[39] With reference to a contemporary theologian of the Reformed tradition, both ecclesiologist and liturgist, and possessed of a similar prophetic enthusiasm, we find the same preoccupation. I refer of course to Jean-Jacques von Allmen. He began his basic study, entitled — in a programmatic fashion — *Célébrer le salut*, by a chapter which dealt with worship as "manifestation of the Church" and towards the end of the book with a lengthy discourse on "worship's partners": the Lord, the faithful, the angels, the world and its sighs.[40] Let us see how things developed on this level, all the time from an ecumenical point of view.

---

[38] *La liturgie après Vatican II*, 241-282.

[39] See the act of worship presented by an American Lutheran Gordon W. Lathrop, "Gottesdienst im lutherischen Kontext," *Handbuch der Liturgik*, ed. Hans-Christoph Schmidt-Lauber, et al., 3rd ed. (Göttingen: Vandenhoeck & Ruprecht, 2003) 151-159. On the particular question of *Allgemeines Priestertum* the article Luise Schorn-Schütte, "Lutheran Offices," *The Oxford Encyclopedia of the Reformation*, I: 332-335. The idea however, looks first of all at the exercise of authority in the Church, and is not primarily liturgical or sacramental.

[40] Jean-Jacques von Allmen, *Célébrer le salut: Doctrine et pratique du culte chrétien* (Geneva/Paris: Cerf, 1984) 37-60 and 223-252. The first chapter that I mention here, beginning with a reminder of the statute of the Church, the

Congar's text is an exposition of what is perhaps the most convincing and the most explicit for our discussion: here the ecclesiologist or the theologian of the Church directly becomes liturgist, and the liturgist honours the theologian of the Church — *maître en théologie* (a title accorded to Congar within his Order) and "friar preacher." Strongly supported by biblical witnesses from both Testaments, together with preaching from the Fathers, Congar reminds us that "the Church is Spouse; the Church is Mother; the Church is Temple"[41] and as such, the "we" of the praying assembly, united in the liturgy, accomplishes the celebration. "The Holy Spirit is in effect, the principle of our communion with Christ, and in Christ among ourselves ... principle in virtue of which the faithful are bonded into *ecclesia* and are ... the subject of liturgical actions."[42] Congar then evokes the disappearance in traditional Catholicism since the Middle Ages, of the original vision of the Church — a celebrating communion — in an institution which dispenses its means of grace. He also judges as insufficiently adequate the reaction of the Reformers, in the essay on the constitution which in the Protestant world is known since as *Gemeinde*.[43]

In his synthesis,[44] Congar points to the founding of Catholic liturgical action on Christological ecclesiology of the encyclical *Mystici Corporis* (1943). Again during the papacy of Pius XII the encyclical *Mediator Dei* (1947), a veritable fore-runner of the Council's theology, had already based itself on this concept: in the liturgy, the faithful are seized upon to be participants of the very mystery of Christ. Now however, after the conciliar Constitutions

Assembly of the Lord, is a more recent development of liturgical theology, already treated in our first paragraph.

[41] *La liturgie après Vatican II*, 257.
[42] *Ibid.*, 259.
[43] *Ibid.*, 265f.
[44] *Ibid.*, 268-282: "Synthèse actuelle de la doctrine traditionnelle."

Sacrosanctum concilium and *Lumen gentium* — the faithful have really become the celebrating community. They assume their liturgical ministry without in any way overshadowing (and vice versa) the ordained ministry of the one who, in the assembly, represents the head of the body, Christ himself. The Amen pronounced collectively by the faithful at the conclusion of the priestly eucharistic prayer, and individually on receiving communion from the hand of the minister, is the supreme example of liturgical propriety fully assumed by each member in the body of Christ.

The second last chapter of the manual of Liturgical and Pastoral Sciences by the Reform professor Jean-Jacques von Allmen, answers in a remarkable revision and an authentically creative development, the idea of Père Congar. I have already announced its plan and structure.[45] Von Allmen begins with the affirmation that the Church's worship indeed has God as object, but especially that it has the Lord as *subject* and that he is the chief partner. "Without God's presence, his action and his welcome, Christian worship would be a farce or a lie."[46] From the human side, it is obviously the baptized who are the bearers or celebrants of worship — all the baptized (including baptized infants). The entire body of the faithful is called to the entire act of worship, to that of each Sunday which normally ought to be a eucharistic celebration with communion of the faithful. The diverse ministries and charisms of the faithful are respectfully finding their place in the assembly. The commissioned or ordained ministers — in particular that of the president, bishop or priest, pastor as we prefer to name him/her, deacons — are assigned their place in the assembly according to

---

[45] The subject in question here is the chapter on "those who partake in worship," von Allmen, *Célébrer le salut*, 223-252. It is an important part of this book of approximately 300 pages.

[46] *Ibid.*, 224.

each one's particular role. Von Allmen is pleased to distinguish three particular liturgies: that of the head or pastor of the community; the liturgy of the people assembled, and as a link between the two, the liturgy of the deacon.[47] We might underline the fact that for von Allmen, participation in the liturgy of a local Church by members of a separated Church, is a real problem that is not only pastoral but ecclesial — this "problem" should be addressed with the institutional or disciplinary attention and the ecumenical consideration which it merits.[48]

I might mention finally that von Allmen considers the angels as liturgical companions of the faithful. But it is also a question — to do the rounds of liturgical requirements — of "the world and its sighs": time, space or natural elements such as water or light. Thus we see in a truly ecumenical perspective, how Congar's words on "the Church ... integral subject of liturgical action" can become concrete and actual in our midst. The imagined celebration, but especially that prepared and ordained by Pastor von Allmen, is a celebration of the whole, communion with the body of Christ, a celebration that is entirely Catholic in its dimension.[49]

---

[47] *Ibid.*, 229.

[48] Here Von Allmen in 1984, *ibid.*, 240-245, treats of the question which to this day remains a stumbling block. He pleads for non-active participation in the sacramental celebration of another Church from which his own is confessionally separated — without however excluding (or considering it a break in communion) "the possibility of eucharistic hospitality in another (Church) on the basis of a mature decision" (245). This corresponded to the proposition of the then Swiss Synod of Catholics, while those Churches belonging to the world grouping of Reformation churches, hold that the Table of the Lord is a welcome-place for all men and women who confess that Jesus Christ is Lord and Saviour. (Decision of World Alliance of Reformed Churches — WARC, in French *Alliance Réformée Mondiale — ARM*, at Princeton in 1954).

[49] Von Allmen, *Célébrer le salut*, 245-252. There is obvious contrast between "the angels, our liturgical companions" and "the world and its sighs" as Von

We can claim then, that this ecclesial and liturgical vision is in no way — as the incredulous person might put it — "a spiritual vision", but that it corresponds in specific places, to a reality lived by the local church. There is no question here of mere anecdote, but of clinging to what is concrete, which is likewise exemplary. The statement is valid for Neuchâtel where von Allmen lived, and for Strasbourg, where Père Congar spent a fruitful period of his life, as it was for the Church of Jerusalem according to the witness of the Acts of the Apostles (Acts 2:42-47). The theological reflection of Père Congar thus becomes — in an ecumenical context — an invitation or exhortation to constitute the assembly which prays and celebrates the Lord, by breaking bread, in order to assume the full vocation of the *Ecclesia communio*.

V. CONCLUSION

It is time to conclude with a text particularly rich, and to which Congar had given much thought. It was written in Jerusalem when he was fifty (the foreword is dated around the middle of the year 1954): *Le mystère du Temple*.[50] It consists of a series of biblical studies on the "gracious initiatives of God with a view to establishing his presence among men and with them."[51] What began at the time of the Patriarchs, led to the Church, the community which is the Temple of God, is realized in the eternity of God, in "the new Jerusalem which comes from on high." Congar's idea on the subject had its origins in his work *Jalons pour une théologie du laïcat*. By biblical references, he wished to highlight "the spiritual

---

Allmen liked to express it. Also, there is a marked difference of style between himself and Père Congar, though their thinking is quite similar.

[50] Congar, *Le Mystère du temple ou l'Économie de la présence de Dieu à sa créature de la Genèse à l'Apocalypse*, Lectio Divina, 22 (Paris: Cerf, 1958).

[51] *Ibid.*, 8.

and living temple which God not alone inhabits, but to which he communicates himself and from which he receives the worship of an entirely filial obedience."[52] The idea anticipates the fundamental thrust of *The Constitution on the Sacred Liturgy* of Vatican II.[53] There is no case here any more for debate about Catholicism or Protestantism, about ecumenism, or even about this or that idea as to what constitutes liturgy, but simply to make an act of faith in the divine presence among us, and so give glory to the Father by the Son in the Holy Spirit.

* Trans. by Marie-Humbert Kennedy, OP

---

[52] *Ibid.*, 7.
[53] *Sacrosanctum concilium*, paras 5-8.

CARDINAL CONGAR'S ECUMENISM
AN "ECUMENICAL ETHICS" FOR RECONCILIATION?

Gabriel FLYNN*

Lecturer in Theology
Mater Dei Institute of Education, a College of Dublin City University

I. ECUMENISM: THE TRIUMPH OF FAILURE

In this article, I consider the ecumenical heritage of Cardinal Yves M.-J. Congar, OP (1904-95), assessing how his ecumenism contributes to the difficult process of Christian reconciliation. His original and transformative contribution to the emergent ecumenical movement in the Catholic Church was part of a wide programme for the renewal of ecclesiology which culminated in the momentous achievement of the Second Vatican Council (1962-65). The Council became the catalyst for change in the Church, its relationship with the other Christian communions, and the world. As Congar commented: "For the first time in history, the Catholic Church is entering into the structure of dialogue."[1] Congar had a quite

---

* Revised version of a paper presented to the Religious Experience and Contemporary Theological Epistemology section of the "Louvain Encounters in Systematic Theology IV," Katholieke Universiteit, Leuven, 7 November 2003. Chair: Professor Mathijs Lamberigts, K.U., Leuven. See *Louvain Studies* 28 (2003) 311-325.

[1] Yves Congar, "The Council in the Age of Dialogue," trans. Barry N. Rigney, *Cross Currents* 12 (1962) 144-151, p. 151; also id., "Vœux pour le concile: enquête parmi les chrétiens," *Esprit* 29 (1961) 691-700, p. 699. See further Paul

definite idea of the close relationship between ecumenism and
ecclesiology. He always viewed the renewal of ecclesiology in conjunction with "wide participation in unitive activities."[2] In harmony with the spirit of a new era that was slowly dawning in inter-
church relations, a spirit he helped to create, Congar regarded his
vocation, from its inception in 1929, as being at once "ecclesiological and ecumenical (*unionique* [*sic*])."[3] He is lauded by the distinguished Dutch ecumenist Dr Willem Adolf Visser't Hooft (1900-
85), first secretary general of the World Council of Churches, as
"the father of Roman Catholic ecumenism."[4] In his *Memoirs*, Visser't Hooft points out that the Church in France was far ahead of
other countries in the field of ecumenism, with Congar as its leading exponent.[5] In the Catholic Church, however, he was regarded
with suspicion, and his eventual elevation to the College of Cardinals on 26 November 1994 came only months before his death at
the *Hôpital des Invalides* in Paris on 22 June 1995. It is important
to recognise that the perception of Congar in the Roman Curia was
for a long time indisputably ambiguous, a point clearly illustrated
in a recent work by his friend and fellow Dominican, the influential French liturgical scholar Father Pierre-Marie Gy who sadly
died on 20 December 2004. He recounts how a prominent Curia

VI, *Ecclesiam Suam: The Paths of the Church* (New York: America Press, 1964)
60-124.

[2] Congar, *Dialogue between Christians: Catholic Contributions to Ecumenism*,
trans. Philip Loretz (London: Geoffrey Chapman, 1966) 9; also id., *Chrétiens en
dialogue: contributions catholiques à l'œcuménisme*, Unam Sanctam, 50 (Paris:
Cerf, 1964) XVIII. Following the initial citation, the page numbers of works in
the original language will be given in parenthesis.

[3] Congar, *Journal d'un théologien (1946-1956)*, ed. Étienne Fouilloux and others, 2nd ed. (Paris: Cerf, 2001) 20. See id., *Une passion: l'unité*, Foi Vivante, 156
(Paris: Cerf, 1974) 14.

[4] W. A. Visser't Hooft, *Memoirs* (London/Philadelphia, PA: SCM/Westmin-
ster Press, 1973) 319.

[5] *Ibid.*, 320.

theologian, Antonio Piolanti, sometime Rector of the Lateran University in Rome,[6] was scandalised on learning that Congar had been named a *peritus* (expert) of the commission for theology in 1960.[7]

In the context of a personal testimony of his ecumenical experience and conversion, published in 1963, Congar situates ecumenism in an eschatological perspective. He writes: "Ecumenism is an effort to rediscover a unity amongst Christians in keeping at once with the unity of its beginnings in the Upper Room of the Last Supper and of Pentecost, and with that of its eschatological culmination."[8] It may be said that this proposed archetypal model of ecumenism is somewhat idealistic, imbued perhaps with the optimistic spirit of the epoch. This consideration gives rise in turn to the question of whether or not Congar, in his passionate desire to advance the cause of Church unity, inadvertently diminishes his own tradition by abandoning Catholicity as the standard of ecumenism, but without succeeding in his grand project to reconcile diversities — those unique elements, sacred to each tradition. So, is the goal of unity, Congar's vocation and life's work, an impossible one after all? Perhaps. Without accepting the *status quo*, and insisting, as he did, on an eschatological perspective in ecumenical dialogue, I hold

[6] See Congar, *Mon journal du Concile*, ed. and annotated Éric Mahieu, 2 vols. (Paris: Cerf, 2002) I: 26-27 (13-17 November 1960). Monsignor Piolanti claimed that since the Church of St John Lateran was the first of all the churches, likewise, the Lateran University should be the first of the universities. See further Gabriel Flynn, "*Mon journal du Concile*: Yves Congar and the Battle for a Renewed Ecclesiology at the Second Vatican Council," *Louvain Studies* 28 (2003) 48-70.

[7] See Pierre-Marie Gy, *The Reception of Vatican II: Liturgical Reforms in the Life of the Church* (Milwaukee, WI: Marquette University Press, 2003) 15.

[8] Congar, "Ecumenical Experience and Conversion: A Personal Testimony," *The Sufficiency of God*, ed. Robert C. Mackie and Charles C. West (London: SCM, 1963) 71-87, p. 83; also id., "Expérience et Conversion Œcuméniques" in Congar, *Chrétiens en dialogue*, 123-139, p. 135. This essay is not available in the English translation of *Chrétiens en dialogue*.

that the vocation to Christian ecumenism is nonetheless an ethical imperative for the Church. In the next section of this article, I consider the rationale of this proposed *modus operandi* for ecumenism. As regards the historical background to Congar's ecumenical vision, I want briefly to refer to its development.

Looking first to the origins of his ecumenical vocation, we find that the circumstances of his early life contributed significantly to its emergence. The way had been prepared by childhood relations with Protestants and Jews, contact with a Russian seminary at Lille, and a lecture given by his friend and mentor Marie-Dominique Chenu on the *Faith and Order* movement of Lausanne.[9] In the years 1927/30, he experienced the first great interior appeal to dedicate himself particularly to the Church and ecumenism.[10] The decisive point that set his course, however, was his retreat in preparation for ordination to the priesthood. As Congar notes:

> To prepare for ordination I made a special study both of John's Gospel and Thomas Aquinas' commentary on it. I was completely overwhelmed, deeply moved, by chapter 17, sometimes called the priestly prayer, but which I prefer to call Jesus' apostolic prayer on Christian unity: "That they may be one as we are one". My ecumenical vocation can be directly traced to this study of 1929.[11]

Following his ordination on 25 July 1930, Congar lost no time in acquainting his superiors with his desire to work for unity and was allowed to visit the principal places associated with the life of Martin Luther (1483-1546). During two visits to Germany in 1930 and

---

[9] See Congar, "Letter from Father Yves Congar, O.P.," trans. Ronald John Zawilla, *Theology Digest* 32 (1985) 213-216, p. 213. See further id., *Dialogue between Christians*, 3-4 (XII).

[10] Congar, "Reflections on being a Theologian," trans. Marcus Lefébure, *New Blackfriars* 62 (1981) 405-409, p. 405.

[11] Congar, "Letter from Father Yves Congar, O.P.," 213.

1931,[12] Congar came in contact with the Lutheran High Church movement. He also attended courses at the Protestant faculty of theology in Paris and became familiar with Karl Barth (1886-1968) and Oscar Cullmann (1902-99). Congar was prepared to give his life for the cause of ecumenism. This is clear from his comments regarding a Catholic understanding of Luther, to whom he was attracted from his earliest years in ecumenical dialogue.[13] He remarks:

> I looked into the question of Luther, whose writings I turn to, in one way or another, almost monthly. [...] I know that nothing really worthwhile with regard to Protestantism will be achieved so long as we take no steps truly to understand Luther, instead of simply condemning him, and to do him historical justice. For this conviction which is mine I would gladly give my life.[14]

Congar had regular meetings during the inter-war period with professors of the *Institut Saint-Serge*, the Orthodox faculty of theology in Paris, including Georges Florovsky, Serge Boulgakov and Leo Zander, a lay theologian.[15] Boris Bobrinskoy, Dean of the *Institut Saint-Serge*, in his address on the occasion of the launch of *Mon journal du Concile* in Paris on 27 September 2002, paid tribute to Congar in the name of the Orthodox Church:

> Father Congar has permanently marked this century [i.e., the twentieth century] and has inspired a theological and spiritual fermentation around the mystery of the one Church and of the division

[12] Congar, *Dialogue between Christians*, 5-6 (XIV-XV).

[13] *Ibid.*, 6 (XV).

[14] Congar, "Ecumenical Experience and Conversion: A Personal Testimony," 74 (126).

[15] See Boris Bobrinskoy, "Le P. Yves Congar et l'orthodoxie," *Istina* 48 (2003) 20-23. Bobrinskoy notes that *Mon journal du Concile* speaks little of the Orthodox and was surprisingly silent on Nicolas Afanassieff, whose Eucharistic vision of the Church had a certain influence on the reflection of the Fathers of the Council.

of Christians. I can say that the Orthodox theological renewal owes much to him and likewise the liturgical renewal at Solesmes or Maria-Laach, or the patristic renewal at "Sources chrétiennes".[16]

Congar also loved the Anglican Church, especially its liturgy. He was captivated by the charm of "evensong" and admired the inheritance and ethos of Anglicanism, but considered its ecclesiological situation to be weak.[17] In his opinion, the Anglican conception of unity failed to give due weight to the unity of faith and, critically, to the visible unity of the Church as the people of God.[18] Congar viewed Anglican theology, like the High Church idea itself, as humanist and nationalist. As he writes of the Church of England: "It seems to have accepted, on the plane of outward order and visible unity, the principle of differentiation, based on human variety and national or cultural diversity, in place of the ultimate universal principle of Catholic unity."[19]

But it was Protestantism which continued to be Congar's primary ecumenical interest. In 1937, he published *Chrétiens désunis: principes d'un "oecuménisme" catholique*, the chief advantage of which, in his view, was that "for the first time it attempted to define 'ecumenism' theologically or at least to put it in that context."[20] He considered the Incarnation to be the means of progress in ecumenical dialogue: "The Incarnation is the key to the whole mystery of the Church and the sacraments. In the degree to which Protestantism can school itself in a profound and realist

---

[16] *Ibid.*, 20.

[17] Congar, *Dialogue between Christians*, 16 (XXV-XXVI).

[18] Congar, *Divided Christendom: A Catholic Study of the Problem of Reunion*, trans. M. A. Bousfield (London: Geoffrey Bles, 1939), 181; also id., *Chrétiens désunis: principes d'un "œcuménisme" catholique*, Unam Sanctam, 1 (Paris: Cerf, 1937) 227.

[19] *Ibid.*, 195 (245).

[20] Congar, *Dialogue between Christians*, 25 (XXXVI).

contemplation of the mystery of the Incarnation will it return to the sphere of apostolic Christianity and prepare itself for reunion in the Church."[21] While the view of ecumenism as a return to Rome is, in some respects, untenable today, the ultimate goal of the ecumenical movement remains the re-establishment of full visible unity among all baptised Christians.[22] But it must be remembered that *Chrétiens désunis* was the first contribution in French to Catholic ecumenism and the first volume of the Unam Sanctam series. This was a new series founded by Congar in 1935, in conjunction with Éditions du Cerf, as part of a Church response to the challenge of modern unbelief. It was dedicated to the restoration of the genuine value of ecclesiology by means of a return to the ancient sources of Scripture and Tradition. Then in 1959, in a text originally published in German, Congar proposed a wide-ranging programme of theological study, with the objective of deepening ecumenical dialogue:

> A whole new chapter will have to be written on the fruit already gathered or made possible by the *Revertimini ad fontes!* [return to the sources] advocated by Pius X. One can only hope for an intensification of work and ecumenical dialogue on all the following subjects, the crucial character of which the above exposé was designed to demonstrate: Christology (and also mariology); redemption and creation, the will and the wisdom of God (analogy of faith and the analogy of being); the economy of salvation and communication or gift (*koinonia*). The kingship of Christ. The relation of his kingship to the world and to the Church, People of God and Body of Christ. What the authority is which Christ wields in his Church, in the midst of the world. The theology of: formal visibility of the Church, apostolicity, era of the Church, tradition, baptism, eucharist and Church. The

---

[21] Congar, *Divided Christendom*, 274-275 (344).

[22] See John Paul II, *Ut Unum Sint: Encyclical Letter of the Holy Father John Paul II on Commitment to Ecumenism* (London: Catholic Truth Society, 1995) par. 77.

Church as an institution and God's "actualism" (institution and event).[23]

From what has been said, it is evident that Congar was indefatigable in his commitment to the advancement of the cause of Church unity. In 1987, he described his involvement in the ecumenical movement in terms of vocation and concern. He writes: "Ecumenism has been my concern, I would even say my vocation, for a very long time; it is a vocation that I can date quite precisely from 1929, though it has antecedents, kinds of preparation in my childhood and youth."[24] As we have seen, his ecumenical vocation rests on profound personal religious experience, perhaps the best support on the difficult path of ecumenism. Congar places ecumenical experience and conversion in juxtaposition, a conviction he expresses as follows:

> It is a way of conversion. It asks not less faith, but more. [...] Ecumenism demands a profound moral and even religious conversion. [...] Ecumenism seeks also a reform within ourselves, for we are full of aggressiveness, clannishness and arrogance, of distrust and rivalry. We must be converted by detachment from all this and from ourselves, and acceptance of a humble submissiveness of what the Lord expects of us.[25]

Such lofty, noble sentiments are very well as far as they go. And even Congar acknowledges that ecumenism is not for everyone since, in his view, only the ecumenically minded can bring it

---

[23] Congar, *Dialogue between Christians*, 356-357 (434-435).

[24] Congar, *Fifty Years of Catholic Theology: Conversations with Yves Congar*, ed. Bernard Lauret, trans. John Bowden (London: SCM, 1988) 77; also id., *Entretiens d'automne*, 2nd ed. (Paris: Cerf, 1987) 99. See Claude Goure, "Conversation avec Yves Congar: un théologien dans le siècle," *Panorama*, 222 (1988) 49-53, p. 53.

[25] Congar, "Ecumenical Experience and Conversion: A Personal Testimony," 83-84 (133-135).

about.[26] So a difficult question arises: was he not naïve in the hoped for *rapprochement* of an earlier and more optimistic stage of dialogue? With the advantage of hindsight, and in light of recent Church history, it is difficult to conclude otherwise. But the attitude implicit in his proposed blueprint for ecumenical dialogue, so profoundly influenced by that of Pope John XXIII, is sound: "Only after eating together, praying and talking together, can the discussion of certain questions be approached in such a way that the other side is both heard and understood. Only then is there any real possibility of rapprochement."[27]

As its relatively short history demonstrates, the success of Christian ecumenism depends on a renewed ecclesiology and on an affective approach that contributes perhaps more than any other to the creation of an environment in which failures, past and present, can be turned into triumphs.[28] But such a course of action calls for an indomitable spirit in ecumenical dialogue, a spirit that must also be firmly rooted in reality. In this regard, I am convinced that the normally difficult experience of political dialogue in situations of violence, mistrust and betrayal provides inspiration and a new impetus for Christian ecumenism. There cannot be any doubt, therefore, that participants in ecumenical dialogue, like their political counterparts, also require fortitude. As the Catholic philosopher Josef Pieper reminds us: "Fortitude presupposes vulnerability; without vulnerability there is no possibility of fortitude."[29] The principal lesson of the present fragile peace in Northern Ireland,

---

[26] *Ibid.*, 82 (134).

[27] Congar, "Conquering Our Enmities," *Steps to Christian Unity*, ed. John A. O'Brien (New York: Doubleday, 1964) 100-109, p. 108.

[28] See Flynn, "The Role of Affectivity in the Theology of Yves Congar," *New Blackfriars* 83 (2002) 347-364; also id., "Le rôle de l'affectivité dans la théologie d'Yves Congar," trans. Jean Prignaud, *La Vie spirituelle* 157 (2003) 73-92.

[29] Josef Pieper, *The Four Cardinal Virtues: Prudence Justice Fortitude Temperance* (Notre Dame, IN: University of Notre Dame Press, 1966) 117.

for instance, is that of vulnerability. The architects of that dearly won peace, politicians and Church leaders, deserve respect for their courageous acceptance of vulnerability, and for their perseverance and fortitude.

Concerning the *praxis* of ecumenism, it can no longer be seen as optional or occasional. It is rather a moral imperative, not so much for the sake of the Church and its unity, as for the world and its salvation. It is important to bear in mind that the foregoing proposals are based on the vision of unity presented at the Second Vatican Council, which remains the model and norm for Catholic ecumenism. As we read in the decree on ecumenism, *Unitatis Redintegratio*: "The concern for restoring unity involves the whole Church, faithful and clergy alike. It extends to everyone, according to the talent of each, whether it be exercised in daily Christian living or in theological and historical studies."[30] Significantly, the Council proposes a practical, affective approach to ecumenism; that is, one based on love and a profound Christian concern for the other, and so it places an important obligation on Catholics to make the "first approaches" towards their "separated brethren."[31]

II. ECUMENISM: AN ETHICAL IMPERATIVE

Ecumenism is an ethical imperative for Christians. The acceptance of an anti-ecumenical or a pre-ecumenical state by any Christian denomination is tantamount to a rejection of Christ's call to unity.[21] And since disunity is a grave obstacle to belief in God, it would be both contradictory and disingenuous for Christians to remain

[30] "Decree on Ecumenism, Vatican II, *Unitatis Redintegratio*, 21 November 1964," *Vatican Council II: The Conciliar and Post Conciliar Documents*, ed. Austin Flannery, 7th ed. 2 vols (New York: Costello, 1984) I: 5.

[31] *Ibid.*, 4.

[32] See John 17:11b.

immured from the Gospel vision of unity and the concomitant moral obligation to engage in dialogue. Congar, in fact, identifies a decisive link between unbelief, as a consequence of the division of Christendom, and the significance of ecumenism for the future of the Catholic Church in a hostile world:

> Historically, the divisions among Christians, the fiercely cruel wars, carried out in the name of dogmatic differences, are largely responsible for the genesis of modern unbelief (Herbert of Cherbury, Spinoza, the *Philosophes* of the eighteenth century). Concretely, the division among Christians is a scandal for the world. The world is exonerated, to a degree, from the duty to believe.[33]

In a seminal article published in 1961, "Vœux pour le concile: enquête parmi les chrétiens," Congar stresses the importance of ecumenism for the future of the Church and the advancement of its mission in the world.[34] He was convinced that the face (*visage*) presented by the Catholic Church is crucial for evangelisation and also determines, in large measure, the hoped-for reconciliation between the Christian Churches.[35] An urgent task for the Second Vatican Council would, then, be the pursuit of unity, in order to redress the indifference and hostility which result directly from unbelief.[36]

Congar's vision for ecumenism was part of a grand plan for renewal and reform in the Church and in the world. In the overall framework of his ecclesiology, ecumenism rests within the widest possible setting. It has profound implications for theology, worship, and the Church's apostolic life. Congar, fully cognisant of inherent weaknesses in the Churches, identifies internal Church reform as a precondition of Christian unity, a point he articulates as follows: "It very soon occurred to me that ecumenism is not a

[33] Congar, "The Council in the Age of Dialogue," 148 (696).
[34] *Ibid.*, 146-148 (694-696).
[35] *Ibid.*, 146, 149-150 (694, 697-699).
[36] *Ibid.*, 148 (696).

speciality and that it presupposes a movement of conversion and reform co-extensive with the whole life of all communions."[37]

But it may be objected that Congar's vision of ecumenism has failed, while Christian unity remains an unrealised goal. This objection brings us to a very large and weighty problem: what are the possible consequences of stagnation or a breakdown in ecumenical dialogue? It is certain that the failure of ecumenism results in the sequential triumph of religious intolerance, racial discrimination and wars of religion. At the same time it should also be easy to understand that ecumenism appeared to a number of theologians to be a dangerous and seductive influence. In a doubtless salutary caveat issued in 1974, Congar observes that, with the Second Vatican Council, the Catholic Church "knows today a kind of *Aufklärung* [Ger. "Enlightenment"] which unquestionably brings it nearer to what is good, but also to what is more questionable, in Protestantism."[38] He accepts that it is legitimate to speak of "a 'Protestantisation' of the Catholic Church."[39] As evidence of this, he points to the use of the vernacular in the liturgy, the study of Scripture, collegiality, increased initiative on the part of local Churches, and the acceptance of lay charisms, which, he asserts, sometimes involve a diminution of the position of ordained priests.[40] While Congar sees these developments as more positive

[37] Congar, *Dialogue between Christians*, 21 (XXXI).

[38] Congar, *Une passion: l'unité*, 106.

[39] *Ibid.*, 104. See Congar, "A Last Look at the Council," *Vatican II by those who were there*, ed. Alberic Stacpoole (London: Geoffrey Chapman, 1986), 337-358, p. 353; also id., "Regard sur le Concile Vatican II à l'occasion du 20e anniversaire de son annonce," *Unterwegs zur Einheit: Festschrift für Heinrich Stirnimann*, ed. Johannes Brantschen and Pietro Selvatico (Freiburg: Herder, 1980), 774-790, p. 790.

[40] See Congar, *Une passion: l'unité*, 104-105. See further Flynn, "*Mon journal du Concile*: Yves Congar and the Battle for a Renewed Ecclesiology at the Second Vatican Council," 66-69.

than negative, nonetheless he echoes a warning which Karl Barth repeated to Catholics on more than one occasion during his last years: "Do not participate in the pathological experiences that we have undergone and from which we have emerged with such great suffering."[41] But Congar would not be deflected from his vocation to ecumenism, whatever the difficulties or dangers. It is to his credit that he was open to dialogue with all, including the *integristes* — extreme right wing conservative Catholics.[42] He viewed dialogue as a permanent element in the Church's mission to the world. In the course of his lifetime, he was personally responsible for an impressive and wide-ranging series of ecumenical initiatives and is appropriately remembered as the Catholic Church ecumenist *par excellence* of his era. In the present period, following the first great pioneers of Catholic ecumenism, we must ask, how can the hope of unity continue to shine forth in our darkened "post-modern" world, a world dominated by secular materialism and the principles of modernity?

III. Ecumenical Ethics:
"Reciprocal Respect for Final and Divisive Choices"

Jean Guitton, the French philosopher and lay observer at the Vatican Council, was Congar's fellow prisoner of war during the Second World War. A friend of Pope Paul VI, he is known for his *Dialogues avec Paul VI*.[43] What is perhaps less well known is that

---

[41] *Ibid.*, 105.

[42] See Congar, *Vraie et fausse réforme dans l'Église*, Unam Sanctam, 20 (Paris: Cerf, 1950), Appendix III, "Mentalité 'de droite' et Intégrisme en France," 604-622. See further Francis Wilyte, "Action Française and Action Catholique: a brief explanation," Appendix IV, Congar, *Challenge to the Church: The Case of Archbishop Lefebvre* (London: Collins; Dublin: Veritas, 1976) 88-90, p. 88.

[43] Jean Guitton, *Dialogues avec Paul VI* (Paris: Fayard, 1967).

in 1949, along with Congar, the Jesuit theologian Jean Daniélou, the Dominican Jérôme Hamer, who was to become the executive secretary of the Vatican's Secretariat for Unity, and the Marist Maurice Villain, a renowned ecumenist and member of the "Groupe des Dombes",[44] he participated in a confidential and unofficial ecumenical meeting with members of the World Council of Churches at the Istina centre in Paris.[45] Guitton's penetrative and realistic view of ecumenism is relevant to the present discussion:

> Ecumenism has two faces, the one radiant and full of hope, of the love which seeks to overcome the conflicts of Christians, the other pained and full of anguish, one which compels lofty consciences smitten with truth either to condemn on the one hand or to break away on the other. It is easy to express these dismemberings in terms of passionate emotion, ignorance or pride. In the final analysis, the reason Christians are divided is the conviction that they are being faithful to Jesus Christ. All ecumenical ethics require this reciprocal respect for final and divisive choices.[46]

Before commenting further on Guitton's position, something more needs to be said about Congar's perception of ecumenism, his unique contribution to its development, and the evolution in his ecumenical thought from 1937 to 1984. He rejected a utilitarian notion of ecumenism viewed in terms of programmes and projects. The manifestation of its true nature is, rather, to be found in the Church animated by the Holy Spirit.[47] A noticeably consistent feature of his ecumenism is the claim that progress towards unity cannot be measured by the criteria of confessional triumphs or the

---

[44] The "Groupe des Dombes" is a Franco-Swiss ecumenical group, founded in 1937 by two Catholic theologians: Fathers Paul Couturier and Laurent Remilleux.

[45] See Visser't Hooft, *Memoirs*, 319-320.

[46] Guitton, "The Future of the Council," Appendix III Congar, *Challenge to the Church*, 82-87, p. 82.

[47] Congar, *Divided Christendom*, 272-273 (340-341).

absorption of one communion by another. As Congar suggests, what is required is respect, patience, and dialogue. Ecumenism is seen as a discovery of another spiritual world which "does not uproot us from our own, but changes the way we look at many things."[48] On the subject of ecumenical dialogue, Congar makes a valid suggestion which he hopes will contribute to a consensus on truth, thereby also helping to avoid conflict and useless polemics. He comments: "In their sociological form, the 'orthodoxies' which nourish endless controversies, prevent one from seeing and incorporating the element of truth contained in what they combat and which must be reabsorbed into that total truth."[49] This is one way of looking at an obvious problem which has the decided advantage of contributing towards a consensus of opinion. But there is another. Congar's view of "orthodoxies," despite his legitimate concern for "total truth" in ecumenical dialogue, could be interpreted as contributing to an inevitable weakening of orthodoxy for the sake of a possible consensus.

The evolution in his ecumenical thought, already fully documented,[50] is summed up by Congar in the following terms: "My confrère and friend J.-P. Jossua finally analysed a change in the key concept from 1937, *Chrétiens désunis* and this book [*Essais oecuméniques*]: the passage from 'Catholicity' to 'diversities' and

[48] Congar, "Ecumenical Experience and Conversion: A Personal Testimony," 72 (124).

[49] *Ibid.*, 74 (126).

[50] See Jean-Pierre Jossua, "L'oeuvre oecuménique du Père Congar," *Études* 357 (1982) 543-555; Joseph Famerée, "'Chrétiens désunis' du P. Congar 50 ans après," *Nouvelle revue théologique* 110 (1988) 666-686; Alberic Stacpoole, "Early Ecumenism, Early Yves Congar, 1904-1940: Commemoration of the half-century of the beginnings of the World Council of Churches, 1937-1987," *Month* 21 (1988) 502-510; also id, "Early Ecumenism, Early Yves Congar, 1904-1940," Part II, *Month* 21 (1988) 623-631; Gabriel Flynn, *Yves Congar's Vision of the Church in a World of Unbelief* (Aldershot, Hampshire: Ashgate, 2004).

'pluralism'."[51] In *Chrétiens désunis*, Catholicity is viewed in dialectical terms as the universal capacity for the unity of the Church and the guarantee of respect for what is finest and most authentic in the diversity of languages, nations, and religious experiences.[52] Congar argues that while there may be a non-Roman ecumenism, since no other exists, "there cannot be a 'non-Roman Catholicity'."[53] This is an indication of how ecumenism has changed since 1937. In *Diversités et Communion* (1982), however, the focus is no longer on Catholicity, but on the necessity of diversity at the heart of communion:

> It was the idea of Catholicity which at the time seemed to me to encompass the diversities; today I am more aware of the diversities, as is evident from my recent book *Diversity and Communion*.[51]

Congar goes even further to give a qualified acceptance to the expression "reconciled diversities."[55] The term "reconciled diversity" (*"Versöhnte Verschiedenheit"*), was proposed by the Concord of Leuenberg — a statement of concord between the Lutheran and Reformed Churches of Eastern and Western Europe, signed at Leuenberg, Switzerland on 16 March 1973, allowing the joint possibility of different doctrinal theses, previously considered irreconcilable — and adopted by the assembly of the World Lutheran Federation at Dar-es-Salaam in June 1977.[56] The question must be

---

[51] Congar, *Essais œcuméniques: le mouvement, les hommes, les problèmes* (Paris: Centurion, 1984) 6. See further Jossua, "In the Hope of Unity," in the present volume.

[52] Congar, *Divided Christendom*, 108, 114 (137, 148).

[53] *Ibid.*, 101 (126).

[54] Congar, *Fifty Years of Catholic Theology*, 81 (104).

[55] *Ibid.*

[56] See Congar, *Diversity and Communion* (London: SCM, 1984) 149; also id., *Diversités et Communion: dossier historique et conclusion théologique*, Cogitatio Fidei, 112 (Paris: Cerf, 1982) 221.

asked whether the shift in Congar's ecumenism from Catholicity to pluralism/diversities, which involves the danger of relativism, also entails the recognition of the division of Christianity as permanent and irreversible. As we have seen, this is the position adopted by Guitton in his call for mutual respect for final divisive choices. Congar, in fact, criticises his view of ecumenism as lacking realism. In *Mon journal du Concile*, we find the following guarded welcome for Guitton's address to the Council, the first by a layperson: "I find his discourse quite good, though too academic, too optimistic and at the same time too beatific (*béat*) on ecumenism. It is not very real."[57] Congar was deeply concerned that ecumenism was perceived to be an affair between experts, like the quarrels between clerics in the fifteenth century, having little contact with the real world.[58] There is one further point which can be alluded to briefly. In *Diversités et Communion*, Congar endorses an ecumenism which he had earlier warned against in *Chrétiens désunis*, that is, the recognition of a certain unity in diversity. He states this caveat unambiguously in *Chrétiens désunis*:

> What is today called "oecumenism" is the introduction of a certain unitedness into an already existing diversity — oneness in multiplicity ("die Einheit in der Mannigfaltigkeit"), as Archbishop Söderblom called it: it is but a mirage of Catholicity (*catholicité*) for those who cannot recognise among "the Churches" *the* Church of Jesus Christ, visibly one with that visible unity which Christ willed and prepared for her.[59]

[57] Congar, *Mon journal du Concile*, I: 586 (3 December 1963).
[58] *Ibid.*
[59] Congar, *Divided Christendom*, 101 (125). See Joseph Ratzinger, "Catholicism after the Council," trans. Patrick Russell, *Furrow* 18 (1967) 3-23, p. 21. See further Daphne Hampson, *Christian Contradictions: The Structures of Lutheran and Catholic Thought* (Cambridge: Cambridge University Press, 2004). In a carefully researched and scholarly study, Hampson argues that Catholicism and Lutheranism are totally incompatible. She shows how Lutheran and Catholic

Ecumenism, reduced to a common denominator without unity, lacks Catholicity.[60] In seeking to reconcile diversities, has Congar failed to respect the divisive choices of others as final? To respond positively would probably be to claim too much. But Congar, whose early works did much to change the frozen ecumenical atmosphere of the time, has allowed a controversial, perhaps anomalous, element into his developed ecumenical thought. To argue on this basis that his vision for unity cannot be applied universally as an adequate ecumenical ethics for reconciliation invites an obvious rejoinder, that an ecumenical ethics for reconciliation is necessarily limited, both geographically and historically, operating as it does in the twilight zone of dialogue and conflict. It seems to me, however, that Congar's concern to reconcile diversities remains largely unrealised, as the current state of the ecumenical movement clearly demonstrates. I suggest that the cause of ecumenism may be better served by respecting diversities, rather than attempting to reconcile them, thus upholding the integrity of the disparate views of all the partners in ecumenical dialogue.

Some remarks on the approach to ecumenism pursued by the distinguished English theologian Bishop Basil Christopher Butler (1902-86), sometime Auxiliary Bishop of Westminster, are here in place. Dr Butler, a founder member of the Anglican/Roman Catholic International Commission (ARCIC) and one of the principal theologians of the Vatican Council, was engaged in the formulation of its Dogmatic Constitution on the Church. In his book *The Church and Unity*, he rejects the view that Christianity is one

theologies are based on different philosophical presuppositions, embodying divergent conceptions of self and God. This book presents a formidable challenge to decades of ecumenical rapprochement, not least the Roman Catholic/Lutheran "Joint Declaration" of 1999.

[60] Congar, *Divided Christendom*, 101 (126).

among many of the versions of the human quest for God and argues instead that the Christian religion springs from a divine initiative that is disclosed primarily in the unique fact of the Incarnation of the Word of God in Jesus Christ. Butler concludes, on the basis of his assertion of the uniqueness of Christianity, that the Church and its unity are integral to the divine economy of redemption.[61] He is at pains to point out to his "ecumenical friends" that his "essay" on ecumenism does not call into question the principle underlying the ecumenical movement or betray its integrity. He, nonetheless, adheres tenaciously to the principle of catholicity as a defence against the delusion of false hopes in ecumenical dialogue. As Butler writes: "Christianity is meant for everyone, and so the Church is meant for everyone; it is 'catholic', universal of right, even when it is not yet universal in fact."[62] Furthermore, in his vision for the embryonic ecumenical movement, Bishop Butler calls for the reform of "extreme centralization" in the Church but without departing from the principle of catholicity.[63]

> Is it possible to say that the Catholic Church must "die" in order to live? This essay has been devoted to arguing that there is a limit to such a suggestion: the Catholic Church, in loyalty to itself, its mission and commission, and to Christianity itself and the world to which Christianity is sent, cannot barter away the principle that God's Church "subsists" in the Roman Catholic Communion.[64]

Ironically, such sentiments are echoed by the American Methodist theologian Stanley Hauerwas who identifies an obvious weakness

---

[61] See B. C. Butler, *The Church and Unity* (London: Geoffrey Chapman, 1979) 24-25.

[62] *Ibid.*, 221.

[63] *Ibid.*, 4.

[64] *Ibid.*, 228.

in the ecumenical endeavours of some Catholic theologians: "I want you to be Catholics. I also believe that there is nothing more important for the future of the unity of the Church than for you to be Catholic. [...] You have been so anxious to be like us that you have failed in your ecumenical task to help us to see what it means for any of us to be faithful to the Gospel on which our unity depends".[65]

IV. CONCLUSION

In spite of its defects, Congar's ecumenism is a remarkable achievement. Nonetheless, the Church continues to be affected by serious obstacles to unity and belief. In this article, I have argued that the acceptance of ecumenism as an ethical imperative for the Churches would give new impetus to ecumenical endeavours. It is clear, however, that the continuance of ecumenical dialogue necessitates a "dialogue on the dialogue,"[66] to borrow Guitton's phrase. A fresh consideration of dialogue must include an honest appraisal of new Church problems, notably thorny issues concerning sexuality, orders and Eucharist, issues which have profound implications for inter-church relations. It cannot be denied that such discussion raises again the familiar problem of reconciling the Gospel standard of unity and the apparently irreconcilable differences between the Christian Churches, differences which bloody history and the passing of time appear to have solidified. It is clear that careful avoidance of such difficult issues reduces ecumenical dialogue to the level

[65] Stanley Hauerwas, "The Importance of being Catholic: A Protestant View," *First Things* 1 (1990) 23-30, p. 25.
[66] Guitton, *Dialogues avec Paul VI*, 195.

currently afforded the annual octave of prayer for Christian unity. This observance, for which Congar and others had such high hopes,[67] has become little more than polite and powerless exchanges between the few, deprived of universality, an important element of the psychology of the octave.[68] But, then, is not all prayer powerful? And do not all Christians believe in prayer? To follow our line of argument to its logical conclusions entails the acceptance of "reciprocal respect for final and divisive choices."[69] This view of ecumenism clearly encapsulates an important part of Pope John XXIII's vision for the Council. As he writes: "Everything, even human differences, must lead to the greater good of the Church."[70] The fact that dialogue is difficult, and rarely in the history of Christianity has it been as difficult as now, does not mean that it should be abandoned. On the contrary, it is at such moments that dialogue must be pursued with energy and enthusiasm. In the midst of much disappointment and failure, there are signs of hope that the cause of ecumenism may yet triumph. The excellent doctrinal work of the "Groupe des Dombes", together with its commitment to prayer, though obfuscated, particularly in the Anglo-Saxon world, is a case in point and inspires renewed hope in the ecumenical movement. As we look forward, the witness of Congar inspires still greater hope. Unequal to the task — his great vocation to unity — he moved forward, sometimes falteringly, always courageously, moved by the fire of love, love of truth and love of the other. This article can perhaps be

[67] Congar, Review of Maurice Villain, *L'Abbé*, *Revue des sciences philosophiques et théologiques* 41 (1957) 590.

[68] See Geoffrey Curtis, *Paul Couturier and Unity in Christ* (London: SCM, 1964) 63-68.

[69] Guitton, "The Future of the Council," 82.

[70] Cited in "Comment," *New Blackfriars* 46 (1965) 206-209, p. 206.

fittingly brought to a close with some remarks by Pope Paul VI from his first encyclical letter, *Ecclesiam Suam*:

> The spirit of dialogue is friendship; even more, it is service. All this we must remember and strive to put into practice according to the example and commandment that Christ left to us. But the danger remains. The apostle's art is a risky one. The desire to come together as brothers must not lead to a watering-down or subtracting from the truth.[71]

[71] Paul VI, *Ecclesiam Suam*, 90-91.

PART IV

**YVES CONGAR:
HISTORIAN OF ECCLESIOLOGY**

YVES CONGAR AS HISTORIAN OF ECCLESIOLOGY

John W. O'MALLEY, SJ

Distinguished Professor of Church History
Weston Jesuit School of Theology, Cambridge, Massachusetts

I first began reading Yves Congar in 1963 while I was in Rome
writing my dissertation "On Church and Reform" as found in
Egidio da Viterbo, Prior General of the Augustinian friars in the
early sixteenth century. *Vraie et fausse réforme dans l'Église*
seemed pertinent to my topic, and I set about trying to find a copy.
The task was more daunting than I had anticipated. The Second
Vatican Council was already in its second year, but the new atmosphere it had already generated could not overnight repair the effects
of the repression that followed in the wake of the encyclical
Humani generis, promulgated in 1950, the same year *Vraie et
fausse réforme dans l'Église* was published. The encyclical and its
aftermath, as we know all too well, left Congar and his works
highly suspect. After much searching I finally located a copy of
Réforme in the library of the Angelicum, the Dominicans'
athenaeum in the centre of the city. That copy was, as far as I could
ascertain, the only one available in any library in Rome.

Réforme helped me clarify my thoughts about Egidio and his
attempts to reform the Augustinians on the eve of the Reformation.[1] My study of him, as the title indicates, dealt in large part

---

[1] John W. O'Malley, *Giles of Viterbo on Church and Reform: A Study in
Renaissance Thought* (Leiden: E. J. Brill, 1968).

with ecclesiological issues, which led me several years later to pick up *L'Église: De saint Augustin à l'époque moderne* (1970), reissued by Éditions du Cerf in 1996. Once I opened it I devoured it. I was not only impressed by the stunning erudition it seemingly so effortlessly embodied but was also persuaded by its general line of argument.

I know that the book has ever since influenced me in a number of ways, but I have not looked at it for at least two decades. Before I began working on this paper, I had not read the earlier, more circumscribed study, *L'Ecclésiologie du haut moyen âge: De saint Grégoire le Grand à la désunion entre Byzance et Rome*, published in a revised edition by Éditions du Cerf in 1968, nor had I except in a casual and unsystematic way read any of Father Congar's other works. Unlike the other contributors to this volume, therefore, I am not an expert on this great theologian. Nor am I even a theologian. My field is history.

It is as an historian that Dr Flynn invited me to examine for this volume the two works mentioned above — *L'Église* and *L'Ecclésiologie*. What he asked me to do was simply to assess them as works of historical scholarship. How do they stand up from that perspective, and after all these years? It seemed like a simple task and within my competence, so, after some gentle persuasion, I accepted the invitation. I now realize that to do justice to the assignment would require much more time than I have at my disposal and also require somebody with an erudition as vast and an intellect as acute as Congar's. I am far from being that somebody, and to use Bernard of Chartres' image, I at the moment feel like a very small dwarf sitting on the shoulders of a very big giant. I will do, however, what I can, beginning with *L'Église*.

As I worked my way through it once again, I was struck with the same admiration I felt the first time. This is a work of synthesis of the first order. Nothing quite like it previously existed, and in many ways it has never been surpassed. That fact alone testifies to its extraordinary importance. As with any work of synthesis, of course, some important figures and issues necessarily fall by the wayside. Why just eight pages for all the Protestant reformers of the sixteenth century? The reformers were perhaps a subject on which Congar felt less well informed, but, more likely, they, like others, such as Schleiermacher and Ritschl, are just as well understood as casualties of the genre. That's the problematic side of a synthesis like *L'Église*.

Such slights and omissions point also, however, to the Roman Catholic framework in which the book was conceived. That framework is of course understandable and perfectly legitimate, but in the light of the theological exchanges between Catholics and Protestants in the last thirty years, exchanges that Congar so much wished for and helped set in motion, the framework seems limited and outdated. In a book of almost five hundred pages, less than a hundred deal with the period from the seventeenth century to the present, whereas in Eric G. Jay's history of ecclesiology published a few years after *L'Église* over half deals with those later centuries.[2] Jay is a Protestant.

Nonetheless, even with limitations like those I've mentioned, *L'Église* remains impressive as a work of historical synthesis. While the erudition is almost breathtaking, in its detail, it never overwhelms the text. Indeed, one of Congar's great gifts was his ability to analyze complex historical movements and events and then, in masterly fashion, summarize the results. On pages 124-125, for instance, he lists the "general traits" of the early twelfth century, and on pages 202-203 he offers a superb summary of the ecclesiological significance of the "spiritual and anti-ecclesiastical

[2] Eric G. Jay, *The Church: Its Changing Image through Twenty Centuries*, 2 vols. (London: SPCK, 1977-78).

movements" like the Waldensians. It would be difficult even today to improve upon these summaries, but they are only two among the many that populate both this volume and *L'Ecclésiologie.*

What I find most remarkable, however, given the period in which *L'Église* was written, is the breadth of inquiry that Congar brought to the subject. Although quite properly Congar expends most of his effort on theological texts that in one way or another speak directly about the church, he did not fall into the trap of writing a history of ideas or, in this case, a history of the "doctrine" of the church in the sense of a history of concepts utterly divorced from their context. In deft, though admittedly limited ways, he incorporated into his study concrete realities in the life of the church, and from them he drew the ecclesiological consequences. In the early pages, for instance, he calls attention to the ecclesiological significance of the basilica form in the West, which by its very architecture promoted processions from the portico through the nave to the sanctuary. The architectural form thus suggested, helped solidify an understanding of the church as the pathway to God and as a people on pilgrimage (pp. 40-41). Congar further on clarifies how the offertory presentation of the gifts indicates the active role the whole congregation of the faithful was meant to play in the church (p. 43), and he elucidates the contrasting significance of the later practice of the priest's silent recitation of the canon (p. 57). He thus makes history of the liturgy a component part of the history of ecclesiology. He does so by drawing out the significance of actions. What the church does is as significant for ecclesiology as what the church says. We might today regard that axiom as a truism, but it was not a truism two generations ago.

This attention to liturgical practice is coupled with an appreciation for what the "movements" mentioned above mean for ecclesiology, as well as what in the thirteenth century something like the disputes between "the regulars and the seculars" at the University of Paris mean (p. 250). What Congar aimed at, I believe, was a history of appreciations of the church derived from the very life of the church. He called attention, for instance, to the import for ecclesiology of the church's resort in the later Middle Ages to "the secular arm" to deal with misbelievers (p. 208). He wanted to include, in other words, the history "from below" in so far as that yielded information about how people, quite ordinary people, thought and felt about the church and how they were treated in it. These were dimensions of a lived ecclesiology that never made their way into ecclesiological manuals.

This dimension of Congar's work effectively highlighted the efforts especially of his generation to move theology in all its aspects out of the arena of timeless truths to an enterprise in which history, including so-called institutional and social history, conditioned all its expressions. True, *L'Église* remains for the most part a history of *ideas*, but, as the very structure of the book indicates, it at least in a generic way ties those ideas to the great historical epochs in which they were produced, modified, or radically transformed.

I suppose we should not be too much surprised at Congar's openness to a more inclusive approach since it was characteristic of schools of historiography that originated and flourished in France long before they became popular elsewhere and that were in their most exciting stages when Congar was maturing as a thinker. It would be difficult to disagree with Peter Burke's assessment that "a remarkable amount of the most innovative, the most memorable and the most significant historical writing of the twentieth century has been produced in France."[3] He was referring of course to the *Annales*, begotten in Strasbourg in the 1920s by Lucien Febvre and Marc Bloch, but also to the religious sociology of Gabriel Le Bras

[3] Peter Burke, *The French Historical Revolution: The Annales Schools, 1929-89* (Stanford, CA: Stanford University Press, 1990) 1.

begotten there at about the same time. Perhaps more important for Congar was the work of the priest Étienne Delaruelle, who in 1929 published his first article on "popular religion." For the rest of his life Delaruelle waged a campaign through his many publications to enrich church history with the history of the ordinary believer. Congar in fact cites him (p. 54). I venture to say that a book like *L'Église* could only have been written by a Frenchman and could hardly have been produced before historiography in France took a turn away from an almost exclusive focus on great men, great events, and, if you will, "great ideas" to a more expansive scope, which would include, at least in passing, "the little people" and the practices of the Christian life that were open to all alike.[4]

Along somewhat the same lines, Congar was sensitive to the impact of literary genres on content and to the necessity of taking that factor into account in interpreting texts. This may seem like an obvious step to take, hardly worthy of comment, except that even today proof-texting has not disappeared from theological writings and official ecclesiastical documents. He realized that the literary form in which the Fathers expressed themselves about the church resulted in two traits that would characterize their thought: the extensive use of images and metaphor and the largeness of their vision (pp. 44-45). Congar does not make explicit the relationship of the forms to the *paideia* or *institutio* that was the training the Fathers received in school, which was literary rather than philosophical, but he understands its impact. The Fathers were not scholastic theologians, and therefore they cannot be interpreted as if they were.

It was this sensitivity, I believe, that allowed him to see St Bernard of Clairvaux's homilies on the Song of Songs as an ecclesiological text. The word church hardly occurs in them, yet

---

[4] See the now classic review, John Van Engen, "The Christian Middle Ages as an Historiographical Problem," *The American Historical Review* 91 (1981) 519-532.

throughout they bespeak an appreciation of the church as the place where persons are gripped by the realization that they must be engaged in the spiritual combat and are called to holiness. It is the place where they will experience the delights of divine love. This is the church of the garden of spiritual joy where one is embraced by the saints and the Lord. But, as Congar indicates, Bernard, contemplative though he was, took an active role in some of the great issues that troubled the church of his day. Bernard's "actions and reactions," as well as his homilies about love, had ecclesiological consequences (pp. 127-128).

When Congar introduced his illuminating discussion of the impact of the treatises on the sacraments that the early scholastics, younger contemporaries of Bernard, began producing, I wish that he had paid more attention to the impact of the new form of these treatises — just how much, in other words, was the medium the message? Theology moved from its literary stage to its "scientific" stage, moved from poetry to analysis, moved from the "formless form" of the homily to tightly structured treatises — from the "spirit of finesse" to the "geometric spirit."[5] Congar manages, nonetheless, to describe with his usual conciseness the great shift in *mentalité* that the scholastic enterprise produced, a transition to essences and definitions from something that was more tolerant and expansive (pp. 169-176).

Congar was certainly not original when he noted that with the Counter Reformation theologians not only increasingly described the church with vocabulary ever more reminiscent of a state but also that the church also began to act more in accord with that description, with its implicit tendency to absolutism. What I find interesting, however, is how at about the same time Congar was

[5] The expressions come from H.-I. Marrou, *A History of Education in Antiquity,* trans. George Lamb (Madison, WI: The University of Wisconsin Press, 1956) 90-91.

writing the English Catholic historian H. Outram Evennett portrayed the popes of that era not as great reformers in the Triden-
tine mode, which was how they were almost invariably portrayed
by Catholic historians of the time, but as the first modern bureau-
crats.[6] The idea was later developed at length and with a certain
acclaim by the Italian historian Paolo Prodi.[7]

Even more important is the emphasis that historians have in
recent years been placing on "social disciplining" as a feature of
all the religious confessions of the early modern era, as well as of
the early modern state. The churches needed the state to effect
the disciplining of their own members, and the state needed
the churches to provide legitimacy for many of its own measures.
Each adopted the tactics of the other. This phenomenon was perhaps more noteworthy in Catholicism simply because the pope was
both head of the church and head of a state. From a historiographical viewpoint, therefore, Congar's observations in this regard seem
even more on target today than they did thirty-five years ago.

No book is perfect. This one rushes to conclusion in the final
pages, yet lacks a proper conclusion. The book also lacks an introduction, which means Congar does not here directly address the
crucial issue of method. And what a disappointment that he, of all
people, spends only five pages on the Second Vatican Council!

While he pays attention to the ecclesiological dimensions of
liturgy, he makes only a passing reference to painting (p. 111).

---

[6] H. Outram Evennett, *The Spirit of the Counter-Reformation*, ed. John Bossy
(Cambridge: Cambridge University Press, 1968), esp. 108-125, first delivered as
lectures in 1951.

[7] Paolo Prodi, *The Papal Prince, One Body and Two Souls: The Papal
Monarch in Early Modern Europe*, trans. Susan Haskins (Cambridge: Cambridge
University Press, 1987); English translation of *Il sovrano pontefice: Un corpo e
due anime. La monarchia papale nella prima età moderna* (Bologna: Il Mulino,
1982).

I think this especially unfortunate for it was through the material culture of church building and church decoration that Christians, most of whom were illiterate until quite recently, formed their ideas — or, better, their images — of the church. They were images not found in books but in the milieus to which they returned week after week all their lives.

The baroque era is especially pertinent here because in the post-Tridentine period Catholicism undertook such a massive programme of refurbishing old churches and building new ones. The decoration of these churches was so extensive and integral to the interior of the building that no worshiper could avoid seeing it. It surely had an impact on how people imagined their *église*. Baroque art, once typified as overwrought and "triumphalistic," is now receiving a more appropriate assessment as bright and hopeful. The frescoes are often filled with playful cherubs and happy saints, and they offer glimpses of the joys of heaven. As one entered the church, one could hardly avoid this "eschatological dimension." Both the architecture and the decoration suggested, indeed, that one had already entered heaven.

Given Congar's gift for seeing the ramifications that practice should have on theory, I am somewhat surprised that, as a Dominican, he did not make more of the "democratic" structures and the emphasis on ministry of the Word that was common to all the mendicant orders and surprised that he did not see (or at least did not mention) a connection between that phenomenon and the ecclesiology of the Protestant Reformers, so many of whom had been mendicants. He does not comment on the great missionary activities of the mendicants especially in the early modern era. Catholics thought of the church as a missionary reality and sent their brightest and best overseas to strange and exotic lands in great evangelizing enterprises, yet that reality never got a foothold in formal ecclesiologies. Ecclesiologists were studying texts not actions, documents not life.

With the invention of printing came the publication of catechisms, surely an ecclesiological genre "from below." Once the question and answer format began to prevail in the early sixteenth century, the question "What is the church?" was invariably asked. The traditional answer was "The congregation of the Christian faithful, governed and illumined by God our Lord," but by the middle of the century something like "under legitimate pastors, especially the Roman Pontiff" was regularly and then inevitably added. A more subtle but equally important ecclesiological implication in the Catholic catechisms was their almost universal inclusion of the gifts of the Holy Spirit and the seven spiritual and corporal works of mercy. To receive those gifts and to engage in those actions was what it meant to be a member of the church.

It would be easy to continue listing features "from below" that Congar does not touch upon or at least does not develop. That would be unfair because every author must make painful exclusionary choices, most especially in a work of synthesis. It would be unfair because this dimension was just beginning to be developed by historians. We need, rather, to be grateful that, though we might wish for more, Congar gave us as much as he did. What I am trying to say here is that Congar pointed the way to how fruitful an ecclesiology might be when it took even fuller account especially of social history and art history, took fuller account of "popular religion," if I may use that problematic term.

In the thirty-five years since *L'Église* was published, moreover, there have been a number of historiographical developments that have opened up even further aspects of this more inclusive approach. I will mention three of them because they are important in themselves but also because I think Congar would have been extremely sensitive to them. The first is detailed studies of the practice of ministry, especially of how the sacrament of Penance was celebrated in the early modern period and of how authorities took measures to ensure that the faithful confessed their sins regularly and properly.[8] Those measures are now commonly described as one of the most important articulations of the social disciplining I mentioned above. Such studies, perhaps especially those done from the perspective of social disciplining, have fairly obvious ecclesiological repercussions — the "model" of the church as stern monitor of morals and enforcer of predetermined patterns of behaviour.

The second development is the great avalanche of studies in the past twenty years about late-medieval and early-modern confraternities, those voluntary associations usually of laymen and lay women, which we now see to have been the principal locus in which ordinary Christians practiced their religion, especially in urban centres. It was not the parish that was the centre of their lives as Christians but the oratories and chapels where the confraternities met, prayed, and carried on their "social ministries" in a somewhat egalitarian and even "democratic" fashion. They for the most part functioned altogether independently of the hierarchy, hired their own chaplains, and determined their own scope and statutes.

The confraternities had their counterpart in the Third Orders of the mendicants. Together these two types of institutions framed the lives of the most religiously vital and engaged segments of the population. By the beginning of the sixteenth century in Italy, for instance, confraternities might number fifty to a hundred in a given city, depending on the size of the population, and they included practically every social class. Nothing has changed my own thinking about "church history" more dramatically than these studies, which continue to pour off the presses. The Third Orders of the

---

[8] See, e.g., Wietse de Boer, *The Conquest of the Soul: Confession, Discipline, and Public Order in Counter-Reformation Milan* (Leiden: E. J. Brill, 2001).

Franciscans and of the Dominicans, Congar's own religious family, were especially important. In such gatherings we see vivid models of the church as "the people of God."

The third development is the new attention historians are now paying to the role women played in the church. Of course even in earlier generations church histories have mentioned outstanding women like Monica, Countess Matilda of Tuscany, Catherine of Siena, Teresa of Avila. What is new is the realization that especially in France in the seventeenth century, women began to have an impact on the church not only as individuals but as corporations of pro-active agents in what can generically be termed social ministries — especially the operation of schools and hospitals. Women thus organized began to have a systemic impact on what the church is principally about — ministry.

The Ursulines are the best known of these *compagnie*, but there were many more even in the seventeenth century and incomparably more in the nineteenth and early twentieth centuries. This was a phenomenon altogether peculiar to Catholicism. One of its most characteristic forms was the "convent school" for girls, a characteristic of Catholic life almost around the globe. Many Catholics knew "the church" most intimately in their most formative years not through priests but through sisters. Nuns were the "face" of the church.[9]

Most of the comments I make about *L'Église* are equally applicable to *L'Ecclésiologie*, but I must address it specifically because the most extensive review the book received was highly critical of Congar's method. According to Ovidio Capitani, the reviewer, the method was not historical — or at least not historical enough.[10]

---

[9] See, e.g., Elizabeth Rapley, *The Dévotes: Women & Church in Seventeenth-Century France* (Montreal/Kingston: McGill-Queen's University Press, 1990).

[10] Ovidio Capitani, "Attualismo storiografico e metodo storico (a proposito di un libro di Y. M. Congar)," *Studi Medievali*, ser. 3, 11, no. 2 (1970) 867-883.

Capitani had already published an important study of Peter Damien and another on Berengarius of Tours, as well as an analysis of the historiographical direction medieval studies were then taking in Italy. He was a young historian at the time but highly qualified to deal with Congar's book — his period of specialization practically coincided with the period covered in *L'Ecclésiologie*. Capitani has continued to publish extensively up to the present. Almost thirty years after his review of Congar appeared, he took up the subject once again.[11] This time, without altogether retracting his earlier criticism, he dwelt on Congar's positive contributions. Our concern here, in any case, must be to deal with the problems Capitani saw with Congar's method in 1970.

Before addressing Capitani's criticisms, however, we need to recall the origins of *L'Ecclésiologie*. It was originally published in 1955 as a fascicule in the Herder *Dogmengeschichte* series, and then again in a thoroughly revised French edition in 1968 while Congar was already at work on *L'Église*. The chronological limits of *L'Ecclésiologie* from Gregory the Great until the Gregorian Reform were set not by Congar but by the editors at Herders. Congar found no difficulty, however, in justifying this period of "the early Middle Ages" as a "period of transition" between the age of the Fathers and the period beginning in the mid-eleventh century. He gives the impression in fact of finding it congenial for his agenda of showing how rich and polyvalent the ecclesiological tradition is.

In his introduction Congar argues for the usefulness of a history of ecclesiology like the one he here undertakes for a theology of

---

[11] Ovidio Capitani, "Congar et l'ecclésiologie du haut Moyen Âge: Quelques réflexions," trans. Cécile Caby, *Cardinal Yves Congar 1904-1995: Actes du colloque réuni à Rome les 3-4 juin 1996*, ed. André Vauchez (Paris: Les Éditions du Cerf, 1999) 41-49.

the church today as well as for ecumenical dialogue. Such a history will show the relativity of some theses held in the present and the usefulness of values in the tradition that have been forgotten. In that regard he specifically mentions the development of the papal office and of certain ideas or doctrines related to it. Although he does not say so in quite so many words, he more than implies that he will be dealing with *ideas* and *images* but not with the social, cultural, and institutional catalysts and embodiments. This approach is altogether appropriate for a book appearing in a series entitled *Dogmengeschichte* and is consonant with how the history of dogmas or doctrines was generally done. The title of the book is, after all, *L'Ecclésiologie*.

In fact, however, Congar from time to time shows his awareness of precisely the social, cultural, and institutional catalysts and embodiments pertinent to his subject, as, for instance, when he describes how the actions of St. Boniface, Charlemagne, and others contributed to the development of papal authority (pp. 195-205). But I detect fewer nods toward an incorporation into his synthesis of such elements, which would include history "from below" than in *L'Église*.

We come back, then, once again to the question of method and to Capitani's review. As Capitani would certainly admit, some of his criticisms are not so fundamental as others. He began his review, for instance, with reservations about the scope and style of the bibliographies Congar provides, which he found undiscriminating and sprawling. I could, I believe, defend Congar's practice in several ways, but I will simply call attention to J. Lecler's observation that in *L'Église* Congar had for every issue with which he deals assembled bibliographies that contain "all the essential works and the most recent scholarship."[12] I think that, although one might

---

[12] Review in *Études* 333 (1970) 157.

wish for some pruning of the bibliographies in *L'Ecclésiologie,* the same positive assessment could be given them.

But Capitani's basic objection to this "*histoire des doctrines ecclésiologiques*" is, as I indicated, that it is not history as an historian would do it. For Capitani Congar's method was defective in two ways. First of all, real history, though it may deal with ideas or concepts, always sees them as produced by concrete historical circumstances arising in very specific contexts. Otherwise they become abstractions, a series of themes that float above reality. For Capitani the very fact that Congar consistently speaks of "*notre époque,*" the period under consideration, indicates that Congar does not take into account the immense diversity that reigned in it. The result is a book that, while it purports to be a history of ecclesiology, is more of a synthesis of certain themes ungrounded in the messy diversity that is the human story. The book gives a more homogeneous view of the early Middle Ages than is justifiable.

Congar's method is also defective in that he has an agenda beyond simply understanding "what really happened." As Congar indicated in his "*Introduction,*" and as I mentioned, he wanted the book to be useful for ecumenism and for reshaping contemporary church thinking and practice (p. 10). No doubt, such an agenda is, to say the least, dangerous for it perforce leads the historian to see the past through lenses that highlight some aspects of it and block out others. It runs the danger of losing objectivity and becoming simply a covert argument for a certain course of action in the present.

Capitani's criticisms must, therefore, be taken seriously. Congar was not trained as an historian but as a theologian. He writes a history of ecclesiology *as a theologian.* Despite what I said above, I at certain points wanted him to be more aware of the social milieu and not move so fast to synthesis. A trained historian would, at least at certain points, be more cautious and specific. In the main, however, I not only do not find Congar's approach objectionable,

I find it helpful. As a theologian he brought to his task a sensitivity that the "lay" historian as such would lack. Only somebody with scientific training can write a history of science! In 1970 few "real" historians would be much concerned with how liturgy, for instance, reflected and helped form ecclesiological sensitivities. There can be no doubt that Congar was fully aware of the contingency inherent in the historical process, even though he may not usually make patent how that contingency affected the development of an idea.

Moreover, *L'Ecclésiologie* is, like *L'Église*, a work of synthesis. The presupposition expressed in the very title of the work is that there is a certain homogeneity in the era, otherwise it makes no sense to begin at one point and to end at another. We all realize that the past can be divided up in any number of ways and that all our attempts at assigning "periods" to it are open to challenge, depending on the discipline or concerns with which one approaches the material. Almost a half century after the publication of the first edition of *L'Ecclésiologie*, church historians and other historians still see the category of "early Middle Ages" as valid and helpful.

But if we do not grant that generalizations for the era we are considering are legitimate, there is no point in attempting a synthesis. Historians are rightly suspicious of the Big Picture, but without a Big Picture, or maybe a series of competing big pictures, we are left with a history that Arnold Toynbee purportedly once characterized as "just one damn thing after another."

Does Congar take insufficient account of the historical milieus? I wish he had done more. But that is a wish, not in itself a criticism. Moreover, as I mentioned, we must not lose sight of the series in which the volume appeared, which not only implied that the substance of the treatment would be "dogmas" or ideas but imposed a certain conciseness that precluded developing even important aspects of the subject. This was, after all, a "fascicule," not an eight-hundred page monograph, and the revised French edition, though expanded, was still only a revision of the original relatively small work. We must also realize that the "history of ideas" — or "intellectual history" — was in Congar's day very much in vogue among historians whose legitimacy was not open to challenge. Although today we historians are more aware of the limitations of such an approach, we have colleagues who still practice the history of ideas and produce useful studies.

Did Congar's agenda vitiate his historical scholarship? As we today read the great works of scholarship produced by Congar's generation of Catholic theologians and liturgists, we can detect that they often had an eye on the present with a view to changing it in the light of the historical evidence and arguments they were producing. Historians see such an agenda as risky business: what is most important in the past may have no relevance to the present, yet it is the historian's task to focus on that and not be distracted by what might seem "relevant." Historians must, that is to say, do their best to be aware of their prejudices — aware of their hopes and fears — and take measures to try to ensure their prejudices do not unduly shape their research and their conclusions.

The fact is, however, that many of the works of Congar's generation are still the standard works on their respective subjects. These great scholars wanted to bring history into the study of theology in a new way. History was no longer just an "auxiliary discipline," a storehouse of "examples" to illustrate or confirm a theory, which was the older rhetorical way of understanding its function going all the way back to antiquity. Since the nineteenth century, history had developed its own critical methods that had transformed it into a sharp instrument for relativizing the past. Congar and the others were keenly aware of this. They saw history as critical in two senses: in itself as a discipline and in its application to received ideas. What they were doing with "doctrines" was what other historians were doing — and are doing — with other historical phenomena.

Moreover, although my experience is limited, I have met few historians in whom I did not detect an agenda of some sort driving their scholarship. Yes, the pure desire to know "what happened" is our ideal, but usually it is something beyond that ideal that keeps us going, even if that something is only to prove our critics wrong. History might read as if it is a neutral chronicle, but it derives its energy from the conviction that the "chronicle" has an importance beyond satisfying idle curiosity.

Capitani's objection to Congar does raise, however, the issue of how any form of "church history" might be different from history pursued from a professedly "lay" stance, which is what Capitani says he practices. The issue was much discussed by German Catholic historians at just the time Congar was writing these two books, though there is no particular reason to believe he was influenced by the debate that ensued. One group maintained that church history was a properly theological discipline, pursued somehow in service to the truths of faith and guided by them, whereas the other maintained it was simply the materials studied that distinguished church history from other kinds of history.

A leader in the former group was the great historian of the Council of Trent, Hubert Jedin, whom Congar certainly came to know during Vatican II where they were both *periti*. Whatever one thinks of the debate and of the many different positions one might take in trying to resolve it, the fact that the issue was so hotly discussed at least raises the question of the legitimacy within a faith-context of a use of history beyond simply conveying a sense of "what happened."[13] Church historians from the group to which Jedin

---

[13] Papers read at a conference on the subject in Rome were published in *Römische Quartalschrift* 80 (1985). My contribution is entitled "Church Historians in the Service of the Church," 223-234. For Jedin's position, see my *Trent and*

belonged would probably not have recognized Congar as a church historian because what they meant by that term was an historian of the church as institution. Congar was not that nor did he pretend to be. He was an historian of ecclesiology. But because of the motives with which he pursued that history, Jedin and other historians like him would have recognized Congar's pursuit as legitimate history.

I do not think that, in balance, Capitani's criticisms substantially damage Congar's historical achievement in *L'Ecclésiologie* and even less in *L'Église*. As I hope is clear from what I have said, the criticisms raise important questions. They serve as a warning to those who would today attempt what Congar did. But, as Capitani now seems to admit, they should not detract from the stunning achievement.

A final question perhaps needs to be asked. Congar was convinced that a proper study of the past shows the contingency of the way ideas and institutions took shape and then developed over the course of time, and he tried to show how this happened. Things could have developed differently. For Congar such a realization had import for the present and seems to have implied for him a certain freedom and flexibility in the church for reshaping mentalities and institutions.

This seems, however, to be precisely where history and a certain kind of theology clash even today. We say ideas and institutions are contingent and that they "develop" over the course of the centuries, but what does such contingency and development imply? There has been evolution, no doubt. Can there be devolution? Can processes be reversed?

The obvious case in point for Catholics and quite specifically for Congar, as is clear in both his books, is the papacy. From the

All That: Renaming Catholicism in the Early Modern Period (Cambridge, MA: Harvard University Press, 2000) especially 57-59.

acorn has grown the mighty oak, to use a frequently applied analogy. The analogy implies a course was from the beginning determined for the future. The acorn can produce only the oak. The very expression "development of doctrine" often seems to do the same. So we come back to the basic question undergirding Capitani's review and Congar's enterprise: what are the legitimate uses of history in the context of Catholic theology and institutions? To what extent can the results of historical research be corrective of "developments," that is, of changes that have with time firmly established themselves in the tradition? The answer to that question must of course be theological. It is a question that goes to the heart of what concerned Congar in both of these historical works, which are thus also works of theology. It is the question that goes to the heart of much of the disagreement in the church today — and that thus renders Congar's work almost as relevant now as when it was first published.

AN HISTORIAN'S REFLECTIONS ON YVES CONGAR'S *MON JOURNAL DU CONCILE*[1]

J. J. SCARISBRICK

Professor Emeritus of History
University of Warwick

The *Diary* which Yves Congar kept during the Second Vatican Council is of extraordinary importance to the historian not only of the Council itself but, in a sense, of the Church in the twentieth century. This is true for two fundamental reasons. First, unlike most of the other conciliar diaries which have been discovered, its 1100 pages cover in great detail the whole of the Council, including much of the preparatory period from November 1960, the *intersessions* and the immediate post-conciliar period.[2] Second, Congar

[1] Ed. Éric Mahieu (Paris: Cerf, 2000). Hereafter cited as *Diary*.

[2] See Alberto Melloni, "Les Journaux privés dans l'histoire de Vatican II," in Marie-Dominique Chenu, "*Notes quotidiennes du Concile: Journal de Vatican II 1962-1963* (Paris: Cerf, 1995) 7-54 for information about other private diaries of the Council which have so far come to light. For detailed analysis of Congar's *Diary* see the long Introduction by Mahieu (note 1 above) and (especially) Gabriel Flynn, "*Mon Journal du Concile*: Yves Congar and the Battle for a renewed Ecclesiology at the Second Vatican Council," *Louvain Studies* 28 (2003) 48-70. Giuseppe Alberigo had access to the *Diary* before it was published and makes extensive use of it in his *History of Vatican II*. This present essay inevitably repeats some things already said by others but is concerned to assess the value of the *Diary* as an historical document, especially as it reports its author's changing perceptions of people and events as the Council unfolded, and to reflect on his conciliar legacy. I am very grateful to the editor of this volume, Fr. Gabriel Flynn, for thc generous help he has given me.

himself, alert and observant, and passionately engaged in the Council's mission, was uniquely equipped to give the inside story — or much of it — of how the Catholic church underwent a revolution in the mid-1960s. Of course, Vatican II's proceedings were enormously complex and there was much also happening all the time that Congar scarcely knew about. But insofar as he was a member of the Doctrinal Commission — preparatory and conciliar — which was the Commission responsible for most of the Council's major documents, and contributed to the work of other Commissions (notably the Commissions for the Missions and the Clergy and the *Commissio Mixta*, drawn from the Doctrinal Commission and the Secretariat for Unity, which produced *Gaudium et Spes*) he probably had as complete a view of the inner workings of the Council as did anyone.

His *Diary*, largely written up from notes made during daytime meetings of his Commissions or while listening to plenary sessions in St Peter's, is what every good *Diary* should be: pithy, spontaneous, uncensored. No wonder he forbade its publication until 2000. It races along. Written in the heat of the moment it records the author's frequent mood-swings from indignation to delight, extreme pessimism to elation. Exclamation marks abound, as do the "*oufs.*"

There are some wonderful thumb-nail sketches of events and people: the sessions of the Preparatory Theological Commission, for instance, presided over by the formidable Alfredo Ottaviani, prefect of the Holy Office, at which Congar was a mere consultant and required to sit in silence with other distinguished theologians like Henri de Lubac on a row of chairs against a wall, while the Commission discussed what Congar and his fellows regarded as a thoroughly unsatisfactory schema, and to speak only if asked to do so by a member of the Commission. Then there are often merciless pictures of individuals: the "tyrant" Dutchman, Sebastian

Tromp, SJ, secretary of that Commission and its conciliar successor, for instance, an "imbecile" and "fascist" (while Archbishop Parente, a member of the Commission, was both these and "monophysite" as well), who hunched his shoulders when being most dictatorial and was all the more dangerous as Ottaviani's underling because so able and possessed of excellent Latin.[3] Charles Balić, a Croatian Franciscan in the Holy Office and enthusiastic mariologist, is a devious "clown."[4] Cardinal Leger of Montreal is a tense loner, drumming his fingers, his "tragic" face lined by grimacing, melodramatic and needing people around him; Archbishop Marty of Rheims makes little impression in the Council and speaks like "a little girl timidly reading a text"; Cardinal Spellman comprehends little and is incomprehensible; Cardinal Feltin at meetings continually looks at his watch and is giving little leadership; an 85-year-old reduces the Fathers to laughter with his simple pieties and another does so by coughing into the microphone.[5]

There are exquisite Gallic acerbities: Cardinal Browne, head of the Dominicans, but "a mule," causes a "mass exodus of bishops to the bar" when he speaks; Bishop Fulton Sheen's first intervention at the Council, rather theatrical but polished, was much applauded, "but not by me"; would that Archbishop Parente, we are told, "were resident in his diocese" — a see in Egypt that had long since disappeared; Taizé's Roger Schutz goes on and on about

[3] *Diary*, i, 6-7, 69, 82-84, 182, etc.

[4] *Diary*, i, 561; ii 92.

[5] *Diary*, i, 197 and ii, 341; ii, 204 [une petite fille récitant une leçon timidement]; i, 236 and 433; i, 200; i, 554-555. But Congar's most violent remarks concerned Cardinal Giuseppe Pizzardo, prefect of the Congregation for Seminaries and Universities and hence president of the conciliar Commission for Seminaries, Studies and Catholic Education: a miserable, ignorant "runt" [avorton], we are told, who lives with two 80-year-old sisters, wears red pyjamas and briefs, is without "culture, vision or humanity" and is scandalously unworthy of his post. *Diary* i, 377-378 and 298.

the need to dialogue and listen to others.[6] At the end of the Council Pope Paul VI gave every bishop a gold ring and all the non-Catholic observers expensive engraved handbells (so much for poverty, Congar snorted), while the expert theologians who had done all the real work received only a Latin New Testament — "rather stingy."[7] And Congar has a nose for good gossip: John XXIII, Schutz reported, once called Ottaviani "a child"; the ultra-conservative Cardinal Siri of Genoa has apparently forbidden the Italian bishops to talk to the French; the American bishops have long been intimidated by their apostolic delegate.[8]

All this adds piquancy to the narrative. The latter's real substance, however, is much more important. Congar's *Diary* gives a vivid account of the battles which went on over months, in some cases for several years, in the Commissions and the sub-Commissions in preparing the schemas for the Constitution *De Ecclesia* (*Lumen Gentium*) which, of course, encompassed the crucial issues of collegiality and the role of the laity; *De Revelatione*, which had to find consensus on the vexed question of the meaning of Tradition and its relationship to Scripture; schema XVII (later renumbered XIII) which faced the equally explosive issues, the bomb and contraception (but eventually did not deal with them, much to Congar's chagrin); *De Oecumenismo, De Missionibus* and *De Beata,* the contentious schema on Our Lady. Essentially two theologies (and especially two ecclesiologies and two mariologies), the one Roman, curial and rooted in the scholastic manuals of the nineteenth century, but reaching back to Bellarmine and beyond,

[6] *Diary*, i, 167 and 221; ii, 248; i, 227 [qu'il aille résider dans son diocèse!!!]; ii, 490.

[7] *Diary*, ii, 513.

[8] *Diary*, i, 468; i, 236; i, 258. The same Apostolic Delegate, Congar adds, continued to control the US bishops during the first session, not allowing them "an inch" [une semelle] of independence.

the other biblical and patristic and deeply critical of its opponents' authoritarianism, collided head-on. Stalwarts like Cardinals Ottaviani, Siri, Cicognani, Ruffini, and Agagianian, supported by ardent integrists like Tromp, Parente, and the eventual secretary to the Council, Pericle Felice, confronted "modernising" German theologians like Karl Rahner and Joseph Ratzinger, the Swiss Hans Küng, the American John Courtney Murray, the formidable contingent from Louvain, headed by Charles Moeller, Albert Prignon, Gustav Thils and, above all, Gerard Philips; and the French Marie-Dominique Chenu, Henri de Lubac, Jean Daniélou and, of course, Congar.

Eventually appointed as experts of the Council, these came with varying support of their local episcopates and mostly enjoying sincere, if sometimes hesitant, approval of both John XXIII and Paul VI. They eventually won the day. The story of how they did so is being told in Alberigo's monumental *History of Vatican II*, and indeed, was reported almost at the time in more popular accounts like Xavier Rynne's *Inside the Council*. But Congar provides extra excitement. He enables us to experience the intensity of the battle, the uncertainty about the outcome — sometimes right up to the last moments — the battle of wits, the lobbying, the intrigues. There were even dirty tricks. Ottaviani regularly tried to ignore Congar at meetings of the Doctrinal Commission and to stop him speaking.[9] Felici, apparently on his own authority, tried to halt the printing of the draft of *De Oecumenismo* in February 1965 but his action was intercepted by the Pope himself.[10] An unknown hand,

[9] E.g. *Diary* i, 239 and 521. On 13 March 1964 he complained "for the fourth time I tried in vain to speak" at the Doctrinal Commission and was reporting in October 1965 that Ottaviani was still rarely giving him an opportunity to do so. *Diary*, ii, 51 and 421.

[10] *Diary*, ii, 320.

possibly Tromp's, had attempted at the last minute to make a crucial alteration to *De Revelatione* after it had been solemnly approved by the Fathers. Only immediate appeal to Ottaviani defeated the attempt to tamper with the definitive text.[11] Perhaps the most startling story of all occurred in the first session when there was a heated debate in the Doctrinal Commission concerning which draft text of *De Ecclesia*, that of the Preparatory Commission produced by Parente or the major revision by Philips, should be taken as the *textus receptus*. A sub-Commission was appointed to settle the matter. It met at the Holy Office. Cardinal Ottaviani opened proceedings by saying that the Parente text was excellent and he expected it to be approved. He then left. The sub-Commission voted by five to two in favour of the Philips text. When it reported to the next meeting of the full Commission, Ottaviani declared that it had acted *ultra vires* and attempted (unsuccessfully) to have its verdict overturned.[12]

Congar had arrived in Rome for the first meeting of the Preparatory Theological Commission on 15 November 1960 still deeply suspect to the likes of Cardinal Ottaviani and still smarting from the humiliation of having been silenced and exiled by the Holy Office. "Since 1938," he wrote, "I have been constantly suspect, pursued,

[11] *Diary*, ii, 514. The strange story runs thus. On 7 December 1965, a fellow-expert told Congar that in section 7 of *De Revelatione* where it speaks of Christ's commandment to preach the Gospel to all, thus "communicating divine gifts to them," the Latin "communicantes" had been changed to "communicans." The singular participle, agreeing with "Christ," implied that the Apostles (and therefore their successors) had a secondary or, as Congar put it, a merely "gnoseological" role. This attempt to diminish the status of the episcopal college (it can hardly have been a slip of someone's pen) provoked immediate, and successful, protest to Ottaviani. The printed text has "communicantes."

[12] The story is told twice in the *Diary* (i, 339 and ii, 283-4) — with slight variations between the two accounts. The second is Bishop Garrone's eyewitness report two years after the event.

sanctioned, restricted, crushed";[13] and though promotion from the rank of consultant to official expert of the conciliar Commission was implicit rehabilitation, he could not forget that he had been marginalised — even persecuted. Nor did Ottaviani. Even as the Council got under way the latter could warn that, since he was so "watched and suspect," he would do well to be especially obedient to the Magisterium.[14] Moreover, by then his initial high hopes for the Council had long since collapsed. It was twenty years too soon, he wrote. The bishops were theologically quite unprepared for it. The "stifling satrapism" of Pius XII's day lived on and would so suffocate the Council that the latter would achieve only 5 per cent of what had been hoped for. The Curia regarded John XXIII as a liability and was determined that the Council would achieve little. Either it would be a "prefabricated" Council that simply rubber-stamped the schemas produced by the Preparatory Commissions consisting of condemnations and papal "effata" from the time of Pius IX to that of Pius XII, or it would talk about everything and nothing — and flounder.[15] In either case the Curia was determined that it would have only one session. It would last only a few weeks, Felici himself said. That being so it had even been proposed that it could be held in a big tent at the back of St Peter's.[16]

[13] *Diary* i, 466 [SANS CESSE suspecté, poursuivi, sanctionné, limité, écrasé].

[14] *Diary*, ii, 279-280. The rector of the Lateran (who was consultant of the Holy Office and a member of the Theological Commission) was reported as saying Congar has "three heresies per page." *Diary* i, 27. — *Diary* i, 4, 6, 9-10, 201. There was of, course, the obvious danger that it would become a Council "de omnibus" (*Diary* i, 374) because its purpose was overall *aggiornamento* and *ressourcement*. Hence Cardinal Tardini, Secretary of State, could reply loftily to a journalist that it would "deal with everything, and much else besides." For him, as for many in the Curia, it would be at best an ill-considered waste of time, at worst a dangerous adventure launched by a pope in his dotage.

[15] *Diary*. i, 39; ii, 464. *Effatum* (*effata*): This Aramaic word (Mk 7:34) refers here ironically to the untimely interventions of the popes.

[16] *Diary*, i, 10 and 13.

Pope John had been disappointingly ambivalent. As well as leaving the chief figures of Pius XII's reign, like Cardinals Ottaviani and Tardini, in post, he had made the capital mistake (the "original sin" — which he later discovered had been forced on the pope) of setting up preparatory Commissions which corresponded to the curial Congregations and allowed the latter to control them. Hence Ottaviani saw the Theological Commission as simply an extension of the Holy Office and, since this was the heart of the Curia, assumed, as of right, that he and his Office would dominate the Council's business. Thus, Congar lamented, "the pitiless Roman machine" had set out to emasculate and dominate the "newborn child," a task made all the easier by the fact that the bishops were timid and used to doing what Rome told them, would not have read the documents and would betray the "conciliar spirit" as they did in 1854 and 1950, at the time of the Marian definitions. To make sure of its victory, Rome insisted on maximum secrecy, and would stop episcopates, or even individual bishops, from talking to each other. Rome, he predicted, would divide and rule by "atomisation" of the Fathers.[17] Even the appointment of himself and de Lubac as consultants has been Rome's way of marginalising potential troublemakers. They were stooges ["figurants"]. Later, he would rebuke himself for having been too timid in the preconciliar days; but at the time he had been convinced that there was little point in trying to improve the woefully inadequate schemas which had been drawn up. They were *faits accomplis*.[18]

That deep pessimism and near-paranoia had been largely dispelled by 1965. By then he was being lionised from all sides.

[17] *Diary*, i, 10, 13 [machine ... impitoyable], 19. So disillusioned was he that Congar had at one time seriously considered resigning as a consultant. *Diary*, i, 74.

[18] *Diary*, i, 181 and 466.

As they dispersed after the final session in December of that year, numerous Fathers heaped praise and thanks on him. The Council had had four sessions after all. The bishops had quickly wrested control of its work from the Curia. Constitutions like *Lumen Gentium* and *Gaudium et Spes*, decrees on Ecumenism and relations with non-Christians which would probably have been rejected in 1962 — and been unthinkable for many — had been passed by overwhelming majorities. Opinions for which Congar had been censured were now the proclaimed teaching of the Church. The contrast between the opening ceremonies for the first and last sessions symbolised the astonishing transformation which had taken place. On 11 October 1962 John XXIII had been carried into St Peter's like a Renaissance potentate wearing the triple tiara and flanked by flabelli, to preside over a 4-hour ceremony of baroque magnificence while the 3000 Fathers and Observers looked on in silence. Scandalised, Congar escaped from St Peter's soon after the papal Mass began. "Pius IX still reigns. Boniface VIII still reigns," he wrote indignantly in his *Diary*. "All this has been imposed on Simon Peter, humble fisher of men."[19] Three years later there was a very different ceremony. On 14 September 1965 Paul VI walked into St Peter's wearing only a mitre (the triple tiara having been sold for the poor) making an "entry of a bishop, pastor and priest, not a prince" for a dialogue Mass concelebrated by the presidents, moderators and secretaries of the Council.[20]

The story of how the Council came alive and began to develop its own personality and momentum is well known. Congar's sharp eye provides telling detail, especially about the changing fortunes of key individuals: Ottaviani losing authority to Cardinal Bea even in the first session and attending the general Congregations less

[19] *Diary*, i, 109.
[20] *Diary*, ii, 389.

frequently.[21] As the bishops then begin to "live the Council seriously"[22] and discover their collegiality, the old guard are forced onto the defensive: Cardinal Cigognani, who insisted that the doctrine of collegiality was heresy, totally outvoted on the Central Commission; Cardinal Siri broken and "bewildered"; Felici's influence waning.[23] But most gratifying of all was the side-lining of Tromp. By the middle of the first intercession (March 1963) Congar is reporting that the man who had dominated the Doctrinal Commission, hectoring and bullying, was losing control. He was now "poor Tromp." By the time the second session was under way, he had effectively been replaced by the assistant secretary, the Belgian Gerard Philips. By January 1964 he is like an "aged, broken chatelaine living on in a large empty castle"; by February 1965 he is a feeble old lion who "has lost his claws and coughs like an old man."[24]

Congar was unfair to Pius XII.[25] He was probably also unfair to the Curia, overestimating its power, villainy and rigid conservatism. He was probably unfair to Ottaviani, but eventually had the generosity of heart to admit that he possessed "a certain nobility of the faithful old servant."[26] He seems to have forgotten that Vatican I's work had been left unfinished and that, by common consent,

[21] *Diary*, i, 254, 257.

[22] *Diary*, i, 431 (but the Council's procedure, he notes, is very clumsy and disorderly, and many of the Fathers' interventions leave him "very oppressed." *Diary*, i, 260, 271).

[23] *Diary*, ii, 59 and 61.

[24] *Diary*, i, 351, 549; ii, 10, 315.

[25] For example, he seems to overlook the fact that that pope's encyclical *Mystici Corporis*, for which he had harsh words, had been hailed at the time by the avant-garde as a Magna Carta for the laity.

[26] *Diary*, ii, 459. He had also to admit that Ottaviani's chairmanship of the Doctrinal Commission had enabled it to accomplish a great deal of work.

a definition of episcopal collegiality, to balance that of papal infallibility, was overdue. He had underestimated the bishops, among whom there were distinguished, accomplished leaders who would quickly challenge any curial domination. He had certainly not expected the Belgian *équipe* — the bishops, led by Léon-Joseph Suenens, Archbishop of Malines-Brussels and Émile de Smedt, bishop of Bruges, and their Louvain theologians — to exercise the often decisive influence that they did both in the Council aula and in the Commissions.

It is intriguing to chart Congar's reactions to his fellow experts. Rahner has his sincere respect throughout, but he talks too much, monopolises discussions and could be indiscreet. Laurentin speaks "in an imperious manner and does not listen." Küng is impetuous and radical and "worries me a bit." Daniélou falls low in his esteem: he is superficial and essentially a journalist. Eventually "he gets on my nerves."[27] On the other hand, Ratzinger is modest, clear-headed and helpful, and Courtney Murray "a true gentleman" with amazingly good Latin.[28] But most praise goes to the Belgians such as Moeller, a theological giant, Prignon, "a good Christian, theologian and tactician" and quite selfless; and, above all, the incomparable Gerard Philips, assistant secretary to the Doctrinal Commission, who effectively silenced Tromp and, thanks to his extraordinary skill and charm, enabled the Commission to achieve what would have been impossible if Tromp and Ottaviani had had their way. He came to be trusted even by those two. Always down-to-earth and eirenic, he was able to express his ideas with perfect precision (praise indeed from an intellectually fastidious Congar), and in perfect Latin. What he said won immediate consent. He

[27] *Diary*, i, 382; ii, 463; i, 466; i, 328 and ii, 312 and 434.
[28] *Diary*, i, 356; ii, 539. Congar also admired Courtney Murray's calm reserve — "more British — even Oxfordian — than American!" *Diary*, ii, 340.

could so focus others' attention on detail that larger issues slipped past without their noticing and always had a solution to problems. His disarming "If it is the Fathers' wish" hid the fact that they were being led by him. This man was "providential."[29]

Though never more than five or six strong, as Congar marvelled, the Belgian experts dominated because they worked as a team and in close liaison with their bishops, especially Suenens and de Smedt. They and the bishops were all Louvain alumni or professors. They knew one another well and trusted each other. Unlike the French experts, who were mainly religious and not always at ease with their bishops, the Belgians were secular priests. They and their bishops were bold, ready to intervene and challenge. They were everywhere — Moeller, for instance, on three Commissions and in the Secretariat for Unity (though Congar had been refused admission to that Secretariat on the ground that he was on the Doctrinal Commission!). Above all, they thought ahead and planned every move. Congar recalls how lunch with the Belgians would always be a working lunch at which the latest developments would be eagerly assessed and tactics agreed — unlike the French, whose bishops would often chat without much purpose. Though better organised than the "anarchic" Spaniards, the French bishops never became the effective block that they could have been — as did the Germans and Chileans, who alone could begin to match the effectiveness of the Belgian team. Truly, Congar remarks, this was "the First Council of Louvain, held in Rome." And why was Louvain so dominant? Where were all the bishops and experts from those much-vaunted *Instituts Catholiques*?[30]

---

[29] *Diary*, i, 549 and 567: ii, 55-56. But Congar could add there that Philips' texts were "a bit pale and lacking in bite" [pâles et manquent de nerf] and that he was a very able man, but not profound.

[30] *Diary*, ii, 53-57.

Congar's pages show vividly how involved in the Council's affairs, albeit often behind the scenes, were both John XXIII and Paul VI. Both followed events closely, both were subject to intense lobbying from all sides. John was reluctant to intervene directly; Paul much more interventionist — often deeply disturbed, especially after an onslaught from, say, Ottaviani — sending his own *modi* to Commissions and exercising his canonical right to prohibit discussion of issues such as clerical celibacy and, of course, contraception. Congar came to understand Pope John's (at least public) ambivalence and to see its wisdom.[31] His successor's extraordinary intelligence and courage won respect over and above that due to his office. But Congar never quite made up his mind about him. He had given the tiara to the poor, but what about those gold rings for the bishops? He had agreed to replace the formula "Paul ... with the approval of the Council" used in promulgation of conciliar documents with "We ... with the Venerable Fathers ... approve." But a year later, on 6 November 1964, when Paul attended a plenary session of the Council in person the event was "stultifying ... A triumphalist display."[32] The famous *nota praevia* which Paul requested to be added to the statement on collegiality — protecting the papal primacy — and 13 "emendations" to *De Ecclesia*, which came at least indirectly from him, would effectively have placed the pope "not in the Church but above the Church."[33] Similarly, while opposing the desperate moves of the "mariologues" to have Mary proclaimed mediatrix of all graces and co-redemptress — to which Congar was ferociously opposed — Paul dismayed many, including most of the non-Catholic Observers

[31] But Pope John remained a "mixture" [mélange] of the "agreeable and the regrettable" [le sympathique et le regrettable]. *Diary*, i, 207.

[32] *Diary*, ii, 241. He came like "a marshall reviewing his troops." *Diary* ii, 243.

[33] *Diary*, ii, 86.

and Congar himself, by naming her "Mother of the Church" in his farewell allocution at the end of the third session.[34] Paul could tell de Smedt that the declaration on religious liberty, over which there had been fierce battles, was "capital" and, following a late night visit by Willebrands, intervene to support the vote on 21 September 1965 despite having been under tremendous pressure by intractable opponents who warned that it contradicted predecessors' teaching and would lead to indifferentism, religious relativism, even anarchy.[35] But the same Pope had obviously been bewildered when Congar had a private audience with him (which Congar had never thought he would be allowed) and talked of the Church as a communion of churches. "There is only one Church. Our Lord intended only one" was the Pope's response.[36] And it was the same Pope who insisted that separated Eastern bishops have no (authentic) jurisdiction. He resisted intense pressure to halt the decree on Ecumenism and gave a profoundly moving farewell address, composed by himself, to the Observers in St Paul's Without the Walls at the end of the final session. But it was Gerard Philips' opinion that Pope Paul remained at heart authoritarian; and he lacked an ecclesiology for his grand ecumenical gestures, Congar remarked — perhaps rather cruelly.[37]

[34] *Diary*, ii, 290. What does the title mean, Congar asks — almost angrily? All his life, he said, he had been fighting "Mediterranean and Irish" Marian excesses. *Diary*, i, 66. Later he wrote of "fanatical mariologists" [mariologues fanatiques]. *Diary*, ii, 114.

[35] *Diary*, ii, 401 and 415.

[36] *Diary*, ii, 115.

[37] *Diary*, ii, 325; ii, 269, 291. But how providential, he suggests, that Pius XII did not make him a cardinal, else he would surely have succeeded immediately and continued in his predecessor's tradition. Instead, he underwent the extraordinary "opening up" [ouverture] brought about by John XXIII. *Diary*, i, 386. Later (in 1980), however, he wrote very warmly about Pope Paul's ecclesiology. See Congar, "Moving towards a pilgrim Church," *Vatican II by Those Who Were There*, ed. A. Stacpole (London: Geoffrey Chapman, 1986) 129-152.

Above all, the *Diary* reveals the stupendous amount of work which Congar undertook during those hectic years after he first joined the Preparatory Theological Commission. He boasted that he had worked harder than anyone else.[38] Until — if this is ever possible — the scores of successive drafts for the schemas in which he was involved have been analysed we will never know the full extent of his contribution to the Council's work. Many of his drafts were either discarded or amended out of recognition. But he himself lists for us those parts which he knew were truly "his."[39] But the drafting and re-drafting of texts at innumerable meetings of sub-Commissions or sub-sub-Commissions or alone for the three Commissions of which he was eventually a member required an enormous toil on the part of him and other experts, because thousands of *modi* submitted by the Fathers on the schemas presented in St Peter's — 4000 for *De Ecclesia* and 9700 for *De Presbyteris,* for example[40] — and hundreds of pages of other comments by the Fathers had to be digested and incorporated, as appropriate, into the texts. This absorbed much time during intersessions and required Congar to be frequently passing to and from Rome, and too often frantic activity during the sessions themselves, when he would be dashing around Rome from one rendez-vous to another, one Commission to another.

The French hierarchy might suddenly ask him to produce a statement for them on this or that. Many individual bishops asked him to draft their speeches they were due to make in the aula (one, a complete stranger, did so on one of the coaches which took

---

[38] *"Plus omnibus laboravi." Diary*, ii, 510.

[39] *Diary*, ii, 511. See Flynn, *"Mon Journal du Concile*: Yves Congar and the Battle for a renewed Ecclesiology at the Second Vatican Council," *Louvain Studies* 28 (2003) 51-53 for a detailed analysis of Congar's contributions to the conciliar documents.

[40] *Diary*, ii, 11 and 482.

the bishops back from St Peter's every lunchtime[41]) or to comment on their own drafts. Congar was tireless in lobbying bishops whom he trusted and proposing ideas to them. Small groups of experts — such as Rahner, Ratzinger and he — often met to discuss ideas and put them on paper. The experts exchanged drafts, Congar ever ready to comment on colleagues' work.

There was an unremitting programme of conferences (workshops) which he gave to groups of bishops during the council sessions: Brazilian, Canadian, francophone African, French, Polish, Vietnamese and Melchite. Fellow-experts did likewise. In some respects this may have been their most influential role. Bishops taught themselves, of course, but the single most important factor which transformed the Council and resulted in the rank-and-file voting overwhelmingly for, say, collegiality, ecumenism, religious liberty, were those sessions when Congar and others were able to inform, explain and answer questions.

The *Diary* shows vividly how busy he could be. In a single evening (7 October 1963), for instance, he composed three texts — on local churches, the priesthood and the "ex sese" clause in the 1870 definition of papal infallibility.[42] In the morning of 28 February 1965 he wrote a piece on St Thomas for the Commission *De Studiis*, a "*relatio*" on a new introduction to the *De Libertate* and a declaration on the subject for the French bishops, and in the afternoon embarked a critical analysis of comments of over 500 bishops on *De Presbyteris* which had to be submitted by 22 March.[43]

He was also doing a considerable amount of his own writing all this time, including regular contributions to *Informations*

---

[41] *Diary*, i, 441. Congar later complains about bishops who asked him to write their speeches but then did not use them! He composed for several cardinals, e.g. Ragumbwa, Liénart and Marty.

[42] *Diary*, i, 441-442.

[43] *Diary*, ii, 341.

Catholiques Internationales, a very successful periodical. He had a heavy daily post to contend with single-handedly and when he came back from Rome to Strasbourg would find letters, requests for reviews, proofs piled on his desk, every chair and even the floor. During the conciliar sessions in Rome, apart from incessant networking with his huge circle of friends and acquaintances and being especially attentive to the Observers, he was pursued by admirers, students wanting advice on their theses (often on aspects of his writings), and the media.

What is truly remarkable is that this heroic endeavour was accomplished even as that disease which eventually killed him was taking remorseless toll of his body. Again and again he exclaims: "I have no strength … I am killing myself. I can hardly put one foot in front of another or carry my bag up the steps."[44] He dragged his right leg and moved — with a stick — with increasing difficulty. Sometimes he lost use of his right arm and could scarcely hold a pen or do more than type with one finger. There were nosebleeds during one session and serious insomnia and cramp towards the end. He suffered from whistling in an ear (tinnitus?) which was increasingly distressing in the poor acoustics of some of the meeting-places of Commissions and sub-Commissions. His back and sacrum had also begun to hurt. And finally, there was the death in December 1963 of a mother he revered.

"The First Council of Louvain, held in Rome": if he had been asked, he would probably have added that the individual who

---

[44] E.g. *Diary*, i, 400, 531. Once it took him half an hour to tie up his shoes (*Diary*, ii, 40). He was often at a very low point. On 2 November 1963 he could cry out: "I am spent … crushed … The world is too big … I am old, empty" [je me suis débordé … écrasé … le monde est trop vaste … Je me sens vieilli, vidé].Were such an idea not "stupid," he could think that it was better if he departed this life now. *Diary*, i, 516-517.

deserved most credit for it was Gerard Philips. But really it was Congar's Council. Vatican II saw the triumph of Congarism.

The Church which he had served and continued to serve selflessly had re-discovered her true identity: hierarchical institution, yes, but also mystery, sacrament, *communio*, servant of the World and the poor, and pilgrim. She now understood herself once more in biblical, kerygmatic and eschatological terms rather than juridical and scholastic ones. Ultra-conciliarism and ultra-papalism had both been finally laid to rest by the doctrine of episcopal collegiality.

The Church is the People of God, the new Israel, empowered by the Spirit to bring the light of Christ to the World. The Kingdom comes. By baptism the laity share in Christ's prophetic and priestly kingship. All Christians, and especially those in full communion with the Vicar of Christ, must work ceaselessly to end the scandal of disunity and for a reconciliation which represents a victory only for Christ and the truth.

Vatican II was an incomparable blessing. Undoubtedly, however, it was followed, at least in the West, by some wholly unexpected, unintended and lamentable events: the departure from the active ministry of tens of thousands of priests, for instance; the emptying of so many houses of nuns, monks, friars and brothers; large-scale decline in Mass attendance — and so on. When Newman observed that every Council was followed by a period of turbulence he was thinking primarily of the often noisy departure of those against whom judgement had been given. But Vatican II did not condemn. It liberated. Unwittingly it also released, many would say, much that was wrongheaded, if not perverse. Some have argued that the "explosion" would have been even greater if there had been no Vatican II. We will never know. As we have seen, Congar (often the pessimist) had judged that it came twenty years too soon. But an alternative judgement is that it came a decade too late. The combination of the heady wine of Vatican II and the "spirit of the Sixties" was devastating. Had the Council taken place in the 1950s, the Church would have had enough time to recover its equilibrium before the affluence and sexual revolution of the Sixties hit the West.

To the end, Congar remained convinced that the real threat to the Council's success came from the "right," not the "left." Ever suspicious of the Curia, he feared that a conservative backlash launched from Rome would result in bishops losing "the spirit of the Council" when they returned home.[45] True, he had become increasingly wary of Küng and German radicalism. Even before the first session he had warned against simply rejecting the first schemas out of hand and starting afresh. He preferred the conciliatory ways of a Gerard Philips. And he had refused to take part in an unofficial meeting of experts in Rome immediately before the first session to plan their campaign lest this was seen as a "paracouncil" of theologians over and against the true Council of bishops. He would come only if the "intégristes" were represented.[46] The simplistic Küng "goes like an arrow," he later remarked, and has the heedlessness of a "revolutionary."[47] Sensing the latter's neo-Donatism, he reminds himself that the Catholic Church includes the Ottavianis, Parentes and Tromps, and "we must live with them."[48] He was obviously taken aback by the intensity of complaints about *Schema XVII* by a group of Dutch and German theologians (including Küng), several of them newcomers, at a meeting in September 1965, just before the final session opened.[49]

---

[45] *Diary*, ii, 465.

[46] *Diary*, i, 101.

[47] *Diary*, i, 465. Cf. ii, 498. Congar deemed "profound" Paul VI's remark to Willebrands that Küng was "without love." *Diary*, ii, 336.

[48] *Diary*, i, 466.

[49] *Diary*, ii, 406.

But such experiences sounded no warning bells. Seven months earlier, he had agonised over the Declaration on religious freedom which the experts had finished and which was due to go to the Council in the Autumn. Was it as dangerous as its critics warned, he asked himself? Could it be abused? Yes, there was that danger. But the document had to be taken in the context of the whole work of the Council.[50] That, some would say, is precisely what many did not do. Later appeals to "the spirit of Vatican II" too often (and increasingly) had little grounding in what the Council actually said.

It is unfair to blame Vatican II — let alone Congar — for that. There was a deeply prudent side to him. After all, he knew the difference between true and false reform! A large body like the Church "must move with a measured rhythm," he had warned himself.[51] Küng and other radicals wanted confrontation and complained about the Council's apparently slow progress. Congar knew that patience was necessary. "I believe profoundly in the delays," he declared.[52]

Nevertheless, when the Dutch theologian Schillebeeckx reported that there was a real danger of schism in Holland, Congar's only response was that the situation was simply "worrying."[53] He did not explore the warning. And when Cardinal Suenens asked if he thought there was a crisis of faith in the Church, he replied "not in France." There were some unacceptable things being said in some places — about the Eucharist, for example — but no crisis. There

[50] *Diary*, ii, 340 (February 1965). "The Declaration will be abused to support false liberations" [libérations frauduleuses].

[51] *Diary*, i, 467.

[52] *Diary*, i, 466. Typically, Küng was critical of what had been achieved by October 1963, while Congar marvelled at the immense progress made. Küng even wanted to have Ottaviani removed. Congar knew that the "opposition" had to be respected — if possible, won over.

[53] *Diary*, ii, 448. He was reassured by Cardinal Alfrink's optimistic verdict on the Dutch situation.

could be one, he predicted, but it would be because of the under-mining of the historicity of the Gospels (by Bultmann and his fol-lowers) and would therefore not be attributable in any way to the Council. That was how he still saw things in October 1965.[54] Was he overlooking an important fact of History, which England dis-covered in the 1640s, France in the 1790s, Russia in 1917 (and which had been all-too obvious to Luther and Calvin, for that mat-ter), namely, that the greater threat to the success of major but ordered change can come from the left rather than the right? Rad-icals often hijack revolutions. Radical liberals have striven hard to hijack Vatican II. Congar seemed to be only half-aware of their threat, continuing to believe, as he has said, that the greater threat was of a conservative backlash.

Hindsight is notoriously easier than prescience. No one could have predicted the size of the disasters which befell the Church in the wake of the Council. But we can legitimately ask whether Con-gar was as sensitive as he should have been to the seriously unset-tling effect on many good, devout souls of the rapid changes which he had vigorously promoted. In a very revealing passage early in the *Diary* he reports that Italian bishops were said to be "bewil-dered" because the Council has thrown into doubt so much that they had taken as "classiques et sacrées."[55] What they were say-ing was truly ominous. One cannot help wondering whether it was exactly such feelings, more intense perhaps, which later caused so many priests and religious, male and female, to quit. So much that they had been taught to regard as important, distinctive, precious and, if not *de fide*, then non-negotiable, had been discarded or demoted, that it was easy to wonder whether much else would soon be jettisoned. It was equally easy to feel cheated, therefore. Faced

---

[54] *Diary*, ii, 435. Obviously unconvinced, Suenens suggested that what Con-gar predicted was more likely to happen in Germany or Holland.

[55] *Diary*, i, 351-352. These words are not easy to put in English.

with the Italians' dilemma, Congar showed neither comprehension nor sympathy. Renewal, he said rather obscurely, will have to come from the laity, but that seemed unlikely.

Similarly, when asked by the head of a Jesuit house that he was visiting in January 1965 whether he thought that John XXIII had done "a lot of harm to the Church" Congar can assume that this referred only to the Pope's softening of the Vatican's attitude to Soviet Russia and the Communists.[56] What was really being asked passed him by. He had been thinking, praying and writing for so many years — decades even — about so many of the changes then taking place that he did not appreciate the distress which their suddenness caused among those who had been little prepared for them. He tended to interpret their bewilderment as mere conservatism.

He was acutely sensitive to the Catholic Eastern bishops and fully aware of the difficulties facing the reunion of the Roman and Orthodox churches. It was one thing to lift the excommunications of 1054; quite another to overcome centuries of fear and even hatred. That will require "much patience."[57] He knew enough history to appreciate why this was so. How far did he understand that Orthodox antipathy to the Latin West was only a part of the problem? Orthodox hostility towards Uniates was matched by centuries of rivalry between Constantinople and Moscow and feuds within Greek and non-Greek churches. Rapprochement with, say, Athens would automatically alienate Jerusalem, even as the Council's *Declaration on the Jews* — which had faced the very delicate issue of "Deicide," that is, the charge of "God-killing" levelled against the Jews who put Christ to death — ran the risk of alienating either Jews if it was judged anti-Semitic and alienating both Orthodox and Jews if the Arab world and particularly Palestinian Arabs thought it was not.

[56] *Diary*, ii, 303-304.

[57] *Diary*, ii, 247. Elsewhere he spoke of the "immobilisme" of the Orthodox. *Diary*, i, 468.

Though surprisingly hostile to the idea of dialogue with non-Christians[58] Congar had, of course, been passionately committed to the cause of Christian unity for decades and was elated when *De Oecumenismo* was at last approved. The Church must practice a "living ecumenism," he wrote, which informs all its thought and actions.[59] When a euphoric Cardinal Heenan on 20 November 1963 had declared on behalf of the bishops of England and Wales that they were "absolutely ready for dialogue" with non-Catholics Congar was overwhelmed. This declaration is "sensational" he wrote in capital letters in the *Diary* and poured out his thanks to the cardinal for "so beautiful, moving and important an intervention: a historic act" which he would never have imagined could happen.[60] He was a devotee of Taizé and the Benedictine monastery of Chèvetogne. He respected the World Council of Churches. He was an assiduous friend of many of the Observers, especially Oscar Cullmann, the distinguished Protestant professor.

But was he facing reality squarely? In the *Diary* he never seems to ask: how influential was Taizé? Was not the World Council of Churches moving away from Rome rather than towards it? Like many continental Catholic theologians Congar probably never really grasped the true nature of Anglicanism, i.e. that it is an 'ism' in a cultural sense more than a theological one and so "broad" that it could contain Protestant fundamentalists at one end, high churchmen at the other and in between lay people, ministers and even bishops who denied the divinity of Christ, let alone the Resurrection. Dialogue with such a diffuse body would never be easy.

[58] What dialogue can there be with Buddhism or Confucianism, he asked, rather indignantly? *Diary*, ii, 21.

[59] *Diary*, ii, 413.

[60] *Diary*, i, 552-553, 555. But later he could remark of Heenan that he likes "to act the fool a bit" [faire un peu le pitre]. *Diary*, ii, 378.

Recent happenings in the Anglican communion, which Congar would never have thought possible, have made dialogue even more difficult.

The same has been true of Continental Protestantism. The subjectivism and denial of the historicity of the Gospels which climaxed in the work of Bultmann has meant that, even as sincere attempts were being made on both sides to heal the divisions caused by the Reformation, much of the Protestant world was drifting away so fast from its former orthodoxy that there was ever less common ground between it and Rome. Bultmann's Christianity has no objective doctrinal content. It says that stories about a man who claimed to be God and performed miracles, etc. are true only insofar as one chooses to believe them.

Congar, of course, knew about this. His friend Cullmann deplored the way in which the young were being seduced by Bultmann's disastrous ideas.[61] But did Congar really face the fact that these posed an increasing obstacle to ecumenism? And there were perhaps two other matters his *Diary* did not address. First, how exactly does one reconcile the goal of ecumenism, which is corporate union or reunion, with the fact that faith requires an individual, free act of assent (under the influence of the Holy Spirit)? How precisely can corporate assent occur? No doubt there is an answer. But what is it? Secondly, given that ecumenical dialogue consists in discovering precisely what issues really divide Christians (as distinct from what are thought to do so), what authority is there in non-Catholic communities which can declare that what agreed statements say is agreed truth is indeed what those communities believe? And what authority is there in those communities which can declare that what has been agreed is sufficient to enable those communities to come into full eucharistic communion

[61] *Diary,* i, 390, ii, 9 and 534.

with one another, the remaining differences between them being matters where diversity is legitimate?

Did Congar admit any of this into his thinking? There is no sign in the *Diary* that he did.[62] Did he appreciate that the familiar slogan of "unity in diversity" is often immediately misunderstood, especially by Anglicans, to mean ecclesiastical federalism — which is the enemy of authentic ecumenism? It was easy to be naïve as Vatican II drew to its remarkable close.

And how has collegiality fared? Congar, who was clearly in favour of a relaxing of the Church's teaching on contraception, would have blamed Paul VI — at least at the time — of highhanded papalism when he confronted the world with *Humanae Vitae* in 1968, and perhaps would have been tempted to blame Rome for the regrettable failure then of most of the college of bishops to rally round its head. But he could never have guessed that, for many episcopates, collegiality has meant the dominance of national conferences of bishops, and that often these both have inhibited individual bishops' ability to act and have produced a plethora of local commissions and secretariats, all with expensive staffs! It is difficult to see what else collegiality could have meant in practice — other than the regular meetings of the Synod of bishops in Rome which have taken place since the Council.

Congar could not have foreseen the catechetical failure of the post-conciliar Church, due in large measure to the collapse of religious orders that previously sustained Catholic schools, which has

---

[62] There is an intriguing entry in the *Diary* (i, 560) for 21 November 1963, a day on which he had listened to the debate in St Peter's on *De Oecumenismo*. Congar writes in capital letters that he sees the ambiguity in the word ecumenism: for some it means reunion, i.e. a return to the Church (of separated brethren); for others "something new facing all of us" and demanding profound reform [quelque chose de neuf en avant de nous tous]. Surely he had not just discovered this crucial distinction?

resulted in widespread ignorance of the Good News and hence widespread lapsation. But in view of the disregard of many Catholics, married and unmarried, for much of the Church's teaching on sexual and related issues, his hopes for a revivified laity now seem rather naïve. Not all is gloom, of course. There is much vitality in the Western Church: holiness among priests and laity, thriving new religious foundations and ecclesial communities for instance, and catechetical initiatives. But it is a striking fact that these have sometimes encountered reluctance, if not worse, from local hierarchies, and have received most support from Rome. Similarly the prolife movement, a worldwide groundswell of "ordinary" people, without parallel in recent history, has been largely a lay Catholic achievement — with sometimes only hesitant support of local ordinaries. Once again it is Rome which has discerned and inspired.

Congar pleaded for dialogue with the World — a phrase also beloved of Paul VI. But what does it mean? It poses many difficulties. In the first place there is, of course, the fundamental ambiguity of "World": the World that God so loved, because it is His Creation, that he sent His only-begotten Son to redeem it, and the World that has been judged and from which the Christian must remain untainted. Which is the World with which there must be dialogue? Next, what is this dialogue? Did Jesus Christ engage in it? Is not the Church's role to preach the Gospel, to convince the World of sin and call it to repentance, to be a sign of contradiction, a sacrament of unity? The Church loves the World, is concerned for all humankind and all Creation, is no one's enemy, benefits from the achievements of the World (e.g. modern communications) listens to and learns from the World.[63] But none of this is *dialogue*.

---

[63] It learnt something from Marxism, for instance. It has learnt something from modern feminism. It has recently taken Enlightenment ideas on human rights and

Consider today's Western World — so much given over to hedonism and consumerism, much of its popular culture nihilistic and aggressively de-Christianised. In what sense does the Church engage in dialogue with it? None. The word does not signify anything. It smacks of sentimentality. Dialogue with the World can easily become conforming to it. Was Congar, then, like *Gaudium et Spes*, too optimistic?

Insofar as his purpose was to help the Church to rediscover her full, authentic self-understanding, he could be described as a radical *conservative*. Much of what happened in the post-conciliar years distressed him deeply. Even by 1967 he was asking: "Where do we go from here? Where shall we be in twenty years? I, too, feel almost every day a temptation to anxiety in the face of all that has changed or is being called into question".[64] That was two years after the Council ended. Early on in his *Diary* he said that it would take one or two generations for the Council's work to bear full fruit, that is, for a true *ressourcement* to be achieved.[65] Yes, perhaps it is still too early to pass final judgement on Vatican II. We must wait in Christian hope for Congar's prediction to be fulfilled.

baptised them in a way which would have astonished both the Enlightenment and Pius IX.

[64] Congar, "Theology's Tasks after Vatican II," *Renewal of Religious Thought*, ed. Shook (New York: Herder and Herder, 1968) i, 50. Elsewhere he spoke of the "negative aspects" of the Council, but strongly denied that "the present crisis in the Church is the result of Vatican II." Congar, "A last look at the Council," *Vatican II by those who were there*, 351. He continued to insist that the Council was "not responsible" for any crisis — without making a distinction between direct and indirect responsibility. And did he not think that the greater problem was the Lefevristes and other right-wingers rather than the radical liberals?

[65] *Diary*, i, 467. He argued that it would take so long because the exegetes of Jerusalem and the *Institut Biblique* had been excluded from the Council.

THE SYSTEM AND THE TRUTH IN THE DIARIES OF YVES CONGAR

Alberto MELLONI

Professor of History at the University of Modena-Reggio Emilia
and A member of the John XXIII Foundation of Religious Science, Bologna

It is often the case that the diaries of ecclesiastics attract at the same time the interest of ecclesiastics themselves, of the general public and of historians. Some suppose that there will be, or they search for, first-hand accounts, that the immediacy that comes from having put aside the dressings of propriety will break open the crust of the style characteristic of religious writing and reveal truths that are unconfessed or which cannot be confessed; others instead scrutinise these writings — more often than not destined to be made public only after the death of their authors — in search of evidence for an unfailing sense of loyalty towards the ecclesiastical institution. There are still others — and *per se* this should get the approval of scholars — who look with disenchantment at a source that, even if it avoids the trappings of propriety, nonetheless needs to be "decoded" from within its own codes of communication. Only after this intense work of criticism has been done will the text be able to uncover sources, connections, a dynamism and, in some cases, broad glimpses of the position of the church in the broader picture of its time.

Often among the reasons that motivate the keeping of a diary there is the desire — more or less acknowledged — to satisfy one or other of these types of reader. It is in this way that one can read those fierce pages penned by Monsignor Tardini during the years

between the wars and beyond; in these pages the idiosyncrasies of
the most illustrious personages he met are firmly set in deadly
aphorisms;[1] or one can find final evidence of a vision of reality —
often limited — in so many of the diaries that were begun by the
fathers of the Second Vatican Council. The best of these were influenced by older models,[2] certainly in some of these (it is enough to
go back and read the large autobiographical diaries of the twentieth century from Baudrillart to Buonaiuti, from Wyszyński to Ron-
calli — to mention but a few) there is the clear awareness that their
pages would provide material destined to make a mark on the public opinion of the future and supply historical data that scholars
would not be able to neglect.

THE CONGAR DIARIES

Yves Congar was very well aware of this complex function of
diaries when, as a Dominican friar, he decided to take up once
again the keeping of a diary. I say, yet again, because almost "con-
strained" by the gentle firmness of his mother, Lucie Desoye, the
infant Congar had started keeping a jotter diary during the First
World War and he succeeded in giving an objective account of the
war that was being carried on under his window as a child. He did
this in a jotter that is complete and accurate. It is full of the cultural stereotypes of his time and reveals a very bright intelligence;
it was here that the little boy acquired some of the fundamental
techniques required for keeping a diary: precision in dating, completeness in the telling of a story, the identification of one's sources

---

[1] Carlo Felice Casula, *Domenico Tardini (1888-1961. L'azione della Santa
Sede nella crisi fra le due guerre* (Rome: Studium, 1988).

[2] See my introduction to "Les journaux privés dans l'histoire du Vatican II,"
in Marie-Dominique Chenu, *Notes quotidiennes au Concile* (Paris: Cerf, 1955) 7-
54.

and the relevance of impressions. He would not be slow in taking these up again when he was an adult.[3]

As a preacher, in fact, Congar would take to keeping a diary again, not continuously but when he happened "de faire une expérience nouvelle, d'entrer en contact avec un monde nouveau; quand j'ai été mêlé à des événements d'importance historique."[4] So among his papers at the Convent of St James in Paris there are diaries about his travels, in England 1936-1939, in Rome in 1946, in Spain in 1950, in the Middle East in 1953-1954. These were dedicated to an investigation in person of the terrain that would be the object of his reflexion on and his support for ecumenism.[5] These diaries follow at close quarters the difficulties that arise from the lack of unity among Christians. First of all, they mark the course of his ecumenical preaching at Montmartre in January 1936, on which he based the plan for the volume that marks in a new way the series *Unam Sanctam*;[6] he then follows the useless negotiation of May 1938 with Cardinal Baudrillart in search of a coverage, which he does not get; and finally, one year later, to recall the colloquies with Cardinal Verdier about the collections that he had promoted with the du Cerf publishing house. At the end of these are again found the diaries of war and imprisonment of 1939 and 1944.[7]

---

[3] *L'enfant Yves Congar, Journal de la guerre 1914-1918*, ed. S. Audoin-Rouzeau & D. Congar (Paris: Cerf, 1997).

[4] This is in the memoir "Appels et cheminements 1929-1963," added as a preface in 1964 to *Chrétiens en dialogue,* and then revised in *Une passion: l'unité Réflexions et souvenirs 1929-1973* (Paris: Cerf, 1974), and now in Cardinal Yves Congar, *Écrits réformateurs*, ed. J-P. Jossua (Paris: Cerf, 1995) 264.

[5] See Étienne Fouilloux, "Présentation générale," in Y. Congar, *Journal d'un théologien 1946-1956* (Paris: Cerf, 2000) 13.

[6] See Étienne Fouilloux, *Les catholiques et l'unité chrétienne du XIXe au XXe siècle: Itinéraires européens d'expression française* (Paris: Centurion, 1982).

[7] This consists of a *carnet de guerre* that covers the tragic days from September 2nd 1939 to March 8th 1940, and in addition there are five notebooks of his imprisonment (May 27th 1940 to January 14th 1942) and of what happened in the years 1942 to 1945, see Fouilloux, "Présentation générale," 14n.

Along with these unedited diaries of the adult Congar,[8] in the years after the war he produced the large series of notebooks that have recently been published: on the one hand there is the one that Étienne Fouilloux has called the *Journal d'un théologien*[9] that contains fragments from the years 1946 to 1956. Then there is the long and very rich account of the Vatican Council, *Mon journal du Concile*;[10] this has been printed reproducing the typewritten transcription carried out in the seventies and re-read by Father Congar himself. Although they have appeared posthumously, these diaries that cover almost twenty years are often the basis on which the postconciliar Congar produced a critical revision of his theological journeys,[11] autobiographical accounts[12] and records that were then taken up again in the colloquium with Jean Puyo in the mid-seventies.[13]

[8] There is a list of these in Étienne Fouilloux, "Yves Congar, témoin de l'église de son temps," *Cardinal Yves Congar (1904-1995)*, ed. A. Vauchez (Paris: Cerf, 1999) 77-78.

[9] Only a fragment of this had been published by Congar in 1977, "La question des observateurs catholiques à la conférence de Amsterdam, 1948," in *Die Einheit der Kirche. Dimensionen ihrer Heiligkeit, Katholizität und Apostolizität. Festgabe Peter Meinhold zum 70. Geburtstag*, ed. L. Hein (Wiesbaden: Franz Steiner, 1977) 241-246; on the Fouilloux affair, *Les catholiques*, 781-798.

[10] Yves Congar, *Mon journal du Concile*, ed. É. Mahieu, 2 vols. (Paris: Cerf, 2002). Congar did not publish any of this, even if the chronicles in the series *Le Concile au jour de jour*, 4 vols. (Paris: Cerf, 1963-1966) include in many passages its substance and his opinions almost to the letter; on the reasons for this permit me to refer to my own contribution "Yves Congar à Vatican II: Hypothèses et pistes de recherche," *Cardinal Yves Congar (1904-1995)*, 117-165.

[11] See "Appels et cheminements 1929-1963," quoted above.

[12] On his youth see "Enfance ardennaise," *La Grive* (October-December, 1965) 14-16 and "Enfance sedanaise 1904-1919," *Le pays sedanais* 9 (1978) n. 5, 27-31; then "Trois années à la Faculté de philosophie," *Le livre du centenaire 1875-1975* (Paris: Beauchesne, 1975) 245-258; for the connections with the Maritain circle of Meudon, "Souvenirs sur Jacques Maritain," *Notes et documents de l'Institut Jacques Maritain* (April-June, 1962) 5-7.

[13] *Une vie pour la vérité, Jean Puyo interroge le Père Congar* (Paris: Centurion, 1975).

The decision to give a privileged place to these two sets of notes is amply justified because they constitute a source of great importance for both historical and theological studies.

The most recent diary — the one kept from the time that Congar appears in the preparatory theological commission right up until the day after the close of Vatican II — is a document of primary importance for getting to know Vatican II and the role played by the Dominican ecumenist within the council. *Mon journal du Concile* gathers together precise and detailed information accompanied by indications of the sources and (in the manuscript version which, through some inexplicable editorial whim, has not been taken as the basis for the edition) of hundreds of accompanying documents. It is a diary in which Congar, while giving free rein to his own thoughts and judgements,[14] records accurately the facts, the speeches and the discussions. It also records his own fidelity: his fidelity to the council as a moment of a "true reform" of the church, free of any yielding or indulgence towards any of the protagonists in the great body of the assembly; fidelity to his own gradualist theological position which he declared and defended with loyalty and courage both in front of his ecclesiastical persecutors and in the face of the theological audacity of younger colleagues; fidelity, and this not the least, to the greater discipline of the church, practised without indulgence and without mitigating compromises on the level of intellectual honesty. *Mon journal du Concile*, therefore, is a witness to the importance of the Second Vatican Council; while maintaining a very entertaining literary side in the encounters between the theological adversaries, from the Assessor of the Holy Office

---

[14] They would have documented some comparisons with the numerous diaries of Vatican II that are now available. See my own, "Les journaux privés dans l'histoire de Vatican II", to which should be added the observations and the information periodically collected by Massimo Faggioli, "Concilio Vaticano II: bollettino bibliografico (2000-2002)," *Cristianesimo nella Storia* 24 (2003) 335-360.

(described as a "fascist monophysite"), onwards, it increases to a considerable degree our knowledge of the rhythm of work in the preparatory sessions and in the discussions in the general assembly.

Completely different are the older notebooks — written in the years 1946 to 1956 — and edited under the title *Journal d'un Théologien*: here the background is not the disordered re-awakening of a church on the move towards an unknown equilibrium both institutional and doctrinal, but the harsh persecution in which Congar is one of the victims. The diaries that document this provide not so much detailed information about individual events, but a heart-breaking and shattering witness to a *status ecclesiae* perfectly aware of its own procedures and its own aims. The diary of the persecution is at one and the same time a diary of war, a diary of imprisonment and a diary of journeying. The war that this diary describes is, in fact, the war carried out against Congar, the motivation for which was never made clear; the imprisonment is one of impalpable silence, of reticent solidarity, of polite and senseless procedures that surround him to the point of bringing him to the brink of despair; the journey is the one that takes Congar away from his own theologising right into the mechanism of condemnations of the ecclesiastical institution, against which Congar protests, not in the name of individual rights, but in the name of Gospel truth.[15] The *Journal d'un Théologien* gives a clear picture of the dialectic between two dimensions of the church that were well known to Congar the scholar: on the one hand, the church of Tradition, sensitive to the unceasing relating of the needs of the time to the Gospel and vice versa, the "great church" of which he will become a voracious listener in the complex event of the Second Vatican Council; and on the other hand, the church of the condemnations,

---

[15] See Jean-Pierre Jossua, "Signification théologique de quelques retours sur le passé dans l'œuvre d'Yves Congar (1904-1995)," *Cardinal Yves Congar (1904-1995)*, ed. A. Vauchez (Paris: Cerf, 1999) 93-103.

ready to confuse the little space of Vatican territory with the world, paying no attention to the mixture of diversities that make up the church, a parallel church that Congar does not hesitate to define as a regime and uses very harsh expressions to describe it.

There is no other ecclesiastical document of the twentieth century, as far as I know, that has such force of direct personal witness: it is not a public denunciation or a public gesture of rupture made by a liberal, but it is precisely because it expresses his obligation to be faithful to the truth,[16] that it creates an even greater impression. What the persecuted Dominican sees and describes is all within a system that, even though he allows concessions that are certainly not insignificant at the level of the magisterium (the encyclicals *Divino Afflante Spiritu* on exegesis, *Mediator Dei* on the liturgy, and in a certain way even *Mystici Corporis* on ecclesiology) clings to its own power with a way of acting that he — Congar, Cardinal Congar, — likens to a totalitarian regime.

THE CHURCH "OF" PIUS XII

The disturbing force of this *Journal,* that publishes eight memoirs or diaries written between around 1946 and 1954,[17] springs not only from the consideration of the scathing vocabulary that Congar uses, but especially from the comparison between the account of Roman

[16] "L'or pur de la vérité" is the phrase he will use in a conversation to indicate history as the "moyen irrécusable" in this research. See Charles MacDonald, *Church and World in the Plan of God: Aspects of History and Eschatology in the Thought of Père Yves Congar OP* (Frankfurt: Peter Lang, 1982) vii.

[17] The section *La crise de 1954* had been used by François Leprieur, *Quand Rome condamne: Dominicains et prêtres-ouvriers* (Paris: Plon-Cerf, 1989). Étienne Fouilloux has used other parts in a number of studies cited later.

power of the final years of the pontificate of Pacelli that it provides and the one that is in circulation among modern historians.

In fact, the research that is going on about Pius XII often takes for granted that to his pretensions to be "the" master of truth for the church there was a corresponding factual reality, and that in any case he can and ought to be judged on the basis of this axiom. It is a fact that under Pope Pacelli the concentration of power (from the church to the episcopate, from the episcopate to the Curia, from the Curia to the person of the pope) was significantly increased, even at the expense of the College of Cardinals, forced by the decisions of the pope towards a progressive impoverishment and an inevitable senescence. However, it has to be proved that such a process permits reducing the decisions of the greater Vatican "machine" to the pure *voluntas* of the pope, without taking into account the internal dynamics of a court that was narrower and more complex than the typical court of the Roman tradition.

A typical product of this historiographical point of view — according to which, in a certain sense, the pope "is" the church — is the research into the position of the Vatican on the *Shoa':* from the mid-sixties onwards this has concentrated on the silence of Pius XII, and there have arisen polemics that have seen serious scholars gathering around the figure of the pontiff in search of a documentation that has for too long been denied, superficial denigrators for whom the few fragments of sources in circulation were enough, and embarrassed official advocates who were dedicated to the camouflage of the decisions and reasons of the pontiff.[18] Today, on the contrary, it has become ever clearer that the historical point is to be found elsewhere with regard to the axis of these polemics: because, after one has reconstructed the personal dilemmas and

---

[18] For a historical account, see Renato Moro, *La Chiesa e lo sterminio degli ebrei* (Bologna: II Mulino, 2003).

decisions of Pius XII, there remains the problem of understanding how and why the whole body of the church had accepted that silence and — notwithstanding the number of "just" Catholics that could be counted — took it over as its own.

In a way analogous to what happened in the historiography about the *Shoa'*, the research into the crises that hit the church in the years after the war, into the purges that weakened its theological culture, already impoverished by the anti-modernist campaign, into the decisions by which the prestigious moral patrimony of the church was dissipated in triumphalism — this research runs the risk of attributing the reasons and the mistakes in these decisions to Pius XII in person, to the point that even the official Roman historiography has come seriously to revise the spiritual and cultural stature of Pius XII,[19] and it does not face the question about how around and under this man, who was surrounded by an aura of omniscient omnipotence, there was unleashed a war, in which no quarter was given, to impose on the whole church theological and disciplinary uniformity.

The *Journal d'un Théologien*, on the contrary, provides an extraordinary source for understanding that period that already has been seen in the above mentioned *Appels et cheminements*. Congar does not deal with the whole of the Pacelli pontificate, but begins precisely with the second half of 1946.[20] The Dominican theologian, who from that time onwards had to go through a silent and harsh persecution, recognises the intellectual dignity of Pius XII:[21] and on the contrary, he singles out the institutional elements of the Roman authoritarianism as a system, made up of functionaries who,

[19] See Philippe Chenaux, *Pie XII, pasteur et diplomate* (Paris: Cerf, 2003).

[20] Reprinted in *Écrits réformateurs*, 294.

[21] May 15th 1946, *Journal d'un théologien*, Voyage à Rome avec le Père *Féret*, 84. In his conciliar diary too his polemical models on papal government are Boniface VIII and Pius IX, *Mon journal du Concile, ad indicem*.

under cover of that mysticism of the pope that they accepted and promoted, carried out acts for which they could not be called to account before anyone. This portrait brings to light a new pair of antinomies that — similar to true/false reform, Tradition/tradition — seems to me of great importance for getting to know that period, but also the life of the church in the following decades: that is, the system/the truth.

THE PERSONS

Congar did not like Rome. This is clear, but I do not think that one can say he suffered from an anti-Roman complex (about which he had already written in 1937).[22] On the contrary, he distinguishes carefully between the people who appear on the scene to block the new edition of *Chrétiens désunis*,[23] then to slow down the publication of *Vraie et fausse réforme,* and finally to get Congar involved in the experience of the worker priests: although he was describing the tunnel in which he found himself, while suffering from extreme spiritual and psychological pressure, Congar is not content to scatter the responsibility without distinction on the pope or on others in a general way; he provides detailed profiles.

In the front row, in this parade, are the Dominicans considered "Romans" for various reasons, either because they were employed in the general Curia or because they had posts of responsibility in the congregations. Congar would encounter Cordovani and

---

[22] This arose from an expression used in "Loyauté et correction fraternelle," *Problèmes de l'œcumenisme* (Paris: Cerf, 1937) I: 4-5. A reflection on other signs is given in Hans Urs von Balthasar, *Die antirömische Affekt* (Freiburg i. Br.: Herder, 1974).

[23] Already on March 22nd 1940 Cordovani had attacked this volume in the *Osservatore Romano*, without naming the author or the work.

Philippe, Suarez and Browne, Ciappi and Gagnebet, as well as many others less well-known, teachers at the Angelicum or elsewhere.[24] Apart from Cordovani, irremediably disqualified by the Chenu affair, or those he considered theologians of the school of the Servite Cardinal Lépicier (classified by the simple expression "Pouah"), Congar is open to explain without any excessive use of tactics his own position. What he found intolerable was the free and easy way in which some people — especially the Master General — considered the possibility of compromising the intellectual autonomy of the Order in the name of a servile attitude that went against the very raison-d'être of the Friars Preacher, whose intellectual freedom constituted, according to Congar, their particular way of serving the church.

Much more interesting, however, is the picture that Congar paints of the Roman Curia: the Roman congregations are a world foreign to him and which will always continue to be remote, both on the intellectual level and on that of his own experience. But even so he does not exempt himself from trying to understand the nuances and the differences. Congar has no prejudices about the heads of the Curia (this is documented in the memoir of his first visit to Rome in 1946 with his fellow Dominican Henri-Marie Féret, in which one can feel the esteem in which some sections of the Curia were held). Congar compares the shared opinions of diplomats and theologians with his own personal impressions that he had accumulated in the course of time.[25]

---

[24] The interrogation with Gagnebet is recounted in *Journal d'un théologien, Affaires de Rome [Séjour à Babylone]*, 14 December 1954, 313-315.

[25] For a broad picture of this, see Jean-Dominique Durand, "La 'furia francese' vue de Rome: peurs, suspicions et rejets des années 1950," *Religions par-delà les frontières,* sous la dir. De Michel Lagrée-Nicholas-Jean Chaline (Paris: Beauchesne, 1997) 15-35.

1. Montini

In some cases this allowed him to dismantle some pretty solid myths, such as the one that surrounded Monsignor Giovanni Battista Montini. An outstanding personage in the Ordinary Affairs section of the Curia of Pius XII, both before and after the death of the Secretary of State, Cardinal Maglione, Montini enjoyed a reputation that went beyond the walls of the Vatican.[26] His sensitivity to the theology and the political philosophy of the French-speaking world had gained for him the respect of important intellectuals who had a cautious correspondence with him about their preoccupations about the future of research and of the church.[27] In 1946 Congar approached him, encouraged by the opinion of Monsignor Devreesse, who acknowledged in the "Substitute" an intellectual openness and "perception des problèmes du monde qui cherche et qui pense," shared by no one else, apart from Pius XII himself.[28] Other members of the French colony in Rome, like Monsignor Arata, explained to the Dominican in his forties, who was coming to Rome for the first time, that there were in the Curia places that were intellectual deserts (for example, the Congregation for Studies after the departure of the biblical scholar, Monsignor Ruffini, who had been appointed archbishop of Palermo and who would be the future champion of the minority at the Council, but who was

[26] See Renato Moro, *La formazione della classe dirigente cattolica (1929-1937)* (Bologna: Il Mulino, 1979).

[27] See Philippe Chenaux, *Entre Maurras et Maritain: une génération intellectuelle catholique (1920-1930)* (Paris: Cerf, 1999), and by the same author, *Paul VI et Maritain: rapports entre 'montinianisme' et 'maritainisme'* (Brescia: Istituto Paolo VI, 1994).

[28] May 15th 1946, *Journal d'un théologien*, V*oyage à Rome avec le Père Féret*, 84. Devreesse explained to him that "sauf Pie XII, Mgr Montini et quelques rare autres, il n'y a ici aucune ouverture intellectuelle, aucune perception des problèmes du monde qui cherche et qui pense; qu'à la Congregation des Universités et Séminaires, en particulier, c'est à cet égard le néant."

still described as having an open mind in 1946), but that one could still find persons like Montini from whom one could expect an intelligent hearing.[29] In circles who moved, however prudently, in the ecumenical field the reputation of Montini was less positive: the *Unitas* group spoke of the insuperable limits of the "Substitute" as far as ecumenism was concerned;[30] he was also alerted to this by Fr. Dumont.[31]

With this information Congar approached his conversation with Montini: the theologian appreciated the ability and the culture that impressed all who had dealings with the "Substitute," but he understood that as far as ecumenism was concerned he was guarded — nothing more. Congar had a clear intuition that what guided Montini was *fear*: fear of indifferentism, fear of an overestimation of the faults committed by the church — but in any case, fear.[32] However, while he was able to grasp the inner core of the personality, his conversation with Montini interested Congar because it permitted him to see at close quarters the effects of two methods of judging on the basis of secret accusations, about which he also knew the cost. In fact, Montini complained about the attacks of the most authoritative French liturgical review on the new translation of the breviary, explaining that the pope took offence at seeing French theology opposing Rome in a conservative manner in the name of the proto-Christian Latin of the Vulgate, "pour une fois

---

[29] *Journal d'un théologien*, Voyage à Rome avec le Père Féret, May 1946, 93.

[30] *Ibid.*, 104: also Montini "lui paraît étroit en ce domaine."

[31] *Ibid.*, 134-135. Fr. Dupont said that from his conversation with Montini he got the impression "que Rome est très sur la réserve dans les questions œcuméniques" and he told him that the prelate had warned the general that "dans l'Ordre de saint Dominique, tout le monde ne gardait pas une fidélité doctrinale assez rigoureuse; que tous n'étaient pas d'aussi bons théologiens que le P. Cordovani…"

[32] *Ibid.*, 107-108.

que Rome entreprenait une réforme..."[33] Still more, having learned in this way, casually, about the *querelle* against *Maison-Dieu* let Congar see that the division between closed prelates and open prelates did not adequately describe the situation which was much more rigid: in fact, this conversation alone allowed him to clarify a number of points that otherwise would have been kept hidden with unforeseeable consequences.

There are objective elements that explain Montini's adopting this way of proceeding: as he was told by Tisserant, an active and convinced participant in the "system," we are for sure under a monarchical regime;[34] for sure the supremacy of the Holy Office over everything and over everybody makes it credible that Montini was taking risks by certain little things that he did or his interest in a popular apostolate about which rumours were in the air.[35] But Congar was not content with this psycho-sociological approach that would explain away everything: so much so that in the course of the years ahead he suspected Montini of being behind the false information concerning the Catholic presence in Amsterdam at the founding session of the ecumenical Council of Churches,[36] he notes that in the great purge of 1952 the prelate — whose difficult situation he ignores — accuses the Dominicans of not having obeyed the request of the pope,[37] he does not give great weight to his disquiet over the effects of the condemnations in France,[38] he is

[33] *Ibid.*, 108.

[34] *Ibid.*, 121-122.

[35] *Journal d'un théologien, Premières alarmes (1946-1950)*, 137, 139 and 156.

[36] *Ibid.*, 148.

[37] *Ibid.*, 166: "Mgr Montini lui a répondu une fois: Le Saint Père a parlé en 1946 au chapitre général [*sic*] des Jésuites, moins fort au chapitre générale des Dominicains; on n'en a pas tenu compte. Alors, il est devenu nécessaire de sanctionner."

[38] D'Ormesson had written to Michelin to let him know that he had informed Montini "de l'émotion suscitée en France par mon affaire; Mgr Montini s'en est

displeased by his justification of the condemnations on the grounds that a hypothesis in Paris becomes a theory in Madrid and then is accepted as doctrine in Buenos Aires,[39] he scorns the promises of reparation that he knows will never come,[40] he distrusts the words of excessive praise of himself by the "Substitute."[41] Congar noted the explanation given by Fr Gy according to whom the pope's illness benefited the reactionaries in the Curia and those who wanted no change while it paralysed men like Montini;[42] his own reading of the situation is different and was derived from "une peine et aussi un scandale profound"[43] that went beyond the person, so much so that Congar was not at all moved by the plot that got Montini out of Rome, and he saw in it nothing similar to what he had had to go through from 1946 onwards.

2. Pizzardo

If his observations about Montini show his understanding of a white legend that was destined to grow grey, the passages about the cardinal from Savona, Joseph Pizzardo[44] are passages in which there runs a sense of intellectual repulsion for this Curial figure who was

montré affecté, et a manifesté son désir de s'informer, de voir cela," *Journal d'un théologien, Vraie et fausse réforme dans l'église menacé*, February 1952, 201.

[39] *Ibid.*, 202.

[40] May 4th 1952, in *Journal d'un théologien, Vraie et fausse réforme dans l'église menacé*, 206.

[41] October 15th 1952, in *Journal d'un théologien, Vraie et fausse réforme dans l'église menacé*, 219.

[42] September 21st 1954, in *Journal d'un théologien, La crise de 1954*, 276-277.

[43] On May 13th 1952, in *Journal d'un théologien, Vraie et fausse réforme dans l'église menacé*, 211.

[44] See Andrea Riccardi, *Il 'partito romano' nel secondo dopoguerra (1945-1953)* (Brescia: Morcelliana, 1983), and by the same author, *Roma "città" sacra? Dalla conciliazione all'operazione Sturzo* (Milan: Vita e Pensieri, 1979).

destined to remain at his post for more that thirty years. Pizzardo, Cardinal Prefect of the Congregation of Seminaries since 1937, along with Ottaviani, was part of that group of functionaries who passed from the Secretariate of State of Gasparri and Pacelli to the major congregations without any great theological formation and without long international experience, in a logic of the vertical movement of power and of a uniformity in the language of government. Fashioned in the ideological machine of Vatican dimplomacy (he had been in Bavaria and was president of the *pro Russia* committee), Pizzardo very astutely managed the first conversation with Congar and Féret on May 25, 1946 — to the point of accepting with seductive *souplesse* the suggestions of the two Dominicans on the place that should be given to the Bible in priestly formation and asking for their opinion in view of a document that was in preparation for the Italian seminaries! However much it may seem paradoxical, it was the Franciscan Agostino Gemelli, founder of the Catholic University and compromised by his support for fascism, who explained to Féret and Congar that it was not worth their while talking to Pizzardo.[45] On the Congregation of Seminaries, that led the field in having Chenu placed on the Index, Congar's judgement would deepen with the passage of time: and for him it was not the conservatism of Pizzardo that mattered, but because he was a complete nonentity and in this he expressed and characterised the "grand village" that Rome was in that "fin de pontificat."[46]

[45] In a conversation on May 31st 1946, *Journal d'un théologien*, 131.

[46] On April 16th 1952 Michelin was "navré de voir la petitesse de la Rome papale dirigeante" that surrounded a pope "influencé par son entourage. Et pas même toujours par son Brain Trust jésuite. Mais par sa gouvernante et par le cardinal Pizzardo;" he said that cardinal Pizzardo "est une nullité totale; à Rome, tout le monde rit de lui. Mais c'est un parfait domestique ... C'est étrange qu'il ait été créé cardinal par Pie XI, qui jugeait autrement les hommes ..." *Journal d'un théologien*, 200-201.

3. Ottaviani

Different still is Congar's judgement on Alfredo Ottaviani — who also came from the Secretariat of State before embarking on the Holy Office and becoming the carrier of a political image of doctrinal control to this highest point of Roman power. If the Ottaviani of the council and the post-council period has the reputation of being a defeated ultra-conservative,[47] the Ottaviani of the years immediately after the war had a better reputation: Fr Boyer of Unitas did not hesitate to describe him as "assez ouvert" and in April, 1952, Monsignor Blanchet spoke to Congar of an "ouverture croissante" in the Assessor[48] of the Holy Office, that in those months became and not by accident the point of reference for the brothers of Taizé-le-Cluny in their search for interlocutors. Ottaviani would send messages to Congar, sometimes cool and sometimes warm, in a negotiating strategy which the Dominicans in the Holy Office made use of to make their interrogations externally as pleasant as they could.[49]

Once again, however, Congar does not abandon his strategy of judging from the facts, the texts: and those of Ottaviani were "pieux et pissotants," bereft of any "préoccupation dominante de la Parole de Dieu," marked by that "autojustification de 'l'Église' (= la hiérarchie), entourée de jus pieux, dégoulinant de 'bon

---

[47] See Emilio Cavaterra, *Il prefetto del Sant'Offizio: le opere e i giorni del cardinale Ottaviani* (Milan: Mursia, 1990).

[48] *Journal d'un théologien*, 211 (Ottaviani said in advance that if Congar would come to Rome "on ne pourra rien lui dire") and p. 218 (Ottaviani asked Veronese to say "au P. Congar que nous l'aimons beaucoup, que nous souhaitons ici qu'il continue à travailler; que, personnellement, je m'intéresse beaucoup à ses travaux et serais enchanté de faire sa connaissance, s'il vient à Rome").

[49] *Journal d' théologien*, 251: Congar is referring to texts that had appeared in *La Documentation catholique*, February 7th 1952, col. 130-150; March 7th 1952, col. 263-315; March 21st 1952, col. 327-328.

esprit'..."[50] For Congar this was simply "tragique," and it was proved by the web of relations in which the *affaire* of the worker priests got tangled up, according to him, and about which new accusations would be made against him, and this time bereft of any factual evidence, and completing a sense of isolation that had begun years before.[51] The weaving together of bonhomie from across the Tiber and institutional impartiality that progressively characterized Ottaviani convinced Congar that the problem was much deeper than one can possibly imagine: the point, in fact, was not the humanity of the office-holders. It was the system.

THE SYSTEM

The prosopography of the Roman Curia that the *Journal d'un théologien* puts together, therefore, shows the inadequacy of the description of people as being open or being closed: what was more serious was that the nonentity of the characters, the intellectual mediocrity and the unconscious stupidity that was not lacking in the Curia of Pius XII, was that this was required by the system, quite apart from the intentions and ways of acting of individuals, and for this reason dangerously disturbed any equilibrium that had been formed in the course of time. For Congar the condemnations — first of all, that of Chenu, and later of himself — showed up the difficulties and the corruption that went deeper still: he did not suffer from (or enjoy) the narcissism of being the misunderstood theologian. The person, who in the first note of *Chrétiens désunis* had

---

[50] *Journal d'un théologien*, 251. According to Congar, Ottaviani was the leader in the persecution of the worker-priests. He was related through his sister with the brother of the Nuncio in Paris: *Journal d'un théologien*, 255-256; according to a recent article on Ormesson in "Chrétiens et sociétés," 2000 or 2001 (?) this was simply untrue.

[51] See Leprieur, *Quand Rome condamne. Dominicains et prêtres-ouvriers.*

projected a great "Catholic philocalia" on an ecumenical foundation, did not accept being confused with being a heretic. Although
he was striving to get to the theological meaning of the modernist
crisis, of the contemporary lack of belief, of protestant theology,
there was in him the desire "to love and be loved" not only in the
circle immediately surrounding him,[52] but also in the church. Therefore he thought that his condemnation was an act of injustice that
he had to undergo (analogously with what Chenu had had to suffer), through the serious fault and the factions of an uncultured and
malevolent ecclesiastical governing class.

The formation of such injustice uncovers the characteristics of a
system that enfolded, shaped and transcended individual limitations,
very serious and considerable though these were; concerning individuals he often expressed himself in extreme tones and sometimes
(as in the case of the Jesuits) with statements of fact that were not
always beyond question. Congar throughout the whole of his life as
a theologian and a believer trusted in the practice of the truth — even
when this had to be used to describe the errors of the church. In an
analysis carried out in accordance with the truth about the facts and
with rigour of language, this meant finding oneself inside a system that
was "totalitaire et paternaliste."[53] This diagnosis came to him when
he saw in Rome's action both the desire to subdue the church in
France "en quête de liberté" and in the implicit plan to reduce the very
statutes of the Dominicans to juridical dependence constructed on the
model of congregations of priests, showing contempt for their vocation to the loyal service of the truth that was characteristic of the order.

This judgement developed over the years: *in principio* there was
the case of Chenu. Putting on the Index of forbidden books the lecture on theological method by the master of the Saulchoir was the

---

[52] *Journal d'un théologien*, 419 and 428.
[53] *Ibid.*, February 12th 1954.

archetypal move in a whole season of suspicion.[54] The leaders in this were a "coterie misérable de gens médiocres, ignorants et sans caractère"[55] whose agent was the Congregation of Seminaries. However, the unmoved mover in this mentality appeared to him to be the Holy Office,[56] whose judgements were beyond discussion even when they wanted to spread as doctrine what were arbitrary impositions of personal theses or those of a particular school. Congar did not attack Pius XII, but he maintained that in the Supreme congregation, which everybody knew had the pope as prefect, "il y a toujours un acte initial arbitraire, parfois faux et mensonger, que le système empêche qu'on remette jamais en question, et qui déclenche en chaine une série d'ennuis et de stupidités."[57]

Such a condemnation, as is clear, is as yet only an intermediate one. In fact, Congar did not look for a negotiated solution to his own difficulties, but at the ecclesiological centre in which they originated.[58] In the *Journal d'un théologien*, against the background of immense personal suffering, there is no attempt to defend individual rights, not even the right to disobey that Congar himself, along

---

[54] On this see Giuseppe Alberigo, *Introduction*, in Marie-Dominique Chenu, *Une école de théologie: le Saulchoir [1937]* (Paris: Cerf, 1985); also R. Guelluy, "Les antécédents de l'encyclique 'Humani generis' dans les sanctions romaines de 1942: Chenu, Charlier, Draguet," *Revue d'histoire ecclésiastique* 81 (1986) 421-497.

[55] *Journal d'un théologien*, 54.

[56] This is the point of Féret's memoir, that Frings used on November 8th 1963, on which see *Storia del Concilio Vaticano II diretta da G. Alberigo*, III. Italian edition by A. Melloni (Bologna: Il Mulino, 1988); the text will be found in *Acta Synodalia Concilii oecumenici Vaticani II* (Roma: Libreria editrice Vaticana, 1966), Pars II, vol. 4, 616-618.

[57] In *Journal d'un théologien*, *Vraie et fausse réforme dans l'église menacé*, February 1952, 221.

[58] Joseph F. Fameréé, *Histoire et Église. L'ecclésiologie du père Congar de 'Chrétiens désunis' à l'annnonce du Concile (1937-1959)* (Louvain-la-Neuve: Peeters, 1991).

the lines of the studies of Brian Tierney, would set out to develop in the early eighties.[59] His criterion was completely ecclesiological: did this way of exercising authority represent "the" truth of the church? Congar was convinced that in his own condemnation there was the aim to put across as the church's magisterium what was simply the theology of a particular school,[60] and for this reason he was convinced that the accusations against himself were simply that he thought and wrote about what Rome thought should have been accepted in servile silence.[61] For Congar this was not just an episode, but the expression of a regime "policier, autocratique, totalitaire, crétin."[62]

[59] "Le droit au désaccord," *L'Anné canonique* (1981), now in *Écrits réformateurs*, 157-167.

[60] Congar criticises his censors on the grounds that they judge him according to purely personal criteria and he disputes those points precisely on which he questions their theses: "Le tragique de la situation actuelle et de la façon dont s'exerce concrètement le magistère ordinaire romain, c'est que ce magistère fait sans cesse de la théologie et exprime, avec l'autorité du magistère catholique, des positions d'école théologique." In *Journal d'un théologien*, Vraie et fausse réforme dans l'Église menacé, February 1952, 221.

[61] The accusation, as Congar understood this on February 8th 1954, was to have written about the worker priests: "En réalité, ce qu'on a écrit est juste et vrai, mais il aurait fallu ne *rien* écrire. Régime invraisemblable: policier, autocratique, totalitaire, crétin. Car ce qui me frappe le plus, c'est le crétinisme, l'invraisemblable indigence en intelligence, en caractère. Le système a fabriqué des serviteurs à son image. C'est d'une pauvreté!', *Journal d'un théologien*, La crise de 1954, 9 February 1954, 233; a little more than two years later he describes the regime of Pius XII as "un régime paternaliste" which reduces theologians to the level of "à commenter ses discours et à n'avoir surtout pas la velléité de penser quelque chose, d'entreprendre quelque chose en dehors de ce commentaire," *Journal d'un théologien, Lettre à sa Mère*, 10 September 1956, 425.

[62] Totalitarian appears 6 times in *Journal d'un théologien* (not at all in the conciliar diary...), one can note also the twelve occasions when Gestapo is used to describe the Holy Office, three times he uses the word Cretins and twice the expression, cretins.

In this regime there were at play, according to Congar, at least
three elements against the truth, that he drew from his experience
as a scholar and from his direct observation: one was theological,
one was anthropological and one was ecclesiological. On the theological level the painful point was caused by mariology: because
the unlimited devotion to Mary[63] was based on an idea of tradition
in which there was hidden "a conspiracy against the truth."[64] On
the anthropological level the system was based on contempt for the
human aspect; this was partly visible in the way the victims were
treated,[65] but more seriously it arose from a denial of the status of
the subject and more widely a denial of the experience and the history of Christian life.[66] At the ecclesiological level the contrast is
the one that arises from a Catholicism that believes in the truth as

[63] On this point see Joseph Famerée, "Formation ecclésiologique du 'premier'
Congar," *Cardinal Yves Congar (1904-1995)*, 65-66.

[64] Congar realised that his views here were not those of the Roman Church
("encore que je les croie absolument catholiques," 302) and he saw in this confessional degeneration "une véritable conspiration contre la vérité" (303), both in
ecclesiology and in mariology: "Et je dis: Non! Je dis *non* au nom de l'Évangile
et de toute l'histoire d'Israël. Marie n'est pas notre rédemptrice, Marie n'est pas
l'Objet de notre culte. Toute l'action des prophètes contre l'association des Baals
à Yahvé ou contre la baalisation de Yahvé vaut ici," *Affaires de Rome [Séjour à
Babylone]*, 11 décembre 1954, 303.

[65] The accusation against the "system" did not spring from an anti-Roman
complex, but from an intellectual analysis of its procedures, that for Congar was
first of all anthropological: "L'anthropologie, sinon théorétisée *[sic]* par les spé-
cialistes, du moins pratiquée de fait. C'est celle du Grand Inquisiteur. Manque d'in-
térêt à l'homme, de considération de l'homme, de respect de l'homme. [Mon cas
présent est ici typique]," *Journal d'un théologien, Affaires de Rome [Séjour à
Babylone]*, 11 December 1954, 303.

[66] See *Journal d'un théologien, Mon Témoignage 1946-1949*, 59 where there is
a significant reference to the analysis of modernism proposed by Fr. Chenu. On
the status of human beings in relation to the mystery of the Incarnation in Congar, see Monika-Maria Walff, *Gott und Mensch. Ein Beitrag Yves Congar zum
ökumenischen Dialog* (Frankfurt: J. Knecht, 1990).

the fruit of research that as such is able to react to human needs and to the ecumenical appeal,[67] and a system that is satisfied with its own procedures and that shelters behind a devotion to the pope that is used for its own manipulating purposes.[68]

What appears from this is a veritable "Appareil tyrannique de Rome,"[69] a thirsting after authority that wants to bring everything into submission,[70] a system with tentacles that Congar in a psychedelic nightmare saw represented by Bernini's colonnade.[71] Yes, a system — and indeed in the phrase of Congar "the" Roman system. A system that according to Congar (not very generous concerning the difficulties of Fourvière) has in the Society of Jesus a perfect support,[72] and in the Holy Office its highest

[67] The theologian is annoyed by the Roman devotion to the Marian Year: "Vérité de tout cela? Néant! Valeur de réponse aux problèmes et aux besoins des hommes, néant! C'est le ronron de la machine, qui tourne doucement sous le signe de la double et unique dévotion au pape e à la Madone," *Journal d'un théologien, Affaires de Rome [Séjour à Babylone]*, 27 November 1954, 294.

[68] Congar declares his disagreement with the image of Catholicism in which everything is perfect and the ecclesiological problem of ecumenism is reduced to the logic of returning: "Je suis frappé partout de cette irréalisme d'un système qui a ses thèses et ses rites, ses serviteurs aussi, et qui chante sa chanson sans regarder les choses et les problèmes tels qu'ils sont. Le système est satisfait de ses propres affirmations et de ses propres célébrations." *Journal d'un théologien, Affaires de Rome [Séjour à Babylone]*, 28 November 1954, 295.

[69] Congar, who at the time of his interrogation with Gagnebet in December 1954 had rejected the idea of passing over to Protestantism or to Orthodoxy or to the Anglican Communion, but only after he had considered the possibility of his doing so, returned to the question almost a year later: what should he do "si je ne puis servir Dieu, servir la vérité, qu'en passant outre à certaines dispositions canoniques de l'Appareil tyrannique de Rome?," *Journal d'un théologien, Et Lazarus similiter mala*, 13 November 1955, 404.

[70] *Journal d'un théologien, Lettre à sa Mère*, 10 September 1956, 426.

[71] *Journal d'un théologien, Affaires de Rome [Séjour à Babylone]*, 27 November 1954, 293.

[72] *Journal d'un théologien*, p. 89: "Ce qui frappe ensuite, c'est l'accord parfait de style et d'esprit qu'il y a entre la Compagnie et le système romain de la

point.[73] His overall judgement on this system, that makes him think of the antifascist prisoner in Carlo Levi's novel, *Christ Stopped at Eboli*,[74] is expressed in one of the sharpest and most desperate passages in the whole of his theological diary in which Congar refutes the accommodating explanations of his brother Dominican Forestier. According to Congar, Forestier underestimates the injustices committed that threatened him with "un ensemble de sanctions, qu'on ne m'a jamais fait connaître, portées à l'issue d'un procès auquel je n'ai pas assisté." This is a "régime policier" that acts with "la sévérité du bourreau qui appuie sur le déclic de l'appareil à tuer" and from whom the victim "ne puis espérer aucune justice." And he explains why:

> C'est un système. Le système est dominé par la "Suprême Congrégation" — à laquelle ils ont le front de donner le qualificatif de "saint" (office). C'est un système policier, où la décision policière, ni n'a à donner de raison, ni n'est accessible à quelque mise en question. Elle est sans appel. Qui est atteint par elle est comme versé dans un autre monde, où il n'y a plus ni justice ni miséricorde; où, avec la plus grande bonne foi et en toute candeur, tous les Browne vous piétinent. Ils ne se doutent même pas, n'étant que système, qu'ils marchent sur du vivant. Vérité. Désaccord intellectuel avec le système romain. Découverte (1950-51, puis à Rome, 1954-55) que ses bases textuelles ou historiques sont fabriquées ou truquées, ou gauchies. Etc. Ma philosophie actuelle, coexistant avec un certain

---

Curie. Ce système des Congrégations, cet appareil d'autorité et de gouvernement qui est comme la croûte de l'Église vivante, évangélique et pneumatique; pour ce système et cet appareil de la Curie, dans lequel nous ne serons jamais à notre aise, la Compagnie est comme faite sur mesure. Elle en représente l'instrument exactement approprié, le service parfait. Il y a, entre les deux systèmes, une sorte d'accord profond."

[73] *Journal d'un théologien, Affaires de Rome [Séjour à Babylone]*, 11 December 1954, 303.

[74] See "Appels et cheminements 1929-1963," and now in *Écrits réformateurs*, 302.

"absolu," avec la satisfaction de quelques joies élémentaires, mais aussi avec mon effort spirituel de fidélité à la Foi et à la Croix, est: je suis un type foutu.[75]

Epilogue

Congar, the future cardinal Congar, was not by any means out of the game. On the contrary, he was about to start out on a very fruitful period for himself and for the great church within a great world in which he would feel himself firmly situated: the long period of the council for Congar that opened 26 months after the dismal conclusion of the *Journal d'un théologien*, is described in a diary in which Congar, in his own way, became a leading figure and earned for himself that very cardinalate that at the end of his life would honour his service to the truth. The Congar of Vatican II — you can see this especially in the months of preparation when the monopoly of the Curia over the documents and the timidity of the episcopate left no hope that anything good would come of it — remained coherent and courageous: and above all he would be able to take part in the council as an opening up of the diversity in the church, as the consecration of his ecumenical striving and as a confirmation of his faith in the Lord of history, all of which put right what had preceded in the institution.[76] During the council the antagonism between system and truth continued to exist but this was in a context that was completely different from what had gone before. The presence of the episcopate and of the observers and of many others put in crisis the omnipotence of the system that he had singled out as his own persecutor.

[75] *Journal d'un théologien, Et Lazarus similiter mala*, 9 December 1955, 433.
[76] See my *Yves Congar à Vatican II: Hypothèses et pistes de recherche*.

It is not by chance that the expression "système romain," that
in the fifties was repeatedly hammered out to describe the *status*
of the church, appears only once in the council diary. This was on
January 30th 1964 when the passivity of the council on the publication of Paul VI's *motu proprio* on the liturgy made him fear that
all that had been successfully done to "gagner sur le système
romain en place!"[77] could be lost. He would allude to it again at
the beginning of the seventies when he would join in the cry of
alarm at a new revival of doctrinal politics of condemnations in the
Catholic church in a gesture that would cost him the revocation of
the cardinalate that had already been decided upon.[78]

Those whom Congar had criticized in telling them that one cannot condemn problems[79] would have been more content with his
being taken off the list than by the decision of John Paul II finally
to make him a cardinal, *in limine vitae*, on November 26th 1994.[80]
The intellectual rigour of the reforming cardinal, however, had
already shown all its strength and its ability to upset a system that
in retaining itself to be necessary and necessarily coextensive with
the truth constituted for that very reason a most terrible menace.

* Translated from the Italian by Clarence Gallagher, SJ

[77] At the institutional level see the note of February 27th 1965 on the inclusion of new cardinals in the plenary sessions; this was a sign of a possible way
of getting out of the "régime des Pizzardo et autres crétins," *Mon journal du Concile*, II: 341 (but Pizzardo is left out of the list of names).

[78] On this episode, see Jean-Pierre Jossua, "Avant-propos," *Écrits réformateurs*, 12.

[79] *Journal d'un théologien, Et Lazarus similiter mala*, 9 December 1955, 415.

[80] See Étienne Fouilloux, "Frère Yves, Cardinal Congar, Dominicain. Itinéraire
d'un théologien," *Revue des Sciences Philosophiques et Théologiques* 89 (1995)
379-404 and Jean-Pierre Jossua, "Yves Congar. La vie et œuvre d'un théologien,"
Cristianesimo nella storia 17 (1996) 1-12.

I BELIEVE IN THE HOLY SPIRIT
THE ROLE OF PNEUMATOLOGY IN YVES CONGAR'S THEOLOGY

Richard P. MᴄBʀɪᴇɴ

Crowley-O'Brien Professor of Theology
University of Notre Dame, Indiana

There are more than 1700 separate items in the complete list of Yves Congar's published works, and a relatively substantial portion of them have at least something to do with his understanding of the relationships existing among ecclesiology, pneumatology, Christology, and theological anthropology, or any combination thereof. Accordingly, I shall not attempt in this single chapter a comprehensive examination of the role of pneumatology in Congar's entire corpus of theological writings, nor even in his exceedingly numerous ecclesiological writings alone. The task is beyond my limited purpose here, which is to reflect only schematically on how Congar's evolving understanding of the Holy Spirit impacted his understanding of the nature and mission of the Church.[1] For

---

[1] Congar's major work on the subject is, of course, his three-volume, *Je crois en l'Esprit Saint* (Paris: Cerf, 1979-80); ET, I *Believe in the Holy Spirit*, trans. David Smith (New York: Seabury, 1983; Crossroad, 1997). This was followed by his *La Parole et le Souffle* (Paris: Desclée, 1984); ET *The Word and the Spirit*, trans. David Smith (San Francisco, CA: Harper and Row, 1986). See also, but only by way of example, his "The Idea of the Church in St. Thomas Aquinas," *The Thomist* 1 (1939) 331-359, later re-published as "L'idée de l'Église chez saint Thomas d'Aquin," *Revue des Sciences Philosophiques et Théologiques* 29 (1940) 31-58, reprinted in *The Mystery of the Church*, trans. A. V. Littledale (London:

Congar is — first, last, and always — an ecclesiologist, not a pneu-
matologist nor a specialist in any other area of theology. Indeed,
by today's standards, even in the West, his pneumatology would
seem to be fairly conventional.[2] Congar was indebted to several

Geoffrey Chapman, 1960) 97-117 (which, in turn, was originally published as
Esquisses du Mystère de l'Église, Unam Sanctam, 8 [Paris: Cerf, [2]1953]);
"L'Esprit-Saint dans l'Église," *Lumière et Vie* 10 (1953) 51-73; *Le Mystère du
Temple ou l'Économie de la Présence de Dieu à sa créature de la Genèse à
l'Apocalypse* (Paris: Cerf, 1958); ET, *The Mystery of the Temple or the Manner
of God's Presence to His Creatures from Genesis to the Apocalypse*, trans. Reginald Trevett (London: Burns and Oates, 1962); "La pneumatologie dans la théologie catholique," *Revue des Sciences Philosophiques et Théologiques* 51 (1967)
250-258; "La tri-unité de Dieu et l'Église," *Vie spirituelle* 128 (1974) 687-703;
"Pneumatologie dogmatique," *Initiation à la practique de la théologie*, ed.
Bernard Lauret and François Refoulé (Paris: Cerf, 1982), 2: 485-516; "Les implications christologiques et pneumatologiques de l'ecclésiologie de Vatican II," *Les
Églises après Vatican II: Dynamisme et prospective*, Actes du Colloque international de Bologne, 1980, ed. Giuseppe Alberigo (Paris: Beauchesne, 1982) 117-
130; and "Actualité de la pneumatologie," *Credo in Spiritum Sanctum*, ed. P. José
Saraiva Martins (Vatican City: Libreria Editrice Vaticana, 1983) 15-28, re-
published as "Pneumatology Today," *American Ecclesiastical Review* 167 (1973)
435-449. Two of the most recent works on the connections existing among theological anthropology, pneumatology, and ecclesiology in the writings of Yves
Congar are Elizabeth Teresa Groppe's "The Contribution of Yves Congar's Theology of the Holy Spirit," *Theological Studies* 62 (2001) 451-478, which is based
on her doctoral dissertation at Notre Dame University (1999), subsequently published as *Yves Congar's Theology of the Holy Spirit* (New York: Oxford University Press, 2004) and also the unpublished dissertation of Sally Vance-Trembath,
*The Pneumatology of Vatican II with Particular Reference to Lumen gentium and
Gaudium et spes* (Notre Dame, IN: Department of Theology, 2003). I am indebted
to both of them in this article.

[2] See, for example, Congar's somewhat convoluted definition of pneumatology towards the end of the first volume of *I Believe in the Holy Spirit*: "By pneumatology, I mean something other than a simple dogmatic theology of the third
Person. I also mean something more than, and in this sense different from, a profound analysis of the indwelling of the Holy Spirit in individual souls and his
sanctifying activity there. Pneumatology should, I believe, describe the impact, in
the context of a vision of the Church, of the fact that the Spirit distributes his gifts

different sources for much of its shape and content: Thomas Aquinas, Johann Adam Möhler, and various Orthodox and Protestant theologians.[3]

Congar's ecclesiology, however, was anything but conventional, particularly on such key issues as mission, ministry, authority, reform, ecumenism, the role of the laity, religious freedom, and salvation outside the Church. He was undoubtedly the greatest ecclesiologist not only of the 20th century but of the entire history of the Church as well. Indeed, his impact on the Second Vatican Council was so profound that Avery Dulles suggested that it "could almost be called Congar's council."[4]

I. *I BELIEVE IN THE HOLY SPIRIT*

Many readers are generally familiar with Yves Congar's last major work, *I Believe in the Holy Spirit*. However, since it is the single most important source for his pneumatology and provides the main element of the title for this paper, one should not be surprised to find herein a full and relatively detailed synthesis and critical evaluation of that three-volume work.

1. The Experience of the Spirit: An Overview of Volume I

The first volume presents a history of the most significant interpretations of the activity of the Holy Spirit in the economy of ˙

as he wills and in this way builds up the Church" (p. 156). My former student, Elizabeth Teresa Groppe, in her recently published book on Congar's pneumatology, may prove my assertion wrong, which, of course, would not be the first time that a student effectively rebutted his or her teacher.

[3] For a helpful synthesis of the impact of these sources on Congar's developing theology of the Holy Spirit, see Elizabeth Teresa Groppe's recent book, cited above in n. 1.

[4] "Yves Congar: In Appreciation," *America* 173 (July 15, 1995) 6.

salvation, focusing initially on the way the Spirit was understood
and presented in both testaments of Sacred Scripture, then on the
post-biblical history of the Church, where Congar contrasts the balanced views of Irenaeus and Augustine, for example, with those of
the Montanists, Joachim of Fiore, and some of the 16th century
Reformers as well as those whom they influenced. Finally, Congar
reflects on the Counter-Reformation and pre-Vatican II periods
where Catholic ecclesiology was largely uninterested in pneumatology, limiting the Spirit's role to the personal sanctification of
the Church's individual members and to the guidance of the hierarchy in its teaching and disciplinary functions.[5]

Although Congar acknowledges that Pope Pius XII's encyclical,
Mystici Corporis Christi (1943), "contains a profound theology of
the Holy Spirit,"[6] he pays relatively little attention to the encyclical's remarkably enlightened observations about the role of the
Holy Spirit in the Church. Congar's reason is that the approach
taken in the encyclical "never reaches the point where it becomes
a full pneumatology because it is restricted by its concentration on
the institution."[7] Even with this limitation, however, the encyclical points out that "after Christ's glorification on the cross, his

---

[5] Even in the best of the Latin manuals in common use in seminaries and pon-
tifical universities before Vatican II, there is only a glancing reference to the Holy
Spirit as the "quasi-soul" of the Church. See, for example, Joachim Salaverri,
"Tractatus III: De Ecclesia Christi," *Sacrae Theologicae Summa*, vol. 1 (Madrid:
Biblioteca de Autores Cristianos, 1962) 488-976. The following constitutes the
sole reference in the tract on the Church to the role of the Holy Spirit in the life
and mission of the Church: "Quasi-anima appellatur Spiritus Sanctus, quia in
Corpore Christi Mystico anima proprie dici non potest, quatenus Spiritus Sanctus
nequit substantialitier Corpori Mystico uniri; *analogice* vero anima appellatur, ex
similitudine ad humani corporis animam, quatenus nempe Spiritus Sanctus *effi-
cienter* et *quasi-formaliter* in Ecclesia peragit vitae effectus similes iis, quos anima
hominis operatur in humano corpore" (830).

[6] I: 157.

[7] *Ibid.*

Spirit is communicated to the Church in an abundant outpouring, so that the Church and each of its members may become daily more and more like to our Saviour."[8] It is the Spirit who, as "an invisible principle," creates and sustains unity among all parts of the Body and with their risen and exalted Head, "for the whole Spirit of Christ is in the Head, the whole Spirit is in the Body, and the whole Spirit is in each of the members."[9] Citing an earlier pope, Leo XIII, the encyclical insists that the Holy Spirit is not just the "quasi-soul" of the Church, but is its very soul.[10]

On the other hand, Congar went beyond even that point, insisting that the Spirit is not simply the animator of the Church — its structures, its ministries, and its missionary activities — but also the co-institutor of the Church along with Jesus. The Church is the product of two inseparable divine missions of the Word and the Spirit.[11] As such, Jesus laid the foundations for the Church during his earthly life, and the Spirit has guided, and continues to guide, the Church throughout its subsequent history until the end of time. The Spirit does so in a variety of ways, not least of which is in

---

[8] *The Christian Faith in the Doctrinal Documents of the Catholic Church*, ed. Jacques Dupuis (New York: Alba House, 1996; 6th rev. ed.) 303. See also H. Denzinger and A. Schönmetzer, *Enchiridion Symbolorum, Definitionum et Declarationum de rebus fidei et morum* (Freiburg im Breisgau: Herder, [36]1976), n. 3807.

[9] *The Christian Faith*, 303; DS, n. 3808.

[10] See Leo XIII, *Divinum illud*, ASS (1896-97) 650. Cited by *The Christian Faith* and DS, as in n. 5 above.

[11] See "Pneumatologie dogmatique," 496 (full citation at n. 1 above). To be sure, the question of Jesus' founding or instituting of the Church always needs to be qualified. He did not institute the Church in the sense that he provided a kind of ecclesiastical blueprint for it, but rather he gathered disciples, conferred on them a mission to the Jews, and urged them to gather regularly for eucharistic meals in memory of him. See my *Catholicism: Completely Revised and Updated* (San Francisco, CA: Harper-SanFrancisco, 1994) 577-579. Similar qualifications might be in order with regard to the Holy Spirit's co-instituting of the Church.

guaranteeing the efficacy of the sacraments, forming and re-forming the members into a coherent community, and providing wisdom and courage for the fulfilment of their mission and ministries in the face of frequent and often enormous obstacles.[12]

Congar concludes the volume with a too-brief summary of the pneumatology found in various documents of the Second Vatican Council (see below at 1.2), and with only a glancing mention at the end of Pope John XXIII's historic call for a new Pentecost for the Church.[13]

1.1. *Mary and the Holy Spirit*

In one of his most insightful, even if not entirely original, observations in this first volume, Congar points out that certain pre-Vatican II styles of devotion to Mary, the Mother of the Lord, were actually a displacement of what should have been a liturgical and theological focus on the Holy Spirit. He concedes, therefore, a basis for the Protestant criticism that Catholics have attributed to Mary what really belongs to the Holy Spirit, for example, the titles and

---

[12] Elizabeth Groppe argues that "Congar developed not simply a pneumatological ecclesiology but rather a pneumatological ecclesiology that was inseparable from a pneumatological anthropology. He did not develop this theology as comprehensively or as systematically as he might have done, in part because of the many demands on his time and talents, but also because of his theological temperament." She cites an interview with Congar's fellow Dominican theologian, Hervé Legrand, who suggested to her that Congar was not a systematic theologian in the traditional sense of the term, but that he was "a genius" and a "*sourcier*," someone who could point others "towards a well of living water." E. Groppe, *op. cit.*, 370. She regards this pneumatological weaving together of anthropology and ecclesiology as "one of the most significant contributions of his theology of the Holy Spirit." Groppe, "The Contribution of Yves Congar's Theology of the Holy Spirit," 457 (see n. 1 above).

[13] I: 167-173.

functions of comforter and advocate, and of the "soul of the Church."[14] Similarly, Mary's maternity is such that, thanks to her, we are not left as orphans. She reveals Jesus to us, who in turn reveals the Father. And she also forms Jesus in us. In each instance, she is said to perform roles that are appropriately reserved to the Holy Spirit alone.

Viewing Mary as the Mediatrix of all grace has been one of the main elements of a maximalist approach to Marian devotions.[15] By way of example, Congar cites a text from the Franciscan friar, Bernardino of Siena (1380-1444), which was later incorporated into an encyclical by Leo XIII, *Iucunda semper* (1894): "All grace that is communicated to this world comes to us by a threefold movement. It is dispensed according to a very perfect order from God in Christ, from Christ in the Virgin and from the Virgin in us."[16] Bernardino had also added that Mary had at her disposal "a certain jurisdiction or authority over the temporal procession of the Holy Spirit, to such an extent that no creature has ever received the grace

---

[14] I: 161. In this regard, Congar agrees not only with Protestant criticisms on this point but also with the views of other Catholic theologians. See, for example, René Laurentin, "Esprit et théologie mariale," *Nouvelle Revue Théologique* 89 (1967) 26-72; Heribert Mühlen, *Una mystica persona: Die Kirche als das Mysterium der Identität des Heiligen Geistes in Christus und den Christen* (Munich: Schöningh, 1968) 461-494; and Léon Joseph Cardinal Suenens, "The Relation that Exists between the Holy Spirit and Mary," *Mary's Place in Christian Dialogue,* ed. Alberic Stacpoole (Wilton, CT: Morehouse-Barlow, 1982) 69-78. More recently, Congar's position has been taken up and reaffirmed by Elizabeth A. Johnson in her *Truly Our Sister: A Theology of Mary in the Communion of Saints* (New York: Continuum, 2003) 80. For a feminist critique of Congar's view, see Sarah Coakley, "Femininity and the Holy Spirit?," *Mirror to the Church: Reflections on Sexism,* ed. Monica Furlong (London: SPCK, 1988) 124-135.

[15] For a comparison of Marian maximalism and Marian minimalism, see my *Catholicism,* 1104-1106 (full citation at n. 10).

[16] *ASS* 27 (1894-1895) 179.

of any virtue from God except through a dispensation of the Virgin herself."[17] Congar's comment: "This is clearly unacceptable."[18]

At the same time, Congar notes, Mary and the Holy Spirit do have an inseparable role in the economy of salvation. She is a model of the Church and of universal intercession. Although this is the result of the activity of the Holy Spirit within her, she is "the first recipient of [the] grace [of Christ] and the first to have been associated with the sovereign action of the Spirit in Christ."[19] Congar appropriately cites here Pope Paul VI's excellent apostolic exhortation on Marian devotion, *Marialis cultus* (1974), as a theologically balanced corrective to various devotional excesses.

1.2. *The Pneumatology of Vatican II*

Notwithstanding the unusual brevity of the volume's final chapter, Congar does have some important points to make about the council's pneumatology and, at least indirectly, about his own. He observes that, although there are 258 references to the Holy Spirit in the conciliar texts, together they do not provide a sufficient basis for a coherent pneumatology. Congar preferred instead "to draw attention to the elements of true pneumatology that were present at the Second Vatican Council and have since then been active in the Catholic Church"[20] He cites six elements in particular:

First, the council preserved the Christological basis of pneumatology, stressing always that the Holy Spirit is the Spirit of Christ.[21] The council's pneumatology, therefore, is decidedly not pneumatocentric.

---

[17] I: 163-164.

[18] I: 164.

[19] I: 164.

[20] I: 167.

[21] See, for example, *Lumen gentium* (hereafter, *LG*), n. 7, para. 1 (hereafter, 7,1); 8, 1; and 14, 2.

Second, the council broke free from the pre-conciliar tendency to regard the Mystical Body of Christ as the only appropriate definition of the Church and also from the commonly employed, contemporary notion of the Church as the prolongation of the Incarnation. According to the council, it is the Holy Spirit who animates the Church "as an event here and now."[22] Congar cites *Lumen gentium* (8,1) in support: "Just as the assumed nature inseparably united to the divine Word serves him as a living instrument of salvation, so, in a similar fashion, does the communal structure of the Church serve Christ's Spirit who vivifies it by way of building up the body."[23]

Third, the council went beyond what Heribert Mühlen called a "pre-Trinitarian monotheism."[24] On the contrary, the council had a theologically robust understanding of the mystery of the triune God, viewing the Church, in Cyprian of Carthage's terms, as the "people made one with the unity of the Father, the Son and the Holy Spirit".[25]

Fourth, one of the most important ways in which the Holy Spirit was restored to the pneumatological ecclesiology of the council was in the sphere of charisms.[26] For Congar, this meant that the Church is built up not only by institutional means but also by the infinite variety of the gifts that each person "has the right and duty to use in the Church and in the world for the good of mankind and for the upbuilding of the Church... in the freedom of the Holy Spirit who 'breathes where he wills' (John 3:8)..."[27] Consequently,

[22] I: 168.

[23] See also *LG* 7,7, and 9,3; *Sacrosanctum Concilium*, 5; and *Presbyterorum ordinis*, 2 and 5,1.

[24] Work cited in I: 173, n.1.

[25] Cited in a footnote to *LG*, 4.

[26] See, for example, *LG*, 4; and 7,3, and also *Ad gentes* 4; 23,1; 28,1.

[27] *Apostolicam actuositatem*, 3; cited by Congar, I: 170.

we can call the Holy Spirit, "who makes the Church by these means, 'co-constitutive' of the Church."[28] All of the Church's social structures are at the service of the Spirit, who makes the Gospel a contemporary reality and enables people to understand the Word of God, who prompts developments in religious life and in the Church's missionary activities, and who inspires the ecumenical movement and indeed the renewal of the Church as a whole.[29]

Fifth, the council also retrieved the traditional importance of the local churches. Indeed, another great contemporary theologian whom Congar cites at this point, Karl Rahner, insisted that the most valuable new element introduced by the council was its teaching that the local church is the realization of the one, holy, catholic, and apostolic Church. "The Church as a whole," Congar writes, "is presented as a communion of churches, with the Holy Spirit as the principle of that communion."[30]

Sixth, the Spirit is already active in history, even before the Incarnation, filling the whole earth and renewing its face.[31]

"Pneumatology, like ecclesiology and theology as a whole," Congar concludes, "can only develop fully on the basis of what is experienced and realized in the life of the Church. In this sphere, theory is to a great extent dependent on praxis."[32]

He closes the first volume with a prescient quotation from Pope Paul VI, given a few years after the council's final adjournment: "The Christology and especially the ecclesiology of the Second Vatican Council should be followed by a new study and a new cult of the Holy Spirit, as an indispensable complement of the conciliar

[28] I: 170.
[29] I: 171, with pertinent conciliar citations.
[30] *Ibid.*, with pertinent citations.
[31] See *Prebyterorum ordinis*, 22,3; and *Gaudium et spes*, 11,1; 26,4.
[32] I: 172.

teaching."[33] Congar indicates in the volume's last sentence that Paul VI's words "to a very great extent justify the attempt that I make in the rest of this work to provide such a pneumatology."[34]

2. Lord and Giver of Life: An Overview of Volume II

The second volume reflects on the presence and activity of the Holy Spirit in the Church, as co-institutor and as the source of its unity, catholicity, apostolicity, and holiness (Part One), in individual members of the Church (Part Two), and in the charismatic renewal (Part Three). The Church, he insists, is the product of a two-fold mission: that of the Son and that of the Holy Spirit. But he rejects the simplistically false opposition between what is of the Spirit (charisms) and what is of the Son (institutional elements). If such a false opposition is accepted, "the unity of the Church as the Body of Christ is destroyed and the claim is made that everything can be regulated and conducted, on the one hand without spirituality and exclusively in the name of power and, on the other, anarchically, in the name of the Spirit."[35] It would also eliminate the "essential element of pneumatology" from ecclesiology, "and it is precisely this element," he writes, "that I am attempting at least to suggest in this work."[36]

---

[33] General audience on June 6, 1973, cited in *Documentation catholique* 1635 (July 1, 1973) 601. Paul VI made a similar point in his apostolic exhortation, *Marialis cultus* (1974), in which he invited theologians and others to "think more deeply about the activity of the Spirit in the history of salvation" (n. 27).

[34] I: 172.

[35] II: 11. Here, again, Pius XII makes the same point in *Mystici Corporis Christi*, although not with the same emphases and nuances that Congar provides: "There can, then, be no real opposition or conflict between the invisible mission of the Holy Spirit and the juridical commission of ruler and teacher received from Christ. Like body and soul in us, they complement and perfect one another, and have their source in our one Redeemer..." See *The Christian Faith*, 304-305.

[36] *Ibid.*

314 RICHARD P. MCBRIEN

Until recently, Congar reminds us, the tendency was not only to separate the two activities — charismatic and institutional — in the Church, but also to subordinate the former to the latter. He warns, however, of our going to the opposite extreme, that is, of claiming that the Church should have only a charismatic structure, with the institutional element playing a secondary and supplemental role.[37] Congar rejects the false dichotomy of "either/or" in favour of the more balanced "both/and." Each type of gift and activity, he argues, "has its place in the building up of the Church."[38] The joint activity of Christ and the Spirit cannot be "reduced to a mere making present of the structures of the covenant proposed by Christ while he was on earth, that is, before he ceased to be visibly and tangibly present." We are dealing here, he insists, with a wholly "new element in history."[39]

2.1. *The Four Notes of the Church*

2.1.1. Unity

Congar's pneumatological treatment of the four notes, or marks, of the Church helps to illuminate his understanding of the relationship between pneumatology and ecclesiology. The Spirit is

[37] He criticizes Hans Küng for holding just such a view in *The Church* (New York: Sheed & Ward, 1968) 179-191. At the same time, he acknowledges his own past excesses in this regard, particularly in making too radical a distinction between the institution as derived from Christ and the free interventions on the part of the Spirit. He admits that the criticisms he received from both Protestant exegetes and Catholic theologians were well-founded. His intentions were good, he insists, but poorly directed. He wanted to give the Holy Spirit "his full worth," but in the process lost sight of the unity that exists between the activity of the Spirit and that of the glorified Christ. See II: 11-12.

[38] II: 11.
[39] II: 12.

given to the whole ecclesial community and to the individual members who constitute it, without violating the individuality of local churches and their members. The Church is not simply the sum total of those who belong to it by faith and baptism. "It is a communion, a fraternity of persons. This is why a personal principle and a principle of unity are united in the Church. These two principles are brought into harmony by the Holy Spirit."[40]

Unfortunately, "excessive emphasis" has been placed in the modern era on the role of authority in the Church, along with a "juridical tendency to reduce order to an observance of imposed rules, and unity to uniformity."[41] As a result, creative individuals have been marginalized by being forced into silence and inactivity. Theology has been "devalued," especially since the Middle Ages and in various documents of the papal magisterium of the 19th and 20th centuries. Congar refers specifically to the six pontificates from Pius IX to Pius XII, but stopping short of the pontificate of John Paul II. The three volumes were published in 1979-80, just as the new pontificate was getting underway, but not before the withdrawal in late 1979 of Hans Küng's canonical mission to teach as a Catholic theologian. That act signalled a new, more adversarial attitude towards theologians than prevailed in the two immediately previous pontificates of John XXIII and Paul VI. Only the Spirit, who is the principle of unity, Congar suggests, can overcome such divisions, past and present, between the hierarchical magisterium and the theological community.

2.1.2. Catholicity

The Holy Spirit also "makes the Church Catholic," but it is always "the Spirit of *Jesus Christ*. He does no other work but that *of Jesus*

[40] II: 16.
[41] *Ibid.*

Christ ... The catholicity of the Church is the catholicity *of Christ*. The soundness of any pneumatology is its reference to Christ."[42] The catholicity of the Church is also the catholicity of Christ. It is a catholicity in space, in the world, and in time itself, or history.

2.1.3. Apostolicity

With regard to the note of apostolicity, Congar walks a fine line between exaggerating the role of bishops, on the one hand, and ignoring them entirely, on the other. "The tradition/transmission of the Spirit, which enables the Church to be faithful to and united in its faith," he insists, "is tied to the function of the bishops," as "successors of the apostles." But apostolic succession also applies to the whole Church. The tendency in an earlier, juridical ecclesiology — and particularly after the French Revolution — was to focus on the authority of the hierarchy over against secular powers. But in the light of more recent developments within society at large and especially within the Catholic Church itself — both with regard to scholarly research and episcopal malfeasance — pressure exists to move the pendulum in the opposite direction and, for the moment at least, closer to the centre.

2.1.4. Holiness

Finally, the Spirit is the principle of the Church's holiness, not just of its individual members but of the Church as a whole, which is "the holy temple in which, through the strength of the living water that is the Holy Spirit, faith is celebrated in baptism and love or *agapē* is celebrated in the Eucharist."[43] The New

---

[42] II: 35. Emphases in original text.
[43] II: 54.

Testament, he points out, speaks of an indwelling in the Church, not simply of "God," that is, the Father and the Son, but explicitly of the Spirit (John 14:15-17; 1 Corinthians 3:16-17; 6:19; 1 John 4:12-13).

At the same time, Congar acknowledges that this holy Church is also a Church of sinners, but he fails to make it clear that the Church itself can be called sinful. On the other hand, he does speak of the pride and hardness of the Church throughout history, its addiction to creature-comforts and to wealth and power, and its vulnerability to the sins of the flesh. The Spirit, he writes, is with us now, but also ahead of us, as the promised one. The Spirit draws us to our eschatological inheritance in the Kingdom of God.

Congar notes that in several ancient manuscripts which contain the words of the Lord's Prayer, "Thy kingdom come" is rendered as "May thy Spirit come upon us and purify us." As such, the Spirit "furthers the cause of the gospel ... encourages great initiatives to renew the Church, missions, the emergence of new religious orders, great works of the mind and heart ... inspires necessary reforms and prevents them from becoming merely external arrangements, so that they are able to lead to a new life according to the spirit of Jesus."[44]

The Church, finally, is a communion of saints whose solidarity in Christ is rooted, again, in the Holy Spirit. It is the Spirit who concelebrates with us in every Eucharist. Indeed, we call upon the Spirit to do so, according to the early anaphora of Serapion: "May the Lord Jesus and the Holy Spirit speak in us and may he sing in hymns through us."[45] The Eucharist, he writes, is "the supreme realization here on earth of the communion of saints ..." Because the Church "lives, through the activity of the Holy Spirit, in the

[44] II: 57.
[45] Cited in II: 60.

unity and the communion of spiritual good things ... should we not dare to believe and profess if the Holy Spirit, personally and identically the same, is in God, in Christ, in his Body and in all members of that Body?"[46]

3. The Indwelling of the Spirit

The seven chapters of Part Two of this second volume dwell on such themes as the Holy Spirit as principle and end of our sancti-fication, the eschatological nature of the Spirit's indwelling within us, the Spirit's relation to Christian prayer and the human struggle against the flesh, and the gifts and fruits of the Spirit. Part Three is perhaps the most difficult to fathom because it tends to exag-gerate, at least in this author's judgment, the importance of the so-called charismatic movement within the Catholic Church, a move-ment which has lost most of its original momentum and popularity. To be sure, Congar invests more space in raising "critical ques-tions" about the movement than in reflecting on its "positive con-tribution" to the Church. The concluding chapter, however, has once again an unfortunately homiletical tone to it, reinforcing the sense that, while this three-volume work represents another signif-icant milestone in Yves Congar's theological journey, it is, in the final analysis, a highly uneven piece of work.

4. The River of Life Flows in the East and in the West: An Overview of Volume III

Volume III offers a lengthy and detailed comparative analysis of Western and Eastern approaches to the study of the Trinity, with

---

[46] II: 61.

particular reference to the Third Person. Following the long-standing emphasis of the East, Congar shows that our access to knowledge of the Holy Spirit comes through our experience of the effects of the Spirit's action in the world, that is, in the economy of salvation. Even though no one can have any direct insight into the inner workings of the Godhead itself, much of Western theology, at least until the middle of the 20th century, seems to have been predicated on the assumption that we can.

4.1. *The Motherhood of God and the Femininity of the Holy Spirit*

There is an odd excursion in this volume into the questions of the motherhood of God and the femininity of the Holy Spirit. Congar acknowledges that recent insistence on the latter is a reaction to centuries of male-dominated imagery of God. He refers to various feminine characteristics attributed to God in Sacred Scripture, and particularly to the Person of the Holy Spirit. In one of the main ironies inherent in his treatment of the subject, Congar repeatedly affirms the femininity of the Spirit while using, at the same time, the male pronoun in referring to the Holy Spirit. Thus, for example, "In Gen. 1:2, the Spirit is shown, in a sense, as God's *rûah*, hatching the egg of the world. *He* is likewise the principle of the second creation, as if realizing the Father's plan in a maternal manner ..."[47] Or again: "The part played in our upbringing by the Holy Spirit is that of a mother ... The Spirit also enables us to invoke God as our Father and *he* reveals to us Jesus our Lord ... Finally, *he* teaches us how to practise the virtues and how to use the gifts of a son of God by grace. All this is part of a *mother's* function."[48] Congar refers here to his brief, but incisive, reflections on Mary and

[47] III: 161, my emphasis.
[48] I: 161.

the Holy Spirit in volume I, and deplores once again the fact that "the maternal function of the Holy Spirit has often been replaced in recent Catholic devotion by the Virgin Mary."[49]

4.2. *The "Filioque"*

Congar also reviews the dialogues between Orthodox Christians and Roman Catholics on questions pertaining to the Holy Spirit. He cites a number of areas where common ground has been achieved. One example, mentioned by other reviewers, concerns the Latin word, *procedere* (*processio*), that expresses the Spirit's "proceeding" from the Father *and* the Son (*Filioque*). The Greek term, *ekporeuesthai* (*ekporeusis*), refers to a single principle, namely, the Father, from whom both the Son and the Spirit proceed. Some of the Greek Fathers were willing to say that the Spirit *receives* from the Son, but not that the Spirit *proceeds* from the Son. Congar suggests that the Catholic Church suppress the *Filioque* in the Nicene-Constantinopolitan Creed, not only because of the non-canonical way in which it was imposed, but also because it is theologically misleading.

4.3. *The Holy Spirit and the Sacraments*

In the second, and much shorter, part of the third volume, Congar reflects on the intimate connection between the Holy Spirit and the sacraments, focusing mainly on Confirmation (an obvious choice) and the Eucharist. Although explicitly an exercise in sacramental theology, he insists that the section is intended "as a chapter of pneumatology."[50]

---

[49] III: 162. See again I: 163-164.
[50] III: 217.

He points out that the "Church as a whole is sacramental in its nature."[51] It is an institution "of a very special kind" that "acts in the present on the basis of past events and in the prospect of a future which is nothing less than the kingdom of God, the eschatological City and eternal life in communion with God himself."[52] The unity of all three aspects is insured by the Holy Spirit, and not by an "earthly means" nor by the institution of the Church. Indeed, the entire "life and activity of the Church" on this earth and in human history "can be seen totally as an epiclesis," a constant calling down of the Holy Spirit upon itself and the world it serves.[53]

4.3.1. Confirmation

Congar agrees with other theologians that Confirmation is really a completion of the sacrament of Baptism rather than a new and different sacrament. Following St. Thomas Aquinas, he suggests that, although the Holy Spirit is already given in Baptism, there is still a need for its "sealing," a way of "marking responsible entry into the communal and missionary life of the Church ..."[54] Confirmation makes possible "a personal act of commitment to the service of Jesus Christ, in the Church, in the presence of witnesses, made at the beginning of adolescence or on the threshold of adult life."[55]

4.3.2. Eucharist

Congar regards as a false dichotomy whether the consecration of the bread and wine into the eucharistic body and blood of Christ is

[51] III: 271.
[52] *Ibid.*
[53] *Ibid.*
[54] III: 222.
[55] III: 224.

322 RICHARD P. MCBRIEN

effected by the priest as representative of Christ, using the very words of Christ, or by the Holy Spirit as invoked in the epiclesis. The consecration and invocation apply to the whole of the anaphora, or Eucharistic Prayer, and not only to the actual words of consecration or to the words of the epiclesis. "The consecration of the sacred gifts," Congar writes, "is the act of Christ, the sovereign high priest who is active through his minister *and* through the Holy Spirit."[56] He notes that in the Eastern rite the epiclesis is spoken in the plural, indicating clearly that the whole community invokes the Spirit. The Roman canon, on the other hand, contains the words, *"Memores offerimus"* and *"Supplices te rogamus"* — both in the plural as well. "We are not very far apart," he observes.[57]

Congar notes that the Second Vatican Council gave life — or perhaps *restored* life — in the Catholic Church "to a spirit in accordance with that of the Fathers and has been preserved in the Orthodox Church."[58] All of the new eucharistic prayers contain an epiclesis before and after the words of institution, asking first for the gifts to be sanctified and consecrated, and then for the fruits of the sacrament to be communicated through the action of the Holy Spirit.[59]

For Congar, the Eucharist "follows the structure of the economy of salvation."[60] The Holy Spirit had to sanctify, anoint, and guide Jesus, the Word made flesh. "It was necessary for the Holy Spirit

[56] III: 234.
[57] III: 236.
[58] III: 241.
[59] Congar elaborates upon this important point in the third chapter of this Second Part, III: 258-266. Following Augustine he insists that to live in the Spirit one must belong to the Body of Christ, which is the Church. It is not enough to receive the body of Christ in Holy Communion; one must also be given life by the Holy Spirit. And for Thomas Aquinas, too, the spiritual eating of the sacrament is a participation in the Holy Spirit. See III: 260-261.
[60] III: 264.

to 'pneumatize' him, according to the teaching of Paul in, for example, Rom 1:4; 1 Cor 15:45; 2 Cor 3:17-18. The Christ whom we receive in sacramental communion is the Christ of Easter who has been 'pneumatized' or penetrated by the Spirit."[61] The Spirit thereby made Christ Head of the Body, the Church, and at the same time has made it possible for its members to complete and sanctify the Body. "There is only one economy of grace in which the same Spirit sanctifies the body of Christ in its three states" [the earthly Jesus who died, rose, and has been glorified; the eucharistic Lord in the consecrated elements of bread and wine; and the communion or Body of which we are the members], Congar concludes, and these are "differentiated but at the same time dynamically linked together and this is to the glory of God the Father: 'Through him, with him, in him, in the unity of the Holy Spirit', as we say at the end of every eucharistic prayer."[62]

4.3.3. The Life of the Church as One Long Epiclesis

Congar reminds us that the Holy Spirit is directly involved in the celebration of every sacrament, not only those of Christian Initiation (Baptism, Confirmation, and Eucharist).[63] Thus, the process by which a minister is ordained to the diaconate, presbyterate, or episcopate is also subject to the invocation of the Spirit. In each

---

[61] *Ibid.*

[62] III: 264-265.

[63] Congar reflects on the role of the Spirit in the act of baptism, with special reference to the New Testament, in II: 189-190. Here in Volume III he links the Spirit with the symbolism of water, which is "like the womb of our mother the Church, in which the Spirit gives birth to the Body of Christ" (III: 267). In the Easter Vigil service, the lighted paschal candle, representing the risen Christ, is plunged three times into the water and, at the same time, the Spirit is invoked, as at the baptism of Jesus in the Jordan.

ordination rite there is a laying on of hands, which is in itself a
gesture pointing to the communication of the Holy Spirit.[64]

The Spirit is similarly engaged in the celebration of the sacrament of Reconciliation. In the words of the so-called "Johannine
Pentecost:" "Receive the Holy Spirit. If you forgive the sins of
any, they are forgiven; if you retain the sins of any, they are
retained" (John 20:19-23). Congar notes here that the Spirit is mentioned more than twenty times in the *Praenotanda* of the new ritual promulgated by Pope Paul VI in 1973. The renewed formula of
absolution is no longer simply a declaration of the forgiveness of
sins but is implicitly in the form of an epiclesis and explicitly Trinitarian in content.[65]

Marriage, too, has a pneumatological dimension. In the Eastern
Churches, the celebration culminates in the crowning of the bride
and bridegroom by the priest, symbolizing the descent of the Holy
Spirit upon the couple. The priest's gesture and the prayer that follows correspond to the invocation of the Holy Spirit in the celebration of the Eucharist.[66] Congar also extends the pneumatological reference to other, non-sacramental rituals within the Church:
religious profession, the reading of Sacred Scripture, and preaching.[67] In the end, the Holy Spirit is "the principle of unity," not
only for Christian communities but for all of humankind.[68]

Congar concludes his three-volume opus with the expressed hope
that it will somehow contribute to "the holy work of restoring
Christians to unity — a unity not of uniformity and imperialism, but
of communion through the one who, distributing his charisms of

---

[64] See III: 268.
[65] See III: 269.
[66] See *ibid.*
[67] See III: 270.
[68] III: 272.

every kind, wants to lead everything back to the Father through the Son."[69]

II. Congar's Pneumatology: Concluding Reflections

On the basis of this limited review of Yves Congar's writings, with special reference to his three-volume *I Believe in the Holy Spirit*, one can identify the following principal pneumatological elements of Congar's ecclesiology:

1. The Holy Spirit is not simply the animator, much less the *quasi*-animator, of the Church; the Spirit is co-institutor of the Church with Jesus Christ. This insight is congruent with Congar's view of the historic *Filioque* controversy. The Spirit does not proceed, in subordinate fashion, from the Father *and* the Son. The Son and the Holy Spirit are co-equal principles which proceed from the Father within the Godhead.

2. As co-institutor of the Church, the Holy Spirit ensures the efficacy and fruitfulness of the sacraments, especially the Eucharist, forms and re-forms the members of the Church into a community, confers charisms upon the institutional Church and its individual members, and inspires and guides the Church's mission and ministries. There is no opposition, therefore, between Christ as the institutor of the structures of the Church, and the Holy Spirit as the source of the Church's charisms. The institutional and charismatic dimensions of the Church are integrated within the mystery of the whole Church.

3. The entire life of the Church is "one long epiclesis," that is, of the Church's calling down of the Holy Spirit upon itself and upon the world it has been sent to serve. The epicletic character of

[69] *Ibid.*

the Church is evident in many realms of ecclesial activities, but especially in its sacramental life.

4. The Holy Spirit is both with the Church now and ahead of it, as the promised one, drawing the Church forward in history towards its eschatological inheritance in the final Reign, or Kingdom, of God.

5. The Church universal is a communion of local churches, with the Holy Spirit as the source and ground of that communion. Indeed, the Holy Spirit is not only the source and ground of the unity of the Church, but also of its holiness, catholicity, and apostolicity.

6. The Church is the Body of Christ, and the Holy Spirit is the Spirit of the Risen and exalted Lord. The primary basis of pneumatology, therefore, is Christology.

To be sure, Yves Congar's evolving understanding of the role of the Holy Spirit in the life, mission, ministries, and structures of the Church, culminating in his *I Believe in the Holy Spirit*, stands in stark contrast with the pneumatology prevalent in Roman Catholicism prior to the Second Vatican Council. In comparison with the *present* state of Roman Catholic pneumatology, however, Congar's seems less extraordinary, even conventional. This is not to say that the pneumatological dimension of Congar's ecclesiology is without importance. On the contrary, what was often only implied in the work of other contemporary ecclesiologists was made much more explicit in Congar's theology of the Church, and that will always be to his credit. At the same time, one can at least raise the question whether the Holy Spirit merited a separate three-volume treatise — by Yves Congar or by any other theologian.

In my own synthesis of Catholic theology and doctrine, I deliberately excluded a separate section on the Holy Spirit, even in the formal treatment of the triune God.[70] I did so for two principal reasons: first, the preoccupation of the New Testament is with God the

[70] See my *Catholicism*, 396.

Almighty Creator and with Jesus Christ, who comes among us to manifest and to do the Father's will, that is, to proclaim, practice, and hasten the coming of God's Reign at the end of history; and, second, the Holy Spirit is never an object of that proclamation in the New Testament, whether on the part of Jesus or the Church. Rather, the Spirit is the power through which the proclamation is made and fulfilled.

On the other hand, the Holy Spirit is at issue, whether explicitly or implicitly, in every major theological discussion: the divinization of humanity by grace, the renewing and reconciling presence of God in history, the mystery of the Church, the celebration of the sacraments, and the exercise of Christian witness.

Nevertheless, "[t]he Holy Spirit cannot become a formula, a dogma apart," the Greek Orthodox theologian, Nikos Nissiotis, has written. "Pneumatology is the heart of Christian theology, it touches all aspects of faith in Christ. It is a commentary on the acts of the revealed triune God, the life of the Church, and of the man who prays and is regenerated ... Orthodox pneumatology does not allow the doctrine of the Holy Spirit to become a separate chapter of dogmatic theology."[71]

In the end, it is not what Yves Congar wrote about the Holy Spirit that will endure for decades and even centuries to come, but what he wrote about the Church. If, indeed, he had wished to do a synthesis of his thought in the twilight of his long and illustrious ministry and career as a theologian, it would have been far more useful if it were in the form of a three-volume work entitled, *I Believe in the Church.* I can think of no one more qualified to write it than Yves Congar.

---

[71] Cited by Patrick Corcoran, *Irish Theological Quarterly* 39 (1972) 277.

CONGAR ON TRADITION

Jonathan ROBINSON

The Oratory of St. Philip Neri, Toronto
Formerly Lecturer in Philosophy
McGill University, Montreal, Quebec

In this essay I want to examine Fr. Congar's analysis of the function of tradition in the Church from the standpoint of the questions
raised by Catholic life today.[1] I am not, that is, so much concerned
to rehearse a tale about the richness and depth which his work
brought to theological studies in the forties and fifties of the last
century because this has already been done with authority and
scholarship over the years by many noted theologians; and recently
both Fr. Aidan Nichols, O.P.[2] and Fr. Fergus Kerr, O.P.[3] have given
us authoritative interpretations of the great Dominican's thought
from an historical perspective. What I am going to do in this essay

[1] I am grateful to Fr. Romanus Cessario, O.P. and Fr. Derek Cross of the
Toronto Oratory who read earlier drafts of this article and who made many helpful suggestions. I must also add the usual disclaimer that the substance of the
work with its defects is my own.

[2] Aidan Nichols, *Yves Congar* (Wilton, CT: Morehouse-Barlow, 1989); id.,
*From Newman to Congar: The Idea of Doctrinal Development from the Victori-
ans to the Second Vatican Council* (Edinburgh: T.&.T. Clark, 1990), amongst
others.

[3] Fergus Kerr, "French Theology: Yves Congar and Henri de Lubac," *The
Modern Theologians: An Introduction to Christian Theology in the Twentieth
Century*, ed. David. F. Ford (Oxford: Blackwell, ²1997) 105-117, where there is
a discussion of the political context in France of the work of de Lubac and Congar. See also id., *Immortal Longings* (London: SPCK, 1997) 167-173.

is to ask to what extent Congar's own theory is capable of sustaining the view of Christianity to which he himself subscribed. I shall conclude that it is not adequate to this task. Congar's thinking is at once too radical and not radical enough. The form of my argument is: if p then q, but not-q, therefore not-p; that is, if Congar's theory of tradition is adequate it should be capable of sustaining the traditional sort of Catholicism to which he seems to have subscribed, but it is not capable of sustaining this traditional Catholicism; therefore the theory is not adequate even for his own purposes. This inference, *modus tollens*, does not show that Congar's theory about tradition is right or wrong in itself; it only shows that it cannot sustain his basically orthodox and sacramental view of Catholicism.

IM ANFANG WAR DIE TAT

In *Tradition and Traditions* Congar says that the idea of tradition involves three elements: "a deposit handed on, a living authority, a transmission by succession."[4] Tradition, he is quite clear, has different meanings, and he saw his task as "distinguishing between the different aspects and various components of a rich and complex reality."[5] Nonetheless, there is some sort of family resemblance between different usages, and he does maintain that the word has a "primary meaning" which is "broad yet precise":

> Tradition comes from the Latin *traditio*, the noun of the verb *tradere*, to transmit, to deliver. It was a term of ratification in Roman law: for example, the legal transfer of a shop or house was accompanied by

---

[4] Yves M.-J. Congar, O.P., *Tradition and Traditions* (New York: MacMillan, 1967) 24 (*T.&T.*).

[5] Yves Congar, *Tradition and the Life of the Church*, Faith and Fact Books, 3 (London: Burns & Oates, 1964) 14 (*T.L.*).

the act of handing over its keys, *traditio clavium*; the sale of a piece of land was accompanied by the act of handing over a clod of earth. *Tradere, traditio* meant to hand over an object, with the intention, on the one hand, of parting with it, and, on the other, of acquiring it. *Tradere* implied giving over and surrendering something to someone; passing an object from the possession of the donor to the receiver. In Greek, *paradidonai*; aorist *paradounai*, had the same meaning. An equally good simile would be that of a relay race, where the runners, spaced at intervals, pass an object from one to the other, a baton, for example, or a torch.[6]

Tradition, then, is a transmission from person to person and implies as Congar says "a living subject"; and from the point of view of content, tradition requires in its "most primitive and general sense ... merely a deposit of some sort." This deposit or content, he makes clear, "can include writings, as well as words, actions, rules of conduct and institutions."[7] Then he draws what he seems to think follows as a conclusion from the above:

> In short, tradition is not primarily to be defined by a particular material object, but by the act of transmission, and its content is simply *id quod traditum est, id quod traditur*.[8]

In other words, the active side of tradition is what gives tradition its distinctive character as an element in Christianity, and this statement is based on the fact that while the content of several acts of transmitting something may vary, the act, as an act of handing over something, does not. The contention is central to Congar's thinking, but it is a claim that must be scrutinized with care. Certainly the argument here moves very quickly. It is quite true that the something handed over, which may vary enormously in character, cannot ("primarily") define the nature of tradition; but, on the other

---

[6] *Ibid.*, 14-15.
[7] *T.&T.*, 296.
[8] *Ibid.*

hand, neither can the bare act of transmission, which is nothing if there is no content handed over. Because some tea drinkers may prefer Indian to China this does not show that tea drinking is defined primarily by the action of drinking rather than by the fact that it is tea of one sort or another that is being drunk. Although Congar is clear that "the act does not exist without its content, nor the content without the act of transmission,"[9] he persists in speaking as if there is an essence to Christian tradition called "handing over" in abstraction from any content whatsoever. To say that "handing over" is a necessary element for an adequate understanding of tradition is quite true, but that does not turn "handing over" into a sufficient condition for understanding how tradition functions.

Mathematical functions of the form $y = f(x)$ do tell us something, but only in a hypothetical form; and a mathematical function devoid of content in fact says nothing about the real world. If we take y to be tradition as an activity of handing on, and x as what is handed on, then y has no definite value until x is specified.[10]

It is not too difficult to see what Congar would say at this point. He maintains that in its "basic, exact, and completely general sense, tradition or transmission is the very principle of the whole economy of salvation," and this economy "begins by a *divine* transmission or tradition."[11] In other words the "series of acts planned by God for the salvation of mankind" (to use Congar's own gloss on the meaning of *the economy of salvation)* is what gives content to the fundamental use of *traditio.* Furthermore this God is a Trinity, the Persons of which are defined by the two Processions of the Son from the Father, and the Holy Spirit from both the Father and Son:

[9] *T &T.,* 297.

[10] See, for example, W. Kneale and M. Kneale, *The Development of Logic* (Oxford: Clarendon Press, 1962) 395ff.

[11] *T.L.,* 15.

> Tradition [as the principle of the economy of salvation] encloses and dominates [the economy] completely, from its very beginning, which is none other than God; God as the word is understood in the New Testament, referring to the Father, the absolute Origin, the uncreated Principle, the primordial Source, not only of all things visible and invisible, but of the very divinity of the Son and the Spirit, by procession.[12]

This is certainly a very compelling and beautiful expression of Congar's conviction that "the economy begins by a *divine* transmission or tradition," but it does nothing to shore up his contention that the primary meaning of tradition is to be understood as *tradere*; all he has shown is that you cannot understand the Christian economy if you leave out of account the activity of God. Furthermore, this activity has to be understood as activity of the *Christian* God, as he himself says; and this Christian God delivers[13] to us Jesus Christ to do the work of the Father: "in and by the men chosen and sent out by God for that purpose. The sending of Christ and of the Spirit is the foundation of the Church, bringing her into existence as an extension of themselves: 'I came upon an errand from my Father, and now I am sending you out in my turn' (John 20:21)."[14]

Congar's statement as to how we are to understand tradition presupposes a firmly stated and orthodox understanding of the activity of God in the redemption of the world, and it is precisely this firmly stated and orthodox understanding which is the foundation of his understanding of tradition. But he has done nothing to show that the active side of tradition is the essential, or the most important aspect of tradition. What he says might be true, but there is no argument for it.

---

[12] *T.L.*, 15.

[13] *Ibid.* Congar makes good use of the fact that *paradidonai* — handing over — is the word St. Paul uses (in for example Romans 8:31-32) to describe God's delivering over to us of the Son.

[13] *Ibid.*

How then are we to understand "the series of acts planned by God"? According to St. Thomas, the plan for redemption was from all eternity in the intellect of God. Only from the point of view of what has been created and redeemed, do before and after have a relevance. The divine plan was always there in a way that the external effect of the act, was not:

> We have to say ... that though the creative act, as it exists in God, is eternal and identical with the divine nature, the external effect of that act, namely the world, is not eternal but that it came into existence in such a way that there is an ideally first moment of time. God eternally willed that out of all possible worlds this particular world should begin to exist in such a way that the temporal order is what it is.[15]

St. John says at the start of his Gospel that in the beginning was the Word, and the Word was God — not the plans of God (if it makes any sense to talk this way). By the 19th century, though, things had begun to change. At the beginning of Goethe's *Faust* there are the famous lines:

> "In the beginning there was the Word" — thus runs the text.
> Who helps me on? Already I'm perplexed!...
> The Spirit speaks! And lo, the way is freed,
> I calmly write: "In the beginning was the Deed".[16]

Im Anfang war die Tat — in the beginning was the deed or the action. The whole of the philosophy of Goethe's younger contemporary Fichte was based on the effort to work out the consequences of his belief that "reason is not a thing which *is* and *exists*, but rather a doing — pure, simple doing ... reason cannot contemplate itself otherwise than as what it is; hence as a doing."[17] His problem then was to generate some content for this activity without a

---

15 F. C. Copleston, *Aquinas* (Harmondswoth: Penguin Books, 1953) 139.

16 *Faust*, 1: 3.

17 From *New Exposition of the Science of Knowledge*, as cited by George A Kelly, *Idealism, Politics and History* (Cambridge: Cambridge University Press,

subject. I am not suggesting that Congar would have had much patience with Fichte, but if we were to take Congar's arguments *au pied de la lettre* we would have to conclude that he is faced with the same problem; that is, he ought to show us how *tradere* is capable of generating "the plan of God." Of course, he is not faced with the same problem because he was a Christian, but his Christianity is required for his discussion of tradition to have any content; and, consequently, I would contend that a satisfactory theory of Christian tradition must place the content of tradition on an equal basis footing with its transmission, and this precludes the acceptance of even a sanitized version of *im Anfang war die Tat*. In his day Congar's writing may have opened up rich fields of historical data for theological exploration, but one cannot put off forever — and I would suggest one can no longer put off — facing the theoretical perplexities his uneasy synthesis entails.

In the end, does not Congar necessarily lead us to some sort of process theology; the theory, that is, that God is developing? To make room in Thomistic ontology and classical theology for historical thinking is one thing, but to erect no bulwark against historicism is another.

THE SUBJECT OF TRADITION

By "the subject of Tradition," Congar, in line with the usual scholastic usage, does not mean the subject matter of tradition, but rather where we find tradition, and who operates with it; sometimes the Latin *subjectum* is translated as *seat*.[18] "The subject of

1969) 184. See Frederick Copleston, S.J., *A History of Philosophy*, Vol. VII (London: Burns and Oates, 1963), Chapter I. The most accessible introduction to Fichte's work in English is his *Science of Knowledge with the First and Second Introductions*, ed. and trans. Heath and Lachs (New York: Appelton, 1970).

[18] "... caritas est in voluntate sicut in subjecto ... charity resides in the will, as in its subject or seat." 2, 2ae, 24, 1. (Blackfriars' *Summa*).

Tradition is the living being who carries it and is answerable for it: the subject of an action always bears a measure of responsibility."[19] The transcendent subject of tradition is the Holy Spirit, while the Church "visible and historical" is what, I suppose, a Scholastic would call the proximate subject of tradition.

Now the Church "is not principally a social and hierarchical organization … but a living organism in which all are members and all take part in the life of the whole."[20] The idea of the state or of the Church as an organism is an old one and has much to commend it. However, the Church does have a structure around which it is organized and which distinguishes it from other organisms such as the state or a multi-national corporation. It is the hierarchical and juridical elements of the Church which provide this structure.

So far so good, and of course Congar accepts and teaches what I have just written. The Visible Church is the proximate subject of tradition, and this visible Church is hierarchically organized. On the other hand, the Church is not *principally* a social and hierarchical structure because it is an organism; or, to put it in the language of the Council, it is the people of God. So, he wants to hold that the proximate subject of tradition is the Church as an organism; and this organism is in some sense prior to, or more important than, the hierarchical Church. It is at this point that matters become more complex.

There is no doubt as to Congar's *attitude* towards the hierarchical Church — for obvious historical reasons he was not enamoured of it and often identified the visible structured Church with what he called the Constantinian Church. On 11 October 1962, the day the Second Vatican Council opened, he wrote in his diary:

---

[19] *T.L.*, 48.

[20] *Irenikon* 12 (1935) 327. Cited in Geoffrey Hull, *The Banished Heart* (Sydney: Spes Nova, 1996) 204.

I see the weight, never disowned, of the period in which the Church played the master, in which the popes and the bishops were lords, had a court, protected artists, and aspired to a pomp equal to that of the Caesars. The Church has never repudiated all this, from Rome. Moving on from the Constantinian Church has never been its intention. Poor Pius IX [...] was called by God [...] to bring the Church out of the miserable donation of Constantine, converting it to an evangelism that would have permitted it to be less "of" the world and more "in" the world. He did exactly the opposite. He was a catastrophe; he didn't even know what ecclesia was [...] And Pius IX still reigns. Boniface VIII still reigns: he has placed himself above Simon Peter, the humble fisher of men.[21]

Cardinal Jean Daniélou summed up the consequences of this attitude in the following way:

On this view, the essential thing is that the Church should bear witness and make sure of satisfying the first requirement for this, which is purity. Attempts are made to keep it clear of civilization lest its purity be compromised. There is a nostalgia for the times of the martyrs and talk of the end of the Constantinian era. To protect the Church's purity, those who hold this view would go so far as to risk the abandonment of the crowd of baptized Christians for whom Christianity is hardly anything more than an external routine.[22]

When Congar and Daniélou considered this issue, with their varying emphasis, it was still perhaps a matter of adjusting the inner attitudes of certain churchmen. But today, as the last remnants of Constantinianism slip away we may question the prudence of those who would encourage this trend.[23]

[31] Congar, *Mon journal du Concile*, ed. and notes Éric Mahieu, 2 vols. (Paris: Cerf, 2002), I, 108-109 (11 October 1962).

[22] Jean Daniélou, *Prayer as a Political Problem*, trans. J. R. Kirwin (New York: Sheed and Ward, 1967) 9.

[23] "Alasdair MacIntyre ... has argued that Western people did not first cease to believe in God and subsequently withdrew their consent from the morality defended by the Church. Rather, they lost any global agreement on their manner

The Monuments of Tradition

The consequence of Congar's attitude towards the actual Church as found in history was to emphasize the Holy Spirit at work in the Church as the subject of tradition. Of course, he did not accept the distinction between the real Church as invisible and pure and the Church of Pius IX (or John XXIII) as somehow unreal or irrelevant. On the other hand, his attitude towards the visible Church left what he called the *monuments of tradition* particularly vulnerable to reformulation. This reformulation of the monuments of tradition leads inevitably to a decrease in the importance of tradition itself in the life of the Church. Here again Congar's thinking confronts us with the paradoxes of historicism.

Congar says the expression *monuments of tradition* is attributed to Franzelin, and that in the Middle Ages the word would have been *documenta*: "realities connected with and having a value for teaching":

> ... the documents of Tradition are not Tradition itself; they are expressions in which Tradition is, at least partially, fixed and contained, and in which as a result it can be grasped and analyzed. Tradition is logically at least, prior to its monuments, since they are only expressions of it.[24]

These monuments are what he calls "objective historical realities," but tradition itself is "a theological reality which supposes an

of living together and only subsequently rejected the authority of the Church. Of course, if this be true, then, not only will it be the case that the response to the gospel's preaching which ... a Christendom society requires ... the re-evangelisation of majorities; it will also be the case that only by putting (or retaining) in place *some* features of a Christendom society, with its particular configuration of practical reason, can render evangelical believing possible again on a demographically massive scale." Aidan Nichols OP, *Christendom Awake* (Grand Rapids, MI: Eerdmans, 1999) 79.

[24] *T.&.T*, 425.

action of the Holy Spirit in a living subject, and this subject is the Church, the people of God and the body of Christ."[25]This living active side of tradition whose subject is the Church produces realities which are historical, but which are not in themselves tradition, but only monuments or witnesses to tradition. The principal monuments or witnesses are the liturgy, the Fathers, and "ordinary expressions of Christian life," and I want to say a few words about the first of these.

There is no doubt that Congar, as a priest, took the liturgy very seriously. Before joining the Dominicans he had thought profoundly about becoming a Benedictine, and there are lovely passages in his works about the importance of the liturgy in the life of the Church and of the believing Catholic. In *Tradition and Traditions* he writes that he wants the pages on the liturgy to be "a hymn of filial homage and respect."[26] The liturgy, he writes, is:

> A privileged custodian and dispenser of Tradition, for it is by far the principal and primary thing among all the actions of the Church. It is, indeed, the active celebration of the Christian mystery in its fullness, it transmits all the essential elements of this mystery ... the liturgy is a *locus theologicus* of a special kind ... due to the very nature of the liturgy, which is worship and consequently has the character of a witnessing to or a profession of faith.[27]

The liturgy is not tradition itself, but, on the other hand, it has a particularly privileged character as a witness to the content aspect of tradition because it is a ritual action which is handed down over the centuries. The liturgy, he says, is not "a dead monument, a kind of Pantheon to be visited as one visits a museum" and this is so because it is "a home which is always lived in, the conditioning

---

[25] *Ibid.*, 452.
[26] *Ibid.*, 428.
[27] *Ibid.*, 354.

envelope or atmosphere of its whole life," yet at the same time he maintains that "as a ritualized activity, the liturgy has a monument's power of conservation. Ritual is a fixed thing, transmitted and performed in a fixed manner."[28] Ritual is not "mere" ritual, it is a monument or witness to tradition that is preserved and transmitted through the action; "ritual preserves: while everything else changes and we ourselves pass through phases which are not always those of continuous growth, ritual remains."[29] Even if Congar's analysis of tradition, as I have argued, is unsuccessful in explaining the abiding content of what is handed on, the liturgy in effect performs the saving synthesis that delivers us from time:

> How do we fare in the twentieth century, living after so much demolition work? But we need only step into an old church, taking holy water, as Pascal and Serapion did before us, in order to follow a Mass which has scarcely changed, even in externals, since St. Gregory the Great, or we may open our missals at the pages which give the Paschal Triduum ... Everything has been preserved for us, and we can enter into a heritage which we may easily transmit in our turn, to those coming after us. Ritual, as a means of communication and of victory over devouring time, is also seen to be a powerful means for communion in the same reality between men separated by centuries of change and affected by very different influences.[30]

Those words were written before the far-reaching changes in the liturgy imposed by the magisterium after the Second Vatican Council. However one judges the changes themselves, there is no doubt that the liturgy as a *monument* to tradition has been somewhat effaced. Liturgical worship until after the Second Vatican Council developed over time, that is to say, through history. In the aftermath of the Council, however, a rite was devised which

---

[28] *T.&T.*, 428.
[29] *Ibid.*
[30] *T.&T.*, 429.

broke with the organic development of the liturgical life of the Church. Dom Alcuin Reid has meticulously studied the way the principle of the organic development of the Roman liturgy was set aside.[31] Fr. Aidan Nichols also points to the phenomenon I am talking about:

> ... Church authority gave the professionals what almost amounted to a blank check, enabling them to redesign the Liturgy in just that inorganic way against which such reflective commentators as Bishop Sailer had warned.[32]

This has left the way open to endless experiment and change and has called forth, correspondingly, ever-renewed warnings and read-justments on the part of ecclesiastical authority. The net result of this has been to increase the importance of the magisterium at the expense of tradition. If the monuments, that is, are not monuments in the sense that their very existence has to be taken seriously (because they are witnesses to tradition), then their preservation or abandonment is no longer organic development but is determined by the magisterium. Tradition as exercising any "control of the object" has in fact disappeared,[33] in this case.

Congar himself, in spite of his claim that liturgy is an important monument to tradition, seems to have accepted the new liturgical dispensation in good part. His analysis of tradition would allow him to argue that the changes in the liturgy were the work of the principal subject of tradition, that is, the Holy Spirit working in the

---

[31] See Alcuin Reid, O.S.B., *The Organic Development of the Liturgy* (Farn-borough: St. Michael's Abbey Press, 2004), for a well documented discussion of this question.

[32] Aidan Nichols, O.P., *Looking at the Liturgy* (San Francisco, CA: Ignatius Press, 1996) 48.

[33] I have worked this point, about the "control of the object," in more detail in Jonathan Robinson, *On the Lord's Appearing* (Washington, DC: Catholic University of America Press: 1997) 13-28.

Church. And in fact he does seem to have lost his balance when he applied the most radical reading of his theory of tradition to justify the new rites:

> Tradition isn't the past, it isn't old habits kept up by *esprit de corps*. Tradition is actuality, simultaneously handing on, receiving and creating. Tradition is the presence of a principle at every moment of its development. We don't accept the break. The Church never stops innovating, by the grace of the Holy Spirit, but she always takes from the roots and makes use of the sap which comes from them. In the beautiful words of Gertrud von Le Fort: "Man must always have earth under his feet, otherwise his heart dries up."[34]

So much for ritual which "preserves: while everything else changes." Now "the Church never stops innovating," and Congar now finds intolerable what he once loved:

> I loved the Latin Mass, which I celebrated [in the Dominican Use] for nearly forty years, but I don't want to go back to it. I recently assisted ... at a "St. Pius V" Mass on the occasion of the burial of a friend. To be honest it was intolerable. Those present didn't say a word; they saw nothing and heard almost nothing of what the priest, his back to the people, was doing at the altar.[35]

Fr. Gelineau said in 1976: "This needs to be said without ambiguity: the Roman rite as we knew it no longer exists. It has been destroyed."[36] If that is true then the Church seems to have set aside

[34] Congar, *Challenge to the Church: The Case of Archbishop Lefebvre*, trans. Paul Inwood (London: Collins, 1976) 57. There was more than theology at work here; there was also the "the bitter struggle that dominated politics in France in the later nineteenth and early twentieth centuries between supporters of the Third Republic, with their increasingly anti-clerical 'laicism', as it was called, and adherents of traditional Catholicism, with their monarchist nostalgia and ultramontanist inclinations."

[35] *Ibid.*, 53.

[36] Hull, *The Banished Heart*, 1.

one of its most important monuments to tradition, and that can only diminish the *de facto* importance of tradition in the life of the Church.[37]

It is a familiar criticism of Catholic theology that it substitutes the magisterium for tradition. For example, R. P. C. Hanson, whom Aidan Nichols called "one of the most classically Anglican theologians of recent times" writes:

> Their [Catholics'] religion is a religion which looks to the present, and to the future for its revelation, indeed one which may confidently expect new revelations and new fundamental doctrines of Christianity to emerge in the future into public gaze ... In this insistence it has entirely deserted the whole emphasis and outlook of primitive Christianity, it has reversed the current of original faith.[38]

I do not really think Congar wanted to draw this conclusion, but it is difficult to see how he can avoid doing so. If the most important monument of all, the liturgy, could be radically restructured with so little regard for tradition as content, then it does seem as though the active side of tradition is in danger of becoming a self-propelling activity which generates its own content — rather like Fichte's original *act* or *deed*.

It seems to me that "radical restructuring" should be distinguished from "organic development" along the lines established

---

[37] "I am convinced that the crisis in the Church that we are experiencing today is to a large extent due to the disintegration of the liturgy, which at times has even come to be conceived of *etsi Deus non daretur:* in that it is as matter of indifference whether or not God exists and whether or not he speaks to us and hears us." Joseph Cardinal Ratzinger, *Milestones: Memoirs 1927-1977, trans. Erasmo Leiva-Merikakis* (San Francisco, CA: Ignatius Press, 1998) 148-149.

[38] Cited in Nichols, *From Newman to Congar: The Idea of Doctrinal Development from the Victorians to the Second Vatican Council*, 2.

by Dom Alcuin Reid. The latter is not opposed to adaptation and change, subject to objective limits which would preserve the traditional identity of content. Even if one does not accept Reid's criteria for organic development one might still recognize how the weakening of the authority of the monuments of tradition forced Congar, as an apologist of the new rites, ineluctably towards a Fichtean formulation of his thesis.

The identity of an individual or of an institution, as we noted above, requires a physical aspect, although that is not to say that identity is wholly constituted by physicality. I think that the same thing has to be said about the Church as the proximate subject of tradition. In addition to the structure provided by the magisterium, the Church as an organic and sacramental reality depends for its identity on the monuments of tradition which are visible, tangible and continuous, and these monuments ought to exercise some control over the development of doctrine and practice.

REVELATION AND TRADITION

We have seen that tradition, for Congar, is fundamentally transmission, and what is handed on from the Apostles and the Church living in history is the saving activity of God. Of course, Congar would say, this saving activity is formalized and canonized (primarily in the Scriptures), but in itself revelation is not verbal any more than tradition is essentially content. This, I think, requires some unpacking.

The traditional Catholic view of revelation is based on the belief that God has shared with us the "mystery of faith." If we affirm, for example, that God is a Trinity of Persons in one God we claim that our belief is based on God's communication of himself to us through his Son. The economy of salvation is not a kind of metaphysics about the "meaning of life" created by the philosophers, nor, much less, is it the result of any sort of empirical survey.

God, the Catholic believes, has shown himself in a unique and definitive way through Jesus Christ, and this revelation imparts, as St. Paul says it, "a secret and hidden wisdom"[39]; a "secret and hidden wisdom" that could be expressed in human language. It is this question of the verbalization of revelation that is the nub of the matter. It is one thing to think that God may have communicated, or shared, himself with us, but it is quite another to affirm that this communicating and sharing has some necessary connection with nouns, adjectives, verbs and adverbs. It seems a bit crass, and, for many, unbelievable, to say that what revelation *means* is God's conveying a verbal message which then gets written down by different people in various ways. A great deal has been made of this difficulty, but before saying anything about it, we should see that we are really faced with two questions. The first of these is: what, in this activity of revealing, are we to understand by God's initiative and the human person's response? Secondly, what is the result of this activity?

The first question is treated in a learned and fair way in a recent article by John Montag, S.J.,[40] in which he shows that the activity of God's revealing, and of our acceptance or (possibly) cooperation in this activity, is best understood by developing some of St. Thomas' ideas in the latter's questions on prophecy in the

---

[39] I Cor 2:7, "But we impart a secret and hidden wisdom of God, which God decreed before the ages for our glorification."

[40] "Revelation: The false legacy of Suarez," *Radical Orthodoxy*, ed. John Milbank, Catherine Pickstock and Graham Ward (London and New York: Routledge, 1999) 38.

Summa Theologiae. These questions concern in part the idea of the prophet's participating in God's own knowledge, rather than receiving a written or spoken message which he then hands on. But this *how* of revealing is not really our concern here. What we do want to see is that the second question, that is, *what* is revealed, is very much of interest to us. St. Thomas never wrote a treatise on revelation but we can find out something about his position on the *what* of revelation in the questions on faith in the *Summa Theologiae*. The assent of faith is our response to God as the first truth; but the first truth is not a complex of statements (or a complex of anything else). Thomas insists that it is our adherence to God as the first truth which provides us with the means to believe in the particular assertions of Christianity, such as God is a Trinity, or Christ as true God and true man and born of the Virgin Mary. So, it is true and important to say that the part God plays in revelation cannot really be adequately understood as the dictation of a series of propositions; and, from our point of view our faith is faith in the living God who cannot be grasped or understood through conceptual thinking:

> With regard to faith, then, if we look to its formal objective, it is the first truth, nothing else. The reason: faith as we mean it here assents to anything only because it is revealed by God, and so faith rests upon the divine truth itself as the medium of its assent.[41]

On the other hand, God as the first truth is simple and we have no way of knowing anything about this nature except that it is. If God is to reveal something about himself that we can grasp then it will have to be in a way which is suited to our capacities. We understand things by using *enuntiabilia*, that is, what can be enunciated, or expressed as propositions or words:

[41] 2, 2, 1, 1.

... the human mind knows in a composite way things that are themselves simple; this is quite the opposite of the divine mind, which in
a non-composite manner knows things that are themselves composite. To apply this: consider the object of faith from its two perspectives. First, from the perspective of the reality believed in, and then
the object of faith is something non-composite, i.e. the very reality
about which one has faith, Second, from the perspective of the one
believing, and then the object of faith is something composite in the
form of a proposition. This explains why earlier theologians were
correct in maintaining either alternative; there is a sense in which
each is true.[42]

The purpose of this revelation by God is not merely to convey
information, but to teach us how to live if we are to appropriate
for ourselves the fruits of Christ's redemption. In the *Summa
Theologiae* St. Thomas teaches that revelation was necessary for
salvation. Human beings were created for a purpose which sur-
passes anything they could have known if left to their own spec-
ulations about the meaning of existence. He quotes the words of
Isaiah to the effect that ear has not heard nor eye seen what things
God has prepared for those that wait on Him,[43] and understands
this to mean that unless the nature of this destiny is revealed to
us then we could never do our part in seeking to obtain it for ourselves:

... the end must first be known by men who are to direct their
thoughts and actions to the end. Hence it was necessary for the salvation of man that certain truths which exceed human reason should
be made known to him by divine revelation.[44]

This was put very clearly by a French Dominican of the last century in his commentary on questions 1-7 of the treatise on Faith in

---

[42] 2, 2, 1, 2.
[43] Isaiah 64:4, in the Vulgate.
[44] 1a Pars, 1,1.

the *Summa*.[45] Revelation and the faith which believes and accepts the revelation are not ends in themselves.[46] Faith, St. Thomas says, will pass away when the vision of God is attained, and the purpose of revelation is to make possible the attainment of this vision:

> The God of faith is a God who has spoken. He has spoken to tell us what is [or what is real, or what is the case]. He has spoken to tell us the truth and to have it become a part of us.[47]

God's revelation of himself in Jesus Christ is given to us so that we might inherit eternal life. But that does not alter the fact that this revelation is presented to us through *enuntiabilia*, or propositions. It is by means of these propositions that we are enabled to put our faith in Christ Jesus and him crucified. It is in the Bible and the Creeds that we find what God wished to communicate to us, and the Bible and the Creeds require the tradition of the Church both for their safekeeping and for the way they are to be understood. Kierkegaard, who I suppose paid sufficient attention to the personal and existential to acquit him of soulless objectivity, put what I take to be the Christian position on this question very clearly.

---

[45] R. Bernard, O.P., *La Foi*, vol. I (Paris: Desclée, 1963).

[46] "L'objet de la foi n'est pas que je puisse acquérir des vérités sur Dieu, c'est que Dieu fasse pénétrer en moi sa vérité à lui, c'est qu'il fasse chez-nous lui-même oeuvre de vérité." Bernard, *La Foi*, 316.

[47] "Le Dieu de la foi est un Dieu qui a parlé. Il a parlé pour dire ce qui est. Il a parlé pour nous dire le vrai et pour nous le faire passer dans l'esprit." Bernard, *La Foi*, 328.

In the *Summa Contra Gentiles*, St. Thomas says that the human person can know divine things in three ways. In the first place he/she can, by the light of human reason, rise to the knowledge of God from the world of creation. In the second, divine truth comes down to us by way of revelation not like a proof to be analysed, but like a truth to be believed. In the third way the mind is raised to a perfect vision of what has been revealed. Revelation then was instituted to lead us to the blessed vision of God where our eyes shall see him and be satisfied. *Summa Contra Gentiles*, IV, 1.

He wrote in one of his efforts "to seek out experimentally an interpretation of existence":[48]

> I scarcely suppose that anyone will deny that it is the Christian teaching in the New Testament that the eternal happiness of the individual is decided in time, and is decided through the relationship to Christianity as something historical.[49]

Many people seem to find this position to be naïve and somehow unspiritual, and even, as the Cardinal de Bernis suggested, in bad taste;[50] although it is also true that a great many people in the eighteenth century, and today as well, do not come out and say it very directly.

Andrew Shanks who has written on Hegel and is interested in literature and poetry is a striking example of someone who does not shirk drawing the consequences of non-propositional revelation. Faith he says "in the true theological sense, is not a metaphysical opinion." Shanks means, I take it, that when someone says: "I believe in God" or "I believe in Jesus Christ, his only Son our Lord," he is not making any claim about reality; he is not saying "look here, this is what I believe to be true." Those kinds of statements have no place in a discourse about faith, because, Shanks says, "Faith is what saves." He then goes on to say that "no metaphysical option, not even the most orthodox or the most enlightened, can ever save."[51] In itself, this last sentence is unexceptionable, but I don't think anyone ever seriously thought that the words

[48] Søren Kierkegaard, *Concluding Unscientific Postscript*, trans. Swenson and Lowrie (Princeton, NJ: University Press, 1943), Book 2 Chapter IV section 1, no. 1, 322.

[49] *Ibid.*, no. 2, 330.

[50] "Cardinal de Bernis noted in his *Memoirs* that by 1720 it 'was no longer considered well-bred to believe in the Gospels'." Cited in Peter Gay, *The Enlightenment: An Interpretation* (London: Weidenfeld and Nicolson, 1967) I: 339.

[51] Andrew Shanks, *What Is Truth, Towards A Theological Poetics* (London and New York: Routledge, 2001) 5

themselves did the saving. It is not sentences or propositions that save, but whatever it is they refer to that matters most. Catholics, and I would have thought most Christians, believe it is Jesus Christ who does the saving. No matter what theory we might have as to how we are made aware of this truth,[52] we think it is true.

We are, however, confused according to Shanks, although we must be shown patience as the confusion is "quite easily under-standable." The confusion of thinking that statements in the Creed, for example, have any reference to truth has arisen because faith, in every culture, is always found associated with "certain opinions" and it is the opinions themselves that make truth claims. For exam-ple, Baal wants the sacrifice of children, Jehovah wants circumcision, Allah wants total abstinence, Jesus wants chastity, and so on, are all opinions *associated* with faith, but they have no intrinsic connec-tion with faith. In itself faith contains no elements of opinion at all:

> Thus, what is faith? I go back to what I said above: faith, surely, is
> a community-building or community-transformative appropriation of
> the very deepest poetic truth.[53]

So poetry through the good offices of the community provides us with the content of faith. The people of God as it develops through history, respectful of the past, no doubt, but not tied down by dead doctrines and experiences moves on towards a richer and more complex experience of Christian living. This picture presented by Shanks, and many like him, of a constant in human experience, called faith, which is without a fixed content, might have been acceptable to the Cardinal de Bernis, but I am not suggesting that it would have evoked much sympathy in Congar. Anyone who has

[52] See for example John Montag, S.J., "Revelation, The False Legacy of Suárez," *Radical Orthodoxy*, ed. John Milbank, Catherine Pickstock and Graham Ward (London and New York: Routledge, 1999) 38-63 who ably shows how complex this subject is.

[53] *Ibid.*

read *The Mystery of the Temple* or *Jesus Christ* will immediately sense he is reading the work of a serious and devout Christian. On the other hand, the unwillingness to lay any emphasis on the truth that language is an indispensable element in the communication of revelation effectively removes tradition as an essential factor in the proclamation of the Christian Gospel. Again, the result of Congar's writing has been to enhance the importance of the magisterium and decrease the importance of tradition. This point is further illustrated by considering the moral dimension of the Gospel.

THE MORAL DIMENSION OF CHRISTIANITY

St. Thomas discusses morality as an integral part of theology; and he begins the *prima secundae* with a discussion of beatitude. If we think this is the correct approach to the question of Christian living, then the consequences of a theological position for morality are relevant to the theory itself. That is, it is not open to a disciple of St. Thomas, at least, to say he is doing dogmatic theology and leave unconsidered its consequences for human action.

The weakness of Congar's analysis of tradition shows itself again in connection with arguments about sexuality. What revelation and the tradition of the Church tell us about marriage and homosexuality is becoming less and less acceptable outside traditional Christian circles. Those who argue that these questions have to be "rethought" in every generation often claim to understand Christianity better than those who maintain, for example, that Christian marriage means a life-time union between a man and a woman that involves sexual intercourse open to having children, or that homosexual activity is intrinsically wrong. Often today we find the arguments against the traditional Catholic stance on these questions presented with a Christian vocabulary. When we look at the arguments it is easy to see they are based on the conviction that the Holy Spirit

is leading the people of God into a more mature and humane attitude towards moral questions and this leaves the way open for a
radical restructuring of Christian morality.

Once again, I am not suggesting that Congar would have wanted
to lend support to the sexual revolution, but if tradition is essentially
movement forward under the influence of the Holy Spirit, then the
only way he would be able to defend the traditional viewpoint on
these matters would be to ascribe a radical importance to the teaching of the ordinary magisterium. If, for example, the exegetes tell
us there are no conclusive arguments against homosexuality to be
found in the Bible, and that many rules of conduct with apparently
equal authority have been set aside, then clearly the Bible itself
requires an authoritative, and an *on-going* interpretation by the
magisterium. Where else, that is, is a rule of life about this and
other sexual matters going to be found?

K. J. Dover is an acknowledged expert on homosexuality in
ancient Greece who understands Christian revelation as not binding in its historical form. That does not mean he is actively promoting homosexuality, but it does mean that if he is correct in his
views about revelation and Christian tradition, then there are no
specifically Christian arguments against homosexuality in abstraction from the teaching of the *Church*.

In a book on what morality actually meant, and how this morality was lived, by the ordinary Greeks living in the century from the
birth of Plato to the death of Aristotle Dover writes:

> Belief that the events and utterances reported in the Bible are cor-
> rectly reported, and with it the belief that God has revealed himself
> in injunctions which we disobey at our peril, has substantially
> declined in the course of the last two hundred years.[54]

---

[54] K. J. Dover *Greek Popular Morality* (United States of America: reprinted,
with corrections by Hackett Publishing, 1994) XII.

History, then, has shown us that there has been a decline in specifically Christian beliefs. The basis of this decline, Dover contends, is an increasingly sophisticated understanding of the problematic character of the different elements which lie at the basis of an unqualified commitment to the doctrines of Christianity:

> Many people find (reasonably, in my view) that the more they know and the more they think about documentation, tradition, religious experience and theological argument, the less inclined they are to commit themselves to acceptance of the claims of Christianity.[55]

Although Dover believes that the decline in belief in specifically Christian doctrines is solidly based, nonetheless, Christian belief can be useful in promoting moral living, although it does not necessarily do so:

> The history of Christianity from the beginning of the Christian era to this day suggests to me that whether Christian belief makes an individual morally better or morally worse depends on how he interprets ambiguous and enigmatic passages of the New Testament, what criteria he employs as a means of distinguishing between valid and invalid religious experiences, how he applies general injunctions to particular cases, and (above all) the relative importance which he attaches to different elements in Christianity.[56]

Dover's views on the disappearance of belief in the explicit teachings of Christianity, together with his contention that Christian morality may still possess elements of value is a familiar position. The criterion, or standard, for the acceptability and interpretation of Christian moral teaching is no longer Christianity itself, but principles drawn from the modern world.

There are those like Charles Taylor who think that the modern world is better suited to advancing the values of Christianity than

---

[55] *Ibid.*, XIII.
[56] *Ibid.*, XIII.

is the institutional Church. Taylor contends that secular society has become the bearer of the values of the Gospel. The Church may have carried the message of Christianity in the past, but a necessary condition for doing so in the future will be taking Christian values away from the care of the Church so that they will be able to flourish more effectively in secular society. I think a great many people do believe something like this, and it is therefore worthwhile to examine Taylor's position more closely.

We live in a world in which the language of human rights seems to be more important (even to Catholics) than the affirmations of the Creed. Part of the reason for the success story of "rights" talk over "Church" talk is just this failure, as it is judged to be, of the visible ecclesiastical structure to understand, much less live up to, the treasures of the Gospel:

> The view I'd like to defend, if I can put it in a nutshell, is that in modern, secularist culture there are mingled together both authentic developments of the gospel, of an incarnational mode of life, and also a closing off to God that negates the gospel. The notion is that modern culture, in breaking with the structure and beliefs of Christendom also carried certain facets of Christian life further than they ever were taken or could have been taken within Christendom. In relation to the earlier forms of Christian culture, we have to face the humbling realization that the breakout was a necessary condition of the development.[57]

Is such a position compatible with the way Congar's principles about tradition have worked out in the post-Vatican II Church and world? I think it is. If tradition is essentially activity; if the subject of tradition is a spiritual organism which is not confined to the limits of the hierarchical and visible Church; if the monuments of

---

[57] Charles Taylor, *A Catholic Modernity?* (New York/Oxford: Oxford University Press, 1999) 16.

tradition are not binding on the movement of the Spirit; if revelation as the activity of God is prior to the language in which the Church receives God's word; then that leaves the way open for fundamental changes in the way Christians should live their lives and think about their destiny.

I am not arguing that this is what Congar thought; but as I indicated in the first paragraph of this essay I just don't think Congar's analysis of tradition is an adequate basis for what he quite clearly did in fact believe. On the other hand, if the reader wants to construct an argument, *modus ponens*: if p then q, but p, therefore q, along the lines that if liberal Catholicism is true it can be seen as based on Congar's theory of tradition, and, as liberal Catholicism is true then Congar's theory of tradition (being the basis of liberal Catholicism) is also true, he would be quite entitled to do so.

PART V

YVES CONGAR AND THE THEOLOGY OF INTERRELIGIOUS DIALOGUE

NOTES ON THE THEOLOGY OF RELIGIONS

Georges CARDINAL COTTIER, OP

Theologian of the Pontifical Household
Formerly Visiting Professor at the University of Montreal
and the University of the Catholic Institute in Paris

1. The Constitution, *Lumen Gentium*, has set out a series of principles, of which the theology of religions must necessarily take note. As we read in paragraph 13:

> All humankind is called to belong to the new People of God.
> This people therefore, whilst remaining one and only one, is to
> spread throughout the whole world and to all ages in order that
> the design of God's will may be fulfilled: he made human nature
> one in the beginning and has decreed that all his children who
> were scattered should be finally gathered together as one (cf.
> John 11:52).

Thus was affirmed the unity and the oneness of the people of God
and the sense of history, which is ours: the time of the Church is
the time of mission.[1]

Then the important details follow on: "All men [and women] are
called to this catholic unity which prefigures and promotes universal peace. And in different ways to it belong, or are related:

---

[1] See also "Decree on the Church's Missionary Activity: Vatican II, *Ad Gentes
Divinitus*," 7 December 1965, trans. Redmond Fitzmaurice, OP, *Vatican Council
II: The Conciliar and Post Conciliar Documents*, ed. Austin Flannery, 2 vols.
(New York: Costello, ⁷1984), I, par. 9: Missionary activity tends towards escha-
tological plenitude.

the Catholic faithful, others who believe in Christ, and finally all humankind, called by God's grace to salvation".[2]

All humankind is called to become part of this Catholic unity, that is to say, to participate in the fullness of Christian life given in the Church. All are called to salvation. These two affirmations complete each other; in the case where the fullness of belonging cannot be realized, salvation is not refused. To this unity one can belong in many ways, one can *be ordained* — in the sense of being in relation to the Church. The formula does not impinge upon theological reflection; one could in fact understand this ordination as an imperfect belonging, belonging being understood in that case by way of analogy.

In a manner resembling *Ecclesiam suam*, the Constitution, designs three circles, with regard to this belonging of which it elsewhere indicates several modalities: the Catholic faithful (para. 14), non-Catholic Christians (para. 15), and non-Christians (para. 16). Paragraph 17, coming back to the *missionary* character of the Church, indicates that the situations described in paragraphs 15 and 16 do not correspond to a definitive status, which would make of them constitutive elements of the economy of salvation. By their very nature these situations are provisional. The support, which they might offer to some people, ought to be judged by the function of the unique salvation which is given in Christ Jesus, "because there is no other name under the heavens given to men by which we must be saved"(Acts 4:12).

2. The Declaration *Nostra Aetate* should be read in conjunction with the Dogmatic Constitution *Lumen Gentium* and the Decree *Ad*

---

[2] "Dogmatic Constitution on the Church: Vatican II, *Lumen Gentium*," 21 November 1964, trans. Colman O'Neill, OP, *Vatican Council II: The Conciliar and Post Conciliar Documents*, par. 13.

Gentes. The Council, in fact, had intended to indicate an order of authority among the documents, an order that already constitutes in itself a criterion for interpretation.

Our age is witnessing the links between peoples becoming closer. Thus it behoves the Church to examine its relationships with non-Christian religions. Its goal is to promote unity and charity between persons and among peoples. This is why it examines first of all "that which persons have in common and which moves them to live out their destiny together."

A whole series of affirmations have their basis in Scripture: all peoples form one single community, they have the same origin (Acts 17:25) (*Lumen Gentium* para. 13 has already said it: in the beginning God created human nature in unity); they have only one last end; the providence of God, the pledge of his goodness and his plan of salvation reach out to all (many Scriptural references) "until the chosen ones are reunited in the holy city, which the Glory of God illumines and where all humankind will walk in his light" (See Apocalypse 21:23f).

Having enunciated these fundamental truths, to which the human spirit may, in part anyway gain access by itself, the *Declaration* replies to the question of why have recourse to religions: from these last mentioned, humankind expects to find "the response to the enigmas concealed in the human condition which yesterday, as today profoundly trouble the human heart." The text enumerates the great questions which the individual asks about identity, the human condition, the meaning and the goal of life. These are the questions posed by every reflective person.

As for the religions themselves, they give witness to "a certain understanding by the human spirit of the hidden strength which is present at the heart of things and in the events of human life," going sometimes as far as to recognize the supreme Divinity, or even the Father.

It is not only the questions surging up from the depths of our being that we must envisage, but also the effort that religions make to respond to the anxiety of the human heart by proposing "ways, that is, doctrines, rules of life and sacred rites."

From that follows some principles of interpretation:

(I) The Church "rejects nothing that is true and holy in these religions." In other words, while it welcomes important questions which present themselves to every person, the Church also has recourse to a careful discernment, beginning with the truth that is entrusted to it, regarding its proposed responses.

(II) "It considers with sincere respect (*sincera observantia*) those ways of acting and of living, those rules and doctrines, which, while they differ in many ways from what it itself holds and proposes, nonetheless often carry a ray of truth which enlightens all people." This principle ought to be understood in the light of the preceding one. It is a question of being more precise as to the meaning of the expression "a ray of truth which enlightens all people" which obviously refers to the Prologue of the Gospel of John (Jn 1:9).

(III) Nonetheless "it announces and it is bound to announce ceaselessly, the Christ who is 'the way, the truth and the life' (Jn 14:6) in whom humankind must find the fullness of religious life and in whom God has reconciled all things to himself" (See 2 Cor 5:18-19). The religions and the responses that they bring, could never replace Revelation. The preceding statement could never be understood as if the Mission and the annunciation of Christ had lost their necessity, which is, on the contrary, very strongly reaffirmed.

3. It is in the context of these council documents, without forgetting the decree *Ad Gentes*, the Encyclical *Redemptoris Missio* (1991) and other documents like the Declaration *Dominus Jesus* (2000) that a theology of religions ought to be elaborated.

Nostra Aetate, as already *Lumen Gentium* had done, provides a direction of utmost importance. The religions are presented according to a certain order, which is that of their distance from or proximity to Christianity. In this way, they have treated of Hinduism, Buddhism, traditional religions, then Islam which is a monotheistic religion, and, finally of Judaism and the Jewish people. It is not by chance that in the ecclesial institutions born of the Council, relations with Judaism have been entrusted, not to the *Council for interreligious dialogue*, but to a commission attached to the Council for the Unity of Christians.

This is why, in my opinion, a theology of religions must begin with a theology of Israel or at least incorporate such a theology. To ignore this essential dimension is to lean towards a sort of neomarcionism. The economy of the history of salvation includes the two inseparable moments of the Old and New Testaments.

This last observation leads us to envisage religions, besides the so-called synchronic considerations, according to the greater or lesser similarity of their content, the diachronic dimension, without doubt much more fundamental, which is that of the history of salvation.

The history of salvation is that of the progressive unfolding of the salvific plan of God. It is the salvation willed by God, which makes of historical time, not just a simple succession of moments, but rather a period qualitatively structured and consequently a bearer of meaning, meaning here signifying direction and meaning altogether. Time, which is the time of salvation, is that of the maturing of God's plan. A central event exercises a structural function: the paschal event of the passion, death and resurrection of Christ. It is in relation to the paschal mystery that the diverse religions find their place. It is not without significance that a religion is either before Christianity or, like Islam, after Christianity.

4. Here, however the analysis leads to the introduction of a certain number of precisions.

The great stages of the history of salvation are the age of the Law of nature, the age of the ancient Law, the age of the new Law. The times of the age of the new Law are the "latter times." The glorious return of Christ will signify the end of history. The former stages play a role of preparation by contrast with the subsequent stage. Here, we must explore all the components of the Pauline notion of divine pedagogy, where the experience of sin itself enters into the plan of salvation: "(...) where sin abounded, grace has super abounded" (Rom 5:20).

Before the coming of Christ, grace was given with Christ in view, after his coming and the work of redemption carried out by him, all graces derive from him. There is no salvation outside of him.

This universal presence of the grace of Christ is not the same as the revelation and the knowledge of Christ. *Lumen Gentium* (para. 16) on this point recalls traditional doctrine. It is the will of God that all people are saved (see 1 Tim 2:4). "Those who, through no fault of their own, do not know the gospel of Christ or his Church, but who nevertheless seek God with a sincere heart, and, moved by grace, try in their actions to do his will, as they know it though the dictates of their conscience — those too may achieve eternal salvation." The text continues: "Nor shall divine providence deny the assistance necessary for salvation to those who, without any fault of theirs, have not yet arrived at an explicit knowledge of God, and who, not without grace, strive to lead a good life. Whatever good or truth is found amongst them, is considered by the Church to be a preparation for the Gospel and given by him who enlightens all people that they may at length have life."

The Constitution adds that "quite often" people allow themselves to be led astray by evil, exchanging the truth of God for a lie, serving the creature in preference to the Creator (see Rom 1:21; 25), or again, living and dying without God in this world, they are exposed to the depths of despair. This is why, "concerned about the glory of God and the salvation of all people," the Church is concerned about the Mission.

The situations that have been evoked, suppose on the one hand the working of grace, and on the other the absence of having met with revelation in its integrity. Grace uses the light of a good conscience, which is of the natural order, in order to bring the person along the way of salvation. This is what the notion of implicit faith implies. The presence of grace is broader than that of revelation, even though the normal development of the life of grace, notably by participation in the sacraments, presupposes access to the fullness of revelation. A theology, inspired by the idealistic philosophies of conscience, will tend to make the two realities coincide. The discussion of this point is essential for a theology of religions. The necessity of mission is constantly reaffirmed, which is crucial for understanding the problem. One must equally take account of the seduction and burden of sin, which may be present in religious-cultural traditions.

5. In the prolongation of what has gone before, the theologian is invited to probe the depths of a certain number of questions. I have kept three in mind, which appear to me particularly important.

The first, scarcely formulated, nonetheless weighs heavily on certain theologies of religions. How can we possibly conceive that the great religions, covering vast territories, some of which are older than Christianity, having borne much fruit at the level of culture, of morality and of spirituality, do not enter into the divine plan of salvation? What is meant by that is not — true though it may be — that all human history is led by the Providence of God, and that nothing escapes his will or his permissions. But we are inclined to see in the existence of the great historical religions some components, willed positively by God, of the plan of salvation, offering the means of salvation, analogous with or even equal to those offered by the Church. What God would require of everyone would therefore be to be faithful to the religious tradition into which individuals are born and which would be of itself and for them salutary. The great traditional religions would be therefore, each one for a given part of humanity, paths to salvation. The logic of this reasoning would be to place religious pluralism as a given *by right*, which would lead to relativism: Christianity would then have to renounce its position as bearer of divine truth, which is the same thing as inviting it to renounce itself.

Those who support this position — in reality an extreme one — are inclined to speak of religions in a general manner, without critical examination of their substance. That, from certain aspects, the big religious worlds live *sub umbra mortis*, would appear then to be a judgment that does not make sense.

One will recall here that, in Scripture, the purity of the faith of Israel finds itself threatened even at the very level of religion. That which opposes the affirmation of the transcendence and the unity of God, is the worship of idols. In this context, the Book of Wisdom distinguishes several forms of idolatry and shows a certain indulgence towards those who, seeking God, stopped at his creation, allowing themselves to be taken in by appearances: "What one sees is so very good" (see 13:6-9).

6. The second question ought to be clearly distinguished from the preceding one; it concerns the *status* of these religions *vis à vis* the fullness of salvation in Christ. We have already taken note of the fact that historical considerations are essential. Hinduism is anterior to the coming of Christ, Islam posterior.

It is with reference to Christ that we distinguish in the divine plan of salvation, three successive economies, that of the Law of nature, that of the ancient Law, that of the new Law. All of humanity falls under the economy of the new Law. But this fundamental "given" should not prevent us from asking the question about the sense of the anteriority or posteriority of a religion with regard to the coming of Christ. Here one might introduce the concept of *statute* (distinct from that of *economy*), which would permit us to be more precise about the proximity, or the access, which religions permit with regard to the revelation of the Old and New Testaments. The reservoir of ideas and of religious values which the great Oriental religions dispose of, stem from the Law of nature, while Islam, not without some malformations and a certain hardening, has been able to inherit ideas and values of a Biblical and evangelical origin. Knowledge of the religions cannot ignore these facts.

7. The third question is concerned with the content of that which one understands by religion, considered in its constitutive elements. It has an anthropological dimension.

A phrase from the *Ambrosiaster* taken up by St. Thomas, which deals with grace, is often quoted. "*Omne verum a quocumque dicatur a Spiritu Sancto est*, all truth, no matter who pronounces it, comes from the Holy Spirit."[3]

The objection quotes the *Glossa* which contains the phrase of the *Ambrosiaster* which it attributes to St. Ambrose and which is a commentary on 1 Cor 12:3: "no-one can say Jesus is Lord if it is not by the Holy Spirit." Thus it is a question of a profession of a truth of faith. Now it is by grace that the Holy Spirit dwells in us. Without Grace, consequently we cannot know the truth.

[3] See *Summa Theologica*, q. 109, Ia-IIae.

It is clear that the phrase refers to the truths of faith, and not to all truth. The objection thus grants to it an unwarranted extension, which does not correspond to the intention of the author.

This made St Thomas, who contributes a decisive precision, remark, "It must be said that all truth, no matter who proclaims it, comes from the Holy Spirit in so far as he infuses natural light and that he leads it to an understanding and an expression of the truth. But not in so far as to state that he inhabits [the soul] by sanctifying grace (*gratum facientem*), nor in so far as he dispenses an ordinary gift in addition to (*superadditum*) nature: for this only proves itself true for certain known truths and, above all, for the truths which are linked to faith, of which the Apostle speaks."

It is clear that in transcribing only the first part of the quotation, there is a distortion of meaning. But the distortion is itself indicative of a tendency, fairly widespread, and, in my opinion, quite destructive, *i.e.* that of attributing everything immediately to the causality of grace, while ignoring that which human nature, by its own resources is capable of. We see the consequence: every religious manifestation will be attributed to grace, and consequently regarded as salvific, every truth will be the effect of a revelation. Religion by itself, whatever the form, will therefore be supernatural.

This exaltation of the supernatural to the detriment of nature in reality empties the mystery of grace of its contents. The "religions" will then present themselves as so many expressions of the universal divine action of salvation. And since between one religion and another, there exist differences, contrasts, and oppositions, one will be obliged to define truth as a totality in which "partial" truths are supposed to insert themselves harmoniously. Assuredly, what I am describing in this way, in broad strokes, represents a tendency and more than one author recoils from having to accept the consequences. But whatever about subjective intentions, the strength of tendencies is in the logic of ideas.

8. It is because of this that the theology of religions may not disregard its anthropological foundations. The religious dimension belongs to human nature. The human person is inclined towards the Absolute and, by his or her own strength, is capable of taking significant steps in its direction. These steps are the precious "waiting stones" on the way to welcoming grace. The "most fundamental questions" posed by the human person, and of which *Gaudium et Spes* (para. 10) speaks are also evoked at the beginning of *Nostra Aetate* (para. 1) which refers to "the unsolved riddles of human existence. The problems that weigh heavily on the hearts of men [and women] are the same today as in the ages past."[4] Now these questions to which he or she asks a response from religions, are also the questions posed by philosophy. The responses given by religions, directly concern the relationship with the Absolute, and are accompanied by behaviours, by attitudes, by acts and by gestures, like worship, adoration, supplication, in a word, by prayer. For its part, philosophy is a school of wisdom. Wisdom, which is knowledge, also determines a rule of life. This proximity between religion and philosophy, which does not exclude their distinction, illustrates in its own way the anthropological roots of religion.

The fact that the economy in which humanity lives is the economy of grace does not suppress, but, on the contrary, demonstrates the resourcefulness of nature and its capabilities. One could never minimize these spiritual capabilities. But, by virtue of the economy of salvation, in which humanity dwells, to recognize the highest achievements of nature should not make us ignore the role of possible actual graces or of private revelations, being clear about the

---

[4] "Declaration on the Relation of the Church to Non-Christian Religions," Vatican II, *Nostra Aetate*, 28 October 1965, trans. Father Killian, OCSO, *Vatican Council II: The Conciliar and Post Conciliar Documents*, par. 1.

fact that the "public" Revelation given for all people is that of the Old and New Testaments.

It is necessary also to consider other aspects, such as that of religions in their comparison with the Church, and the danger of placing them on the same plan of ecclesiality. It is essential, for the history of salvation, to stress that only the Church, in the proper meaning of the term, is a subject. But this point alone would call for further development.

I am happy to be able to publish these notes, reflecting an initial appreciation, and as a mark of homage to Yves Congar.

* Trans. by Claire O'Brien, OP.

YVES CONGAR
THEOLOGIAN OF GRACE IN A WIDE WORLD

Thomas F. O'Meara, O.P.

Formerly William K. Warren Professor of Theology
University of Notre Dame, Indiana

We associate Yves Congar with researched essays on the history of ecclesial forms, with pioneering works in the theology of laity in the church or episcopal collegiality, and with pioneering ecumenical encounters with Protestants and Orthodox. Although he not infrequently mentioned that he was not a philosopher, he appreciated the differences between Thomas Aquinas and neo-scholastics, between Maurice Blondel and Jean-Paul Sartre, and, when asked, he could write an essay leading from an existential psychology of faith to a theology of grace.[1] He found his vocation early: he would combine history with ecclesiology to further the unity of Christians. He was a theologian inspired by historical variety, a historian of church forms taught by Biblical origins to pastoral movements. When he was twenty-six, while visiting Germany, he wrote a prayer. "Oh God, why does your church always condemn? If your church were only more encouraging, more comprehensive. The church must make itself intelligible to every human ear. God, enlarge our hearts. Make people understand us and make us understand each other, and all peoples. Times press — there is so much work to be done."[2]

---

[1] For instance, "L'Homme est capable d'être appelé," *La Vie Spirituelle* 51 (1969) 377-384.

[2] *Dialogue between Christians* (Westminster, MD: Newman, 1966) 5-7.

I. GRACE IN A WIDE WORLD

The researcher of medieval texts soon became in the French church between the wars, an explorer of realms in the present and even in the future. Congar published in 1959 a book whose topics looked at the issue of salvation outside of Christianity. Pastoral issues from the exciting years of French Catholicism after World War II led Congar into a creative consideration of the church amid people in the contemporary world, the book he called *Vaste Monde, ma Paroisse*. The opening "Avertissement" is signed Strasbourg, September, 1959 where the bishop had received him after periods of exile in Cambridge and Jerusalem. "In 1959, thanks to Michael Browne, Master of the Order of Preachers, the exceptional censure imposed on him had been tempered. He could assemble some articles."[3] The book's title comes from a phrase of John Wesley, "I look upon the world as my parish," and the book appeared in 1961 in an English translation as *The Wide World My Parish* with the subtitle, "Salvation and Its Problems."[4] (The French title *Vaste Monde, Ma Paroisse* lacked the opening awkward article, and its subtitle "Truth and Dimensions of Salvation" is more direct). Some of the material had appeared in *Témoignage Chrétien*: that journal had been a clandestine periodical of the French Catholic resistance

[3] J. M. R. Tillard, "Introduction," to Cardinal Yves Congar, *Vaste monde ma paroisse* (Paris: Cerf, 2000) I. "But the crisis remains in the background. He will always be marked by what he will call 'the purge of 1954' when, as he will repeat, the Order of St. Dominic was wounded, attacked in its structure of authority, attacked in its representative theologians" (Tillard I).

[4] (London: Darton, Longman & Todd, 1961). There were also translations into German, Spanish, and Italian. "What is essential in the book is, in our view, found in the very dense but nonetheless understandable pages (written in a clear style) on the nature of salvation, the traditional perspective of ultimate goals, the salvific value of other religions, the formula of 'outside the church no salvation,' and the import of our freedom, however weak it might be" (III).

movement in Lyons, and its founder the heroic advocate of children
and Jews, the Jesuit Pierre Chaillet, was a friend of the Dominican.[5]
In the late 1950s, Congar was also working on articles on Anselm,
the ecclesiology of the Eastern church from the sixth to the eleventh
centuries, and the laity, as well as on the historical section of *Tradition and Traditions*. The overall theme of *The Wide World My
Parish* is salvation, salvation understood not simply as the private
state of an introspective individual kneeling in a dim church but as
a human salvation with historical and global contexts. If today we
associate the topic of salvation outside of Christianity with Karl
Rahner or Raimundo Pannikar, we will be surprised to learn that
Congar too has his theology of the vast numbers of men and
women who through an accident of history live outside of the possibility of belief and baptism in Jesus Christ.

Salvation in present and future worlds implies topics like salvation amid other religions, heaven as the goal of history, purgatory
and hell, the end of the world and the resurrection of the body,
while two appendices look at the questions of reincarnation and
extraterrestrials. The themes themselves — person, existence in
history, grace outside of baptism and dogma — recall problemat-
ics important to European theologians, particularly after 1945.[6] The
lengthiest chapter treats salvation outside of Christianity. Francis
Sullivan observes: "Other Catholic theologians have described,
more explicitly than Rahner has done here, the things that can serve
as secular mediations of grace and salvation for people who profess no religion, and consider themselves atheists. Congar, for
instance, observed that among such people one finds those who

[5] On Chaillet and Congar, see Thomas O'Meara, "A French Resistance Hero,"
America 176 (1997) 12-17.

[6] See Stephen J. Duffy, *The Graced Horizon: Nature and Grace in Modern
Catholic Thought* (Collegeville, MN: Liturgical Press, 1992).

unselfishly devote their lives to such transcendent values as Duty, Peace, Justice, Fraternity, Humanity; absolute values are worthy of unconditional love, serve as *incognitos* of God for those inculpably lacking any explicit religion."[7] A minimal Catholicism of hierarchical laws and linguistic propositions controlling and distributing actual graces proffers a salvation extrinsic to the person, and a grace unstable and transitory. A different approach is needed, and Congar observed of theology: "It may be said that the door whereby *one enters on* a question decides the chances of a happy or a less happy solution."[8]

Europeans had learned that growing populations of different kinds of people live on earth: in large cities Christians and members of other religions mixed with agnostics and atheists. How should we ponder "the salvation of 'the others'" (1)?[9] Congar's chapters, far from condemning people, are positive. In a sense the book has one theme considered in existential and historical, biblical and eschatological modes, the presence of God's salvific grace, and the place of salvation is the person. How does each person meet God? Grace and person are presented in a mature way, going beyond the manuals of seminary education where Catholicism is a divine and human mechanics of sins and graces.

Catholics in Europe no longer live in "Christian countries." People are not living in the synthesis of the patristic and medieval worlds where culture and Christian religion intertwined, but in a new time when socialism and communism or the liturgical movement and biblical renewal compete for parishioners' attention (ix).

---

[7] Sullivan, *Salvation outside the Church: Tracing the History of the Catholic Response* (Mahwah, NJ: Paulist Press, 1992) 180.

[8] "My Path-Findings in the Theology of Laity and Ministries," *The Jurist* 32 (1972) 176.

[9] Page references to *The Wide World My Parish* are in the text.

There are new questions and it is hopeless "to try to keep the faithful in a sort of Catholic ghetto, cut off from the outside world and in ignorance of the interests and upheavals of human society" (7). One is not saved from this world, nor is a concert of Gregorian chant the antidote to social misery (37). The very structure of the human intellect involves "dialogue," and so the church like society will find "almost everywhere an effort of the mind, the intellect, of intelligence and understanding" (7). The teachings of Christianity, when they are in dialogue with other people and not only with Christians, do not shrink back but expand in time and space.[10]

The Christian message does not stop with Paul's urging (Romans 12:2) not to be conformed to the world but listens to the call of others, to the countless voices in the world whose destiny is salvation. "Two mediations are joined in the church, one going up, or representative, the other coming down, or sacramental; and through them she is the place where Christ gives himself to the world, and the world gives itself to Christ, the place where the two meet ... The Church and the world need one another. The Church means salvation for the world, but the world means health for the church: without the world there would be the danger of her becoming

---

[10] At the time of the Vatican's repression of the French church Congar wrote: "The tendency to expand in Catholicism all that is determined by the mode of authority too ready to judge and to condemn all that is a reaching out, a research, a questioning of received ideas; there is also an inclination to measure the orthodoxy of everyone and by a quickness to suspect others of heterodoxy. In this approach, however, one is substituting individual judgment for that of the church, and one arrogantly takes on the right to measure the Catholic communion by individualistic constrictions (which are often not much more than the limits of ignorance) (Congar, "Mentalité 'de droite' et intégrisme," *La Vie intellectuelle* 21 [June, 1950] 663). See the still valuable reflections (written before Vatican II) on the church looking to the past and to the future: "... to see church with respect to what it is already and what it is called to be" ("How Christian is the Christian Church?," *Listening* 2 [1967] 92).

wrapped up in her own sacredness and uniqueness" (19, 23). The Christian community is learning out of completeness and holiness to express a hope for redemption in the world. If the church has become smaller, its message is not dogmas holding an anxiety about life in an enclosure of a sect but a consideration of how salvation exists for the world (25). Salvation itself holds a dynamic, an inner drive working to reach people, and the Bible offering a deeper humanism calls Christians to be a leaven influencing society.

The modern person may be pondering salvation out of the goodness in the depths of the human heart even when he or she questions faith and God. The traditional meaning of individual salvation is not set aside but takes on a wider social dimension. We find here echoes of French existentialism present in philosophy, films, literature, and plays in the 1950s where sin is personal destruction. Salvation is deliverance and meaning and fulfillment, and Congar cited the line from Irenaeus about the glory of God shining in the life of men and women. "We must now put away our stupidly superficial, mundane imaginings, and try to understand things in the spiritual context of salvation and the covenant…, for heaven is not the negation of the world but its pattern, the pattern first lost, and then restored by grace" (44-45). Does not salvation unfold within personal existence and human history? If human history is filled with violence and injustice, the earthly current of time is also the place of health and progress towards the more. Persons become whole not from within themselves or from technology or aesthetics but from some deeper, though unperceived empowerment of grace in human life (60).

II. SALVATION OUTSIDE THE CHURCH

A long chapter on salvation outside the church even as it goes beyond the devotional and neo-scholastic texts from the early 1900s does build on principles of earlier theologians, and unfolds its ideas amid new theological approaches of the twentieth century. Congar was aware of theologies expounding a fundamental human orientation towards and within grace (as in the basic psychology and teleology of the adult global choice of Aquinas).[11] He called it a "fundamental direction." There is in each person a "fundamental direction involved in a mass of lesser decisions, in the whole use a man makes of his existence" (88). Christian (and human) life is not solely about knowing the Bible and doing good deeds: there are the milieu and dynamic of life's choices. This does not exist apart from grace. Since God is justice and life, he is inseparable from every act and quest of love and justice (91). Opening historical observations on the topic lead to Aquinas' brief and laconic text about each person choosing a basic option for themselves. The Gospels themselves tell of "faith before faith and grace before grace" (104): often faith in Christ comes at the end of an individual process of human choice. Jesus' parables invite everyone to move towards salvation, not just those observant of Judaism or competent in Christology. While the church is the sacrament of the reality, the presence, the clear promise of salvation, others can find in life an intimation of grace, an incipient salvation. "Those people who walk in the way of salvation through an encounter with God of which the church was not corporeally the minister, those who are at any rate 'related to the mystical Body', such are not strangers to her. They are destined to overtake her at the end ... Spiritually, they exist by the Spirit which is her principle of existence" (112). The Spirit of grace and salvation is not confined within one religious history nor is it a sullen recluse in periods of time before or after Bethlehem. The Holy Spirit, "dominating time as well as space" (112), can be present to many people in many ways.

---

[11] *Summa contra gentes* III, 159. One suspects that among its sources are the texts of Aquinas on implicit faith and the intention of the will reaching the divine, as well as the various neo-Thomisms of the years after 1900 developing those themes.

378 THOMAS F. O'MEARA

Faith comes from the Gospel heard. Both Gospel and faith have a subtlety. What does it mean for the Gospel to be really and effectively preached to and believed by the peoples of the earth? Faith is certainly necessary: the presentation of the Gospel can be subjectively or objectively inadequate, even off-putting. There is what Aquinas calls implicit faith. In the New Testament open and sympathetic contact with Jesus is not produced by an acceptance of an intellectual creed. Each person has a search for the absolute. "It is necessary that the realm in which someone is invited to encounter God without knowing it should have a certain absolute character which may be recognized and really respected" (121). If there is only one resonating word and clear light about God's gift of the world's salvation, Jesus, his influence is not coterminous with the gift itself (112). Life may silently hold a love that challenges false absolutes threatening to swallow up the divine in the human. Congar goes on to treat allied questions which decades later still unsettle Christians. Why is the missionary drive at the heart of Christianity? Is one religion as good as another? Are implicit faith and personal love relativism and indifferentism? Ultimately, salvation is not automatic or extrinsic but occurs within the person. One must not hide behind theories of a divine love which is called universal but is incapable of reaching people.

III. AN EVEN WIDER WORLD

The chapters of *The Wide World My Parish* pass beyond the boundaries of human religion. A chapter treating the end of the world makes two points: first, the Bible teaches that no one knows when the end of the world will arrive; second, the new world will not be totally different from ours, will not be a disconnected replacement of this world. The resurrection of the body is a corrective to both Platonism and to an ideology of the material. Resurrection stands against reincarnation, a philosophy of the soul depicting a spirit independent of corporeality moving about in a world of spirits and then again in matter. Those anthropologies — the one is too material and the other is too spiritual — are foreign to Biblical Christian faith (182).

Hell and heaven, purgatory and limbo are sketched in several chapters not in mythical or fearful terms but as eschatological modalities of a human life. The value of each striving individual transcends sin, punishment, and judgment. Purgatory is not about suffering in an imprisoning fire but affirms a realm of purification and education where an individual's faith and grace are separated from the dross and selfishness surrounding them. A Christian life becomes "clear as crystal to God's shining rays" (68). Two chapters on hell — like the one on purgatory — take as their point of departure not judgment but goodness in the person. Hell, a secondary and purely negative realm, exists as an opposing pole to "the prospect of *the* resurrection ... as the fullness of the glorious fellowship of our whole persons with God, in Jesus Christ who died and rose again for us" (183). Jesus' teaching concerns the resurrection, not the damnation of people, for God is not a punishing judge nor a destroyer of creation. "*There is no predestination to Hell* (against Calvin)" (72). What we call punishment is a response by those freely choosing the solitariness of evil and rejecting the communion offered by God. Hell, a lonely and meaningless existence, is the result of a life of choices (one thinks of Sartre whom Congar does not cite and of Dostoyevsky whom he cites at length). The ultimate question is whether we are free enough to choose evil so firmly and forcefully that we can tenaciously embrace and cling to it eternally: only such a powerful choice can include an eschatological form. "There is always the question of whether man stands alone, absolutely self-governing, or whether he has a relationship, a 'dialogue', with God, his Creator, and is open to the advances of divine love" (35). Hell is not a cosmic threat but a condition lived in opposition to salvation, a free and fundamental choice for evil, egotism and sin in a frozen state.

For Catholics, topics like salvation, the human being, purgatory and hell suggest limbo. What happens to the unbaptized children of Christian parents? This question, so frequently asked in daily life and so starved by a meager theology of the sacraments, puzzles over what happens to children dying prior to consciousness. "Millions of little human beings, our brothers and sisters" are more than numbers in the "statistical tables of 'infant mortality'" (147). Congar falls back at first upon the tradition that these beings, prior to religious choice and ritual, are not in the highest kind of fellowship with God but also are not being punished. He goes on, finding no treatment in the New Testament of the eschatological region of limbo (limbo has no dogmatic definition), to seek for general principles in God's love, a basic Christian teaching. Infants, not being punished, belong to the race redeemed and so exist in the sphere of redemption. Is limbo a fantasy? Perhaps. While there are all kinds of states of interplays between grace and sin and nature on the terrestrial way to the eschaton, after death there are only two. The unbaptized are neither in hell nor in a neutral world in the future; they too are persons seeking grace.

The final pages of *The Wide World My Parish* move beyond the place of human religion and salvation in history, to persons possibly inhabiting planets elsewhere in the universe. This problem was discussed by European theologians in the 1950s because of the claimed sightings of "flying saucers."[12] Congar spotlights what today are main points in a theology of extraterrestrials. Revelation in Christ and the Bible is not about astronomy nor does it treat the

[12] On German and Italian articles of the 1950s, see O'Meara, "Christian Theology and Extra-Terrestrial Intelligent Life," *Theological Studies* 60 (1999) 3-30.

world of sin and grace away from earth. Biblical lines about generosity and lordship may indicate the context for this topic. Persons
on other planets may have been called to a further life of grace. Just
as we know nothing about their existence, we also do not know
anything about the issue of other incarnations of the divine persons
of the Trinity in creatures.[13]

IV. SALVATION AND RELIGION

In Congar's theology, salvation is not a purely intellectual acceptance of Christian teaching nor a positive world-view but choices
about life and goodness empowered by and drawn to God. "*It is
not necessary to recognize God to be able to reject or to love him.*
There is the answer of the Gospel ... God does not of necessity present himself to our free choice with face unveiled" (84f.). Not
everyone sees with the clarity of Jesus where goodness truly lies,
but all do glimpse in the course of a life some degree of the goodness that is proposed by Christian revelation in its sublime and
explicit way. If sinners belong to the church not in an accidental
way but as part of its structure, do not those who are touched by
the Spirit in a variety of religious faiths also belong to Christ's
body.[14] "People can save themselves without having an explicit
knowledge of the Gospel, or even of the existence of God, and
without having any formal connection to the church ... More and

---

[13] In an unnuanced way he spoke of Jesus as the "absolute pinnacle of the
whole Universe, whether existing or possible" (188), and decades later of Jesus
as the Lord, King, criterion of relationships with God, although not necessarily a
savior for them since they might lack sin (*Fifty Years of Catholic Theology: Conversations with Yves Congar* [Philadelphia, PA: Fortress, 1988] 18). If in fact
there are other incarnations, Jesus of Nazareth, the Word of God but the terrestrial Christ, would not necessarily be superior to all of them.

[14] *Vraie et fausse réforme dans l'Église* (Paris: Cerf, 1950) 110.

more there is an active presence of the Word and of the Holy Spirit outside of the institution of salvation begun by the historical mission of the Word in Jesus Christ and of the Spirit in Pentecost, the effect of Easter."[15]

As with his German counterparts like Erich Przywara, Karl Rahner and Heinz Robert Schlette, Congar saw that atheism in the twentieth century, unlike in the times of Medieval Christendom or the Roman Empire — Augustine called it "an insanity of the very few,"[16] had become the faith of millions.[17] In the 1960s, however, the problem of Marxist atheism yielded to the diverse populations of other religions. Religions — Congar said he knew them only from individuals and books — meet each other because humanity is drawn together in a global humanity, and yet, the issue of others and their salvation is not a new problem but one already present a hundred years after Pentecost. Patristic theologians devoted more effort to this issue than did medieval thinkers, although "it is not always easy to clarify [*préciser*] their thought on this question because it is very difficult for us to enter their point of view and, if one can express it in this way, their mental universe."[18] Theologians of the second and third centuries had spoken of a "pedagogical role," and neo-scholastic theologies had mentioned an "evangelical preparation." The church learns "through contacts with

---

[15] *Missionnaires pour demain* (Paris: Centurion, 1966) 13, 30.

[16] *Sermo 69, Patrologia Latina* (Migne) 38, col. 441.

[17] "Au sujet du salut des non-catholiques," *Sainte Église* (Paris: Cerf, 1963) 441.

[18] "Au sujet du salut des non-catholiques," 437. This theme led to an article noting that the not numerous texts from the second and third centuries indicated little interest among the Christians in evaluating or condemning their pagan neighbors, and implied that God's love might touch them too ("Souci du salut des paiens et conscience missionaire dans le christianisme postapostolique et préconstantien," *Kyriakon* [Münster: Aschendorff, 1970] 3-11).

facts" (98), and it is change in global perspective that inevitably stimulates reflection upon this religious topic. Geographical discovery in the sixteenth century and the academic comparative study of religion since the nineteenth century spotlighted the religions of humanity; a new awareness of religions is caused by travel and the media. Although faith affirms Christianity to be absolute, "the Catholic tradition is that Christianity is inclusive" (30). One can cite the New Testament and papal documents to argue that men and women in other religions have a positive capability of transformation, of being freed and purified by Christ through the church, the church that is "the sacrament of the active presence of Christ in the world" (31), while Congar recalls Henri Bergson's view of the *mystiques* of religions and Pierre Teilhard de Chardin's location of Christianity in a long line of divine love capable of renewing humanity.

Congar's principles, Catholic and Thomist, remained the same in lectures and talks after Vatican II. God wills the salvation of all, and "the whole of humanity is therefore (and has been since Adam!) in an objective situation of redemption and of salvation ... In the case of morally guiltless ignorance of Jesus Christ, and even of God, salvation, which presupposes faith and charity, is possible on the basis of an obedience to what conscience presents to us as absolute."[19] While baptism, belief and membership of the church are the means of salvation given in the positive, historical plan of God, it is also true to say that through "the mercy of a God who is just and good, men and women ignorant of the Gospel, when it is not their fault, can arrive (secretly) at faith and at salvation. Their

[19] Congar, "Non-Christian Religions and Christianity," *Evangelization, Dialogue and Development* (Rome: Gregoriana, 1972) 133f.; for more analysis of Congar on religion, see Thomas Potvin, "Congar's Thought on Salvation outside the Church: Missio ad Gentes," *Science et Esprit* 55 (2003) 139-163.

business is the business of God."[20] Since God is infinitely just, it would be absurd to think that salvation would hinge on temporal circumstances beyond a person's control. Salvation is possible in the case of invincible ignorance of the Gospel and, even, of God: a real intention moves towards God and his plan of salvation, taking shape in the consecration of one's life to an absolute religious idea or value recognized by one's conscience. In its broadest contours the Bible describes not a static sect but a field of salvation being expanded at central moments before and after Calvary.[21] Passages from the New Testament support this: for instance there is the person, in the Gospel according to John, who "does the truth" (3:21), acts according to the light which he or she has been granted. However, self-giving as a personal orientation cannot be performed without the help of God, without an elevation of the light of the conscience which can be considered as the equivalent of a revelation

The expansion of our knowledge of world religions is a task just beginning and one requiring effort and time. If *The Wide World My Parish* offered a theological approach to religion in the decades before Vatican II from the perspective of the person outside of the church, Congar's subsequent writings focused more on religion and salvation and on the church as missionary. Already in 1956, he excluded two extremes: the religions are the equal of the church, or the church requires membership for grace. God wills salvation, and the classical distinction between belonging to the church in baptismal ritual or in profound orientation and intent is still valid. A critical confidence in other faiths does not mean indifferentism or relativism but points to the individual's personal search for

[20] Yves Congar, "Principes Doctrinaux," in *L'Activité missionnaire de l'Église* (Paris: Cerf, 1967) 214.

[21] Congar, "Les religions non bibliques sont-elles des médiations de salut?" Ecumenical Institute for Advanced Theological Studies, *Year-Book 1972-1973* (Jerusalem: Tantur, 1973) 84-85, 90-96.

Truth: the truths of Christian belief are found clearly and centrally in the church.[22] In the 1960s, Congar's evaluation of non-Christian or non-Biblical religions followed by billions of the world's inhabitants remains somewhat negative because unfashionably he would not overlook aspects of religions that are destructive, false, or idolatrous. Religions are not an instrument of salvation as Christianity is. Still religions do minister to their adherents, and followers of human religions (and they are very much the creation of their cultures) encounter that mystery we call grace and revelation but not formally and directly as Christianity does. At this time Catholic theologians were expressing a momentous shift in the relationship of religion to grace. Earlier in the first decades of the twentieth century, Catholic theories depicted salvation as coming directly from God to the religious devotee, summoned there not by rite or doctrine but by a moral life and a theodicy pursued by the individual (this, of course, countered the viewpoint that religions were demonic). French Catholics in the 1920s like Louis Gardet and Louis Massignon reversed this by their study and experience of Muslim and Hindu mysticism through which they saw that authentic spirituality necessarily indicated the presence of grace.[23] Religions were not hostile or indifferent to grace, and grace was offered. The Eucharistic Congress in Bombay in 1964 was a turning point, for it passed beyond the theory of a reward for observing the natural law and the approach of the erroneous conscience.[24]

---

[22] "Hors de l'Église, pas de Salut," *Sainte Église* (Paris: Cerf, 1963) [a text from 1956]; for a valuable bibliography of patristic texts and studies on this topic, see pages 417-423.

[23] Thomas O'Meara, "Exploring the Depths: A Theological Tradition in Viewing the World Religions," *In Verantwortung für den Glauben*, ed. Peter Neuner and Harald Wagner (Freiburg: Herder, 1992) 375-390.

[24] The factor of the erroneous conscience was the theology of Abelard and medieval theologians, and textbooks and catechisms from Peter Canisius to the mid-twentieth century ("Au sujet du salut des non-catholiques," 443f.; "Hors de

Were not the large world religions ordinary ways of salvation? Their ideas and rites led hundreds of millions of men and women to seek God as the answer to the mystery of life.

"For Christians, one of the discoveries of this century is the existence of *other spiritual worlds* representing coherent totalities of positive values ... What is profound is the Asiatic or the African man. It is from him that the religions derive their profundity. These men *are at the same time* in search of God, in an objective situation of redemption by Christ, formed and conditioned in depth by their culture, their history, their religion, alienated in diverse ways, subjected to the domination of 'Powers'."[25] First, each religion represents social and historical realities that have influenced those who live and worship within them. A theology of religion would begin with a "historiosophy," a large and accurate knowledge of the facts of the great religions, and proceed to personal impressions and intellectual hypotheses about their role vis-à-vis revelation. Second, there is the plan of salvation of the Father as revealed and realized by the Incarnate Word, through the Holy Spirit. This plan of salvation from the Father embraces all of humankind and its habitat, the cosmos and unfolds in time and space. Finally, the absolute primacy and sovereignty of Christ demands that Christ not be absent from any moment of human history identical to the history of salvation.[26]

Congar said he wanted to steer a course down the middle between what he termed an "optimistic and broad solution" (Rahner, Schlette, Gustave Thils, Hans Küng, Leonardo Boff) and

l'Église, pas de salut," 423) and the sparse ideas of Pius IX (Denziger-Schönmetzer #2866). Summarizing the new theology of the Bombay conference is Eugene Hillman, *The Wider Ecumenism: Anonymous Christianity and the Church* (London: Burns & Oates, 1968).

[25] "Non-Christian Religions and Christianity," 144.

[26] "Les religions non bibliques sont-elles des médiations de salut?," 101.

a "negative and strict solution" (Martin Luther, Ludwig Feuerbach, Karl Barth, Hendrik Kraemer, and Wolfgang Pannenberg). God's salvific will is universal, and his grace prior to the Incarnation is generous; grace lives outside the limits of the church, and the limits between church and religion are not clearly fixed. "Outside the church, in an ignorance that is not culpable, a regime of personal graces perdures, and this does not exclude that the religions of humanity might be habitually an occasion or a canal."[27]

Still, the offer of salvation is not made to individuals living apart from societies. Persons fully exist in groups whose forms penetrate their very being, and persons and peoples contribute to religions. Doctrines, rules of life, and rites express the religious genius of a culture with its traditions and its profound sense of identity. Some of these forms appear stagnant, whereas others offer signs of growth. In the latter case, profound experiences and religious genius have contributed to the development of precious values. In the major religions, we discover progress made in the consciousness humankind has of itself, of its transcendence, its relationship to the world and that which transcends all of this while containing it and permeating it, incorporating a treasure house of mediations, valuable experiences, original expressions. As such, they can become the source or, at least, the occasion of spiritual enrichment even for Christians. If religions are not the Body of Christ, a certain instrumentality seems legitimate, but would not words like "ordinary" or "normal" cover over the distortions of religions? Still, Congar viewed these religions not so much themselves but as aspects of people,[28] and individual grace still kept itself a little aloof from communal religion.

---

[27] *Missionnaires pour demain*, 37.
[28] "Les religions non bibliques sont-elles des médiations de salut?," 91-101.

In the last analysis, it is not easy to see how Congar differs from the "optimistic" theologians, for despite his reservations he did see religions as means or mediations of salvation.

In 1987, Congar looked again at this topic. The implicit faith of Aquinas lives on in a self described by Rahner in the context of a transcendental anthropology. Congar remarked that during some months at the ecumenical institute at Tantur in Jerusalem in 1972, he had come to see that "it is clear that for individuals, the culture in which they live and the religion associated with it are the ordinary ways of salvation, in the sense that 'ordinary' usually has in almost all cases."[29] In light of the approach of French institutions and personality in the Middle East he realized that "to proclaim Jesus Christ is not always to speak of him, or to preach him explicitly."[30] This approach is not "pre-evangelization" but evangelization through sign and word; such corresponds not to a defeatist notion of evangelization or a minimalist Christology but to a richer, broader Gospel. "From the moment when Jesus is God-man in a single person according to a unity of which there is no higher example, it is evident that he is the absolute religion, the fullness and the perfect example of the religious relationship. And he is that not by the exclusion of other factors, possibly other religions, but by inclusion."[31]

V. YVES CONGAR AND KARL RAHNER

The mention of grace coming into the personalities of billions of men and women, a loving plan of God touching all intelligent creatures, and some kind of centrality of Jesus Christ in the history of

---

[29] *Fifty Years of Catholic Theology*, 15.
[30] *Ibid.*, 16.
[31] *Ibid.*, 18.

religion — these recall the theology of Karl Rahner. Congar and Rahner — are they not very different theologians, very different kinds of thinkers? They were born in the same year 1904. One was a Frenchman spending World War II in military camps trying to escape, while the other was a German banished from teaching to pastoral work in Austria. Both were resolute critics of neo-scholasticism even while being gifted interpreters of Aquinas. Both were silenced by church authority: Rahner was usually censored prior to publishing his writings, while Congar's books were not permitted second printings. The accomplishments of the Dominican historian began early when he was barely thirty with studies on Luther and on the Body of Christ, but he offered few original insights after he was sixty-five, while the German philosophical spirit matured later and brought forth dozens of creative essays in the decade leading up to his eightieth birthday.[32]

The Frenchman's writings in the area of wider grace are occasional essays, while Rahner constructs a direct analysis grounded in modern German philosophy and the foundations of Christianity. Each has his own charism. Resonance between the two comes from their sharing the European cultural milieu after World War I and the Catholic ecclesial milieu after World War II. Both are interested in the world of the subject, a literature of existence, theories of the temporality of a culture, and theologies of history, and yet they can write for ordinary church-goers. Their hermeneutics is not one of demythologizing or dismissing Christian traditions but of finding in Scripture and Tradition something deeper, something new, something welcoming and expansive. Both had activities apart from academic theology. Just as Rahner became in the last decade

---

[32] See Thomas O'Meara, "Raid on the Dominicans," *America* 170 (1994) 8ff.; H. Vorgrimler, *Understanding Karl Rahner: An Introduction to His Life and Thought* (New York: Crossroad, 1986) 88-94.

or two a theologian of ordinary life where Absolute Mystery reached out personally through the mysteries of daily life to individual existence, so Congar early in his career had given countless talks to church groups. Rahner's abstract German philosophical language and conceptuality sought to explain the Christian worldview within an expanding understanding of human history,[33] while Congar was cognizant of modern German thought in Johann Adam Möhler's romantic idealism of idea, subject, and life.[34] Congar spoke of the idea of the church and the idea of the world, and that modern thematic lies behind Rahner's systematic theology, a foundational exposition of the idea of Christianity.[35]

Rahner published early in his career historical research into some areas of patristic spirituality and sacramentology, but his life's project was the explanation of what is most basic in Christian revelation and how God acted in the historical life of church and liturgy. Not neglecting a Trinitarian activity reaching from divine mystery

[33] Congar occasionally contrasted his theology of history and sources with the "philosophical spirit" and "speculative elaboration" of Rahner's work (Congar, "Letter from Father Yves Congar, O.P.," *Theology Digest* 32 [1985] 215) and at times found Rahner's theology presenting through thought-forms of subjectivity, freedom, and history from Kant, Joseph Maréchal, and Heidegger too enclosed in specific philosophical forms.

[34] On Möhler and Congar see Thomas O'Meara, "Beyond 'Hierarchology.' Johann Adam Möhler and Yves Congar," *The Legacy of the Tübingen School*, ed. Donald. Dietrich and Michael Himes (New York: Crossroad, 1997) 173-191.

[35] He mentioned Rahner's emphasis upon the conciliar rediscovery of the local church as a gift of Vatican II ("Vision de l'Église chez Thomas d'Aquin," *Revue des Sciences Philosophiques et Théologiques* 62 [1978] 538). On the differences between Rahner and Congar in expressing the external and internal missions of the church, and on the relationships of both modes to the transcendental and categorical in history, see Joseph Famerée, *L'Ecclésiologie d'Yves Congar avant Vatican II: Histoire et Église* (Leuven: University Press, 1992) 348-349, 386-389, 444. "One finds in Rahner the Congarian dialectic that is constitutive of the ecclesial sacrament: the gift of God *and* the visibility of this gift, the presence of Christ *in* the precariousness of the flesh of history" (388).

to the interplay of grace in human intimacy and the extension of salvation-history to a parallel with all of human history, the Jesuit began hundreds of talks and writings with the fundamental orientation of the person towards and within grace, or with the response of someone who freely chooses evil and rejects the offered communion with God.[36] A rare and important facet of Congar's work was that he was fluent in German (a gift of war and prison), and his contact with German theological literature drew him to Rahner's publications early on. For instance, Rahner's ideas on "simul justus et peccator" from 1947 found their way into *Vraie et fausse réforme dans l'Église*,[37] and in 1951 Congar's "Chronique" of ecclesiology had looked at *Die vielen Messen und das eine Opfer*.[38]

Congar welcomed the Jesuit's essays exploring alteration in theological issues and church structures, and just before the opening of Vatican II he found in an essay on the "dangers facing contemporary Catholicism" a helpful perspective with views related to the experience of French renewal, views that have nothing to do with modernist tendencies:[39] "Father Karl Rahner has posed the classic problems of theology in ways capable of renewing them. The gift he has for knowing the ensemble of the issues and for fashioning a synthesis assists him. He brings to this enterprise a reflection of a philosophical type bearing, we would say, on the concepts or notions under consideration."[40] Twenty years later Congar spoke of

[36] See Nikolaus Schwerdtfeger, *Gnade und Welt* (Freiburg: Herder, 1982) Zweiter Teil.

[37] (Paris: Cerf, 1950) 110.

[38] "Chronique" (1951), *Sainte Église*, 612.

[39] "Chronique" (1950), *Sainte Église*, 603.

[40] "Inspiration des écritures canoniques et apostolicité de l'église," *Revue des Sciences Philosophiques et Théologiques* 45 (1961) 32. Rahner's new ideas on the papacy were mentioned positively by Congar, "Chronique" (1962), *Sainte Église*, 693.

Rahner providing "the most original contemporary contribution to
the theology of the Trinity," although the Dominican adds comments that "limit its absolute character."[41]

Jean-Pierre Jossua in his biography of 1967 briefly compared
the two theologians. He found "points of interest common to
the two theologians: the interest in renewing ecclesiology and mis-
siology, in re-introducing biblical categories into theological elaboration, in a theology treating areas formerly abandoned by the
'dogmatists' to apologetics, and in giving a decisive place to
anthropological considerations." Congar, unlike Rahner, came to
anthropology through ecclesiology, and Rahner is much more a
thinker of structure and synthesis. There is a Christian anthropology in Congar, one flowing from the biblical idea of the image of
God as developed by the psychology of Aquinas and the Greek
Fathers. "For Father Congar, a real theological anthropology ought
to pick up this trail and transfigure it Christologically into a historical perspective."[42] An economic view of Trinity is not diminished by but opens out into a history of salvation. He disagreed
with a positivistic view of revelation in which the reality of theology and faith is adequately presented in formulas in which there is
no relationship to anything concrete, and in which the world and
the human person are expressed only in categories of contradiction
to God. "To be saved is to be snatched from an existence that is
meaningless, hopeless and doomed to unending death. To be saved

---

[41] Congar, *I Believe in the Holy Spirit* 3 (New York: Seabury, 1983) 11, 13.

[42] Jossua, *Yves Congar: Theology in the Service of God's People* (Chicago, IL:
The Priory Press, 1968) 48f., 133. For Congar, Christian modernists were not hostile to Christianity but their writings sought too easily to reconcile science and religion. "They also lacked a philosophy that was adequate to deal with such questions. They often thought they had found the answer in a distinction ... between
forms that are relative and subject to all the changes and chances of history, and
a *spirit* that is lasting" (5). These last words recall Rahner's central distinction and
interplay of the categorical and the transcendental.

is for existence to have the meaning that Jesus gave to it ..., the assurance of everlasting life, body and soul, there where everything will be meaningful" (81). While Rahner wrote: "Anyone who contemplating Jesus, his cross and death, really believes that here the living God has spoken to him the final, decisive, irrevocable and comprehensive word, and has thereby delivered him from all bondage to the existential dimensions of his imprisoned, sinful, death-doomed existence, that person believes in the reality of Jesus ... whether or not he or she realizes the fact."[43]

Congar chose as his theme for *Vaste monde* that which Rahner sought to interpret throughout his life: human existence as the place of God's self-communication. We can find a similarity of sources and language, a similarity of attention to the subject in Rahner's existential anthropology of grace and Congar's "feeling for the unique value of every person, the person who is a totality in the individual self" (17). *Vaste monde* is a theology of subjectivity and grace, basically transcendental and existential. Congar's line — "God does not of necessity present himself for our free choice with face unveiled" (85f.) — recalls Rahner's aphorism: "The event of God's free, gracious self-revelation is always in the state of being because this grace is offered to all men in all ages for Christ's sake and is efficacious by the very fact of being offered, and, we may hope, though it is impossible to know for certain, at least the majority of men accept it even when they are unable to reflect on this event happening in the inmost core of their spiritual person."[44] Rahner's position affirming a universal salvific will of God is not original but is generally shared by Catholic theologians treating this topic. As Congar comments:

---

[43] Rahner, "Jesus Christus," *Theological Dictionary* (New York: Herder and Herder, 1965) 187.

[44] Rahner, "Revelation," *Theological Dictionary*, 411.

The originality of this [Rahner's] position consists in placing this universal will of salvation in strict relationship with human *Dasein*, with the human condition; it assures to the human person an existential that is a supernatural horizon of grace like a horizon of the realization of nature; the one is given with the other and they have similar dimensions. The supernatural is implicated in the transcendental framework in which spiritual consciousness experiences being: a history of salvation, of revelation, and of faith coexist with the history of humanity. In accepting himself the person realizes between him and God a transcendental rapport in which God communicates himself in a certain way to the person and in which the person posits supernaturally an act of faith. But such an act, like every personal act, must take bodily form, not only individuals, but as suits human nature, socially. This is what religions do.[45]

"Anonymous Christian" is not a helpful or accurate phrase, for a Christian is one who professes faith and is baptized in the church; nor should the phrase People of God, a term with precise biblical and ecclesial usages, be used of those in other religions. *"That which* Rahner gave the name 'anonymous Christians' is an authentic reality in terms of the condition of people not evangelized but nevertheless justified by the grace of Christ ... It is the term that is questionable, for in fact a Christian means someone who has a reference to and a participation in the positive institution coming forth from salvation, from what Rahner called 'special revelation.'"[46] In an interview Congar dismissed the idea that Rahner's theology caused a decline in missionary zeal. "I am fully convinced that people can be saved without knowing the Gospel and even without knowing God, when they are not to be blamed for this ignorance ... The period reaching from Abraham to the present is nothing in the history of the race. It is certain therefore that there was salvation outside of that time, but I do not like to speak of

[45] "Les religions non bibliques sont-elles des médiations de salut?," 82.
[46] "Les religions non bibliques sont-elles des médiations de salut?," 84.

'anonymous Christians' in this connection ... I criticize the expression but not the idea. I prefer to use the term 'salvation of the non-evangelized.'"[47] Does Rahner do justice to the teaching and witness of the Scriptures? Congar's response is this:

> I know that all these difficulties from one side or another have already been brought to your attention, and you have certainly not failed to give explanations and answers to them! I must say that I agree with your idea of grace as an "existential" of the concrete existing human person, because we do actually live in a supernatural order which encompasses the natural ... An "*objective* redemption," which means that human persons *are* really redeemed; they exist in a real order of salvation. Only if a person rejects this (corresponding to the conditions of their knowledge and their possibilities) do they fall away from the salvation of Jesus Christ. Certainly that seems to me to occur at a *concrete*, existential level. The questions emerge on the level of the analysis of the essential structures of this, on the level of that which you call transcendental anthropology.[48]

Congar found in non-Christian religions a mystical genius and subjective mediations of grace but not "direct salvific value," although religions can be more than accidents and function in the providence of God.[49] Congar struggled with the categorical reality of non-Christian religions. In the issue of the ordinary mediation of religions of salvation, an effect of God's permissive will, Congar

---

[47] Tony Sheerin, "Talking to Yves Congar," *Africa: St. Patrick's Missions* (November, 1974) 7. "Karl Rahner does not merit the reproach of being involved in arresting the missionary dynamic ... although the position of Rahner on the anonymous Christians has been criticized by missionaries" (Congar, "Principes Doctrinaux," 212f.).

[48] Congar, "Loving Openness Toward Every Truth: A Letter from Thomas Aquinas to Karl Rahner," *Philosophy and Theology* 12 (2000) 218 (German original: "Die Offenheit lieben gegenüber jeglicher Wahrheit. Brief des Thomas von Aquino an Karl Rahner," *Mut zur Tugend: Über die Fähigkeit, menschlicher zu leben*, ed. Karl Rahner and Bernhard Welte (Freiburg: Herder, 1979) 124-133.

[49] Congar, "Non-Christian Religions and Christianity," 134-139.

found Rahner more nuanced as he spoke of a legitimate religious institution, considered globally in itself as a positive means of relationship with God, helpful towards obtaining salvation in the plan of God.[50]

Observations on the relationship of Congar to Rahner find their best conclusion in some pages written by the French Dominican for a German volume honouring Rahner's publisher. Congar contributed not a historical study but an entertaining literary improvisation, a letter composed as if it were coming from Thomas Aquinas. In this letter Congar lets Aquinas offer similarities between the medieval Scholastic and the modern Jesuit. The theme of person appears. "You yourself say that your transcendental anthropology is simply an analysis of the human being as spiritual being. As that kind of being, the human person goes beyond all the limits of a determined 'being' and is an openness for the infinitude of being, that is, to God. From that you conclude: under the presupposition that concretely no other order exists than the supernatural order, with Incarnation, grace, being a son and daughter of God, the grace of God is offered in every truly personal activity and is accepted or rejected by each man or woman." In the final lines we find Congar's appreciation of Rahner. "But I don't want to conclude my letter without expressing how very much I value the way, the style in which you have formulated anew so many issues. I am your predecessor. I wear a different habit than you (and some have placed a sun on my chest and a circle of light on my head), but you are my brother, and I embrace you. Vale! Thomas Aquinas of the Friars Preachers."[51]

---

[50] Congar, "Les religions non bibliques sont-elles des médiations de salut?," 85 (reference to Rahner, "Das Christentum und die nicht-christlichen Religionen," *Schriften zur Theologie*, 5 (Einsiedeln: Benziger, 1962) 148, 153. Rahner's position is "very systematic" (Tantur 81).

[51] Congar, "Loving Openness Toward Every Truth," 217, 219.

These are two great contributors to Vatican II. One can suggest that Congar was the most important Catholic theologian leading up to the Council, while Rahner was the most influential thinker in the post-conciliar period. The interaction and friendship of the two theologians indicate the harmony between theological perspectives affirmed at Vatican II. For a *Festschrift* in Rahner's honour, Congar described how Rahner and Joseph Ratzinger prepared during the first session of Vatican II a document criticizing the Vatican's proposed texts. Cardinal Ottaviani angrily confronted Congar who said that he had not worked on the text, and regardless "Karl Rahner was my friend."[52] Each out of his own charism placed grace at the heart of reality and called community to ministry.

VI. CONCLUSIONS

The perspective of Congar is longsighted, but his theological explanations held in common with others had their limits. The ordinary presence of religions is new, while the centrality and superiority of Christianity must be affirmed though remaining general and distant, for instance, in the institution of the church or in the teaching on the Trinity. He sometimes too easily accepts the dichotomy offered

---

[52] Congar, "Erinnerungen an eine Episode auf dem II. Vatikanischen Konzil," *Glaube im Prozess. Christzein nach dem II. Vatikanum* (Freiburg: Herder, 1984] 31-32. Congar wrote his contribution "to honor a magnanimous man and friend, Karl Rahner." Rahner was often with Congar in conciliar meetings, and the Dominican found him brave and valuable. In May of 1963 he wrote: "Rahner monopolizes the conversation a little too much. He is magnificent, he is courageous, he is perspicacious and profound, but ultimately imprudent." *Mon Journal du Concile I* (Paris: Cerf, 2002) 382; a few months before the end of the Council: "Rahner said to me, 'Daniélou gets on my nerves: a minute after someone has made a contribution he speaks as if the idea just expressed was his'. This is true but it must irritate Rahner more than others because of his kind of personality with its marked intellectual honesty" (*Mon Journal du Concile*, II: 440).

by those holding that if you do not have a strong evangelization of an evil world you have no advocacy of the Gospel and no reason for missions.[53] His concluding word, however, is that Gospel and church have a centrality which is not exclusivistic but inclusive; evangelizing other cultures makes the church more catholic.[54] J. M. R. Tillard observed that Congar's theology of wider grace was "rich, both surpassed and always contemporary and prophetic." It was ultimately a theology of church and ministry. The question is not, 'Who will be saved?,' but, 'Who has been commissioned to be a minister of salvation?' The issue is ecclesiological."[55]

How is the Roman Catholic to locate the centrality of the Risen Christ in the vastness of human religion? Each decade this question receives new and increasing attention. The initial contexts are those of the experience of world religions and the analogous and sacramental paradox of Catholicism opposing the Protestant sectarian exclusivism of the baptized. Familiarity with the history of this topic shows at once that this marginal but ancient teaching of Christian thinkers finds little new in either Congar or Rahner except gifted attempts to express a traditional teaching in modern language and ideas. Themes like implicit faith, the will to what baptism symbolizes, the erring conscience, the right of the person by nature — which were present in Aquinas and in his predecessors — remain and lay the foundation for these recent developments. The one new direction, although this was present in

[53] Congar, "Principes Doctrinaux," 211-221.

[54] "Non-Christian Religions and Christianity," 135, 145.

[55] Tillard, "Introduction," VIII, V.

[56] Las Casas wrote that the nation of the Lucayhos were "a most blessed people ... more prepared than any other in the whole of humanity to know and serve God ... What was being transmitted [through their religion] is that this God is the true God" (*History of the Indies*, 161, 232); see Lluis Duch, "Religión y Religiosidad en la 'Apologética Historia' de Fray Bartolomé de Las Casas," *Fides*

Bartolomé de Las Casas,[56] is what occupied Congar's reflections on how God's grace contacts billions of peoples in their own, inevitably present religions.

Congar's remarks on salvation and religion were a quite marginal topic in his career in ecclesiology, and yet a book and a dozen articles treat this minor area. They witness to the breadth of his accomplishment — and so does his diary written during Vatican II. It records towards the end of the Council on December 7, 1965 the latter's approving its final group of documents (*Lumen gentium, De oecumenismo, De missionibus, De libertate religiosa, De presbyteris, De revelatione*). Congar had drafted or contributed significantly to them, and he wrote. "So this morning what has been publicly read [in St. Peter's] comes very extensively from me."[57]

quaerens intellectum. Beiträge zur Fundamentaltheologie (Tubingen: Francke, 1992) 43-46.

[57] *Mon Journal du Concile*, II, 511. At the end of Vatican II, physically debilitated and theologically summoned to a new era, he wrote: "People have no idea of what my life is like and of what I can accomplish in a day, for I have no time to read or to write. They do not see that I am asked to be *everywhere* and what I do in this place or another is actually multiplied by two hundred. Often I think: Only eschatology will resolve the insoluble problem of my poor life!" (525f.).

MEDIATING THE NON-CHRISTIAN RELIGIONS
CONGAR, BALTHASAR, NATURE AND GRACE

Stephen FIELDS SJ

Associate Professor of Theology
Georgetown University, Washington DC

Among thinkers who view Christianity as the absolute religion, discussion of its relation to other religions often revolves — and none too amicably — around the polarity between the "optimistic and broad" inclusivism of the Catholic Karl Rahner (1904-84), crystallized in his notion of the "anonymous Christian;" and the "negative and strict" exclusivism of the Lutheran Karl Barth (1886-1965), centering on his castigation of any natural analogy to the definitive revelation of God in Christ.[1] Presupposed in these approaches are long traditions of Christian reflection that each thinker retrieves and develops. Rahner harkens, for instance, to the tradition of Aquinas, which sees non-Christian religions as useful preparations for the Gospel (*praeparatio evangelii*). Barth harkens to the model prominent in the Reformation, especially in Calvin, that places these religions outside the divine economy of salvation (*cultus degeneres*). Congar presents us with some bold and refreshing insights that chart a middle path between these Titans of twentieth century theology.[2] His insights direct attention

---

[1] *Missionnaires pour demain* (Paris: Centurion, 1966) 30ff, 35, 37; cited in Thomas F. O'Meara OP, "Yves Congar: Theologian of Grace in a Wide World," in the present volume, 386-387.

[2] Congar, *ibid.*

to two relations: that between culture and conscience and between nature and grace. Under Congar's guidance, a consideration of these relations in light of Vatican II and the thought of Hans Urs von Balthasar (1905-88) can help to retrieve a third model based on Justin the Apologist's notion of "seminal reason" (*logos spermatikos*).[3]

---

[3] The *praeparatio evangelii* model, given prominence by St. Thomas (1225-74), splits into two strains. The older is theological and broadens the typological interpretation of Scripture. If the Hebrew covenant has a privileged role because its heroic types and events prefigure Christ and his paschal mystery as the messianic anti-type, so other religions can be seen as vestigially offering types that prepare conscience to believe in Christ as absolute. This strain is carried on in the work of Bacon (1214-92), for instance, and Ricoldus de Montecroce (1243-1320), Ramon Martin (13th century), Suarez (1548-1617), Lessius (1554-1623), the 16th century Jesuit missionaries in China, and de Lugo (1583-1660). The other strain is philosophical. It uses a model of reason as a hermeneutical tool to understand how non-Christian religions are related to Christianity claimed as definitive or superior. It is developed in the thought of Jean Bodin (1530-96)), for instance, and in Malebranche (1638-1715), Leibniz (1646-1716), Kant (1724-1804), Herder (1744-1803), and Schleiermacher (1768-1834).

The *cultus degeneres* model, given prominence in Luther (1483-1546), Calvin (1509-64), Zwingli (1448-1521), and Sebastien Franck (1499-1542), is revitalized in the twentieth century by Protestant neo-orthodoxy in general and by Barth and Brunner (1889-1966) in particular.

The *logos spermatikos* model, originating in Justin (c.114-c.165), is found, for instance, in Clement of Alexandria (150-215), Origen (185-253), Ramon Lull (1235-1316), the Florentine Academy [Manetti (1396-1459), Ficino (1437-99), Pico della Mirandola (1463-95)], Nicholas of Cusa (1401-1464), and Hegel (1770-1831). It is revitalized by J. N. Farquhar (1861-1929), for instance, and N. Mac-Nicol (1870-1952), E. C. Dewick (b.1884), D. W. Soper (b.1910), and P. Tillich (1886-1965).

For a helpful discussion, both historical and systematic, of all three models, see the neo-orthodox work of Hendrik Kraemer (1888-1965), *Religion and the Christian Faith* (Philadelphia, PA: Westminster, 1957).

CONGAR

In his contribution to this volume, Thomas O'Meara helpfully
delineates the development of Congar's thought. Throughout his
career, Congar approached Christianity's relation to other religions
by demonstrating the possibility of salvation outside the Church. In
his earliest considerations, he understood salvation as a function
principally of the "person, existence in history, grace outside of
baptism and dogma."[4] He remained ambiguous about the value of
non-Christian and non-Biblical religions, even "somewhat negative," since he saw false, destructive, and idolatrous elements in
them.[5] Nonetheless, even though they are "the creation of their cultures," they can function as incipient means of grace.[6] As his thinking matured, this last notion — religion's cultural conditioning —
tended to become more positive. The availability of personal graces
outside formal incorporation in the Church "does not exclude
that the religions of humanity might be habitually an occasion or
a canal" of these.[7] Still, Congar continued to view non-Christian
religions "not so much themselves but as aspects of people,
and individual grace kept itself a little aloof from communal
religion."[8] Nonetheless, they mediate humanity's capacity for

[4] O'Meara, "Yves Congar: Theologian of Grace in a Wide World," 373, referring to Congar, *The Wide World, My Parish: Salvation and Its Problems*, trans.
Donald Attwater (Baltimore, MD: Helicon Press, 1961); originally *Vaste monde,
ma paroisse* (Paris: Témoignage Chrétien, 1959).

[5] O'Meara, "Yves Congar: Theologian of Grace in a Wide World," 385.

[6] *Ibid.*

[7] *Missionnaires pour demain*, 30ff, 35, 37; cited in O'Meara, "Yves Congar:
Theologian of Grace in a Wide World," 387.

[8] O'Meara, "Yves Congar: Theologian of Grace in a Wide World," 387, referring to Congar, "Les religions non-biblique sont-elles des médiations de salut?,"
in Ecumenical Institute for Advanced Theological Studies, *Year-Book 1972-73*
(Jerusalem: Tantur, 1973) 91-101.

self-transcendence, and so, although they are not the Body of Christ, they can be "the occasion for spiritual enrichment even for Christians."[9] Significantly, his reflection on the subject concluded with the frank admission that the culture in which people live, and the religions embedded in it, are humanity's usual and "ordinary ways of salvation."[10] These are "inclusive" within Jesus Christ, who as the God-man represents "the absolute religion, the fullness and the perfect example of the religious relationship."[11]

Congar's thought on salvation outside the Church, taken as a whole, shows subtlety in balancing the problem's constitutive elements: personal conscience, culture, sinfulness and error, the necessity of the Church, and the inclusion of all humanity in the Incarnation. O'Meara believes, however, that finally Congar does not differ essentially from Rahner's optimistic school. "Despite his reservations," O'Meara claims, "[Congar] did see religions as means or mediations of salvation."[12] In my judgment, this lack of a difference cannot be sustained in light of Congar's unapologetic diagnosis of idolatry in non-Christian religions. This diagnosis buttresses the visible Church's indispensability, whereas his doctrine of the efficacy of a sincere but errant conscience grounds the possibility of grace's saving ubiquity.

O'Meara is certainly right to draw attention to the discernible shift in Congar's thought from its early emphasis on the person as the locus of salvation to its later crediting of culture as an essential mediation of God's universal saving will. But neither he nor

[9] *Ibid.*

[10] Congar, *Fifty Years of Catholic Theology: Conversations with Yves Congar* (Philadelphia, PA: Fortress Press, 1988) 15; cited in O'Meara, "Yves Congar: Theologian of Grace in a Wide World," 388.

[11] Congar, *Fifty Years*, 18; cited in O'Meara, "Yves Congar: Theologian of Grace in a Wide World," 388.

[12] O'Meara, "Yves Congar: Theologian of Grace in a Wide World," 388.

Francis Sullivan seems fully to appreciate the profound implications of this shift. Ultimately, opines O'Meara, Congar is a Thomist in the solution he offers to grace outside the Church. This is essentially individualist, grounded in the personal conscience in which an invincible ignorance of Christ is no block to "a real intention mov[ing] towards God and his plan of salvation."[13] Sullivan commends Congar on the quality of his individualist solution. Wherever conscience responds with unconditional love to "such transcendent values as Duty, Peace, Justice, Fraternity, Humanity" grace and salvation are mediated outside formal ecclesial incorporation.[14]

It is true that conscience stands a pillar of Congar's solution. But his later thought, in suggesting that conscience itself is mediated by specific, determinate religious forms, represents a key advance. It implies that these forms, despite their errors, can lay some claim to association with the Body of Christ. Surely it can be no accident that so schooled a Thomist as Congar would refer to non-Christian religions as "habitually" a canal of grace. What an adroit pun! Habitual grace in Aquinas is sanctifying grace, the very life of God, that, through Christ, reforms the sinner.[15]

This later shift in Congar's thought is prescient. It underscores the naïveté of centering the problem of salvation outside the Church exclusively on personal conscience. The theological anthropology of *Gaudium et Spes* makes this especially apparent. Vatican II's *Pastoral Constitution on the Church in the Modern World* appreciates the reciprocal mediation obtaining between personal acts of thinking, judging, and willing and the socio-cultural milieu in

[13] *Ibid*, 13.

[14] Francis A. Sullivan, *Salvation Outside the Church: Tracing the History of the Catholic Response* (Mahwah, NJ: Paulist Press, 1992) 180; cited in O'Meara, "Yves Congar: Theologian of Grace in a Wide World," 374.

[15] See *Summa Theologiae* 1a2ae: 110.2, 111.2, 112.1 ad 1. The *Summa* is cited subsequently in the text.

which the person exercises them. Congar's developing thought reflects the Council and may even be the effect of it.

GAUDIUM ET SPES

The *Constitution* frankly acknowledges that "true, full humanity" can "only" be achieved "by means of culture," whose purpose is the development of nature and the refinement of family and civic life.[16] Culture fosters institutions that express humanity's "spiritual experiences and aspirations" so that, in turn, these can inspire others and contribute to their progress (par. 53, p. 958). Culture "flows from [humanity's] rational and social nature" as transcendent spirit embodied in time and space (par. 59, p. 963). Intelligent and creative activity produces symbols such as "literature, art, the humanities, the interpretation of history and even civil law," together with "science and technology [and] the social disciplines" (par. 4, p. 905; par. 5, p. 906; par. 7, p. 908). In addition, culture embraces those phenomena that affect how these symbols change, develop, and are proliferated, such as industrialization, urbanization, mass media, and emigration (par. 6, p. 907).

On the one hand, if the symbols of culture emanate from humanity's rational and social nature, still on the other hand they form the basis for the exercise of that nature. Conditioning the yearnings of the transcendent spirit by time and space, they constitute the milieu "from which [persons of every nation and age] draw the values needed to foster humanity and civilization" (par. 53, p. 958).

---

[16] *Gaudium et Spes*, in *Vatican Council II: The Conciliar and Post Conciliar Documents*, ed. Austin Flannery OP (Northport, NY: Costello Publishing, 1975) 1: 903-1014, paragraph 53, p. 958. *Gaudium et Spes* is cited subsequently in text by paragraph and page numbers.

But cultural symbols not only elevate us from the chaos of brute sensuousness; they also "recoil upon [us], upon [our] judgments and desires, ... upon [our] ways of thinking and acting" (par. 4, p. 905). Changes in symbols, brought about by phenomena like materialism and atheism, disturb traditional "modes of thought" (par. 5, p. 906; par. 7, p. 908). Such disturbances make it increasingly difficult for individual consciences to balance the demands of morality over-against the demands of the society where they must be applied (par. 8, p. 908).

Although the symbols of culture affect the individual conscience, they are not the sufficient cause of moral tension. This results from the fundamental paradox of human nature. Though "untrammeled in [our] inclinations ... for a higher form of life," we are beset by the shortcomings of finitude and sin (par. 10; p. 910). These impair our ability to create symbols adequate to our potential. When impoverished symbols arise, they infect culture with "a host of discords," from the false immanence of scientism to the false transcendence of utopianism (par. 10, p. 910). Nonetheless, these discords recoil upon conscience and serve as a fresh impetus for questions about the destiny of humanity and the meaning of suffering, evil, and death (par. 10, p. 910).

Gaudium et Spes thus offers a sophisticated view of the reciprocity between culture and the individual conscience. If culture springs from humanity's rational and social creativity, still culture necessarily mediates that creativity. But like humanity, culture is ambivalent. Its capacity to manifest the transcendent order is flawed by limitation, error, and sin. Yet even these can spur human aspiration higher and so renew culture.

Moreover, the *Constitution* posits an equally sophisticated view of the Gospel's relation to the interdependence of conscience and the social order. Grace "continually renews," not only the individual human person, but also the "culture of fallen [humanity]" (par. 58, p. 963). In combating sin and error, the Gospel purifies morality, stimulating and advancing "human and civic culture," and thus contributes to the freedom of conscience (par. 58, p. 963). Significantly, grace accomplishes this renovation, not by standing in stern judgment outside of culture, but "from within" it (par. 58, p. 963). Divine revelation "takes the spiritual qualities and endowments of every age and nation," and with its own abundance, "fortifies, completes and restores them in Christ" (par. 59, p. 963, citing Eph. 1.10). Most important, renovating "from within" means that wherever culture's symbols lead humanity to a deeper awareness of truth, goodness, and beauty, conscience is "more clearly enlightened by the wondrous Wisdom, which was with God from eternity" (par. 57, p. 961, citing Prov. 8.30-31). We reach then a significant conciliar teaching. Culture, an essential basis for the exercise of personal conscience, is capable of mediating human transcendence because of the implicit immanence of the divine Logos in it.

If this is true; and if, as Congar says, the culture in which people live, and the religions embedded in it, are humanity's usual and ordinary means to salvation; then it follows that non-Christian religions can implicitly embody, manifest, and communicate the Wisdom of the Trinity. And it is this Wisdom that, through these religions, is able, not only to enlighten personal conscience, but to mediate grace, the very life of God, to the sincere non-Christian conscience. How could it be otherwise if God is implicit in these religions, if they are habitual means to salvation, and if, as the Holy See affirms, salvation is accessible to the invincibly ignorant outside of formal ecclesial incorporation?[17]

[17] See "Letter of the Holy Office to the Archbishop of Boston (1949)," *The Christian Faith in the Doctrinal Documents of the Catholic Church*, ed. J. Neuner and J. Dupuis (New York: Alba House, 1996) 305-307.

Furthermore, if this is the conclusion to which Congar in tandem with *Gaudium et Spes* leads, then we are led further to seek a fresh understanding of the relation between nature and grace that undergirds any solution to the problem of salvation outside the Church. Any understanding that posits a sharp dichotomy in this relation cannot deal adequately with the reciprocity between culture and personal conscience. A sharp dichotomy presupposes the naïve view that centers the solution exclusively on personal conscience. It presupposes that the non-Christian religions of humanity belong to fallen nature incapable of mediating grace "from within" themselves to the individual conscience. In order to seek an understanding of the nature/grace relation that accounts for the interdependence of culture and conscience, we need first to examine St. Thomas's classic articulation.

THOMAS, NATURE AND GRACE

According to Aquinas, humanity before the Fall existed in the state of "integral nature" untainted by sin. In this state, we could do the good of "acquired virtue:" that is, without divine grace, we could do the good proportionate to a sinless human nature (1a2ae, 109.2). This good included knowing what the divine law required and being able to fulfill it (1a2ae, 109.4). We could accomplish these acts of knowledge and will because we received the necessary help of God Who, as the First Mover, inspires us towards "any good whatsoever" (1a2ae, 109.2). The good of integral nature, however, did not include fulfilling the law with the required spirit of charity. This good could only be realized by an "infused virtue" animated by grace, not by nature (1a2ae, 109.2). Thus, even in our prelapsarian state grace was needed in addition to God's activity as First Mover (1a2ae, 109.4). After the Fall, humanity exists in the state of "corrupt nature" in which, without grace, we cannot clearly know all that the law requires, we cannot do its commands, and we cannot do them with the required charity (1a2ae, 109.4). Nonetheless, we continue to need the help of God as First Mover to tend towards any good whatsoever (1a2ae, 109.2). Thus in both states of nature, integral and corrupt, God's activity as redeeming giver of grace builds upon His activity as Creator.

In the state of corrupt nature, under the influence of the First Mover but without grace, we are capable of what might be called the good of utility. This includes "particular" goods, such as erecting buildings, planting vineyards, and other "works leading to a good which is connatural" to fallen nature (1a2ae, 109. 2, 5). Because such works spring from natural virtues, especially the cardinal virtues of prudence, fortitude, justice, and temperance, the good of utility must include the whole culture of acquired virtue such as Aristotle sets out in his ethical treatises, and which St. Thomas incorporates into Christian moral theology. What is important, however, is that the good of utility, as such, is not meritorious before God, because the person performing it is not justified by sanctifying or habitual grace (1a2ae, 109.2). Nonetheless, the good of utility results from the motion of the First Mover by which "everything seeks [God] under the common notion of good" (1a2ae, 109.6). By common, St. Thomas means analogous.

This view of the relation between nature and grace implicitly undergirds the emphasis on the individual conscience as the solution to extra-ecclesial salvation. Non-Christian religions belong to the good of utility. Falling outside of grace, and hence incapable of justifying, they nonetheless spring from the First Mover. As such, God providentially orders all secondary causes, thereby guiding everything to Himself under the common notion of the good (1, 22.2). Because they are capable of leading people to the good proportionate to fallen nature, the non-Christian religions of humanity can rightly be called preparations for the Gospel. But because only the sacramental culture of the Church mediates grace, not the fallen culture of acquired virtue, salvation requires the person, not his/her culture, to be linked to the Church, either explicitly or implicitly. The position of St. Thomas could therefore be summarized as follows: a non-Christian can be saved when the First Mover guides his/her conscience to a state of acquired virtue sufficient, in the judgment of the redeeming God, to attain baptism of desire. A chief problem with this position lies in its understanding of the good. On the one hand, Aquinas says that the movement of the First Cause inspires everything towards a common (analogous) notion of the good. On the other hand, he maintains that the culture of virtue described, for instance, by Aristotle is devoid of any vestigially justifying merit. This position leads inevitably to the claim that goods resulting from the cardinal virtues, when exercised by unjustified nature, are discontinuous from the goods resulting from these same virtues when fallen nature is elevated by grace. It is hard to see how the notion of the good presupposed in this claim is analogous when it tends towards being equivocal. The equivocation can be muted by seeing the preparation for justification that occurs in conscience as indirectly but authentically a participation in the habitual grace to which it leads. But St. Thomas is far from clear on this matter, as Henri Bouillard's study shows.[18] The question needs another look, especially in the light of *Gaudium et Spes*'s claim that grace renews culture from within. A model that understands nature and grace, not as harmonious but separate principles, but as a unity-in-diversity would, I suggest, better understand the reciprocity between conscience and culture and better undergird the efficacy of non-Christian religions as the habitual means of humanity's salvation.

[18] Henri Bouillard, *Conversion et grace chez saint Thomas d'Aquin: étude historique* (Paris: Aubier, 1944) especially 211-219.

BALTHASAR, NATURE AND GRACE

Insights drawn from the work of Hans Urs von Balthasar offer help in developing the suggestion just made. Under the influence of the German Catholic thinker Erich Przywara (1889-1972), Balthasar's concept of nature enters into dialogue with the later position of Karl Barth (1886-1968).[19] According to Barth, original sin causes so radical a breach between God and humanity that the powers of the soul to know the good (and the true and the beautiful) are virtually destroyed. Because of the Fall's damage to the image and likeness of God in the soul, no viable concept of nature can exist after it. Nature's pre- and postlapsarian states are thus avowedly equivocal. Only Christ's redeeming entry into history can restore the soul's divine image and likeness and revivify the human faculties. So utterly gratuitous is this event, and so bereft is postlapsarian nature of divine reflection that after Christ only one concrete order exists, that of grace (TKB, especially 95, 145-47, 164-70).

In responding to Barth, Balthasar uses the Council of Chalcedon (AD 425) as his point of departure. Its doctrine, he argues, contains a more elevated conception of postlapsarian nature than Barth's position acknowledges. Chalcedon defines Christ as the union in one Person of two natures, one human and created, one divine and infinite. The Council thus contends, Balthasar asserts, that even after the fall a viable concept of nature continues to exist. Since

---

[19] Hans Urs von Balthasar, *The Theology of Karl Barth*, trans. John Drury (New York: Holt, Rinehart, Winston, 1971) 217; originally published as *Karl Barth: Darstellung und Deutung seiner Theologie* (Cologne: Jakob Hegner, 1962). This book is based on two articles in *Divus Thomas*, "Analogie und Dialetik" (1944) and "Analogie und Natur" (1945), which Balthasar acknowledges "were prompted" by Przywara's work (TKB, 307, note 2). These articles are studied in James V. Zeitz, "Przywara and von Balthasar on Analogy," *The Thomist* 52 (1988) 473-498. *The Theology of Karl Barth* is cited subsequently in the text as TKB.

Chalcedon is a definitive explication of the Christian faith, it follows that nature cannot be an equivocal concept. It must be analogous (TKB, 221-22). As I interpret Balthasar, this analogy entails
four senses.

According to the first sense, the states of pre- and postlapsarian
nature are analogous. To justify this claim, Balthasar returns to the
Christian datum that creation is spontaneously fashioned by God.
Nature's origins are divine because they flow forth freely out of
nothing from the divine essence, whose omniscience contains the
archetypes of all created forms. If grace is the very life of God
freely given to creation, then the forms of nature must be vestigially graced. Not so cataclysmic as to eradicate these vestiges, the
Fall means that postlapsarian or corrupted nature retains some continuity with its former state of integral nature (TKB, 227, 229).
The soul's divine image is sufficiently in tact so as to form in Christ
the basis for the Incarnation (TKB, 228).

As a consequence of the Incarnation, a second analogy emerges.
In the Incarnation, divinity has irrevocably impregnated postlapsarian creation. It has raised nature to a dignity higher than its
prelapsarian integrity, which ensued from its being made in the
divine image. Nature's postlapsarian and redeemed states are thus
analogous, because both manifest the divine life, although in
markedly different degrees (TKB, 232). A third analogy thus
becomes apparent. If integral nature is analogous to corrupted
nature, and corrupted to redeemed nature, then integral and
redeemed nature are analogous. These three senses of nature's analogy are epitomized in yet a fourth sense.

As Chalcedon teaches, in Christ humanity and divinity,
although distinct, are inseparably united. Because the single Person fuses both natures into a unity-in-diversity, the being of the
divine nature and the being of the human nature are similar
within their uniqueness. The analogy between these natures is

evinced in the doctrine of the "exchange of predicates" (*communicatio idiomatum*). This allows Christ's properly human acts to be applied to his divinity. Thus we say that, in Christ, God is born, suffers, and dies, because in Christ humanity is divinized. As a consequence of these four analogous senses, Balthasar concludes that there can be "no slice of 'pure nature' in this world" (TKB, 232). Created through the Logos, integral nature freely originates in God's life; it retains something of this in spite of the Fall; and in Christ corrupted nature is elevated and perpetually shot through by divinity. In all senses of the analogy, nature is not a freestanding entity separable from the divine life. On the contrary, nature's origins are grounded in this freely offered life that, as a result, is able harmoniously to renew, renovate, and redeem from within what it has, from out of itself, created from nothing.

Any notion, therefore, of nature conceived as utterly independent of grace, to which grace is superadded, is theologically problematic. Nonetheless, because the Incarnation is not imposed by strict necessity on humanity, nature must exist in some manner distinct from grace in order for it to constitute the bare minimum presupposed by a gratuitously given Revelation (TKB, 228-29). But this Revelation, understood as the redeeming act of God in Christ, stands in an analogous continuity with the very origins of creation, understood as the implicit revelation of the Logos, through whom all things were made, and without whom was made nothing that was made (Jn 1:3). It is not possible, says Balthasar, precisely to define what belongs properly to nature and what to grace, any more than in Christ it is possible precisely to delimit his humanity over-against his divinity (TKB, 234-35). It is necessary, of course, to maintain that sin, error, and their effects belong to nature. But because sin, as the Church prays in the Easter *Exultet*, has in Christ become a happy, a fortunate fall (*felix culpa*), exactly where sin ceases and "grace abounds all the more" (Rom 5:20) will always remain an open, an insoluble question for the human mind.

In sum, under the guidance of Congar's insights, our review of *Gaudium et Spes*, St. Thomas, and Balthasar leads to the following conclusions. First, nature and grace, from the beginning of creation, through the Fall, and into the redemption, exist as a unity-in-diversity, distinct but inseparable. This unity-in-diversity obtains as a graded series of analogies in order to account for sin and for the distinction between God's creating and redeeming activity. Both creation and redemption, however, should be understood as freely communicating the divine life. Both are intrinsic moments of God's one saving economy, although they realize different effects in different historical epochs. As a result, nature is vestigially graced by the Logos Who redeems it from within by His Incarnation as Christ. Consequently, non-Christian religions, the habitual means of humanity's salvation, even though they belong to fallen nature, implicitly embody the Wisdom of the Trinity. Moreover, because culture mediates the exercise of personal conscience, non-Christian religions can, in some vestigial way, mediate salvific grace, the life of God, to the sincere but errant conscience baptized by desire. These conclusions develop and support *Gaudium et Spes* by finding in Balthasar a means of overcoming the tendency to equivocation present in St. Thomas.

LOGOS SPERMATIKOS

The claim that culture implicitly embodies the divine Wisdom is not new with Vatican II or Balthasar. It can be traced to Justin the Apologist's notion of the *logos spermatikos* or seminal reason, as echoed in turn by Greek Fathers like Irenaeus (c.149-c.202) and Athanasius (c.295-373). According to Justin, the divine Logos is preeminently "the seed of God" in Christ, Who is also "the seed of Jacob.'"[20] By Logos, Justin means not only Word but also God's speech, design, reason, thought, and plan (p. 233). As "the First-begotten of God," Christ "is the Reason of which every race of man partakes," the End to Whom "every nation" looks "forward to His coming" (s. 46, p. 272; s. 32, pp. 262-63). Consequently, "[t]hose who lived in accordance with Reason are Christians, even though they were called godless" (s. 46, p. 272). Plato, for instance, "borrowed from our [Judeo-Christian] teachers, I mean from the Word [speaking] through the prophets, when he said that God made the universe by changing formless matter" (s. 59, p. 280). For Justin, therefore, the divine Reason incarnate in Christ diffuses itself as the seminal logos or word that speaks in a divinely vicarious way in the reason of every person (p. 233). Wherever authentic rationality obtains, there also obtains "the divine force" impregnating "the universe" (p. 233, citing *Apology* II, ss. 10, 13). "Hence everything good and true really is [Christian] by right" (p. 233). If so, then everything good and true belongs not only to nature but, participating in the Logos, implicitly to grace.[21]

Irenaeus develops Justin by the notion of "recapitulation" (*anakephalaiosis*). In *Against the Heresies*, he says that Christ

---

[20] Justin, *Apology* I, ed., trans., and introd. Edward Rochie Hardy, in *Early Christian Fathers*, ed. Cyril C. Richardson, et al (New York: Macmillan, 1970) 225-89; section 32, pp. 262-263. *Apology* is cited subsequently in the text by section and page numbers.

[21] Justin is writing before Nicea (325) and so the mode of nature's participation in the Logos must be qualified by the Council's doctrine. Because nature proceeds out of nothing, not directly out of the divine essence, the mode of participation is perhaps best called a quasi-formal participation. The qualification spares the infinite distance between Creator and created. See for instance Karl Rahner, *Foundations of Christian Faith: An Exploration into the Idea of Christianity*, trans. William V. Dych (New York: Crossroad, 1987) 120ff; originally *Grundkurs des Glaubens: Einführung in den Begriff des Christentums* (Freiburg-im-Breisgau: Herder, 1976).

"became what we are" that we might become "even what He is."[22] What He is, as Word, means "Creator of the world," Who "in an invisible manner contains all things created and is inherent in the entire creation" (p. 546). As Word, He "governs and arranges all things" (pp. 546-47). What He has become, as "very man," is the communicator of "invisible things" in virtue of His intelligence (p. 547). As God-man, therefore, he recapitulates or "'sum[s] up in Himself all things which are in heaven, and which are on earth,'" thereby "uniting man to the Spirit" (p. 548, citing Eph. 1.10). Thus nature, created by, presided over, and incarnated in the Logos, constitutes, together with the freely offered divine life, a unity-in-diversity. Creation and redemption cohere into a symmetry by their one divine agent, the Word-Wisdom-Son, Who refashions from within what He has fashioned and guides. Primordially, therefore, nature participates in the Logos and thus implicitly in grace.

Athanasius in *On the Incarnation* posits a similar position. Like Justin and Irenaeus, he understands that humanity, being made in the divine image, was given "a portion even of the power of [God's] own Word" in virtue of "having been made rational."[23] Significantly, God "has not only made us out of nothing; but he gave us freely by the *grace* of the Word, a life of correspondence with God," the fullness of such grace being lost by sin (s. 6, p. 59; italics mine). Nature thus exists primordially within the grace of the Word, a measure of which perdures through the Fall. Nonetheless,

---

[22] Irenaeus, *Against the Heresies*, in vol. 1 of *Ante-Nicene Fathers,* trans. and ed. Alexander Roberts and W. H. Rambaut (Peabody, MA: Hendrickson Publishers, 1996; originally Edinburgh, 1868-69) 315-567, p. 526. *Against the Heresies* is cited subsequently in the text.

[23] Athanasius, *On the Incarnation*, trans. Archibald Robertson, in *Christology of the Later Fathers*, ed. Edward Rochie Hardy (Philadelphia, PA: Westminster, 1954) 43-110, s. 3, p. 58. *On the Incarnation* is cited subsequently in the text by section and page numbers.

despite this measure, sin turns humans "back to their natural state, so that just as they have had their being out of nothing, so also ... they might look for corruption into nothing in the course of time" (s. 4, p. 59). Within the cosmic ambit of divine grace, integral and fallen nature are thus distinguished by the tendency of fallen nature to revert to the radical contingency that defines it over-against the radical freedom of God that brings it into being.

Athanasius further draws out his analogy. Only the Word "alone" possesses the "*natural* fullness" to refashion fallen nature, because as "the image of the Father, he [could] create afresh the man after the image" (s. 7, p. 62; s. 13, p. 67; italics mine). "It was *naturally* consequent," Athanasius continues, "that the physician and Savior should appear in what had come to be, in order to cure the things that were" (s. 44, p. 98; italics mine). Creation and redemption, integral nature and redeemed nature, are thus understood as a continuum obtaining under the grace of the Logos that exists "in the whole universe" that "is illuminated and moved by Him" (s. 42, p. 96). In sum, this doctor of the Church, developing Justin and Irenaeus, puts forth a relation of nature and grace consonant with Balthasar's: they obtain analogously as a unity-in-diversity. This view in turn supports Vatican II's understanding of culture and conscience that implicitly underlies Congar's view of non-Christian religions.

SIN AND FAITH

If Balthasar like the Greek Fathers understands nature to be constituted by grace, still following their lead he harbours no naïveté about the toll that sin and error exact from nature. Like Congar, he is aware of the false, destructive, and idolatrous elements in non-Christian religions. Unlike Judaism, whose appreciation of the material cosmos provides the seedbed for the Incarnation, Hinduism, Balthasar avers, dispenses with the dignity of form and structure. For its part, Buddhism climbs towards the divine without waiting for God's own message from above.[24] In short, when non-Christian religions overstress spirit at the expense of matter, they become prone to the delusions of the Gnosticism that Christianity has long countered. Such delusions include pantheism, which stands at odds with the Incarnation; syncretism and claims to esoteric knowledge, which undermine the ecclesial structure of Revelation; and emphases on extraordinary psychological phenomena, which often obviate the redemptive value of suffering epitomized in the cross.[25]

Because of these delusions resulting from the sin of fallen nature, faith in Jesus Christ is essential. For Balthasar, religious experience, like his understanding of nature and grace, is analogous. It emerges from all the faculties of the human person: the concepts and judgments of the intellect, the yearning and choices of the will, the visions of the imagination, and the sensory intuitions of the material world. Unless all the human faculties are reconstituted according to Christ as their formal object, they remain open to the spuriousness of a subjectivity held hostage by the fall. For this reason, Balthasar's notion of faith stresses the truth of its content, *fides quae creditur* (the faith that is believed), rather than its existential

---

[24] Hans Urs von Balthasar, *The Glory of the Lord: A Theological Aesthetics*, ed. Joseph Fessio, et al., 7 vols. (San Francisco, CA: Ignatius Press, 1982-89) 1.217, 314, 336-37, 496; in Louis Dupré, "Balthasar's Theology of Aesthetic Form," *Theological Studies* 49 (1988) 299-318, pp. 315-316. *Glory of the Lord* is cited subsequently in the text by volume and page numbers.

[25] The so-called "new age movement" exemplifies these problems (see *New Dictionary of Catholic Spirituality*, 704). For a contemporary reassertion of Catholic spirituality over-against them, see Anselm Stolz OSB, *The Doctrine of Spiritual Perfection*, trans. Aidan Williams (New York: Crossroad Publishing, 2001); originally *Theologie der Mystik* (Regensburg: Friedrich Pustet, 1936).

activity, *fides qua creditur* (the faith by which one believes) (1, 131).[26] This content refashions humanity because it reveals the Trinity to the person as concrete evidence in and through the incarnation of the Logos (1, 151). Through faith, therefore, the intellect is rendered capable of perceiving the forms of grace as manifested explicitly in Christ and implicitly in creation. Insofar as the intellect is transformed, so are the other faculties, because they are animated by it and subordinated to it. When faith is conceived as a noetic act that confers on all the human powers a share in its formal object, religious experience is spared from the errors of Gnosticism. As permeating the bodily senses and the imagination, it is not purely spiritualized; as divinely revealed knowledge, it is not confined to the myths of mere fancy (1, 131-33, 139-40).

Nonetheless, although Christian faith is necessary, this does not mean that those religious experiences awaiting formal reconstitution by the evidence of the Incarnation are devoid of divine life. If nature and grace obtain as a unity-in-diversity, and if fallen nature is analogous to redeemed nature, then despite sin, error, and delusion, fallen nature bears grace sufficiently implicit to support the existence of some saving truth in non-Christian religious experience. As Balthasar observes in his study of St. Bonaventure, the entire sensible cosmos, although fallen, as grounded "in the generation of the Logos" has been made "a monstrance of God's real presence" (1, 419-20; 2, 296). Truth and error, like the wheat and the chaff, thrive together in nature anticipating a sorting out. As the central point of the Trinity, the incarnate Son alone accomplishes this, drawing creation back to its source. Balthasar's position therefore means that *fides quae creditur* is itself an analogous

---

[26] For Congar's treatment of this distinction, see *Tradition and Traditions: An Historical and a Theological Essay* (New York: Macmillan, 1967) 315ff; originally *La tradition et les traditions* (Paris: A. Fayard, 1960-63).

concept. Wherever authentic truth, goodness, and beauty obtain, including in the forms of non-Christian religious experience, they are, as Justin affirms, Christian by right. They make humanity "more clearly enlightened by the wondrous Wisdom," as *Gaudium et Spes* teaches, "who was with God from eternity."

Balthasar's position can be more fully appreciated by contrasting it with Rahner's notion of faith and its relation to the anonymous Christian. Rahner delineates two types of revelation that show how knowledge of God can be correlated to the faculties of the human person. First, in a philosophical analysis independent of Christian revelation, he shows that humanity is constituted by a "general" revelation of the absolute and infinite Being. This ensues from the "preapprehension of absolute Being," the foundation and summit of human thought. In a dim and unobjectified way, it affirms in the intellect's knowledge of finite realities the unconditioned existence of the Absolute as the intellect's necessary and sufficient explanation.[27] In addition to general revelation, a "categorical" revelation comes to humanity in history. Access to it is given by the act of faith. This manifests Christ as the Absolute's definitive Word who reveals the Trinity and the other data mediated by Scripture and the tradition of the Church.[28]

General and categorical revelation function reciprocally. On the one hand, general revelation is the condition for the possibility of categorical revelation. The person's assent to the grace of the Absolute's self-revelation in Christ represents a development of the

[27] See Karl Rahner, *Spirit in the World*, trans. William V. Dych (New York: Herder and Herder, 1968) especially 387-407; originally *Geist in Welt* (Munich: Kösel, 1957).

[28] Karl Rahner, "The Theology of the Symbol," *Theological Investigations* 4, trans. Kevin Smyth (Baltimore, MD: Helicon, 1966) 221-252, pp. 235-236; originally "Theologie der Symbols," *Schriften zur Theologie*, 16 vols. (Einsiedeln: Benzinger, 1954-84) 4: 275-312.

natural openness to the Absolute, which philosophy shows as constituting the human intellect.[29] On the other hand, categorical revelation is the condition for the possibility of general revelation. Although reason can investigate and affirm humanity's necessary openness to the Absolute independently of grace, still general revelation actually belongs to the graced order.[30]

In agreement with Balthasar, Rahner affirms that, although a distinction can be drawn between nature and grace, only the order of grace concretely exists.[31] Nature subsists as a "remainder concept" necessary to explain what humanity would be like were there no categorical revelation. But since faith posits that such a revelation obtains, faith makes it clear that general revelation exists within the "supernatural existential." This means that categorical revelation shows human intelligence to reach its full term, not in reason's affirmation of the absolute Being as its ground, but in faith's assent to the God whom Christ reveals.[32] The supernatural existential means that through the Incarnation Christ embodies the general revelation of the Absolute in time and space. Christ becomes a mirror in which humanity can see the historical fulfillment of reason's orientation to the unconditioned Cause of all reality.[33]

---

[29] See Rahner, *Foundations of Christian Faith*, especially chapter 4.

[30] *Ibid.*, 55-57; and Rahner, "Nature and Grace," *Theological Investigations*, 4: 165-188, pp. 178-179; originally "Natur und Gnade," *Schriften zur Theologie*, 4: 209-236.

[31] Rahner, "Nature and Grace," 181-183.

[32] Rahner, "Concerning the Relationship Between Nature and Grace," *Theological Investigations* 1, trans. Cornelius Ernst (London: Darton, Longman and Todd, 1974) 297-317, pp. 312-313; originally "Über das Verhältnis von Natur und Gnade," *Schriften zur Theologie*, 1: 323-346.

[33] Rahner, "The Order of Redemption Within the Order of Creation," *The Christian Commitment*, trans. Cecily Hastings (New York: Sheed and Ward, 1963) 38-74, pp. 49-50; originally *Sendung und Gnade* (Innsbruck/Vienna/Munich: Tyrolia, 1961).

The supernatural existential forms the basis for the anonymous Christian. Any assent to the Absolute who in the preapprehension constitutes the goal and term of the human person, is implicitly an assent to the Absolute's historical utterance. Because general revelation obtains as a moment within categorical revelation, the "natural" method of philosophy actually belongs within the world of grace. No qualitative difference seems to obtain, therefore, between reason's assent to general revelation and faith's assent to categorical revelation.[34] This does not make Christ's work any the less gratuitous on the part of God. Nor does it mean that reason's affirmation of the Absolute in any sense logically entails the categorical revelation. It does mean that faith and reason are part of a continuum whose origin is grace. Although reason may seem to function by its own laws, the Christian knows that their root lies, not merely in general revelation, but in the Absolute's freely issued Word.

When contrasted with Balthasar, a number of problems emerge in the anonymous Christian. It is true that both thinkers agree on the relation of nature and grace as a unity-in-diversity. Balthasar says that no slice of pure nature obtains in this world; Rahner calls nature a remainder concept. Nonetheless, their understandings of the relation of faith to this unity-in-diversity present marked differences. Whereas Balthasar emphasizes the transforming content of Christian faith, Rahner emphasizes faith as an existential activity of the human person reaching out to God. As a result, for Balthasar the direct object of faith is the concrete evidence of the incarnate Word, and therefore the triune God as entailed in it. For Rahner, it is the supernatural existential, which holds in a tenuous

---

[34] Rahner, "Anonymous Christian," *Theological Investigations* 6, trans. Karl-H. and Boniface Kruger (London: Darton, Longman and Todd, 1974) 390-398, pp. 393-394; originally "Die Anonymen Christen," *Schriften zur Theologie*, 6: 545-554.

balance — more a juxtaposition — the relation between the divine
aspiration of the human spirit and the divine utterance in history.
In the preapprehension, Rahner's object holds out the necessity of
a "natural" revelation of God so important in Catholic doctrine.
Nonetheless, positing the supernatural existential as the object of
faith blurs the qualitative distinction between nature and grace, min-
imizing and obfuscating nature. The anonymous Christian, as a
corollary of the supernatural existential, does not, therefore, adequately account for sin, error, and delusion in non-Christian religious experience and for the redeeming necessity of Christian faith.

Furthermore, because Rahner stresses *fides quae creditur*,
despite the broad and optimistic inclusivism of the anonymous
Christian, he is unable adequately to handle the reciprocity between
personal conscience and culture. Of itself, the anonymous Christian has little to say about the implicit truth, beauty, and goodness
of non-Christian religions as cultural forms. Finally, it accounts
neither for their delusion nor their value. It belongs to the school
of thought that too naïvely centers the solution to the problem of
salvation outside the Church on the assent of personal conscience.
Accordingly, it underassesses the astute observation of *Gaudium et
Spes* and Congar that the assents of conscience are necessarily
mediated by the socio-cultural nexus in which they are exercised.
In short, if the anonymous Christian is to be rescued from the
anachronous, it needs development robust enough to incorporate
this mediation, together with sin, and the necessity of Christian
fides quae creditur.[35]

---

[35] The problem just described with the anonymous Christian is symptomatic
of a deeper problem in the transcendental Thomism that gives Rahner's theology
its philosophical basis. It has not been developed sufficiently to account for the
intrinsic link between the forms of reason and those of culture. A fuller appro-
priation of Blondel, or something akin to Cassirer's development of Kant is
needed. See some observations in Stephen Fields, "Blondel's *L'Action* (1893) and

A MEDIATING MODEL

This essay began with Congar's insight that the religions embedded in the diverse cultures of the world are humanity's usual and ordinary means to salvation. Furthermore, it asserted that, by developing this insight in light of Balthasar's thought, a mediating course could be charted between Rahner and Barth. It claimed that this mediating course could retrieve a model of *logos spermatikos* consistent with *Gaudium et Spes*. The key insight that fulfills these claims is Balthasar's view of nature as analogous. Although no slice of pure nature obtains in this world, still nature subsists as a sacrament of grace in various grades: prelapsarian, fallen, and redeemed. As analogous, these grades share a similarity that ensues from nature's graced origin; yet each grade maintains a qualitative distinction between nature and grace. This distinction is especially important in fallen nature. It means that fallen nature, while implicitly retaining some grace, is infected by sin, error, and delusion mixed in with grace in ways that, as Balthasar says, are impossible exhaustively to define.

As a result of this distinction, Christian *fides quae creditur* is necessary for redemption, understood as the divine's gratuitous reformation of fallen nature. This augments, restores, and heals "from within" the vestiges of grace in fallen nature. Christian *fides quae creditur* is necessary, because without explicit reception of the concrete evidence of the Incarnation, the vestiges of grace in fallen nature are insufficient to overcome sin, error, and delusion, and hence elevate and justify nature. Still, the vestiges of grace in fallen nature account, on the one hand, for "natural" knowledge of God. This remains accessible to fallen nature, even though it may

Neo-Thomism's Metaphysics of the Symbol," *Philosophy and Theology* 8 (Autumn 1993) 25-40.

STEPHEN FIELDS

426

also be owing to the vestiges of grace remaining there. On the other hand, these vestiges account for an implicit presence of grace in non-Christian religions, understood as cultural forms belonging to fallen nature. Because nature is analogous, these forms remotely participate in the creating Logos who is nature's origin and in the redeeming work of the incarnate Logos.[36] They are thus rightly called by Justin's epithet *logoi spermatikoi*.

Congar and Balthasar move the problem of salvation outside the Church beyond personal conscience and beyond seeing non-Christians religions merely as preparations for the Gospel. Together with *Gaudium et Spes*, they understand on the one hand the reciprocity between culture and conscience. On the other hand, they understand that all the authentically true, good, and beautiful symbols of human culture participate in the Word-Son-Wisdom. Finally, therefore, they not only carry us beyond St. Thomas. They tone down the optimism of the anonymous Christian by a frank account of sin, while still including all that is created within the divine economy. This economy joins creation and redemption together into one integral act of the triune God, who mediates time and space towards the eschaton when the divine life will mediate all in all.

[36] For further studies of nature and grace in Balthasar and Rahner, see Stephen Fields, "Balthasar and Rahner on the Spiritual Senses," *Theological Studies* 57 (1996) 224-41; "The Singular as Event: Postmodernism, Rahner, and Balthasar," *American Catholic Philosophical Quarterly* 77 (Winter 2003) 93-111; and "Nature and Grace after the Baroque," *Creed and Culture*, ed. Joseph Koterski and John Conley (Philadelphia, PA: St. Joseph's University Press, forthcoming).

THE APPEAL TO YVES CONGAR IN RECENT CATHOLIC THEOLOGY OF RELIGIONS THE CASE OF JACQUES DUPUIS

Terrence MERRIGAN

Professor of Dogmatic Theology
Catholic University of Louvain (K.U. Leuven)

INTRODUCTION

Less than three years after the death of Yves Congar, the Belgian Jesuit, Jacques Dupuis, published his *Toward a Christian Theology of Religious Pluralism* (1997),[1] the book that brought him into open conflict with the Vatican and that focused the attention of the Catholic world on the theology of religions. The theme of the relationship between Christianity and the world's religious traditions had, of course, been growing in importance since prior to Vatican Council II, and Congar's *The Wide World My Parish*[2] was one of the books that anticipated the prominence this theme would assume in the years to come. However, Dupuis' conflict with Rome, and more particularly with the Congregation for the Doctrine of the Faith, signified a new and decisive moment in the history of the Catholic theology of religions, and this for two major reasons.

---

[1] Jacques Dupuis, *Toward a Christian Theology of Religious Pluralism* (Maryknoll, NY: Orbis, 1997).

[2] Yves Congar, *The Wide World My Parish: Salvation and its Problems* (London: Darton, Longman & Todd, 1961). The book originally appeared in French as *Vaste Monde ma paroisse* (Paris: Témoignage chrétien, 1959) 131-132.

In the first place, it marked the occasion when the Church[3] authorities felt compelled to make public their alarm with certain tendencies in this area. (It has been suggested that the real object of the Congregation's censure was in fact a movement within Asian theology and that Dupuis, a European theologian with Asian theological roots, so to speak, served as a more high-profile target than his lesser-known Asian colleagues.) More importantly, however, the controversy with Dupuis provided the ecclesiastical authorities with the opportunity to identify what they regarded as the foundational principles of the Catholic theology of religions. In its response to Dupuis and, even more forcefully, with the publication of *Dominus Iesus* in 2000, the Congregation for the Doctrine of the Faith demarcated the boundaries within which it felt the discussion of the Christian understanding of other religions must take place. I have suggested elsewhere that Dupuis is perhaps best characterized as an explorer who tested those boundaries, and there is little doubt that he was instrumental in prompting the authorities to identify them.[4]

In this essay, I would like to enquire where Yves Congar stood (or perhaps, more accurately, would have stood) in relationship to those boundaries, at least as far as we can gather on the basis of his writings. The decision to take Dupuis as our starting point for this discussion is justified not only by the fact that his conflict with Rome constituted a decisive moment in the development of the

---

[3] Since nearly all the references to the 'Church' in this article concern the Roman Catholic Church, I will consistently employ the capital letter 'C' (even if the authors quoted employ a lower-case letter).

[4] Terrence Merrigan, "Exploring the Frontiers: Jacques Dupuis and the Movement 'Toward a Christian Theology of Religious Pluralism'," *Louvain Studies* 23 (1998) 338-359. (This article was reprinted in *East Asian Pastoral Review* 37 (2000) 5-32. (See also "Believer on the Frontiers: A Review of Jacques Dupuis, 'Christianity and the Religions: From Confrontation to Dialogue'," *The Tablet* (9 August 2003).

contemporary Catholic understanding of religions. It is also supported by the fact that Dupuis appeals to Congar's writings, particularly with regard to what is emerging as the most significant issue in the whole debate, namely, the question regarding the precise role of the Church vis-à-vis non-Christians. In what follows, I will make reference to all of the theological issues highlighted by the Congregation for the Doctrine of Faith. However, I will concentrate especially on the question of the Church's role with respect to the salvation of those who do not belong to her. Indeed, there is reason to believe that this question will prove even more intractable than the problematic of Christ's role in the salvation of non-Christians. While the appeal to the Trinitarian character of God's salvific economy has provided some theologians (including Dupuis) with a means to at least "relativize," as it were, Christ's role, little or no progress has been made with respect to the question of the Church's role.[5] Indeed, it may well be that the diminution of Christ's role will only aggravate the problem. After all, while Catholic theology might distinguish Christology and ecclesiology, it can never countenance their separation from one another. It seems to me, therefore, that the future of the Catholic theology of religions

---

[5] Among those theologians who appeal to the Trinity in their attempt to address the place of non-Christian religions in the economy of salvation, see, in addition to Dupuis, the following: S. Mark Heim, *The Depth of the Riches: A Trinitarian Theology of Religious Ends* (Grand Rapids, MI: William B. Eerdmans, 2001); Gavin D'Costa, *The Meeting of Religions and the Trinity* (Maryknoll, NY: Orbis, 2000). Dupuis provides a succinct presentation of his Trinitarian views in his article, "Trinitarian Christology as a Model for a Theology of Religious Pluralism," *The Myriad Christ: Plurality and the Quest for Unity in Contemporary Christology*, ed. Terrence Merrigan & Jacques Haers, Bibliotheca Ephemeridum Lovaniensium (Leuven: University Press & Peeters, 2000) 83-98. For a discussion of this trend, see Terrence Merrigan, "Jacques Dupuis and the Redefinition of Inclusivism," *In Many and Diverse Ways: In Honor of Jacques Dupuis*, ed. Daniel Kendall & Gerald O'Collins (Maryknoll, NY: Orbis, 2003) 60-71.

will be focused mainly on the question of the Church's role in the mediation of salvation to non-Christians. Congar's work, devoted, as so much of it was, to questions of ecclesiology, may have some important lessons to teach us as we move towards that future.[6]

I will proceed by means of four steps. First, I will present the official view on the Church's role in salvation history, especially as this is reflected in Vatican II and in *Dominus Iesus*. Second, I will examine in detail Dupuis' appeal to Congar, in the light of Dupuis' own position on the matter. Third, I will provide a critical assessment of Dupuis' references to Congar. Finally, I will offer some reflections on the broader theological significance of the divergence between Dupuis and Congar regarding the role played by the Church in the salvific economy.

1. The Church and the Salvation of Non-Christians

According to *Lumen gentium*, §13, "all human beings are called to the new people of God," that is, the Church, and all either "belong to it or are ordered (*ordinantur*) to it in various ways, whether they be catholic faithful or others who believe in Christ or finally all people everywhere who by the grace of God are called to salvation."[7] *Lumen gentium*, §16 takes up this theme again, and declares that "all those who have not accepted the gospel are related (*ordinantur*) to the people of God in various ways." Taking his lead from the discussion in this passage (§16), Francis Sullivan points

---

[6] For a recent and comprehensive study of Congar's ecclesiology, with particular attention to the relationship between Church and world, see Gabriel Flynn, *Yves Congar's Vision of the Church in a World of Unbelief* (Aldershot: Ashgate, 2004).

[7] All references to the conciliar documents will be taken from *Decrees of the Ecumenical Councils*, ed. Norman P. Tanner, 2 vols. (London/Washington, DC: Sheed & Ward/Georgetown University Press, 1990).

out that the Council distinguishes five groups among non-Christians, in accordance with "the source and kind of knowledge of God that is characteristic of each group."[8] First among these are the Jews, who know God through divine revelation. Next in line are the Moslems who "acknowledge the Creator," and who "profess to hold the faith of Abraham," and "to worship the one merciful God who will judge humanity on the last day." The third category (presumably the adherents of other non-Christian religions) encompasses those who "search for the unknown God in shadows and images." The fourth and fifth categories are described by Sullivan as "those who do not practice any specific religion."[9] In this case, a distinction is made between, on the one hand, those "who, without any fault do not know anything about Christ or his Church," but "search for God with a sincere heart" and seek to live according to "the dictate of conscience," and, on the other hand, those who, "through no fault of their own, have not yet attained to the express recognition of God," but nevertheless strive ("not without divine grace") "to lead an upright life."

Sullivan attempts to clarify the Council's understanding of the way in which these people can be said to be 'related to' the Church, especially since the same Council says elsewhere (*Gaudium et Spes*, §22) that grace is "secretly at work" in the hearts of "all people of good will," and that "the holy Spirit offers everyone the possibility of sharing in [Christ's] paschal mystery in a manner known to God (*modo Deo cognito*)." Sullivan appeals to the *relatio* drafted by the theological commission that was involved in the composition of *Lumen gentium*, §16, to defend the view that "just as every offer of grace directs the recipient toward salvation, so also every offer of grace directs the recipient toward the Church."

---

[8] Francis Sullivan, *Salvation outside the Church? Tracing the History of the Catholic Response* (London: Geoffrey Chapman, 1992) 154.

[9] Sullivan, *Salvation outside the Church?*, 154.

The *relatio* declares that, "All grace has a certain communitarian quality, and looks toward the Church" (*Omnis gratia quandam indolem communitariam induit et ad ecclesiam respicit*).[10] Taking his lead from the *relatio*, Sullivan goes on to substantiate this claim by appealing to three arguments. In the first place, since grace finds its ultimate fulfillment in the "universal Church" that will be realized in the eschaton (*Lumen gentium*, §2), it "must also be intrinsically ordered toward the Church in its earthly state." Secondly, since saving grace "must make possible an act of saving faith," it is also "intrinsically directed toward the full profession of faith in divine revelation, which is had only in the Church." Thirdly, since saving grace "includes the gift of supernatural love of God and neighbor," it is "intrinsically ordered toward the communion in charity which is the inner life of the Church." Sullivan is of the opinion that "it was for reasons such as these" that the theological commission insisted that "there is an ecclesial character, an orientation toward the Church, in every offer of grace. And since the offer of grace is made to all, all are, by that fact, 'related to the Church'."[11]

Sullivan goes on to note that Congar had made precisely this point in the mid-1950s. In an article published in 1959 (but already prepared in 1956, and republished in 1963), Congar wrote:

> The Catholic Church remains the only institution (*sacramentum*) divinely instituted and mandated for salvation, and whatever grace exists in the world is related to her by finality, if not by efficaciousness.[12]

---

[10] *Ibid.*, 155, 215 n. 18.

[11] *Ibid.*, 155.

[12] Quoted *ibid.*, 156; see Yves Congar, "Hors de l'Église pas de salut," *Sainte Eglise: Etudes et approches ecclésiologiques*, Unam Sanctam, 41 (Paris: Cerf, 1963) 431-432. Sullivan, *Salvation outside the Church?*, 215 n. 18 points out that Congar's text had been prepared in 1956 and that it was first published in the encyclopedia, *Catholicisme*, 5: 948-956 in 1959.

Sullivan is of the view that the Council went beyond this position to propose that "all grace for salvation" is indeed "related to the Church not only by finality, but also, in some sense, by efficacious-ness." He finds a "basis" for this claim in the Council's description of the Church as the "universal sacrament of salvation." Drawing on a variety of conciliar documents (including *Lumen gentium*, §1, 8, 9, 10, 45, 48; *Ad gentes*, §1; *Gaudium et Spes*, 22; *Sacrosanctum concilium*, §2, 10) and the new Eucharistic prayers enjoined by the Council, as well as Pius XII's 1943 encyclical, *Mystici corporis*, Sullivan argues that the Church exercises an "instrumental or medi-atory role" in the salvation of all people, including those who do not belong to her. She does this, above all, by fulfilling her vocation to be a "priestly people," a vocation which finds its fullest expres-sion in her celebration of the eucharist. The eucharist makes present the "unique sacrifice which obtained the grace of redemption for the whole world." As such, it is "the principal channel through which that grace is now mediated to each succeeding generation."[13]

As Sullivan points out, the Council developed a bold analogy between the way in which the humanity of Christ served the incar-nate Word "as a living instrument of salvation," and the way in which the "communal structure of the Church" serves "Christ's Spirit who vivifies it" (*Lumen gentium*, §8). According to Sullivan, "this means that, as the humanity of Christ is the instrument of the divine Word in the total work of salvation, so also the Church can be seen as the instrument of the Holy Spirit in the total work of bringing Christ's grace to every human person."[14] Through its preaching, teaching, service and worship — and its eucharistic wor-ship, in particular — the Church exercises its vocation of "univer-sal priesthood" and makes Christ's saving work present in history,

[13] Sullivan, *Salvation outside the Church?*, 159.
[14] *Ibid.*, 158.

for the salvation of all.[15] This theme reappears in the document, *Dialogue and Proclamation* (1991), the most important statement on the Catholic understanding of interreligious dialogue since Vatican II. There (§86), we read that,

> Through the ministry of the Church, the one Eucharist is offered by Jesus in every age and place, since the time of his passion, death and resurrection in Jerusalem. It is here that Christians unite themselves to Christ in his offering which 'brings salvation to the whole world' (Eucharistic Prayer IV). Such a prayer is pleasing to God who "desires all men to be saved and to come to the knowledge of the truth" (1 Tim 2:4).[16]

This same incarnational vision permeates *Dominus Iesus*, which appeared in 2000.[17] One feature of *Dominus Iesus* which generated comment was its combination of the theology of religions with a discussion of the relationship between Catholicism and other Christian Churches. In fact, there is no discontinuity here. The point of departure is the same in both cases, namely, the universal salvific will of God and its *concrete* realization in human history. The entire argument of the concluding (ecclesiological) paragraphs of *Dominus Iesus* (§16-22) is built on the conviction that "Jesus Christ continues his presence and his work of salvation in the Church and by means of the Church, which is his body" (§16, with references to

---

[15] Terrence Merrigan, "What's in a Word? Revelation and Tradition in Vatican II and in Contemporary Theology," in M. Lamberigts, L. Kenis (eds.), *Vatican II and its Legacy*, Bibliotheca Ephemeridum Lovaniensium, 166 (Leuven: University Press & Peeters, 2002) 59-82.

[16] The text of *Dialogue and Proclamation* can be found in William R. Burrows (ed.), *Redemption and Dialogue: Reading 'Redemptoris Missio' and 'Dialogue and Proclamation'* (Maryknoll, NY: Orbis, 1993) 93-118, see p. 117, §86.

[17] For a fuller treatment of the document, see Terrence Merrigan, "Religious Pluralism and 'Dominus Iesus'," *Sacred Heart University Review* 20 (1999-2000) 63-79.

Col 1:24-27; 1 Cor 12:12-13, 27; Col 1:18).[18] The document repeats the claim of Vatican II that the Church of Christ "subsists in the Catholic Church" (§17), and that other Christian bodies share 'Church-hood', so to speak, to a greater or lesser degree. As far as the degree of sharing is concerned, the issue is once again a matter of *'mediation'*. A community is more or less a Church depending on whether (and to what degree) it possesses the means to mediate effectively. For Vatican II (and for *Dominus Iesus*), the most important of these 'means' are apostolic succession and a valid eucharist (§17). In fact, these two are intimately related, since apostolic succession guarantees the validity of the eucharist. Indeed, we can justifiably say that, for Vatican II and for *Dominus Iesus*, 'Church-hood', so to speak, is, above all, a matter of the validity of the eucharist. In the final analysis, *Dominus Iesus*, like Vatican II, portrays the eucharist as the primary sacramental mediation of the saving work of Christ. Where the eucharist is celebrated, Christ the Savior is most intimately present to his people.[19] This is not to

---

[18] See also the following passages: §16: "The Catholic faithful are required to profess that there is an historical continuity — rooted in the apostolic succession — between the Church founded by Christ and the Catholic Church..." §20: "... The one Christ is the mediator and the way of salvation; he is present to us in his body which is the Church."

[19] See Francis Sullivan, "The Impact of 'Dominus Iesus' on Ecumenism," *America* 183:15 (28 October 2000) 10. Sullivan points out that the Doctrinal Commission of Vatican II allowed for a more positive approach to the so-called "ecclesial communities" than *Dominus Iesus* which says bluntly that they are "not Churches in the proper sense." The Doctrinal Commission said that these communities "are not merely a sum or collection of individual Christians, but they are constituted by social ecclesiastical elements which they have preserved from our common patrimony and which confer on them a truly ecclesial character. In these communities the one sole Church of Christ is present, albeit imperfectly, in a way that is somewhat like its presence in particular Churches, and by means of their ecclesiastical elements, the Church of Christ is in some way operative in them." Sullivan also refers to *Ut Unum Sint* (1995) where it is said that "the one Church of Christ is effectively present in [the other Christian communities]." *Dominus*

say that his saving presence cannot be found elsewhere. It is, however, to proclaim that this presence can be located in space and time, in the Church's celebration of his life, death and resurrection, and to insist that his saving presence elsewhere can never be divorced from the paschal mystery which the Church celebrates and makes present.[20]

2. THE APPEAL TO CONGAR IN THE WORK OF JACQUES DUPUIS

On 24 January 2001, the Congregation for the Doctrine of the Faith issued a so-called *Notification* regarding Jacques Dupuis' book, *Toward a Christian Theology of Religious Pluralism*, which stipulated, among other things, that the text of the *Notification* "must be included in any reprinting or further editions of his book, as well as in all translations."[21] The motivation for this step, according to the Congregation, was a concern "to safeguard the doctrine of the Catholic faith from errors, ambiguities, or harmful interpretations"

Iesus, he notes (p. 11), gives one "the impression that the Church of Christ is present and operative only in those that it calls 'true particular Churches'."

[20] It must be said, however, the theme of the universal priesthood of the faithful is not considered in *Dominus Iesus*.

[21] The text of the *Notification* is contained in the edition of the book published in 2001. With the exception of the three appendices containing the *Notification*, a statement by the Superior General of the Society of Jesus, Peter-Hans Kolvenbach, and the Foreword to the Indian edition of the book (2001), the 2001 edition is identical to the 1997 edition. See Jacques Dupuis, *Toward a Christian Theology of Religious Pluralism* (Maryknoll, NY: Orbis, 1997; 2001). The text of the Notification is found on pp. 434-438 of the 2001 edition. A 'Publisher's Note' on p. 435 points out that, "The requirement to insert the *Notification* was not found in the draft of the *Notification* signed by the author in December 2000. It was added after the author signed it." For a comprehensive discussion of Dupuis' book and the theological issues it raises, see Terrence Merrigan, "Exploring the Frontiers: Jacques Dupuis and the Movement "Toward a Christian Theology of Religious Pluralism," *Louvain Studies* 23 (1998) 338-359.

that "could be derived from reading the ambiguous statements and insufficient explanations found in certain sections" of the book. More specifically, the Congregation identified the "important doctrinal points" about which it was concerned as "the interpretation of the sole and universal salvific mediation of Christ, the unicity and completeness of Christ's revelation, the universal salvific action of the Holy Spirit, the orientation of all people to the Church, and the value and significance of the salvific function of other religions." The *Notification* then proceeds to discuss each of these points separately. With respect to "the orientation of all human beings to the Church," the *Notification* says the following:

> It must be firmly believed that the Church is sign and instrument of salvation for all people. It is contrary to the Catholic faith to consider the different religions of the world as ways of salvation complementary to the Church. According to Catholic doctrine, the followers of other religions are oriented to the Church and are called to become part of her.[22]

In his 1997 book, Dupuis had stated that, while "the Church intercedes undoubtedly for the salvation of all, especially in the eucharistic celebration," its role as an effective 'instrument' of salvation is limited to its own members. Though he acknowledged the attempts by Sullivan and others to extend the Church's mediatory role to non-Christians, he argues that this is not 'mediation' "in

---

[22] Quoted in the 2001 edition of Dupuis, *Toward a Christian Theology of Religious Pluralism*, 436. Regarding the Church as "sign and instrument of salvation for all people," the *Notification* refers the reader to *Lumen gentium*, §9, 14, 17, 48; *Redemptoris missio*, §11; *Dominus Iesus*, §16. Regarding the proposition that there are "ways of salvation complementary to the Church," the reader is referred to *Redemptoris missio*, §36; *Dominus Iesus*, §21-22. Regarding the proposition that "the followers of other religions are oriented to the Church and are called to become part of her," the reader is referred to *Lumen gentium*, §16; *Nostra aetate*, §2; *Ad gentes*, §9; Pope Paul VI, Apostolic Exhortation *Evangelii Nuntiandi*, §53; *Redemptoris missio*, §55; *Dominus Iesus*, §8.

the proper, theological sense." Making use of scholastic terminology, Dupuis argues that whereas Christ's mediation can be characterized as "instrumental efficient causality in the strict sense," the Church's mediation is "derived," and the causality that is "involved" in its intercessory activity "is not of the order of efficiency but of the moral order and of finality." As he puts it, "The proclamation of the word and the celebration of the eucharist constitute a true mediation of the action of Jesus Christ in the ecclesial community. But, it is necessary to add, those factors do not — by definition — reach out to the members of the other religious traditions who receive salvation in Jesus Christ."[23]

Critics of Dupuis' work, including the editors of the *Revue thomiste*, took him to task for this position. In a lengthy reply to their comments, published in 1999, Dupuis reiterated his distinction between "the instrumental causality such is at work in the *opus operatum* of the sacraments on behalf of Church members, and the moral causality operative in intercession..."[24] In his last major treatment of the subject, published in English in 2002, Dupuis reproduced nearly verbatim those segments of his 1997 work in which he had expounded his position. For him, it is clear that the 'orientation' of non-Christians towards the Church that is referred to in *Lumen gentium*, §16 "does not imply a universal mediation of the Church already operative by way of efficient causality."[25]

[23] Dupuis, *Toward a Christian Theology of Religious Pluralism*, 350. See also n. 27 on p. 350.

[24] Jacques Dupuis, "'The Truth will make you free': The Theology of Religious Pluralism Revisited," *Louvain Studies* 24 (1999) 211-263 at 252. This article provides a comprehensive survey of the most important reviews of Dupuis' work and his responses to his reviewers. Regarding the *Revue thomiste*, see n. 43 below.

[25] Jacques Dupuis, *Christianity and the Religions: From Confrontation to Dialogue* (Maryknoll, NY: Orbis, 2002) 213.

Dupuis consistently and explicitly appeals to Congar to defend his views on the limited mediatory role of the Church.[26] His argument in this regard (and his appeal to Congar) revolves around three distinct (but ultimately inseparable) issues, namely, the meaning of the axiom, *Extra ecclesiam nulla salus*, the significance to be attached to the word 'ordinantur' in *Lumen gentium*, §16, and the role played by the non-Christian traditions as efficient channels of grace for their adherents. Let us examine each of these separately.

1. Extra ecclesiam nulla salus

With regard to the ancient axiom, Dupuis notes that Congar does not reject it as meaningless, since "he finds in it a biblical truth,"[27] namely, that "the Church is the only institution created and commanded by God to obtain for people the salvation which is in Jesus Christ."[28] Nevertheless, Dupuis asserts, Congar felt that, "since in its formulation the axiom can no longer be taken *literally* [Dupuis' emphasis] and a correct understanding of it requires long explanations," the axiom should be "abandoned."[29] Dupuis quotes Congar to the effect that:

---

[26] Dupuis' references to Congar, in the three works discussed here, are as follows: *Toward a Christian Theology of Religious Pluralism*, 77, 81, 101, 147, 349 n. 24, 350-351 (the 'Index of Names' does not include the reference on p. 349 n. 24); "The Truth will make you free," 216, 242, 250; *Christianity and the Religions*, 180, 203-204, 211-213.

[27] Dupuis, *Toward a Christian Theology of Religious Pluralism*, 101.

[28] Yves Congar, "L'Église, sacrament universel du salut," *Église vivante* 17:339-355 at 354.

[29] Dupuis, *Toward a Christian Theology of Religious Pluralism*, 101. See also *Christianity and the Religions*, 211. The word, "abandoned," does not occur in the text to which Dupuis immediately refers, namely, Yves Congar, *The Wide World My Parish: Salvation and its Problems* (London: Darton, Longman & Todd, 1961) 98. Moreover, I can find nothing in Congar's text to support the use of this term. See the comments on the translation of Dupuis' reference in the

There is no longer a question of applying the formula to any concrete person ... [The axiom] is no longer regarded as answering the question, "*Who* will be saved?," but ... the question: "*What* is it that is commissioned to discharge the mystery of salvation?"[30]

If the maxim is to be preserved, Congar argues, then it must be interpreted "in a wholly positive sense." He explains this sense as follows:

> ... There is in the world one and only one reality that shows forth the gift given by God for the world's salvation, destining it to life in fellowship with him: that gift is Jesus Christ, foretold by the prophets, suffering death and rising again for us, master of truth, who entrusted to the Church, his Bride and his Body, the treasure of the saving word and the sacraments.[31]

Dupuis takes note of Congar's remarks in this regard, but he also recalls that Congar expressed some hesitation about the efficacy of the Church's mediation with respect to non-Christians. As we have seen, Sullivan maintains that Vatican II resolved any remaining ambiguity about whether the grace that is in the world ought to be referred to the Church "in efficiency," as well as "in finality." Nevertheless, as late as 1999, Dupuis insisted that, "As regards the

following footnote (n. 30). See also Yves Congar, "Au sujet du salut des non-catholiques," *Revue des Sciences Religieuses* 32 (1958) 53-65 at 64-65. Though Congar also discusses the axiom here, he says nothing about 'abandoning' it.

[30] Quoted, in this form, in Dupuis, *Toward a Christian Theology of Religious Pluralism*, 101; see also p. 351; see Dupuis, *Christianity and the Religions*, 203-204, 211-213. In *Toward a Christian Theology of Religious Pluralism*, Dupuis refers the reader to Congar, *The Wide World My Parish*, 98. In a footnote, Dupuis also refers the reader to p. 112 of the same work (*The Wide World My Parish*) and to Congar's, *Sainte Église: Études et approches ecclésiologiques*, 417-432. It is worth noting, however, that the translation provided by Dupuis is his own, and that it does not correspond entirely to the translation found in *The Wide World My Parish*. In *Christianity and the Religions*, Dupuis refers to the original French edition of the book, namely, *Vaste Monde ma paroisse*, 131-132.

[31] Congar, *The Wide World My Parish*, 112.

universality of the Church's efficient instrumental causality in the order of grace, I believe — with Y. Congar, among others — that questions can be legitimately formulated."[32]

2. The Meaning of 'ordinantur' in Lumen gentium, §16

With regard to the term, *ordinantur*, in *Lumen gentium*, §16, Dupuis claims that Congar interpreted it in what we might describe as a 'broad' sense, that is to say, as signifying a general 'orientation' towards the Church rather than giving expression to the conviction that all people are somehow destined to become actual members. The word was 'borrowed' from Pius XII's encyclical, *Mystici Corporis* (1943), where it is said that those who do not belong to the Church are "oriented toward it by a certain unconscious desire and wish" (*inscio quodam desiderio ac voto ad mysticum redemptoris corpus ordinari*). According to Dupuis, both Karl Rahner and Congar were of the opinion that the encyclical deliberately sought to avoid the impression that those who unconsciously yearn for the Church are already actually (*reapse*) a part of it. In Congar's words,

> The encyclical would not favor the idea of invisible *belonging* to the visible Church; or even that they belong 'voto', because, according to the encyclical, what the 'desire' brings about is merely an *orientation* to the mystical Body.[33]

Dupuis contrasts this view with other, more restrictive interpretations of the term, which were born of the fear that the broader view

---

[32] Dupuis, "The Truth will make you free," 250.

[33] Dupuis, *Toward a Christian Theology of Religious Pluralism*, 349 n. 24. The reference is to Congar, *Sainte Église: Études et approches ecclésiologiques*, 431.

might "undermine the doctrine of the necessity of the Church."[34] Responding to a critic who had described Dupuis' reading of *ordinantur* as "minimalist," the latter insists that Vatican II "deliberately chose to speak a different language than that of 'membership', where those of other religions are concerned; and this for the good reason that the members of those religions are simply not members of the Church, according to the definition of the Church given in Constitution *Lumen Gentium* itself (n.8). If, however, they remain 'ordained' to her, this is because Jesus Christ has entrusted to her 'the fulness of the benefits and means of salvation' (*Redemptoris Missio*, n.18; cf.55)."[35]

For Dupuis, the upshot of this line of thinking is clear, namely, that "the relationship between the Church and nonmembers is not of the order of efficiency but of finality: nonmembers are oriented toward (*ordinantur*) the Church," but they are not, and need not become, actual members of it in order to be saved.[36] While they are in the flesh, so to speak, the means by which Christ's grace reaches them is, above all, their own religious traditions.

3. The Non-Christian Traditions as Mediators of Grace

With regard to the role played by the non-Christian traditions in the economy of salvation, Dupuis invokes yet again the authority of Congar. Dupuis writes as follows:

---

[34] Dupuis, *Toward a Christian Theology of Religious Pluralism*, 349 n. 24. Dupuis mentions, in particular, J. J. King, *The Necessity of the Church for Salvation in Selected Theological Writings of the Past Century* (Washington, DC: Catholic University of America Press, 1960) 288.

[35] Dupuis, "The Truth will make you free," 251. The critic is Gavin D'Costa, in his review of Dupuis' *Toward a Christian Theology of Religious Pluralism*, published in the *Journal of Theological Studies* 49 (1998) 910-914, at 913.

[36] Dupuis, *Toward a Christian Theology of Religious Pluralism*, 351.

The council [Vatican II] affirms the necessity of the Church for salvation (*Lumen gentium*, §14), as the "universal sacrament of salvation" (*Lumen gentium*, §48). This necessity does not, however, imply a universal mediation in the strict sense, applicable to every person who is saved in Jesus Christ. On the contrary, it leaves rooms for 'substitutive mediations' (*médiations de suppléance*) [a term used by Congar in his 1959 work, *Vaste monde ma paroisse*], among which will be found the religious traditions to which the 'others' belong. From this one may infer that the causality of the Church in relation to the 'others' is of the order not of efficiency but of finality.[37]

According to Dupuis, the non-Christian religious traditions "contain 'supernatural, grace-filled elements'" and "it is in responding to these elements of grace that [non-Christians] find salvation and become members of the Reign of God [not the Church] in history."[38] To the degree that non-Christian religious traditions exercise a mediatory role, they would appear to do so as "participated forms of mediation," that is to say, according as they participate in the "one, universal" mediation of Christ. Dupuis takes this notion from John Paul II's encyclical, *Redemptoris Missio*. There the pontiff affirms (§10) that "salvation in Christ is accessible to people outside the Church 'by virtue of a grace which, while having a

---

[37] *Ibid.*, 351. Dupuis attributes the notion of 'médiations de suppléance' explicitly to Congar and refers the reader to Congar, *Vaste monde ma paroisse*, 133-147, at 144.

[38] Dupuis, *Christianity and the Religions*, 202. As Dupuis notes (202 n. 12), the phrase, "supernatural, grace-filled elements," is borrowed from Karl Rahner, "Christianity and the Non-Christian Religions," in *Theological Investigations*, 21 vols. (London: Darton, Longman & Todd, 1961-1988) 5: 121, 130. Regarding Dupuis' views on the relationship between the visible Church and the Kingdom of God, see Dupuis, *Christianity and the Religions*, 206-217. See, for example, p. 214 where Dupuis argues that non-Christians "can attain the reality of the Kingdom of God present without belonging to the body of the Church. They can be members of the Reign of God without becoming part of the Church as its members."

mysterious relationship to the Church, does not make them formally part of the Church but enlightens them in a way which is accommodated to their spiritual and material situation'." The encyclical then goes on to recognize the possibility in the order of salvation of participated forms of mediation. The text reads as follows: "Although participated forms of mediation of different kinds and degrees are not excluded, they acquire meaning and value *only* from Christ's own mediation, and they cannot be understood as parallel or complementary to his" [emphasis in the original] (§5). Dupuis comments that "it is not clear whether among the 'participated mediations' contemplated in this text are included, for the benefit of members of the other religions, the traditions to which they belong."[39]

For Dupuis himself, it is clear, the "participated mediation" mentioned by the Pope does extend to non-Christian religious traditions as such. In any case, John Paul II, in *Redemptoris Missio*, provides another avenue for approaching these traditions as genuine mediators when he describes them as loci for the activity of the Spirit. Dupuis cites the encyclical (§28) to the effect that:

> The Spirit's ... presence and activity are universal, limited neither by space nor time ... The Spirit's presence and activity affect not only individuals but also society and history, peoples, cultures and religions.[40]

Commenting on this passage, Dupuis observes that, "Thus, throughout human history, in the religious traditions as well as in

---

[39] Dupuis, *Toward a Christian Theology of Religious Pluralism*, 177.

[40] Quoted *ibid.*, 222. See also Dupuis' discussion (pp. 173-179) of other documents and statements by the Pope (including the encyclicals *Redemptor Hominis* (4 March 1979) and *Dominum et Vivificantem* (18 May 1986) where the active presence of the Spirit in non-Christian religious traditions is affirmed). See also pp. 365-370.

individual persons, the Spirit has been present and active."[41] In this regard, it is interesting to note that, when Dupuis laments Western Christianity's tendency to reduce the Spirit to a "function of the risen Christ," he appeals to Congar.[42] Congar also provides Dupuis with an eloquent testimony to the work of the Spirit outside the Church which Dupuis duly invokes in his dispute with his critics, including the editors of the *Revue Thomiste* who had protested that "the Church is the proper place where grace operates" (*le lieu propre de la grâce*).[43] Dupuis replies that "grace has no 'proper place'. It is operative in all places and salvation can reach out to all people, in whatever historical situation and life circumstances they may find themselves."[44] While "it is true that the Church is in a privileged way 'the locus of the sending of the Spirit', in which the grace of salvation consists," the Spirit is not "so bound to the Church, to its ministry and institutions, that its presence and work of salvation are impaired outside of it." "People saved in Jesus Christ outside the Church are objectively oriented toward it (*ordinati*) but without being members of the Church."[45] To add weight to this claim, Dupuis refers to a remark by the nineteenth-century English cardinal, Manning, which Dupuis borrows from Congar's 1983 work, *I Believe*:

> It is true to say with St. Irenaeus, *Ubi ecclesia ibi Spiritus* — Where the Church is there is the Spirit —, but it would not be true to say,

---

[41] Quoted *ibid.*, 222.

[42] Dupuis, "The Truth will make you free," 242; *Christianity and the Religions*, 180.

[43] Dupuis, "The Truth will make you free," 249. The article to which Dupuis refers is "'Tout récapituler dans le Christ'. À propos de l'ouvrage de J. Dupuis, *Vers une théologie chrétienne du pluralisme religieux*," by 'Le comité de rédaction', *Revue thomiste* (1998) 591-630, at 629. See also Dupuis, *Christianity and the Religions*, 212-213.

[44] Dupuis, "The Truth will make you free,"249

[45] Dupuis, *Christianity and the Religions*, 212.

Where the Church is not, neither is the Spirit. The works of the Holy
Spirit have always pervaded the entire history of human beings from
the beginning, and they are still fully at work among those who are
outside the Church.[46]

In his attempts to defend the real mediatory role played by the non-
Christian traditions, Dupuis makes an extended appeal to the document, *Dialogue and Proclamation: Reflections and Orientations
on Interreligious Dialogue and the Proclamation of the Gospel of
Jesus Christ*, published jointly by the Pontifical Council for Interreligious Dialogue and the Congregation for the Evangelization of
Peoples (19 May 1991). Dupuis describes this as "a first among
documents of the Church's magisterium on the subject of members
of other religions and their traditions." It "goes beyond whatever
Church documents have stated before regarding the role played by
religious traditions in the salvation in Jesus Christ of their followers." The text (§29) declares that, "the mystery of salvation reaches
out to [those who "remain unaware that Jesus is the source of their
salvation"], in a way known to God, through the invisible action
of the Spirit of Christ. Concretely, it will be *in the sincere practice
of what is good in their own religious traditions* and by following
the dictates of their conscience that the members of other religions
respond positively to God's invitation and receive salvation in Jesus
Christ, even while they do not recognize or acknowledge him as
their Savior" (Dupuis' emphasis).[47] Dupuis acknowledges that the
statement is a "guarded one," but he also claims that "a door seems
to be timidly opened here, for the first time, for the recognition on
the part of the Church authority of a 'participated mediation' of

[46] Manning, as quoted in Dupuis, *Christianity and the Religions*, 212-213. See
"The Truth will make you free," 249-250, where the same quotation is employed
and elaborated upon. The text of the quotation is slightly different in the latter
work.
[47] Dupuis, *Toward a Christian Theology of Religious Pluralism*, 178.

religious traditions in the salvation of their members. With such a statement we seem to be definitely moving from the 'fulfillment theory' to that of an active presence of the mystery of Jesus Christ in the traditions themselves."[48] In a commentary on the text of *Dialogue and Proclamation*, Dupuis says of this passage:

> This is, even in its present form, a weighty statement, not found before in official documents of the central teaching authority, and whose theological import must not be underestimated. It means, in effect, that the members of other religions are not saved by Christ in spite of, or beside, their own tradition, but in it and in some mysterious way, 'known to God', through it. If further elaborated theologically, this statement would seem to imply some hidden presence — no matter how imperfect — of the mystery of Jesus Christ in these religious traditions in which salvation reaches their adherents.[49]

Elsewhere, while discussing the limited character of the Church's mediatory role, Dupuis again invokes Congar, this time to the effect that:

> Every Catholic must admit and admits that there have existed and exist gifts of light and grace working for salvation outside the visible boundaries of the Church. We do not even deem it necessary to hold, as is nonetheless commonly done, that these graces are received *through* [Congar's emphasis] the Church; it is enough that they be received in view of the Church and that they orient people toward the Church.[50]

It is clear that Dupuis regards Congar as an important ally in his efforts to ascribe a real (or 'efficient') mediatory role to the

---

[48] *Ibid.*, 178-179.

[49] Jacques Dupuis, "A Theological Commentary: Dialogue and Proclamation," *Redemption and Dialogue: Reading 'Redemptoris Missio' and 'Dialogue and Proclamation'*, ed. W. R. Burrows (Maryknoll, NY: Orbis, 1993) 119-158, at 137.

[50] Yves Congar, "L'Église, sacrament universel du salut," 351, as quoted in Dupuis, *Toward a Christian Theology of Religious Pluralism*, 351. Dupuis also refers the reader to Yves Congar, *This Church that I Love* (Denville, NJ: Dimension Books, 1969). See also Dupuis, *Christianity and the Religions*, 211.

non-Christian religious traditions. However, the references to Congar would seem to indicate that the latter serves, above all, as an ally in Dupuis' campaign to circumscribe the Church's mediatory role. Let us examine whether this appeal is really justified.

3. AN ASSESSMENT OF DUPUIS' APPEAL TO CONGAR

A careful examination of the way in which the references to Congar function in Dupuis' argumentation reveals that the texts involved are not always as amenable to Dupuis' case as a cursory reading might suggest.

So, for example, in discussing the meaning of the term, *ordinantur*, Dupuis recalls Congar's remark (cited in full above) that it is not necessary to hold that the graces enjoyed by those outside the Church are received "through" the Church. Instead, "it is enough that they be received in view of the Church and that they orient people toward the Church."[51] This quotation occurs after Dupuis has clarified his own understanding of *ordinantur*, namely, as being of the order of finality and not of efficiency. In the accompanying footnote, however, Dupuis makes the following observation:

> At the end of the text just quoted, Congar adds: "or that they incorporate them invisibly into it." This final recourse to a Church belonging, similar to Church membership *in voto*, seems to be what *Lumen gentium*, §16 deliberately chose not to resume in its own name.

In other words, Dupuis omits Congar's suggestion that the graces received by those outside the Church might, after all, serve to effect

---

[51] Yves Congar, "L'Église, sacrament universel du salut," 351, as quoted in Dupuis, *Toward a Christian Theology of Religious Pluralism*, 351. Dupuis also refers the reader to Yves Congar, *This Church that I Love* (Denville, NJ: Dimension Books, 1969). See also Dupuis, *Christianity and the Religions*, 211.

their eventual "incorporation into the Church." Moreover, he does this in view of his own reading of *Lumen gentium*, §16, a reading which, according to Sullivan, does not cohere with the teaching of the Council taken in its entirety.

Dupuis is, of course, not unaware of the divergence between his position and that of the Church authorities. Having repeated his claim that the "causality of the Church" in relation to non-Christians is "of the order not of efficiency but of finality," Dupuis immediately adds: "However, according to the recent Magisterium, the Church remains the 'ordinary way' for people's salvation inasmuch as it possesses the 'ordinary means' of salvation or the 'fullness of the means of salvation'." Here, too, though, Dupuis appeals to *Lumen gentium*, §16, to argue that the ecclesial dimension of saving grace, in the case of non-Christians, is subordinate to its "Christic" character. As he puts it, "Saving grace must be called 'Christic'; it may be called 'ecclesial' (*gratia ecclesialis*)." It is in the context of this discussion that Dupuis refers to Congar's expression, "substitutive mediations" (*médiations de suppléance*). As the passage quoted above makes clear, Dupuis formulates the reference in such a way that it appears as if Congar's 'substitutive mediations' include "the religious traditions to which others belong." This reading of Congar is certainly moot. Where the term, 'substitutive mediation', is actually used, it refers to either "an act of love," or to a basic "knowledge" of God's existence and His justice (though Congar says that this "is often a poor sort of knowledge, debased and sadly corrupt").[52] Congar's primary focus is,

---

[52] Congar, *The Wide World My Parish*, 123 (*Vaste monde ma paroisse*, 143). The terms used in the original text are, "une médiation supplétive" and "une mediation de suppléance." See also Congar, "Au sujet du salut des non-catholiques," *Revue des Sciences Religieuses* 32 (1958) 67. In the 1958 article, Congar (discussing the same book that he refers to in *Vaste monde ma paroisse*), asks whether "la consécration à quelque grande cause à laquelle on donnerait la

however, on the underlying attitude of love that comes to expression in the commitment to a whole range of "representations," some of which may be "very inadequate."[53] These representations include "those master-words that stand for a transcendent absolute to which [people] may have given their love, words that are often written with a capital letter: Duty, Peace, Justice, Brotherhood, yes, and Humanity, Progress, Welfare, and yet others."[54] Congar goes on to state the most "privileged" of these representations is "the sacrament of our Neighbor." In Congar's words:

> [The sacrament of our Neighbor] is privileged because our neighbor is a person and therefore something in regard to which one can adopt a commensurate attitude by love; because, too, meeting with a person, differently from meeting with objective realities, is able to be significant of the person of God; and again, because mediation through our neighbor [*la médiation du Prochain*] is more likely to remain unalloyed than that of other things … it is less likely to be contaminated by the efforts of the Evil One.[55]

There is, therefore, nothing particularly novel in Congar's reflections at this point. Indeed, his point of departure for the discussion is a speech of Pope Pius XII to midwives, in 1951, in which he stated that "an act of love can suffice for an adult to obtain sanctifying grace and supply for lack of baptism." As Congar remarks,

valeur d'un absolu: "Justice, Fraternité, Devoir, Progrès, Paix," might not constitute "quelque *substitut* de Dieu" (our emphasis). The book under discussion is R. Lombardi, *The Salvation of the Unbeliever* (London: Burns & Oates, 1956).

[53] Congar, *The Wide World My Parish*, 123 (*Vaste monde ma paroisse*, 143).

[54] *Ibid.*, 124 (145). In "Au sujet du salut des non-catholiques," Congar writes of these 'absolutes' as follows: "Objectivement, ce sont là plutôt des idoles, les idoles du monde moderne. Mais subjectivement, ne peuvent-elles être les espèces sous lesquelles, sans le nommer ni le connaître, des consciences, réellement, honoreraient et chercheraient Dieu?"

[55] Congar, *The Wide World My Parish*, 124 (*Vaste monde ma paroisse*, 145).

the pope "was thinking of an act of love *for God* [Congar's emphasis], but certainly admitting that God can be 'aimed at' through very inadequate representations, and even under other names than his."[56] Though Congar's reflections may be described as, in some sense, anticipating the later notion of "participated mediation" so dear to Dupuis, it is difficult to see how they can simply be incorporated into a defense of the claim that the Church's "relation" to non-Christians is "of the order not of efficiency but of finality."[57]

In fact, Dupuis is aware that Congar does not accept the 'independent' mediatory value of non-Christian religious traditions. In the course of a consideration of Karl Rahner's notion of the "anonymous Christian," Dupuis, in a footnote to his text, states that "Congar does not accept a salvific value or mediation of salvation in the religious traditions *as such* [Dupuis' emphasis], objectively considered, while admitting that these may exercise a de facto mediation for persons who in good faith seek God in and through them. He thus distinguishes between religions in themselves and as they are lived by concrete persons."[58]

---

[56] *Ibid.*, 122-123 (143). The French text of the Pope's words reads as follows: "un acte d'amour peut suffire à l'adulte pour obtenir la grâce sanctifiante et suppléer à l'absence du baptême."

[57] Dupuis, *Toward a Christian Theology of Religious Pluralism*, 351.

[58] *Ibid.*, 147 n. 15. Dupuis refers to Yves Congar, "Non-Christian Religions and Christianity," *Evangelization, Dialogue and Development: Selected Papers of the International Theological Conference, Nagpur (India) 1971*, ed. M. Dhavamony, Documenta Missionalia, 5 (Rome: Università Gregoriana, 1972) 133-145; See also Yves Congar, "Les religions non bibliques sont-elles des médiations de salut?," *Year-Book / Annals / Jahrbuch: Ecumenical Institute for Advanced Theological Studies* (Tantur/Jerusalem, 1973) 77-102. For Congar's thoughts on Rahner's proposal, see Congar, "Les religions non bibliques sont-elles des médiations de salut?," 81-86; see also, "Talking to Yves Congar: Interview by Tony Sheerin," *St. Patrick's Missions* (November 1974) 6-8, at 7-8. See also Congar's remark (p. 7) to the effect that: "God did not will simply the salvation of individual men. He willed that they should be saved in a certain way. Jesus Christ and His Church is the way that He has chosen to communicate His salvation to men."

Congar had made his position in this regard unambiguously clear in a lecture delivered in 1971 (though he still referred his audience to his 1959 study, *Vaste monde ma paroisse*, for a fuller treatment of the problem). Referring once again to the existence of 'absolutes' such as "a love of justice or of fraternity," Congar declared that, "on [the] subjective level, the mediations of salvation are many." Moreover, "One cannot deny that for those men to whom Christ and his Church have not been proposed, or have been proposed in an 'insufficient' way, the religions into which they are born, which they practice and which are, moreover, profoundly linked with all the concrete conditions of their social life and of their culture, are obvious mediations of salvation." However, Congar continues, "One cannot conclude from this that these religions are divinely legitimated *in themselves* and *as such* [Congar's emphasis]. Their value derives from the persons who live them."[59]

Writing in 1997, Dupuis contends that the "foundation" of Congar's distinction between "religions in themselves and as they are lived by concrete persons" is "questionable." Though he does not elaborate on this critique, it is clear what he is referring to. The whole thrust of Dupuis' theology of religions, especially as this comes to expression from 1997 onwards, is, first, that the response to God's universal salvific will necessarily comes to expression in visible, social forms, namely, the world's religious traditions, and, second, that the persistence of these traditions in history means they are best understood as being possessed of an abiding value in

---

[59] Yves Congar, "Non-Christian Religions and Christianity," 139-140. See also Congar, "Les religions non bibliques sont-elles des médiations de salut?," 87: "De la possibilité du salut pour tout homme on ne peut passer *immédiatement* [Congar's emphasis] à une justification des religions en elles-mêmes et comme telles. Ce passage est possible, et nous le ferons, mais à partir des personnes. Les religions sont, pour ces personnes, des médiations du salut, mais elles ne sont pas les seules." See also pp. 85, 88, 94-95, 95-96, 96-97.

the salvific economy. In a lecture delivered at the same conference that Congar addressed in 1971, Dupuis reflected on the "dichotomy that is often established between the subjective religious life of men and the objective religion which they profess, between their personal religious experience and the historico-social religious phenomenon, made up of scriptures and cultic practices to which they adhere." According to Dupuis, this 'dichotomy' is untenable. As he puts it:

> It is then said that, though non-Christians are saved due to the sincerity of their subjective religious life, their religion has for them no objective salvific value. However, the dichotomy on which this restriction is based, is seriously inadequate. Subjective and objective religion can be distinguished; they cannot be separated. Religions are in fact born of the religious life of their adherents; their scriptures contain the record of concrete religious experiments with Truth; their practices result from the codification of religious experiences. Therefore, it appears unpracticable [sic] and theologically unrealistic to maintain that, though non-Christians can be saved, their religion plays no part in their salvation. If no concrete religious life is purely natural [i.e., devoid of authentic religious experience], no historical religion is merely human.[60]

It might well be said that Dupuis' subsequent theology of religions is nothing more (but also nothing less) than the working out of this position. This line of thought reaches its culmination in Dupuis' claim, in his 1997 work, that the world's religions are the visible and social expression of the "distinct modalities of God's self-communication to persons and peoples,"[61] that is to say, of the various covenantal relations established by God with humankind at various times.[62] As such, these religious traditions are possessed of an

---

[60] Dupuis, "The Salvific Value of Non-Christian Religions," *Evangelization, Dialogue and Development*, 169-193, at 185.

[61] Dupuis, *Toward a Christian Theology of Religious Pluralism*, 212.

[62] *Ibid.*, 223-234. On p. 204, Dupuis appears to use the expression, "diverse modalities," to refer to the non-Christian religions. On p. 212, it seems to refer to

"abiding meaning," and "an abiding [and "lasting"] efficacy," in "accordance with God's universal saving design for humankind."[63] Indeed, they may be described as representing "true interventions and authentic manifestations of God in the history of peoples; they form integral parts of one history of salvation that culminates in the Jesus-Christ-event."[64] In line with this view, Dupuis is able to claim that "plurality needs to be taken seriously and to be welcomed, not merely as a matter of fact but in principle. Its place in God's plan of salvation for humankind must be stressed."[65]

From Dupuis' point of view, then, Congar appears, as it were, to shift the centre of gravity *from* the 'religions' which non-Christians practice *to* their (personal) religious 'practice' as such. This would mean (from Dupuis' perspective) that Congar has not sufficiently appreciated the fact that communal forms (religions) are not incidental to the way in which individuals (or, to use Congar's term, 'persons') work out their salvation, but are the *sine qua non* of every saving encounter with God.[66]

the "'pre-Christian' covenants." It is not clear how much of a distinction ought to be made between these covenants and the world's religions in which they appear to find concrete expression.

[63] Dupuis, *Toward a Christian Theology of Religious Pluralism*, 212.

[64] *Ibid.*, 303.

[65] *Ibid.*, 201. See also pp. 11, 210, 252, 268, 294, 322, 373, 379, 388.

[66] It is striking that, in Congar's 1971 lecture, "Non-Christian Religions and Christianity," there are some traces of a tendency to highlight the 'individual' character of the non-Christian's religious practice. So, for example, Congar remarks (p. 139) that, "On this *subjective* [our emphasis] level, the mediations of salvation are many: everything in which *a conscience* [our emphasis] loyally places its absolute and which does not involve in itself a contradiction." So, too, Congar acknowledges that "the religions into which [people] are born, which they practice and which are, moreover, profoundly linked with all the concrete conditions of their social life and of their culture, are obvious mediations of salvation," and that it is "by means of them that they are in communion of faith and love with God." However, he immediately qualifies this endorsement, so to speak, by observing that: "One cannot, however, exclude the idea that, while practicing

4. The Theological Significance of the Divergence between
Congar and Dupuis

Both Congar and Dupuis highlight the importance of the theme of
'mediation' in their theologies of religions. This is a quintessentially
Catholic concern, and might indeed be said to define the Catholic
approach to the theology of religions (or the theology of interreligious
dialogue, as it is increasingly called).[67] Catholicism is a 'sacramental' system. This means that it is structured around the principle that
the divine presence is always 'mediated'. The root of this sacramental orientation is, of course, the doctrine of the incarnation, the assertion that the second person of the Trinity became human in the cause
of human salvation. Catholic thought cannot conceive of the divine
presence without linking it to some sacramental expression. This is
why Christ is sometimes called the foundational sacrament, the first
and ultimate sacrament of God's presence to humankind. In Catholic
theology, the Church exists to perpetuate Christ's sacramental presence, especially through its own sacramental life (and the eucharist
in particular). To affirm the saving presence of God in history is to
affirm His ongoing presence by means of visible, tangible forms.

Seen in this light, Dupuis' interest in the question of how saving grace might be 'mediated' to non-Christians, and his willingness to recognize the mediatory role played by non-Christian religious traditions can be regarded as thoroughly Catholic. These
concerns are completely in keeping with the sacramental (or incarnational) principle. One might, however, inquire whether he also

loyally or candidly these religions, men may be saved by another mediation, for
instance, the gift to a generous absolute love on the philanthropic plane." See
p. 139 n. 18.

[67] Terrence Merrigan, "For us and for our salvation: The Notion of Salvation
History in the Contemporary Theology of Religions," *Irish Theological Quarterly* 64 (1999) 339-348.

does justice to this principle when he suggests that the Church's mediatory role be circumscribed.

It has been suggested that Congar's understanding of the urgency of the Church's missionary vocation was somewhat compromised by his approach to the mediatory value of the non-Christian traditions.[68] It certainly is the case that his views in this regard are not always unambiguous and, as Sullivan indicates, Congar's preconciliar 'hesitation' about the 'efficiency' of the Church's universal mediation was not shared by the Council. Perhaps this latent ambiguity accounts, to some degree, for Dupuis' appeal to a theologian who, in the final analysis, does not share his view on the 'intrinsic' mediatory value of non-Christian religions. Reflecting, in 1971, on the theology of mission, Congar observed that the narrow ecclesiocentrism of the time before the Council had given way to a grander and more dynamic vision of the Church. Speaking in terms that probably would not have endeared him to the authors of either the 'Notification' directed at Dupuis or *Dominus Iesus*, Congar observed that we now acknowledge other mediations than the institutional Church, and recognize that the 'eschatological Kingdom' is the end towards which all of creation, and not simply the Church, are moving. At the same time, he reaffirms the Council's teaching that the Church was founded to serve as the "active sign" of God's saving love for the world, and recalls *Lumen gentium's* description of the Church as "a sacrament or instrumental sign of intimate union with God and of the unity of all humanity." Congar then adds that one may not separate the institutional and the charismatic (or 'graced') dimensions of the Church. The very idea of a sacrament, he comments, mitigates against such a separation.[69]

---

[68] Flynn, *Yves Congar's Vision of the Church*, 41-43.

[69] Yves Congar, "Les missions au service du salut," *Quel missionnaire?*, Museum Lessianum — Section Missiologique, 55 (Bruges, 1971) 13-38 at 33. The reference is to *Lumen gentium*, §1. See also p. 29 where Congar writes as

As Congar well knew, the Church derives its sacramental character from its union with Christ. Its very raison d'être is its service to his work of redemption.[70] To separate the Church from Christ — even for a moment, so to speak — would be to rob it of its 'essential' significance as instrument of his salvific will. This is not to suggest that the Church can simply be equated with Christ, only that it makes present, albeit in a limited (because historical) fashion, his universal saving work. After all, while it is possible to distinguish the sacrament and the reality signified, these can never be divided. To suggest, therefore, that Christ is always 'implicated' in the salvation of all men and women, but that the Church is only implicated in the salvation of Christians, would be to violate the sacramental (or incarnational) principle on which the Church is founded. For that reason, it seems to me, Congar's (somewhat ambiguous) defense of the Church's universal mediatory role may well prove more lasting than Dupuis' more daring embrace of the non-Christian religions.

follows: "L'institution apostolique est fondée, que le Saint-Esprit fera devenir événement à travers l'espace et le temps. Elle sera la représentation, c'est-à-dire la présence active, mandatée publiquement, de l'amour sauveur de Dieu pour les hommes." See, too, Yves Congar, *This Church that I Love*, trans. L. Delafuente (Denville, NJ: Dimension Books, 1968) 59, as quoted in Flynn, *Yves Congar's Vision of the Church*, 42: "If above and beyond the rescue of the individual, salvation consists in the realization of the truth of His being, the Church is the universal sacrament of salvation. From the point of view of individual salvation, the reality (*res* in the sense of classical analysis in sacramental theology) is sometimes bestowed independently of the *sacramentum*. But this unity of mankind, *as God wants it*, cannot be accomplished outside the Church, which is its sacrament." See also Flynn, *Yves Congar's Vision of the Church*, 110-113 for a discussion of Congar's understanding of the Church as "essentially sacramental" (p. 112); for Congar's views on the role of the eucharist in building up the church, see pp. 107-110.

[70] Congar, "Les missions au service du salut," 29.

EPILOGUE
YVES CONGAR'S THEOLOGY
IN THE NEW MILLENNIUM

Gabriel FLYNN

The greatest achievement of the Catholic Church in the twentieth century was the Second Vatican Council, "Congar's Council," as it has been called. As the twentieth century recedes into history, theologians and historians are reassessing the legacy of the giants of Catholic theology who left an indelible mark on the era. This has resulted in the recognition of Yves Congar as an undisputed master of ecumenism, reform and tradition. In the preface to a welcome reprint of Congar's little book *The Meaning of Tradition* (San Francisco, CA, 2004), a masterful summary of one of his most important works, *Tradition and Traditions*, Cardinal Avery Dulles refers to him "as perhaps the greatest master of the theology of tradition who has ever lived." While the substantive question of Congar's role and influence at the Second Vatican Council remains to be answered, the thrust of recent theological/historical scholarship points to his pre-eminence. He was the foremost Christian theologian of the Church in the twentieth century and contributed to a comprehensive renewal in Catholic theology principally through the Unam Sanctam Series, of which he was founder and editor, a renewal that provided the impetus for the reforms of Vatican II and the subsequent flowering in ecumenical activity.

The future reception of the theology of Yves Congar is important since his theology is closely linked with the theology of the Second Vatican Council. The fact that Congar's theological corpus, along with that of the Council, is not widely read today and is regarded by the younger generation as history, but without an adequate appreciation of its historical significance, points to the need for a new reception of the Second Vatican Council. The writings of Hans Küng and Edward Schillebeeckx, perhaps the two most widely read theologians of the post-conciliar period, have contributed little to such a new reception. It seems to me, however, that a renaissance in the theology of Yves Congar would contribute to a rejuvenation in the respective domains of ecumenism, ecclesiology and church life, as it did in the fecund period before the Second Vatican Council. The success of such a new reception depends on the resources, and co-operation of the Christian churches, faculties of theology and, perhaps most important, of publishers — since even Congar's most influential writings on laity, reform and tradition are either out of print or are not readily available, while the documents of the Second Vatican Council remain inaccessible and are, for the most part, unread, even by students of theology. Those who would commit themselves to a new reception of the Council require boldness and courage to begin, as in the spirit portrayed by those words attributed to Johann Wolfgang von Goethe: "Whatever you can do or dream, you can do, begin it. Boldness has genius, power and magic in it. Begin it now."

It is now one hundred years since the birth of Yves Congar at Sedan in the French Ardennes and almost ten since his death in Paris. Is this the propitious moment to render appropriate honour to a paradoxically masterful servant of the Church, the enigmatic star of the Second Vatican Council? The present volume brings together a multinational group of scholars from nine countries, both to outline and assess the work of one of the great Christian thinkers of the twentieth century. The twenty contributors to the volume, Anglican and Orthodox, Catholic and Protestant, encompassing a broad spectrum of theological opinion, have no uniform position regarding their subject, nor was one sought. The purpose of the volume is to permit Cardinal Congar to speak again to the Church and the world.

Yves Congar's life was dedicated to the service of truth and love. The service of such elusive virtues requires eschatological fulfilment. For inspiration in penning a final tribute, one that depicts, through mystical seeing, a joyful Congar, we need look no further than Sacred Scripture, beloved of him whose profoundly ascetical Dominican spirituality is perhaps best illustrated in the beatitude "Blessed are the clean of heart; they shall see God."[1] I leave the last words, words uttered during his bitter exile in England, to Yves Congar:

> Caught by the rain outside, sheltering under a tree waiting for a clearing, I started weeping bitterly. Shall I be forever a poor, lonely fellow, dragging my bags hither and thither, having no friend, despoiled of everything, an orphan? *"Dominus autem assumpsit me"*: these tears: will God notice them? Will he show himself as a Father?[2]

[1] Matthew 5:8 (Knox).
[2] Congar, *Journal d'un théologien (1946-1956)*, 419.

SELECT BIBLIOGRAPHY

SELECT BIBLIOGRAPHY

PRIMARY SOURCES: WORKS BY YVES CONGAR

(A) Books and collections of articles

Chrétiens désunis: Principes d'un "œcuménisme" Catholique, Unam Sanctam, 1 (Paris: Cerf, 1937).

Divided Christendom: A Study of the Problem of Reunion, trans. M. A. Bousfield (London: Geoffrey Bles, 1939).

Vraie et fausse réforme dans l'Église, Unam Sanctam, 20 (Paris: Cerf, 1950); 2nd ed., Unam Sanctam, 72 (Paris: Cerf, 1969).

Le Christ, Marie et l'Église (Paris: Desclée de Brouwer, 1952).

Esquisses du mystère de l'Église, new ed., Unam Sanctam, 8 (Paris: Cerf, 1953).

L'Église catholique devant la question raciale (Paris: UNESCO, 1953).

The Catholic Church and the Race Question (Paris: UNESCO, 1953).

Jalons pour une théologie du laïcat, Unam Sanctam, 23 (Paris, Cerf, 1953); 2nd ed., Unam Sanctam, 23 (Paris: Cerf, 1954); 3rd ed. rev. with additions and corrections, Unam Sanctam, 23 (Paris: Cerf, 1964).

Neuf cents ans après: notes sur le "Schisme oriental" (Paris: Chevetogne, 1954).

La Pentecôte: Chartres 1956 (Paris: Cerf, 1956), trans. "The Church and Pentecost," *The Mystery of the Church: Studies by Yves Congar*; 2nd rev. ed. (London: Geoffrey Chapman, 1965) 146-198.

Christ, Our Lady and the Church: A Study in Eirenic Theology, trans. with an introduction by Henry St. John (London: Longmans, Green, 1957).

Le Mystère du temple ou l'Économie de la présence de Dieu à sa créature de la Genèse à l'Apocalypse, Lectio Divina, 22 (Paris: Cerf, 1958).

Vaste monde ma paroisse: Vérité et dimensions du salut (Paris: Témoignage Chrétien, 1959); new ed., Foi Vivante, 413 (Paris: Cerf, 2000).

Si vous êtes mes témoins... Trois conférences sur Laïcat, Église et Monde (Paris: Cerf, 1959).

Laity, Church and World: Three addresses by Yves Congar, trans. Donald Attwater (London: Geoffrey Chapman, 1960).

La Tradition et les traditions: Essai historique (Paris: Fayard, 1960).

The Wide World My Parish: Salvation and its Problems, trans. Donald Attwater (London: Darton, Longman & Todd, 1961).

The Mystery of the Temple or the Manner of God's Presence to His Creatures from Genesis to the Apocalypse, trans. Reginald F. Trevett (London: Burns & Oates, 1962).

Aspects de l'œcuménisme, Études religieuses, 756 (Brussels: La Pensée Catholique; Paris: Office Général du Livre, [1962]).

La Foi et la Théologie, Théologie dogmatique, 1 (Tournai: Desclée, 1962).

Les Voies du Dieu Vivant: Théologie et vie spirituelle (Paris: Cerf, 1962).

Sacerdoce et laïcat devant leurs tâches d'évangélisation et de civilisation (Paris: Cerf, 1962).

La Tradition et les traditions: Essai théologique (Paris: Fayard, 1963).

Sainte Église: Études et approches ecclésiologiques, Unam Sanctam, 41 (Paris: Cerf, 1963).

Pour une Église servante et pauvre, L'Église aux cent visages, 8 (Paris: Cerf, 1963).

Vatican II: Le concile au jour le jour, L'Église aux cent visages, 3 (Paris: Cerf, 1963).

Le Concile au jour le jour: Deuxième session, L'Église aux cent visages, 9 (Paris: Cerf, 1964).

Power and Poverty in the Church, trans. Jennifer Nicholson (London: Geoffrey Chapman, 1964).

Tradition and the Life of the Church, Faith and Fact Books, 3 (London: Burns & Oates, 1964).

Chrétiens en dialogue: Contributions catholiques à l'œcuménisme, Unam Sanctam, 50 (Paris: Cerf, 1964).

Le Concile au jour le jour: Troisième session, L'Église aux cent visages, 15 (Paris: Cerf, 1965).

The Mystery of the Church: Studies by Yves Congar, trans. A. V. Littledale, 2nd rev. ed. (London: Geoffrey Chapman, 1965).

Jésus-Christ: Notre Médiateur, notre Seigneur, Foi Vivante, 1 (Paris: Cerf, 1965); new ed., Foi Vivante, 1 (Paris: Cerf, 1995).

Le Concile au jour le jour: Qatrième session, L'Église aux cent visages, 22 (Paris: Cerf, 1966).

Tradition and Traditions: An Historical and a Theological Essay (London: Burns & Oates, 1966).

Dialogue between Christians: Catholic Contributions to Ecumenism, trans. Philip Loretz (London: Geoffrey Chapman, 1966).

Priest and Layman, trans. P. F. Hepburne-Scott (London: Darton, Longman & Todd, 1967).

Le sacerdoce chrétien des laïcs et des prêtres, Études religieuses, 777 (Brussels/Paris: La Pensée Catholique/Office Général du Livre, 1967).

Situation et tâches présentes de la théologie, Cogitatio Fidei, 27 (Paris: Cerf, 1967).

Jesus Christ, trans. Luke O'Neill (London: Geoffrey Chapman, 1968).

À mes frères, Foi Vivante, 71 (Paris: Cerf, 1968).

L'Ecclésiologie du haut moyen âge, de saint Grégoire le grand à la désunion entre Byzance et Rome (Paris: Cerf, 1968).

Cette Église que j'aime, Foi Vivante, 70 (Paris: Cerf, 1968).

A History of Theology, ed. and trans. Hunter Guthrie (New York: Doubleday, 1968).

This Church That I Love, trans. Lucien Delafuente (Denville, NJ: Dimension Books, 1969).

Au milieu des orages: L'Église affronte aujourd'hui son avenir (Paris: Cerf, 1969).

L'Église de saint Augustin à l'époque moderne, Histoire des dogmes, 20 (Paris: Cerf, 1970).

L'Église une, sainte, catholique et apostolique, Mysterium Salutis, 15 (Paris: Cerf, 1970).

Ministères et communion ecclésiale (Paris: Cerf, 1971).

Une passion: l'unité, Foi Vivante, 156 (Paris: Cerf, 1974).

Un peuple messianique: L'Église, sacrement du salut, Cogitatio Fidei, 85 (Paris: Cerf, 1975).

La Crise dans l'Église et Mgr Lefebvre (Paris: Cerf, 1976).

Challenge to the Church: The Case of Archbishop Lefebvre (London: Collins; Dublin: Veritas, 1976).

The Church Peaceful (Dublin: Veritas, 1977).

Église catholique et France moderne (Paris: Hachette, 1978).

Droit ancien et structures ecclésiales (London: Variorum Reprints, 1982).

Diversités et Communion: dossier historique et conclusion théologique, Cogitatio Fidei, 112 (Paris: Cerf, 1982).

I Believe in the Holy Spirit, trans. David Smith, 3 vols. (New York: Seabury; London: Geoffrey Chapman, 1983).

Études d'ecclésiologie médiévale (London: Variorum Reprints, 1983).

Martin Luther sa foi, sa réforme: Études de théologie historique, Cogitatio Fidei, 119 (Paris: Cerf, 1983).

Esprit de l'homme, Esprit de Dieu, Foi Vivante, 206 (Paris: Cerf, 1983).

La tradition et la vie de l'Église, 2nd ed., Traditions chrétiennes, 18 (Paris: Cerf, 1984); 1st ed., Je sais — Je crois, 3 (Paris: Fayard, 1963).

La Parole et le Souffle, Jésus et Jésus-Christ, 20 (Paris: Desclée, 1984).

Diversity and Communion (London: SCM, 1984).

Le concile de Vatican II: Son Église peuple de Dieu et corps du Christ, Théologie Historique, 71 (Paris: Beauchesne, 1984).

Essais œcuméniques: Le mouvement, les hommes, les problèmes (Paris: Centurion, 1984).

Thomas d'Aquin: Sa vision de théologie et de l'Église (London: Variorum Reprints, 1984).

Lay People in the Church: A Study for a Theology of Laity, trans. Donald Attwater, rev. ed. with additions by the author (London/Westminster, MD: Geoffrey Chapman/Christian Classics, 1985).

Appelés à la vie (Paris: Cerf, 1985).

Entretiens d'automne, 2nd ed. (Paris: Cerf, 1987).

Called to Life (Slough: St Paul; New York: Crossroad Publishing, 1988).

Fifty Years of Catholic Theology: Conversations with Yves Congar, ed. Bernard Lauret, trans. John Bowden (London: SCM, 1988).

Église et papauté: Regards historiques, Cogitatio Fidei, 184 (Paris: Cerf, 1994).

Je crois en l'Esprit Saint, 1st ed., vol. I and II 1979, vol. III 1980; new ed. (Paris, Cerf, 1995).

Journal d'un théologien (1946-1956), ed. and annotated by Étienne Fouilloux and others, 2nd ed. (Paris: Cerf, 2001).

Mon journal du Concile, ed. and annotated by Éric Mahieu, 2 vols. (Paris: Cerf, 2002).

The Meaning of Tradition, new ed. (San Francisco, CA: Ignatius, 2004).

(B) Articles

"Bulletin de théologie spéculative: Ecclésiologie," *Revue des sciences philosophiques et théologiques* 21 (1932) 680-686.

"Une conclusion théologique à l'enquête sur les raisons actuelles de l'incroyance," *La Vie intellectuelle* 37 (1935) 214-249.

"La pensée de Möhler et l'ecclésiologie orthodoxe," *Irénikon* 12 (1935) 321-329.

"L'Église selon M. Georges Bernanos," *La Vie intellectuelle* 43 (1936) 387-390.

"Pour une théologie de l'Église," *La Vie spirituelle* 52 (1937) 97-99.

"The Reasons for the Unbelief of our Time: A Theological Conclusion," Part I, *Integration* (August 1938) 13-21 and Part II, *Integration* (December 1938) 10-26.

"Sur l'évolution et l'interprétation de la pensée de Moehler," *Revue des sciences philosophiques et théologiques* 27 (1938) 205-212.

"L'Esprit des Pères d'après Moehler," *Supplément à la "Vie Spirituelle"* 55 (1938) 1-25.

"L'hérésie, déchirement de l'unité," *L'Église est une: hommage à Moehler*, ed. Pierre Chaillet (Paris: Bloud & Gay, 1939) 255-269.

"Autour du renouveau de l'ecclésiologie: la collection 'Unam Sanctam'," *La Vie intellectuelle* 51 (1939) 9-32.

"The Idea of the Church in St. Thomas Aquinas," *Thomist* 1 (1939) 331-359.

"Sacerdoce et laïcat dans l'Église," *La Vie intellectuelle* 14 (1946) 6-39.

"Théologie," *Dictionnaire de théologie catholique*, ed. A. Vacant, E. Mangenot and É. Amann, 15 vols. (Paris: Letouzey and Ané, 1946) XV Part 1, cols. 341-502.

"Tendances actuelles de la pensée religieuse," *Cahiers du monde nouveau* 4 (1948) 33-50.

"Le prophète Péguy," *Témoignage Chrétien*, 26 August 1949.

"Notes sur les mots 'Confession', 'Église' et 'Communion'," *Irénikon* 23 (1950) 3-36.

"Il faut construire l'Église en nous," *Témoignage Chrétien*, 7 July 1950.

"Le peuple fidèle et la fonction prophétique de l'Église," *Irénikon* 24 (1951) 440-466.

"Structure du sacerdoce chrétien," *Maison-Dieu* 27 (1951) 51-85.

"Bulletin de théologie dogmatique," *Revue des sciences philosophiques et théologiques* 35 (1951) 591-603.

"L'Ecclésiologie de la Révolution Française au Concile du Vatican, sous le signe de l'affirmation de l'autorité," *L'Ecclésiologie au XIXe siècle*, by Maurice Nédoncelle and others, Unam Sanctam, 34 (Paris: Cerf, 1960) 77-114.

"Les leçons de la théologie," *Le role de la religieuse dans l'Église*, by T. R. P. Liévin and others (Paris: Cerf, 1960) 29-57.

"Comment L'Église sainte doit se renouveler sans cesse," *Irénikon* 34 (1961) 322-345.

"Vœux pour le concile: enquête parmi les chrétiens," *Esprit* 29 (1961) 691-700.

"The Council in the Age of Dialogue," trans. Barry N. Rigney, *Cross Currents* 12 (1962) 144-151.

"De la communion des Églises à une ecclésiologie de l'Église universelle," *L'Épiscopat et l'Église universelle*, ed. Y. Congar and B.-D. Dupuy, Unam Sanctam, 39 (Paris: Cerf, 1962) 227-260.

"Foreword" in Frank B. Norris, *God's Own People: An Introductory Study of the Church* (Dublin: Helicon Press, 1962) III-V.

"Ecumenical Experience and Conversion: A Personal Testimony," *The Sufficiency of God*, ed. Robert C. Mackie and Charles C. West (London: SCM, 1963) 71-87.

"Introduction et notes," *Traités Anti-Donatistes*, Œuvres de Saint Augustin, 28 Quatrième Série, trans. G. Finaert, 5 vols. (Paris: Desclée de Brouwer, 1963) I, 9-125.

"Ministères et laïcat dans les recherches actuelles de la théologie catholique romaine," *Verbum Caro* 71-72 (1964) 127-148.

"L'Avenir de l'Église," *L'Avenir: semaine des intellectuels catholiques (6 au 12 novembre 1963)*, ed. M. Olivier Lacombe and others (Paris: Fayard, 1964) 207-221.

"Preface," in Karl Delahaye, *Ecclesia mater chez les Pères des trois premiers siècles*, trans. P. Vergriete and É. Bouis, Unam Sanctam, 46 (Paris: Cerf, 1964) 7-32.

"L'Église comme peuple de Dieu," *Concilium* 1 (1965) 15-32.

"The Church: The People of God," trans. Kathryn Sullivan, *Concilium* 1 (1965) 7-19.

"Introduction," *La collégialité épiscopale: histoire et théologie,* by Yves M.-J Congar and others, Unam Sanctam, 52 (Paris: Cerf, 1965) 7-9.

"Theology in the Council," *American Ecclesiastical Review* 155 (1966) 217-230.

"La Théologie au Concile: Le *'théologiser'* du concile," *Vérité et Vie* 71 (1965/66) 1-12.

"Christ in the Economy of Salvation and in our Dogmatic Tracts," trans. Aimée Bourneuf, *Concilium* 1 (1966) 4-15.

"The Place of Poverty in Christian Life in an Affluent Society," trans. Theo Westow, *Concilium* 5 (1966) 28-39.

"En guise de conclusion," *L'Église de Vatican II: études autour de la Constitution conciliare sur l'Église,* ed. Y. M.-J. Congar (French ed.), 3 vols. (Paris: Cerf, 1966) III, 1365-1373.

"Le diaconat dans la théologie des ministères," *Le diacre dans l'Église et le Monde d'aujourd'hui,* ed. P. Winninger and Y. Congar, Unam Sanctam, 59 (Paris: Cerf, 1966) 121-141.

"The Laity," *Vatican II: An Interfaith Appraisal,* ed. John H. Miller (Notre Dame, IN: University of Notre Dame Press, 1966) 239-249.

"The People of God," *Vatican II: An Interfaith Appraisal,* ed. John H. Miller (Notre Dame, IN: University of Notre Dame Press, 1966) 197-207.

"Discussion," *Vatican II: An Interfaith Appraisal,* ed. John H. Miller (Notre Dame, IN: University of Notre Dame Press, 1966) 231-236.

"Mother Church," *Theological Burning Points: The Church To-day,* by Joseph Ratzinger and others, trans. M. Ignatius, 2 vols. (Cork: Mercier Press, 1967) II, 37-44.

"Church Reform and Luther's Reformation, 1517-1967," *Lutheran World* 14 (1967) 351-359.

"La Pneumatologie dans la théologie catholique," *Revue des sciences philosophiques et théologiques* 51 (1967) 250-258.

"Le rôle de l'Église dans le monde de ce temps," *L'Église dans le monde de ce temps: constitution pastorale "Gaudium et spes,"* ed. Y. M.-J. Congar and M. Peuchmaurd, Unam Sanctam, 65b, 3 vols. (Paris: Cerf, 1967) II, 305-328.

"Religion et institution," *Théologie d'aujourd'hui et de demain,* ed. Patrick Burke (Paris: Cerf, 1967) 81-97.

"Institutionalised Religion," *The Word in History: The St. Xavier Symposium,* ed. T. Patrick Burke (London: Collins, 1968) 133-153.

"The Council as an Assembly and the Church as Essentially Conciliar," *One, Holy, Catholic, and Apostolic: Studies in the Nature and Role of the Church in the Modern World*, ed. Herbert Vorgrimler, trans. Edward Quinn and Alain Woodrow (London: Sheed and Ward, 1968) 44-88.

"Les tâches de la théologie après Vatican II," *La Théologie du renouveau*, ed. Laurence K. Shook and Guy-M. Bertrand, 2 vols., Cogitatio Fidei, 27 (Montreal/Paris: Fides/Cerf, 1968) II, 17-31.

"Theology's Tasks after Vatican II," *Renewal of Religious Thought*, ed. Laurence K. Shook, 2 vols. (New York: Herder and Herder, 1968) I, 47-65.

"Le sacerdoce du Nouveau Testament: mission et culte," *Les Prêtres*, ed. Jean Frisque and Yves Congar, Unam Sanctam, 68 (Paris: Cerf, 1968) 233-256.

"Entretien avec le Père Congar," *Sept Problèmes Capitaux de l'Église*, by Yves Congar and others (Paris: Fayard, 1969) 9-15.

"L'Église: obstacle ou voie d'accès à la vérité," *Recherches et Débats*, 66; *Chercher la Vérité: Semaine des intellectuels catholiques (1969)*, 205-219.

"Yves Congar," *The Crucial Questions: On Problems facing the Church Today*, by Yves Congar and others (New York: Newman, 1969).

"The Role of the Church in the Modern World," *Commentary on the Documents of Vatican II*, ed. Herbert Vorgrimler and others, trans. W. J. O'Hara, 5 vols. (New York/London: Herder and Herder/Burns & Oates, 1969) V, 202-223.

"Autorité, initiative, coresponsabilité," *Maison-Dieu* 97 (1969) 34-57.

"Vraie et fausse contestation dans l'Église," *Spiritus* 38 (1969) 125-132.

"Pourquoi j'aime l'Église," *Communion: Verbum Caro* 24 (1970) 23-30.

"Church History as a Branch of Theology," trans. Jonathan Cavanagh, *Concilium* 7 (1970) 85-96.

"Apports, richesses et limites du décret," *L'Apostolat des laïcs: décret "Apostolicam actuositatem,"* ed. Y. Congar, Unam Sanctam, 75 (Paris: Cerf, 1970) 157-190.

"Dialogue Entre Les Pères Congar et Girardi 1960-1970: dix années décisives pour l'Église et pour le monde," *Informations catholiques internationales* 351 (1970) 21-36.

"Johann Adam Möhler: 1796-1838," *Theologische Quartalschrift* 150 (1970) 47-51.

"La Personne 'Église'," *Revue Thomiste* 71 (1971) 613-640.

"My Path-Findings in the Theology of Laity and Ministries," *Jurist* 32 (1972) 169-188.

"Renouvellement de l'esprit et réforme de l'institution," *Concilium* 3 (1972) 37-45.

"Renewal of the Spirit and Reform of the Institution," trans. John Griffiths, *Concilium* 3 (1972) 39-49.

"La 'réception' comme réalité ecclésiologique," *Revue des sciences philosophiques et théologiques* 56 (1972) 369-403.

"Non-Christian Religions and Christianity," *Evangelisation, Dialogue and Development: Selected Papers of the International Theological Conference, Nagpur (India) 1971*, ed. Mariasusai Dhavamony, Documenta Missionalia, 5 (Rome: Gregorian University Press, 1972) 133-145.

"Actualité renouvelée du Saint Esprit," *Lumen Vitae* 27 (1972) 543-560.

"Renewed Actuality of the Holy Spirit," trans. Olga Prendergast, *Lumen Vitae* 28 (1973) 13-30.

"Norms of Christian Allegiance and Identity in the History of the Church," trans. John Griffiths, *Concilium* 3 (1973) 11-26.

"Intervention du Père Yves-M. Congar," *Tous responsables dans l'Église?*, by Paul Huot-Pleuroux and others (Paris: Centurion, 1973) 56-72.

"La tri-unité de Dieu et l'Église," *La Vie spirituelle* 128 (1974) 687-703.

"Saint Thomas d'Aquin et l'esprit œcuménique," *Freiburger Zeitschrift für Philosophie und Theologie* 21 (1974) 331-346.

"L'héritage reçu dans l'Église," *Cahiers Saint Dominique* 145 (1974) 229-242.

"St. Thomas Aquinas and the Spirit of Ecumenism," *New Blackfriars* 55 (1974) 196-209.

"Talking to Yves Congar: Interview by Tony Sheerin," Parts I and II, *Africa: St. Patrick's Missions* (November and December 1974) 6-8.

"Tradition in Theology," in "A Symposium on Tradition," reprinted from: *The Great Ideas Today 1974* (Chicago, IL: Encyclopaedia Britannica, 1974) 4-20.

"What Belonging to the Church Has Come to Mean," trans. Frances M. Chew, *Communio* 4 (1977) 146-160.

"Mgr Lefebvre, Champion de 'La Tradition'? Les discernements nécessaires," *Concilium* 119 (1978) 111-120.

"Archbishop Lefebvre, Champion of 'Tradition'? Some Necessary Clar-
ifications," trans. Sarah Fawcett, *Concilium* 119 (1978) 95-105.

"Regard sur le Concile Vatican II à l'occasion du 20e anniversaire de son
annonce," *Unterwegs zur Einheit: Festschrift für Heinrich Stirnimann*, ed. Johannes Brantschen and Pietro Selvatico (Freiburg:
Herder, 1980) 774-790.

"Le Théologien dans l'Église aujourd'hui," *Quatre Fleuves: cahiers de
recherche et de réflexion religieuses* 12 (1980) 7-27.

"L'Église, antique fontaine d'une eau jaillissante et fraîche, *La Vie spirituelle* 134 (1980) 31-40.

"Reflections on Being a Theologian," trans. Marcus Lefébure, *New Blackfriars* 62 (1981) 405-409.

"Classical Political Monotheism and the Trinity," trans. Paul Burns, *Concilium* 143 (1981) 31-36.

"Towards a Catholic Synthesis," trans. John Maxwell, *Concilium* 148
(1981) 68-80.

"Les théologiens, Vatican II et la théologie," *Le Concile: 20 ans de notre
histoire*, ed. Gérard Defois (Paris: Desclée, 1982) 171-183.

"The Conciliar Structure or Regime of the Church," trans. Francis
McDonagh, *Concilium* 167 (1983) 3-9.

"Where Are We in the Expression of the Faith?," trans. Dinah Livingstone, *Concilium* 170 (1983) 85-87.

"Les laïcs ont part à faire l'Église," *Quatre fleuves: cahiers de recherche
et de réflexion religieuses* 18 (1984) 111-122.

"Thomismus und Ökumenismus," *Entwürfe der Theologie*, ed. Johannes
B. Bauer (Graz: Styria, 1985) 41-50.

"Letter from Father Yves Congar, O.P.," trans. Ronald John Zawilla, *Theology Digest* 32 (1985) 213-216.

"The Brother I Have Known," trans. Boniface Ramsey, *Thomist* 49
(1985) 495-503.

"Moving Towards a Pilgrim Church," *Vatican II by those who were there*,
ed. Alberic Stacpoole (London: Geoffrey Chapman, 1986) 129-152.

"A Last Look At The Council," *Vatican II by those who were there*, ed.
Alberic Stacpoole (London: Geoffrey Chapman, 1986) 337-358.

"Dominicains et prêtres ouvriers," *La Vie spirituelle* 143 (1989) 817-820.

"Marie dans ma vie de théologien," Κεχαριτωμένη: *Mélanges René Laurentin*, by Pierre Ouvrard and others (Paris: Desclée, 1990) 239-243.

"Introduction" in John Paul II, *Les Fidèles laïcs: exhortation apostolique de Jean-Paul II* (Paris: Cerf, 1991) I-IV.

"Sur la transformation du sens de l'appartenance à l'Église," *Cardinal Yves Congar, O.P.: écrits réformateurs*, ed. Jean-Pierre Jossua (Paris: Cerf, 1995) 235-247. First published in *Communio* (French language ed.) 5 (1976) 41-49.

"Mon cheminement dans la théologie du laïcat et des ministères," *Cardinal Yves Congar, O.P.: écrits réformateurs*, ed. Jean-Pierre Jossua (Paris: Cerf, 1995) 123-140. (Jossua notes that this article was written in 1970).

SECONDARY SOURCES: WORKS ON YVES CONGAR

(A) Essays in collections

DUPUY, Bernard and others, *Le Père Yves Congar, pionnier de l'unité des Chrétiens, Istina* 41 (1996).

FLYNN, Gabriel (ed.), *This Church that I Love: Essays Celebrating the Centenary of the Birth of Yves Cardinal Congar, Louvain Studies* 29 (2004).

SED, Nicolas-Jean and Jacques MAURY (eds.), *Deux pionniers de l'unité: Yves Congar et Willem Visser 't Hooft, Istina* 48 (2003).

VAUCHEZ, André (ed.), *Cardinal Yves Congar 1904-1995: actes du colloque réuni à Rome les 3-4 juin 1996* (Paris: Cerf, 1999).

(B) Monographs

BLAKEBROUGH, Denise S., *El Cardenal Congar o la libertad teológica: Ensayo sobre su comprensión del Espíritu Santo* (Salamanca: Primera Bibliografía General, 1995).

DUNNE, Victor, *Prophecy in the Church: The Vision of Yves Congar*, European University Studies, 23 (Frankfurt: Lang, 2000).

DUQUESNE, Jacques, *Jacques Duquesne interroge le Père Chenu: "un théologien en liberté"* (Paris: Centurion, 1975).

FAMERÉE, Joseph, *L'Ecclésiologie d'Yves Congar avant Vatican II: Histoire et Église*, Bibliotheca Ephemeridum Theologicarum Lovaniensium, 107 (Louvain: Leuven University Press, 1992).

FLYNN, Gabriel, *Yves Congar's Vision of the Church in a World of Unbelief* (Aldershot: Ashgate, 2004).

GROPPE, Elizabeth Teresa, *Yves Congar's Theology of the Holy Spirit* (New York: Oxford University Press, 2004).

JOSSUA, Jean-Pierre, *Le Père Congar: la théologie au service du peuple de Dieu*, Chrétiens de tous les temps, 20 (Paris: Cerf, 1967).

MACDONALD, Charles, *Church and World in the Plan of God: Aspects of History and Eschatology in the Thought of Père Yves Congar O.P.* (Frankfurt: Lang, 1982).

MACDONALD, Timothy I., *The Ecclesiology of Yves Congar* (Lanham, MD: University Press of America, 1984).

NICHOLS, Aidan, *Yves Congar* (London/Wilton, CT: Geoffrey Chapman/Morehouse-Barlow, 1989).

PELLITERO, Ramiro, *La Teología del Laicado en la obra de Yves Congar* (Pamplona: Servicio de Publicaciones de la Universidad de Navarra, 1996).

PUYO, Jean, *Jean Puyo interroge le Père Congar: "une vie pour la vérité"* (Paris: Centurion, 1975).

VAN VLIET, Cornelis Th. M., *Communio sacramentalis: Das Kirchenverständnis von Yves Congar — genetisch und systematisch betrachtet* (Mainz: Grünewald, 1995).

(C) Articles

ALLCHIN, A. M., "Vraie et fausse réforme dans l'Église by Y. M-J. Congar," 2nd rev. and corrected ed., *New Blackfriars* 50 (1969) 821-822.

BEAUCHESNE, Richard, J., "Heeding the Early Congar Today, and Two Recent Roman Catholic Issues: Seeking Hope on the Road Back," *Journal of Ecumenical Studies* 27 (1990) 535-560.

BEAUCHESNE, Richard, J., "Worship as Life, Priesthood and Sacrifice in Yves Congar," *Église et Théologie* 21 (1990) 79-100.

BEDOUELLE, Guy, "Le Père Congar et l'Église romaine," *Communio* 20 (1995) 113-125.

BOBRINSKOY, Boris, "Le P. Yves Congar et l'orthodoxie," *Istina* 48 (2003) 20-23.

BOULDING, M. Cecily, "Yves Congar: Faithful Critic of the Church in *Mon journal du Concile*," *Louvain Studies* 29 (2004) 350-370.

CAILLON, C., "Y. Congar, *Le Christ, Marie et l'Église*," *Lumière et Vie* 16 (1954) 135-136.

CLANCY, Finbarr, "Breathing With Both Her Lungs: Yves Congar and Dialogue with the East," *Louvain Studies* 29 (2004) 320-349.

DULLES, Avery, "Yves Congar: In Appreciation," *America* 173 (1995) 6-7.

DUPUY, Bernard, "Aux sources de l'œuvre du Père Congar," *Istina* 41 (1996) 117-135.

DUPUY, Bernard, "Le Père Yves Congar: pionnier de l'unité des chrétiens," *Istina* 48 (2003) 5-8.

DUVAL, André, "Yves Congar: un homme, une œuvre," *Choisir* 245 (1980) 12-16.

DUVAL, André, "Yves Congar: A Life for the Truth," trans. Boniface Ramsey, *Thomist* 48 (1984) 505-511.

FAMERÉE, Joseph, "'Chrétiens désunis' du P. Congar 50 ans après," *Nouvelle revue théologique* 110 (1988) 666-686.

FAMERÉE, Joseph, "L'ecclésiologie du Père Yves Congar: essai de synthèse critique," *Revue des sciences philosophiques et théologiques* 76 (1992) 377-419.

FINNEGAN, Gerald F., "Ministerial Priesthood in Yves Congar," *Review for Religious* 46 (1987) 523-532.

FLEINERT-JENSEN, Flemming, "La personnalité et le message d'Yves Congar: Témoignage d'un protestant," *Istina* 48 (2003) 24-28.

FLYNN, Gabriel, "The Role of Affectivity in the Theology of Yves Congar," *New Blackfriars* 83 (2002) 347-364; reprinted in *Theology Digest* 50 (2003) 115-122; French trans. "Le rôle de l'affectivité dans la théologie d'Yves Congar," *La Vie spirituelle* 157 (2003) 73-92.

FLYNN, Gabriel, "*Mon Journal du Concile*: Yves Congar and the Battle for a Renewed Ecclesiology at the Second Vatican Council," *Louvain Studies* 28 (2003) 48-70.

FLYNN, Gabriel, "Cardinal Congar's Ecumenism: An 'Ecumenical Ethics' for Reconciliation?," *Louvain Studies* 28 (2003) 311-325; reprinted in *Theology Digest* 3 (2004) 209-218 and in *Doctrine and Life* 54 (2004) 4-17.

FLYNN, Gabriel, "The Role of Unbelief in the Theology of Yves Congar," *New Blackfriars* 85 (2004) 426-443.

FLYNN, Gabriel, "Yves Cardinal Congar, *un maître en théologie*," *Louvain Studies* 29 (2004) 239-257.

FLYNN, Gabriel, "An Yves Congar Bibliography 1987-1995, with *Addenda*: 1996-2002," in Gabriel Flynn, *Yves Congar's Vision of the Church in a World of Unbelief* (Aldershot, Hampshire: Ashgate, 2004) 229-233.

FOUILLOUX, Étienne, "Comment devient-on expert à Vatican II? Le cas du Père Yves Congar," *Le deuxième concile du Vatican (1959-1965): actes du colloque arganisé par l'École française de Rome en collaboration avec l'Université de Lille III, l'Istituto per le scienze religiose de Bologne et le Dipartimento di studi storici del Medioevo e dell'età contemporanea de l'Università di Roma — La Sapienza (Rome 28-30 mai 1986)*, by John Paul II and others, Collection de l'École française de Rome, 113 (Rome: École française de Rome, 1989) 307-331.

FOUILLOUX, Étienne, "Frère Yves, Cardinal Congar, Dominicain: itinéraire d'un théologien," *Revue des sciences philosophiques et théologiques* 79 (1995) 379-404.

GOURE, Claude, "Conversation avec Yves Congar: un théologien dans le siècle," *Panorama* 222 (1988) 49-53.

GROPPE, Elizabeth Teresa, "The Contribution of Yves Congar's Theology of the Holy Spirit," *Theological Studies* 62 (2001) 451-478.

GROPPE, Elizabeth Teresa, "The Practice of Theology as Passion for Truth: Testimony from the Journals of Yves Congar, O.P.," *Horizons* 31 (2004) 382-402.

GROOTAERS, Jan, "*Yves Congar, Mon journal du Concile*: Vatican II raconté de l'intérieur," *Écritures* 50 (2002) 6-7.

HAUSMAN, Noëlle, "Le Père Congar au Concile Vatican II," *Nouvelle revue théologique* 120 (1998) 267-281.

HENN, William, "The Hierarchy of Truths Twenty Years Later," *Theological Studies* 48 (1987) 439-471.

JOSSUA, Jean-Pierre, "L'œuvre œcuménique du Père Congar," *Études* 357 (1982) 543-555.

JOSSUA, Jean-Pierre, "Yves Congar: un portrait," *Études* 383 (1995) 211-218.

KERR, Fergus, "French Theology: Yves Congar and Henri de Lubac," *The Modern Theologians: An Introduction to Christian Theology in the Twentieth Century*, ed. David F. Ford, 2nd ed. (Oxford: Blackwell, 1997) 105-117.

KERR, Fergus, "Yves Congar: From Suspicion to Acclamation," *Louvain Studies* 29 (2004) 273-287.

LE GUILLOU, M.-J., "Yves Congar," *Bilan de la théologie du XXe siècle*, ed. Robert Vander Gucht and Herbert Vorgrimler, 2 vols. (Paris: Casterman, 1970) II, 791-805.

MCBRIEN, Richard P., "Church and Ministry: the achievement of Yves Congar," *Theology Digest* 32 (1985) 203-211.

MCBRIEN, Richard P., "Yves Congar: Mentor for Theologians," *Louvain Studies* 29 (2004) 258-272.

MACKEY, James P., "Father Congar on Tradition," *Irish Theological Quarterly* 32 (1965) 53-59.

MAHIEU, Éric, "Introduction," *Mon journal du Concile*, ed. and annotated by Éric Mahieu, 2 vols. (Paris: Cerf, 2002) I, XXV-LXVII.

MAHIEU, Éric, "Présentation de 'Mon journal du Concile'," *Istina* 48 (2003) 9-19.

MALLON, Colleen Mary, "Ecclesial Discipleship: Applying the Requirements of the Gospel to the Church as Social Institution," *Louvain Studies* 28 (2003) 344-362.

MELLONI, Alberto, "Congar: Architect of the *Unam Sanctam*," *Louvain Studies* 29 (2004) 222-238.

MULLINS, Patrick, "The Spirit Speaks to the Churches: Continuity and Development in Congar's Pneumatology," *Louvain Studies* 29 (2004) 288-319.

NICHOLS, Aidan, "Yves Congar," *The Modern Theologians: An Introduction to Christian Theology in the Twentieth Century*, ed. David F. Ford, 2 vols. (Oxford: Blackwell, 1994) I, 219-236.

NICHOLS, Aidan, "An Yves Congar Bibliography 1967-1987," *Angelicum* 66 (1989) 422-466.

OLS, Daniel, "Diversités et communion: réflexions à propos d'un ouvrage récent," *Angelicum* 60 (1983) 122-150.

PRUNIERES, Jérôme, "L'ecclésiologie du P. Congar: œuvre témoin d'une crise," *Études franciscaines* 16 (1966) 253-283.

QUATTROCCHI, Pietro, "Bibliographie générale du Père Yves Congar," in Jean-Pierre Jossua, *Le Père Congar: la théologie au service du peuple de Dieu*, Chrétiens de tous les temps, 20 (Paris: Cerf, 1967) 213-272.

RADCLIFFE, Timothy, "La mort du cardinal Yves-Marie Congar: homélie du P. Timothy Radcliffe, O.P.," *Documentation catholique* 92 (1995) 688-690.

SED, Nicolas-Jean and Jacques Maury, "La célébration de deux pionniers de l'unité," *Istina* 48 (2003) 3-4.

SESBOÜÉ, Bernard, "Le drame de la théologie au XXe siècle: à propos du *Journal d'un théologien* (1946-1956) du P. Yves Congar," *Recherches de Science Religieuse*, 89 (2001) 271-287.

STACPOOLE, Alberic, "Early Ecumenism, Early Yves Congar, 1904-1940: Commemoration of the half-century of the beginnings of the World Council of Churches, 1937-1987," *Month* 259 (1988) 502-510.

STACPOOLE, Alberic, "Early Ecumenism, Early Yves Congar, 1904-1940," Part II, *Month* 249 (1988) 623-631.

TORRELL, Jean-Pierre, "Yves Congar et l'ecclésiologie de Saint Thomas d'Aquin," *Revue des sciences philosophiques et théologiques* 82 (1998) 201-241.

VAN VLIET, Cornelis Th. M., "Ministère et charisme chez Y. Congar: l'ecclésiologie entre christologie et pneumatologie," *Communio* 21 (1996) 61-72.

WICKS, Jared, "Yves Congar's Doctrinal Service of the People of God," *Gregorianum* 84 (2003) 499-550.

WINTER, Michael M., "Masters in Israel: Yves Congar," *Clergy Review* 55 (1970) 275-288.

INDEX

INDEX

PRINTED ON PERMANENT PAPER • IMPRIME SUR PAPIER PERMANENT • GEDRUKT OP DUURZAAM PAPIER - ISO 9706

N.V. PEETERS S.A., WAROTSTRAAT 50, B-3020 HERENT